D1130924

THE LOEB CLASSICAL LIBRARY

FOUNDED BY JAMES LOEB, LL.D.

PLUTARCH'S
MORALIA
XV

PLUTARCH'S
MORALIA

IN SIXTEEN VOLUMES

XV

FRAGMENTS

EDITED AND TRANSLATED BY

F. H. SANDBACH
TRINITY COLLEGE, CAMBRIDGE

CAMBRIDGE, MASSACHUSETTS
HARVARD UNIVERSITY PRESS
LONDON
WILLIAM HEINEMANN LTD
MCMLXIX

Printed in Great Britain

CONTENTS OF VOLUME XV

CONTENTS OF VOLUME XV

THE TRADITIONAL ORDER of the Books of the *Moralia* as they appear since the edition of Stephanus (1572), and their division into volumes in this edition.

TRADITIONAL ORDER OF THE BOOKS

TRADITIONAL ORDER OF THE BOOKS

* This work, by Aëtius, not Plutarch, is omitted in the current edition.

TRADITIONAL ORDER OF THE BOOKS

INTRODUCTION

THE surviving works of Plutarch, although they occupy 25 volumes of the Loeb Classical Library, seem on the evidence of the so-called Lamprias Catalogue (p. 3) to represent less than half of his literary output. Some of his lost writings were known to authors and anthologists down to the sixth century A.D.; but I know of no evidence that, when learning revived after the Greek Dark Ages, anyone had any knowledge of any work that we do not now possess.[a] Such scraps of information as occur in writers of the ninth and later centuries reached them at second hand.

The first attempt to offer a complete collection of fragments of Plutarch is to be found in Wyttenbach's edition. A few additions were made by Duebner and others by Bernardakis. The following works deserve mention as dealing with a wide range of fragments, and are referred to by their authors' names.

J. J. Hartman, *De Plutarcho scriptore et philosopho*, Leiden, 1916.

H. Patzig, *Quaestiones Plutarcheae*, Berlin, 1876.

N. Piccolos, " Sur une nouvelle édition des fragments de Plutarque," *Revue archéologique*, 1855.

---

[a] Except that the end of *Quaestiones Naturales* seems to have been lost after the early eleventh century, and Photius (see p. 2) had a few excerpts that have not been preserved.

INTRODUCTION

R. Volkmann, *Plutarch von Chaeronea, Leben und Schriften*, Berlin, 1869.

K. Ziegler, article " Plutarchos " in Pauly-Wissowa, *Realencyklopädie*, xxi (separately printed 1949).

Wyttenbach appended a Latin translation to his edition. So far as fragments from Stobaeus were concerned, he amended that of Gesner. His version is too literal to throw much light on difficulties, but sometimes implies emendations that were not placed in the Greek text. Translations of some fragments preserved by Stobaeus are to be found at the end of the Life of Plutarch added by Sir Thomas North to the third edition (1603) of his *Lives of the Noble Greeks and Romans* ; North's original here was the French of Simon Goulart of Senlis, which had similarly been added to Amyot's *Vies*.

A possible pitfall for the collector of fragments is the existence of another Plutarch, the Athenian neo-Platonist, son of Nestorius, who is often quoted in philosophical commentaries. Our Plutarch is sometimes distinguished from him by the addition of the words ὁ Χαιρωνεύς. I hope, but cannot be sure, that I have left the son of Nestorius in possession of no material that should be claimed for the Chaeronean. The former is often to be identified by the neo-Platonic company he keeps—Atticus, Proclus, and Porphyry. On one topic, however, it is Plutarch of Chaeronea who is associated with Atticus. They both held the unorthodox view that in Plato's *Timaeus* the world had a beginning in time. The work that Plutarch specifically devoted to this (Lamprias 66) is lost. I have not, however, printed the numerous passages in which his opinion is recorded, since they give no details, only the bare fact that he held it. The surviving *De Animae Procreatione* not only informs us of this but also gives a summary of his reasons.

Since the time of Maximus Planudes the "Collected Works of Plutarch" have always embraced a number of spurious writings. It may therefore be logical to include in a collection of fragments those which are in all probability falsely ascribed to him in our sources, but are not the work of any other identifiable author. I follow my predecessors in doing this, but in one respect depart from their practice : I have excluded, for reasons explained in Appendix B, a number of brief " fragmenta incerta " which are referred to Plutarch, but to no specific book, in certain late gnomologia. I have also passed over several *complete* works that are generally recognized to be pseudepigrapha, *viz.*, *De Vita et Poesi Homeri*, *De Metris*, *De Fluviis*, *De Proverbiis Alexandrinorum*, and *De Nobilitate* : on these, together with the Latin fragments of the so-called *Institutio Trajani*, see Appendix A. I have distinguished by an asterisk fragments of which the Plutarchean origin is impossible or doubtful ; the notes show to which category, impossibility or doubt, I should myself assign them.

Of the " fragments " some are verbatim extracts from Plutarch, others reports or adaptations of what he wrote. Unfortunately it has been impracticable to make any typographical distinction between these kinds ; but there should be no difficulty in recognizing them, since the former are always introduced by some other author's words which make it plain that he is quoting literally, or nearly so. Where a fragment is an adaptation, it is often difficult to determine the extent of the Plutarchean material. Here again I have used an asterisk, to indicate sentences which in my view may not contain anything derived from Plutarch.

To establish a text of these fragments is no easy task. Many come from the anthology of Stobaeus [a]; he or his predecessors, when excerpting, could make arbitrary changes or omissions, as appears when we still possess the work excerpted. Others, like those from the spurious *Stromateis* or from the *Commentary on Hesiod's Works and Days*, are the end-product of a process of free modification, which may unintentionally have distorted the meaning of the original. In either case, although it may be suspected that something has gone wrong, conjectural emendation would

[a] Since Stobaeus is a frequent source of these fragments, it will be convenient to give here a brief summary of his manuscript tradition, which is not the same for the first two books and for the latter two. Few fragments, in fact, are derived from the first two. Here F(arnesianus), now Naples III D. 15, of the fourteenth century, is in general much more reliable than P(arisinus 2129), of the fifteenth. Remnants of a longer version are to be found in L(aurentianus 8. 22), of the fourteenth century. For the latter two books the tradition is divided into two branches. The best representative of the first is Vindobonensis phil. gr. 67 (S), of the eleventh century ; many other mss. belong to the same group, but the only one fully known is Marcianus 4. 29, the origin of Trincavelli's edition (Tr.). Tr. has been interpolated from other traditions and by conjecture. The second branch is headed by Escorialensis II. Σ. 14 (M), of the eleventh or twelfth century. Associated with this is Parisinus 1984 (A), of the fourteenth century, which has been affected by conjectures. " Maximus " used for his anthology (see p. 409) a manuscript of this family, which was the source of other anthologies also : Macarius Chrysocephalus (Mac.), Parisinus 1168 (corp. Par.), Laur. 8. 22 (L), and Bruxellensis 11360 (Br.). Hense's conclusion, in the introduction to vol. iii of the edition of Stobaeus by Wachsmuth and Hense, is that S, though abbreviated, has suffered less from other forms of alteration than the manuscripts of the second family.

INTRODUCTION

be out of place. That must be restricted to the correction of copyists' accidental errors. Even this is exceptionally difficult where spurious fragments are concerned. The author being unknown, there is no norm for his style. An editor who is also a translator finds, however, that he must sometimes temper caution with temerity. When error has resulted in patent nonsense, he can feel obliged to introduce sense by means of changes which at the best may not misrepresent the author's intentions, but are not likely to capture his exact wording.

It is a pleasant duty to thank the authorities of the Bibliothèque Nationale in Paris, of the Biblioteca di S. Marco in Venice, and of the Abbadia de el Escorial for allowing me to consult, or obtain photographs of, manuscripts in their keeping. I am also obliged to the Institut de recherche et d'histoire des textes, by whose aid I obtained a microfilm. Of scholars who have helped me I must mention in particular Mr. R. T. Wallis, whom I consulted with profit on the second of Tyrwhitt's fragments, and above all my colleagues at Trinity College, Mr. H. J. Easterling and Dr. R. D. Dawe, who between them generously undertook the reading of the first proofs. To their care and acumen I owe the detection of many errors and inadequacies. For those that remain uncorrected the responsibility is mine.

F. H. SANDBACH

TRINITY COLLEGE, CAMBRIDGE
   April 1965

WORKS BY PLUTARCH
ANCIENT LISTS

A. PHOTIUS

Photius, *Bibliotheca*, 161, p. 103 a Migne, records that he had met the Ἐκλογαὶ Διάφοροι of Sopatros (from Apamea, a pupil of Iamblichus) ; in vols. 8-11 there were extracts from Plutarch, themselves taken from an anthology in a MS. that Sopatros called old. He gives 45 titles, of which eight belong or may belong to lost works. They are :

Epaminondas (Lamprias 7)
Pindar (Lamprias 36)
Crates (Lamprias 37)
Daïphantus (Lamprias 38)
Περὶ ὀργῆς (Lamprias 93, or *De Cohibenda Ira*)
Περὶ πλούτου (perhaps Lamprias 211 ; but *cf.* frags. 149-152)
Περὶ φύσεως καὶ πόνων [a] (see frag. 172)

and finally Ἀνδρῶν ἐνδόξων ἀποφθέγματα ; since *Regum et Imperatorum Apophthegmata* is separately mentioned, this is perhaps to be associated with Lamprias 168, Περὶ ἐνδόξων ἀνδρῶν.

The title Περὶ ποταμῶν probably refers to the spurious work so called (see p. 404).

---

[a] Bücheler, *Rh. Mus.* xxvii (1872), p. 523, rejects any possibility that this might be identical with the spurious Περὶ ἀσκήσεως, which survives only in a Syriac version, and of which he prints a German translation.

2

B. THE LAMPRIAS CATALOGUE

Editio princeps by D. Hoeschel, printed by J. Prae-
torius at Augsburg in 1597, from a transcript made by
Andreas Schottus from the MS. now Neapolitanus III
B 29. Variant readings, taken from some other MS.,
are ascribed to Ful(vius) Urs(inus). A more complete
version, from a " Venetus," identifiable as Marc. 248
(now 328), was given by J. C. Siebenkies to G. C.
Harles, who published it in his edition (1786) of
Fabricius, *Bibliotheca Graeca* (vol. v, p. 187). The
basic facts about the catalogue were established by
M. Treu, *Der sogenannte Lampriaskatalog der Plutarch-
schriften*, Progr. Waldenburg, 1873.

Manuscripts

Paris. 1678 (Plutarch, *Lives*, etc.), described by
Nachstädt, p. vi of preface to vol. ii of Teubner
Moralia, and by Ziegler, *Rh. Mus.* lxiii (1908), p. 239,
has the catalogue on fol. 148 recto and verso, now
only partially legible owing to wear and creeping of
the ink. Through the kindness of the authorities of
the Bibliothèque Nationale I have an ultra-violet
photograph. Ziegler ascribes the hand to the twelfth
century (one may compare Vat. gr. 504, De' Cavalieri
and Lietzmann no. 28, dated A.D. 1105). This list is
not the source of the other, later MSS., since it omits
several titles that they include.

Neapolitanus III. B 29 (Diogenes Laertius), has
the catalogue on fol. 246 verso and 247. A collation
is given by C. Wachsmuth, *Philologus*, xix (1863), p.
577, who ascribes it to the late fourteenth century.
The last title is no. 222, Ἐρωτικαὶ διηγήσεις, ἐν ἄλλῳ
πρὸς τοὺς ἐρῶντας, but this is at the foot of fol. 247

verso ; of fol. 248, which presumably contained the remainder of the list, only a narrow margin survives. From it are derived Vat. gr. 1347 and Paris. 1751.

Marc. 481 (now 863), a miscellany written by Maximus Planudes in A.D. 1302, has on its last folio (123), still in his hand, a list without any heading. Not always easy to read, it gives the titles, first of the surviving *Lives*, then of those *Moralia* that he then possessed, and concludes with nearly all those items of the Lamprias Catalogue that had not occurred previously. The few omissions are probably due to accident. Derived from this are the lists in Marc. 186 (now 601), Marc. 248 (now 328), which was written by John Rhosos, and Pal. Vat. 170. I call it Ven.

In my apparatus I include significant variants only. When Ven. and Neap. alone are cited, I cannot read Par.

Title

The name Lamprias Catalogue has no manuscript authority. The list is preceded in the Neapolitanus by an anonymous introductory epistle as follows :

> I never forget our association in Asia nor your enthusiasm for education and regard for your friends, and now as soon as I received your letter I recognized the name and learned with the greatest pleasure that you were well and remembered me. In return I am glad to send my greetings, and I have dispatched to you the list you want of my father's writings. I hope that all goes well with you.[a]

Whoever composed this may have intended what in

---

[a] οὐδ' ἄλλοτέ ποτε τῆς γενομένης ἡμῖν ἐπὶ τῆς Ἀσίας πρὸς ἀλλήλους συνουσίας ἐκλαθόμενος οὐδὲ τῆς σῆς περὶ παιδείαν καὶ περὶ τοὺς φίλους σπουδῆς καὶ προθυμίας καὶ νῦν εὐθέως δεξάμενος σου τὴν ἐπιστολὴν ἐγνώρισα τοὔνομα καὶ ἡδιαίτατα διετέθην ἐρρωμένον ἐπιγνούς σε καὶ ἡμῶν μεμνημένον, καὶ ἡδέως ἐν μέρει πάλιν ἀσπάζομαί σε καὶ τὴν γραφὴν ὧν ἠθέλησας τῶν τοῦ πατρὸς βιβλίων ἔπεμψά σοι· ἐρρῶσθαι εὔχομαι.

the event happened, namely that the writer should be identified with a Lamprias mentioned by Suidas :

> Lamprias, son of Plutarch of Chaeronea. He wrote a list of his father's works on all Greek and Roman history.[a]

So far as is known, none of Plutarch's sons was called Lamprias. The epistle has some similarity to Pliny, *Ep.* iii. 5, which Ziegler believed to have served as a model for a forger of the xiii or xiv century.[b]

Another account of the list is given by a note of John Rhosos in Marcianus 248 :

> Besides all these titles, there were also found some time ago, as was recorded in an ancient book, summaries of the works listed below, but they have not survived to our times, except for their titles, since I have never yet met with them. But I have set out their titles for the benefit of scholars, so that they may know all the works composed by this sage of Chaeronea.[c]

Rhosos was certainly mistaken about the existence of these summaries, and the origin of his mistake seems to lie in Marc. 186, which after giving a list of the surviving *Lives* and *Moralia* continues :

> All these have been found, and also the summaries of the works marked below with this sign, θ'.[d]

There follows the remainder of the Lamprias Catalogue, including nos. 65, 79, and 121, of which so-

---

[a] Λαμπρίας, Πλουτάρχου τοῦ Χαιρωνέως υἱός. ἔγραψε Πίνακα ὧν ὁ πατὴρ αὐτοῦ ἔγραψε περὶ πάσης Ἑλληνικῆς καὶ Ῥωμαϊκῆς ἱστορίας.   [b] *Rh. Mus.* lxxvi (1927), p. 20.

[c] παρὰ πάντα δὲ ταῦτα πρὸ μέν τινων χρόνων, ὡς ἔν τινι βίβλῳ ἀρχαίᾳ ἐνεγέγραπτο, καὶ τῶν ὑπογεγραμμένων λόγων συνόψεις ηὑρίσκοντο, εἰς ἡμᾶς δὲ οὐκ ἔφθασαν ἢ μόνον αἱ αὐτῶν ἐπιγραφαί· οὐδαμῇ γάρ πω αὐτῶν ἐνετύχομεν. τῶν φιλολόγων δὲ χάριν καὶ ὡς ἂν εἰδεῖεν ὅσα ὁ Χαιρωνεὺς οὗτος σοφὸς συνεγράψατο, τὰς αὐτῶν ἐπιγραφὰς ἐνταῦθα ἐξεθέμεθα.

[d] ταῦτα πάντα εὑρέθησαν (sic) καὶ αἱ συνόψεις τῶν κατωτέρω σημειωθέντων τῷδε τῷ σημείῳ θ'.

called summaries do survive. These and these only, are marked with a sign ; but it is a cross, and not that promised.

Origin

The list begins with " parallel " *Lives*, succeeded by other biographies, including the spurious *Lives of the Ten Orators*. The *Moralia* follow, the only principle of arrangement being that works in more than one book are enumerated before those in a single book ; there are, however, some small groups of works with similar subjects, *e.g.*, four of the anti-Stoic writings are collected together (76-79) and three of those against Epicureans (80-82). Three titles are those of surviving spurious works,[a] while at least twelve surviving genuine works [b] and six spurious [c] are not included. About a dozen titles are of lost works of which the authenticity is supported by other evidence. It follows that just as the presence of a title in the list is no guarantee of the work's genuineness, so its absence is no evidence of spuriousness.

Treu concluded that the list originated as the inventory of some library. The presence of eight volumes of Aristotle's *Topica* (56) is an indication that ancient libraries, like modern, could suffer by the replacement of a book on the wrong shelf. Since the parallel *Lives* are not arranged according to any prin-

---

[a] *Vit. X Orat., Plac. Phil., Parallela Minora.*

[b] *De Amic. Mult., De Fortuna, De Virtute et Vitio, De Cohibenda Ira, De Amore Prolis, An Vitiositas, De Invidia et Odio, Quaest. Conv., Maxime cum Princ., Ad Princ. Inerud., De Monarchia, De Esu Carnium.*

[c] *De Liberis Educandis, Cons. ad Apoll., De Musica, De Fluviis, De Vita et Poesi Homeri, Fragmentum Tyrwhittianum ii.* It is uncertain whether no. 58 refers to *De Fato.*

ciple, the list is likely to be fairly early.[a] The disposition by number of books suggests a library on rolls
rather than in codices. Treu's guess that the list
dates from the third or fourth century may well be
right.

[a] K. Ziegler, *Die Überlieferungsgeschichte der vergleichen-
den Lebensbeschreibungen Plutarchs*, pp. 33-36 ; he holds
that the first ordered collection of *Lives* was made in the fifth
century.

ΤΟΥ ΠΛΟΥΤΑΡΧΟΥ ΒΙΒΛΙΑ

Surviving works of the Moralia *have been distinguished by appending to their title a numeral in brackets ; this refers to the volume of the Loeb Classical Library in which the work is*

THE WORKS OF PLUTARCH

*to be found. The Arabic numerals are those traditionally in
use ; they do not coincide with the medieval numerations
found in some later MSS.*

1. Theseus and Romulus.
2. Lycurgus and Numa.
3. Themistocles and Camillus.
4. Solon and Publicola.
5. Pericles and Fabius Maximus.
6. Alcibiades and Marcius Coriolanus.
7. Epaminondas and Scipio. Frags. 1, 2.
8. Phocion and Cato.
9. Agis and Cleomenes.
10. Tiberius and Gaius Gracchus.
11. Timoleon and Paullus Aemilius.
12. Eumenes and Sertorius.
13. Aristides and Cato.
14. Pelopidas and Marcellus.
15. Lysander and Sulla.
16. Pyrrhus and Marius.
17. Philopoemen and Titus.
18. Nicias and Crassus.
19. Cimon and Lucullus.
20. Dion and Brutus.
21. Agesilaüs and Pompey.

22. Ἀλέξανδρος καὶ Καῖσαρ.
23. Δημοσθένης καὶ Κικέρων.
24. Ἄρατος καὶ Ἀρταξέρξης.
25. Δημήτριος καὶ Ἀντώνιος.
26. Αὐγούστου βίος.
27. Τιβέριος.
28. Σκιπίων Ἀφρικανός.
29. Κλαύδιος.
30. Νέρωνος βίος.
31. Γάϊος Καῖσαρ.
32a. Γάλβας.
32b. Ὄθων.[1]
33. Βιτέλλιος.
34. Ἡρακλέους βίος.
35. Ἡσιόδου βίος.
36. Πινδάρου βίος.
37. Κράτητος βίος.
38. Δαΐφαντος.
39. Ἀριστομένης.
40. Ἄρατος.
41. Βίοι τῶν δέκα ῥητόρων.
42. Ὁμηρικῶν μελετῶν βιβλία δʹ.
43. Εἰς Ἐμπεδοκλέα βιβλία ιʹ.
44. Περὶ τῆς πεμπτῆς[2] οὐσίας βιβλία εʹ.
45. Περὶ τῆς εἰς ἑκάτερον ἐπιχειρήσεως βιβλία εʹ.
46. Μύθων βιβλία γʹ.
47. Περὶ ῥητορικῆς βιβλία γʹ.
48. Περὶ ψυχῆς εἰσαγωγῆς βιβλία γʹ.
49. Περὶ αἰσθήσεως βιβλία γʹ.
50. Ἐκλογὴ φιλοσόφων, βιβλία βʹ.

---

[1] The titles are separated by Par. γάλβας καὶ ὄθων Neap.
[2] Possibly πεμπτῆς should be omitted as a dittography.

22. Alexander and Caesar.
23. Demosthenes and Cicero.
24. Aratus and Artaxerxes.
25. Demetrius and Antony.
26. Life of Augustus.
27. Tiberius. ? Frag. 182.
28. Scipio Africanus. ? Frags. 3, 4.
29. Claudius.
30. Life of Nero. Frag. 5.
31. Gaius Caesar.
32a. Galba.
32b. Otho.
33. Vitellius.
34. Life of Heracles. Frags. 6-8.
35. Life of Hesiod.
36. Life of Pindar. Frag. 9.
37. Life of Crates. Frag. 10.
38. Daïphantus. Frag. 11.
39. Aristomenes. Frag. 12.
40. Aratus.
41. Lives of the Ten Orators. (x)
42. Homeric Studies, 4 vols. Frags. 122-127.
43. Notes on Empedocles, 10 vols. Frag. 24.
44. On the Fifth Substance, 5 vols.[a]
45. On Arguing both Sides of a Question, 5 vols.[b]
46. Stories, 3 vols.
47. On Rhetoric, 3 vols.
48. An Introduction to Psychology, 3 vols.
49. On the Senses, 3 vols.
50. Selections from Philosophers, 2 vols.

[a] Since Plutarch does not show much interest in Aristotle, it is surprising to find him devoting five volumes to this subject. See the critical note.
[b] Perhaps referred to at *Moralia*, 1036 A.

---

[1] The order in Par. Ven. is 50, 53, 51, 52, in Neap. 50, 51,
52, 53. Treu suggested the amalgamation of titles.

[2] τοπικῶν Par. Ven. πολιτικῶν Neap.

[3] καὶ added by Ziegler.

[4] Par. may have a different numeral.

---

[a] Plutarch used this work of Theophrastus for his *Praecepta
Gerendae Reipublicae* (no. 104) ; see Mittelhaus, *De Plutarchi
praeceptis gerendae reipublicae*, pp. 29-55.

[b] Probably included here by mistake, see p. 6. Since
Plutarch shows no interest elsewhere in the *Topics*, it is unlikely that a commentary on that work is meant.

[c] The existing pseudo-Plutarchean *On Fate* (L.C.L. vol.

WORKS BY PLUTARCH

51. Benefactions by (or to) Cities, 3 vols.
52-53. On Theophrastus' work *Opportunist Statesman-ship*, 2 vols.[a]
54. On Neglected History, 4 vols.
55. A Collection of Proverbs, 2 vols.
56. Aristotle's *Topics*, 8 vols.[b]
57. Sosicles, 2 vols.
58. On Fate, 2 vols.[c]
59. On Justice, a Reply to Chrysippus, 3 vols.[d]
60. On the Art of Poetry.
61. On the Views held by Philosophers, a Summary of Scientific Theories, 5 vols. (xi) [e]
62. A Patchwork of Extracts, historical and poetical, 62 sections ; some make it 66.[f]
63. On the Unity of the Academy since the time of Plato.
64. On the Difference between the Pyrrhonians and the Academics.[g]
65. On the Generation of the Soul in the *Timaeus*. (xiii)
66. On the Fact that in Plato's View the Universe had a Beginning.[h]

vii) is in one book, but promises a continuation. If that was ever written, an identification with this entry in the Lamprias Catalogue might be correct.

[d] Mentioned, *De Stoic. Repugn.* 1040 D, and probably used in chaps. 15-16 of that work, see *Class. Quart.* xxxiv (1940), p. 22.

[e] This spurious work is not currently (1965) included in vol. xi.

[f] Possibly the work from which fragment 179 is taken, since it might be called historical : or again, the title may be abbreviated and have once contained the word " philo-sophical."

[g] *Cf.* Sextus Empiricus, *Outlines of Pyrrhonism*, i. 220-235.

[h] Mentioned, *Moralia*, 1013 E ; some of what follows there, down to 1023 B, will be drawn from this book.

[1] Joined to 69 in Ven., omitted by Neap. Joined to 70 by Volkmann, made independent by Ziegler.

[2] The manuscripts of this book have, more correctly, περὶ τῶν κοινῶν ἐννοιῶν.

[a] Plato, *Timaeus*, 53 c ff.

WORKS BY PLUTARCH

67. Where are the Forms ?
68. The Manner of the Participation of Matter in the Forms, namely that it constitutes the primary Bodies.[a]
69. On the Sign of Socrates. (vii)
69a (?). To (or Against) Alcidamas.[b]
70. In Defence of (or About) Plato's *Theages*.[c]
71. That the Academic Philosophy allows for the Reality of Prophecy. *Cf.* no. 131. Frags. 21-23.
72. On Moral Virtue. (vi)
73. On the Face that appears in the Moon. (xii)
74. Whether Odd or Even Number is the better.
75. Whether an Old Man should engage in Public Affairs. (x)
76. On Stoic Inconsistencies. (xiii)
77. On Conceptions, against the Stoics. (xiii)
78. On Common Usage, against the Stoics.[d]
79. That the Stoics talk more paradoxically than the Poets. (xiii)
80. A Reply to Epicurus' Lecture on the Gods.[e]
81. Against Colotes in Defence of the other Philosophers. (xiv)
82. That one cannot even live pleasantly by following Epicurus' Doctrine. (xiv)
83. On Friendship, addressed to Bithynus.

[b] United in the mss. to the previous title, but that work bears no such dedication. Volkmann suggested that the words belong with no. 70. Alcidamas is unknown.
[c] The authenticity of the *Theages* was disputed, and since Plutarch never quotes it as Plato's, Patzig thought this work spurious.
[d] *Cf. Stoic. Rep.* 1036 c-e, *S.V.F.* ii. 109, Pohlenz, *Die Stoa,* i. 29.
[e] Usener, *Epicurea,* p. 103, if the " lecture " is identical with what is elsewhere called a " book." But *On the Gods* ought perhaps to be a separate title.

---

[1] τὸν κόλακα τοῦ φίλου Par. : τοῦ φίλου τὸν κόλακα Neap. Ven.

[2] σχολικοῖς Par. Ven. : σχολαστικοῖς Neap.

---

[a] Without adequate reason Usener, *Jb. kl. Phil.*, 1889, p. 139, *Kl. Schr.* i. 344, identified this with *An Vitiositas*, Wilamowitz, *Hermes*, lxii (1927), p. 296, with *De Virtute et Vitio*.

[b] Probably an anti-Stoic essay, *cf.* Cicero, *De Oratore*, iii.

16

84. Ammonius, or On not finding Pleasure in Involvement with Vice.[a]
85. How to praise oneself without giving Offence. (vii)
86. Is Rhetoric a Virtue ?[b]
87. How to be aware of making Moral Progress. (i)
88. On the Oracles that have come to an End. (v)
89. How we distinguish a Flatterer from a Friend. (i)
90. On the Principle of Cold. (xii)
91. On Delays in Divine Retribution. (vii)
92. On Talkativeness. (vi)
93. On Anger. Frag. 148.
94. Advice on Health. (ii)
95. On Cheerfulness. (vi)
96. On Compliancy. (vii)
97. On Officiousness. (vi)
98. On Brotherly Affection. (vi)
99. On Comets.
100. Which of a Man's three Names is his Proper Name ?[c]
101. On Exile. (vii)
102. On Listening to Philosophers' Lectures. (i)
103. How one should study Poetry. (i)
104. Precepts of Statecraft. (x)
105. On Ways of Life. Another copy has the title On Life's being like a Game at Dice.[d]
106. The proper Use of School Exercises.[e]

65, " (Stoici) soli ex omnibus eloquentiam uirtutem . . . esse dixerunt."

[c] *i.e.*, the Roman praenomen, nomen, and cognomen. *Cf. Life of Marius*, chap. 1.

[d] *De Tranquillitate Animi*, 467 A, ascribes this comparison to Plato (*cf. Rep.* 604 c); see also Epictetus, ii. 5. 2-3.

[e] In rhetoric.

PLUTARCH'S MORALIA

---

[1] Περὶ ἰσχύος σώματος Patzig.
[2] κρινοῦμεν Ven. Neap. κρίνομεν Volkmann.

---

[a] At *Coniugalia Praecepta*, 145 A Plutarch's wife Timoxena is said to have written on this subject. Wilamowitz, *Kl. Schr.* iv. 655, suggested that her authorship was a fiction and Plutarch himself the true writer.

[b] Possibly a metaphorical title; but Volkmann refers to Aulus Gellius, xii. 1, which records Favorinus' advice to wealthy mothers to feed their babies themselves, and not to employ wetnurses.

WORKS BY PLUTARCH

107. A Dialogue on Love. (ix)
108. Sayings of Rulers, Generals, and Monarchs. (iii)
109. On My Own Body.
110. Dinner of the Seven Sages. (ii)
111. A Letter of Consolation addressed to Asclepiades.
112. A Letter of Consolation to his Wife. (vii)
113. On Love of Self-adornment.*a*
114. The Wetnurse.*b*
115. Advice on Marriage. (ii)
116. On the Fact that the Priestess at Delphi no longer gives Oracles in Verse. (v)
117. On the E at Delphi. (v)
118. On the Meaning of the Story of Isis and Sarapis.*c* (v)
119. Explanations of Aratus' *Weatherlore*. Frags. 13-20.
120. Notes on Nicander's *Theriaca*. Frags. 113-115.
121. A Comparison of Aristophanes and Menander. (x)
122. On the Malice of Herodotus. (xi)
123. On the Date of the *Iliad*.
124. How to judge True History. *Cf.* no. 225.
125. Recollections.*d*
126. Brave Deeds by Women (iii) ; in another copy, On the correct Relation of a Woman to her Husband.*e*
127. On Irrational Animals, a poetic work.*f*

---

c The mss. of the work give it the title *On Isis and Osiris*, but it identifies Osiris with Sarapis, 362 B.

d Nachstädt identifies this, without much probability, with no. 108.   *e* Compare the note on no. 222.

f Ziegler would identify this with *Bruta Ratione Uti* (xii), understanding " a work of fiction." A. Gercke, *Rh. Mus.* xli (1886), p. 470, demolishes a house of cards built by O. Crusius, *ibid.* xxxix (1884), pp. 580-606.

---

[1] ἀπ᾽ Bernardakis : ὑπ᾽ Ven. Neap.

[2] φιλοπράγμονος Ziegler : φιλοπραγμόνων Par. Ven. (-ῶν) Neap.

[3] δὲν Patzig : οὐδὲν Ven. Neap.

---

[a] Treu suggested that this was really a different work, identical with *De Amicorum Multitudine*, which is otherwise absent from the list. *Cf.* the note on no. 222.

WORKS BY PLUTARCH

128. Parallel Stories, Greek and Roman. (iv)
129. On Epicurean Inconsistencies.
130. How to profit by one's Enemies. (ii)
131. On the Fact that there is no Conflict between the Principles of the Academy and the Art of Prophecy. *Cf.* no. 71.
132. A letter to Favorinus about Friendship. Another copy has the title, On the Use to be made of Friends.[a] Frags. 159-171.
133. A Reply to Epicurus on the subject of Free-Will.
134. Academic Lectures.
135. Can Animals think ?
136. Platonic Problems. (xiii)
137. How might a Man active in Affairs escape the Reputation of being a Busybody ?
138. Roman Customs Explained. (iv)
139. Foreign Customs Explained.
140. On the Cestos of the Mother of the Gods.
141. Protagoras' *On the First Things.*[b]
142. On the Proverbs in Use among the Alexandrians. See p. 404.
143. That the Epicureans talk more paradoxically than the Poets.
144. What is Understanding ?
145. On " Hing " and " Nothing." [c]
146. That Understanding is impossible.
147. Whether Land-animals or Water-animals are the more intelligent. (xii)

[b] It would be surprising if an otherwise unknown work of Protagoras had survived late enough to be included by error in this list, *cf.* no. 56. Perhaps there are two Plutarchean works, *On Protagoras* and *On First Principles.*

[c] So we may represent Democritus' jesting division of μηδέν as μὴ δέν; see *Adversus Colotem,* 1109 A.

21

---

[1] Στωικῶν] ? ἱστοριῶν.
[2] Βηστίαν Ziegler : Φηστίαν.
[3] τρόπων [so in Christ-Schmid-Stählin, *Griech. Litt.* ii, p. 511] : τόπων.
[4] πολίτης] ? πολιτικός Pohlenz.
[5] οὐ πονήσει after ὅτι deleted by Hoeschel.

---

[a] Conceivably an alternative title for no. 97.

[b] The subject is likely to have been logical rather than political, although Pohlenz, *Moralia*, vol. v, Praef. vi, adopts the latter view.

WORKS BY PLUTARCH

[c] For the controversies concerning the concept of τὸ ἐφ' ἡμῖν see *S.V.F.* ii. 974, 979-984, 988, 1001, 1007.

[d] *De Superstitione* (ii) does not reply to Epicurus. Ziegler suggests that " A Reply to Epicurus," if not a mere mistake, is the title of a separate work.

[e] The classification of 10 " tropes," or methods of procedure, in scepticism was made by Aenesidemus (Sextus Empiricus, *Adversus Mathematicos*, vii. 345), but expounded in his *Outline Introductory to Pyrrhonism.* See Diogenes Laertius, ix. 79-88, Sextus Empiricus, *Outlines of Pyrrhonism*, i. 36-163.

---

[1] Αἰτίαι] ? ἀρεταὶ Nachstädt.

WORKS BY PLUTARCH

166. Greek Customs Explained. (iv)
167. Explanations concerning Women.[a]
168. On Famous Men.
169. Spartan Sayings. (iii)
170. Solutions of Problems.
171. A Collection of Oracles.
172. On Freedom from Pain.
173. On Exercises.[b]
174. On Desire.
175. On the Luck of the Romans. (iv)
176. On Alexander's Luck. (iv)
177. On the Saying " Know Thyself " and the Problem of Immortality.
178. On the Saying " Live in Obscurity." (xiv)
179. On Mental Calm.
180. On Virtue, whether it can be taught. (vi)
181. On the Descent into the Cave of Trophonius.
182. The Suppliant.
183. An Epitome of Natural Science.
184. On the First Philosophers and their Successors
185. On Matter.
186. On Alexander's Virtue. (iv)
187. The Education of Achilles.
188. On the Cyrenaic Philosophers.
189. A Defence of Socrates.
190. On the Condemnation of Socrates.
191. On Earth-eaters.
192. Lecture on the Ten Categories.
193. On Problems.

[a] Nachstädt suggests that this title is corrupt and should be identical with no. 126.
[b] Perhaps rhetorical exercises.

---

[2] διδακτὸν Bernardakis : διδακτέον Ven. Neap.
[3] Κυρηναϊκῶν Bernardakis : Κυρηναίων.

194. Περὶ χαρακτήρων.

195. Πόλεων κτίσεις.

196. Φυσικῶν ἀρεσκόντων.

197. Κατὰ τί εὔδοξοι Ἀθηναῖοι;

198. Περὶ τῶν συνηγορούντων.

199. Τίς ἄριστος βίος;

200. Περὶ ἡμερῶν.

200a.[1] Μελετῶν φυσικῶν καὶ πανηγυρικῶν.

201. Περὶ τῶν ἐν Πλαταιαῖς Δαιδάλων.

202. Φιλολόγων παρασκευῶν.[2]

203. Περὶ εὐγενείας.

204. Ὁ πρὸς Δίωνα ῥηθεὶς ἐν Ὀλυμπίᾳ.

205. Περὶ τοῦ τί ἔδοξεν Ἡρακλείτῳ.

206. Πότερον χρησιμώτερον πῦρ ἢ ὕδωρ.

207. Προτρεπτικὸς πρὸς[3] νέον πλούσιον.

208. Πότερον τὰ ψυχῆς ἢ σώματος πάθη χείρονα.

209. Περὶ ψυχῆς.

210. Εἰ ἄπρακτος ὁ περὶ πάντων ἐπέχων.

211. Περὶ φιλοπλουτίας.

212. Περὶ σεισμῶν.

213. Πῶς δεῖ Λάκωνα μάχεσθαι;

214. Προτρεπτικὸς εἰς Ἀσκληπιάδην[4] Περγαμηνόν.

[1] Title separated from the preceding by Wyttenbach.
[2] Par. Ven.: περὶ φιλολόγων, περὶ σκευῶν. Neap.
[3] πρὸς Neap.: εἰς Ven.
[4] Ἀσκληπιάδην Ziegler: Ἀσκληπιὸν Ven. Neap.

---

[a] Perhaps not to be identified with no. 61, *Placita Philosophorum*, since that work is in five books, and this should by its place in the list be contained in a single one.

[b] There is some error in the mss., for which a possible remedy is to divide, as above, what they give as a single title. But there is still a strange combination in no. 200a.

[c] *Cf.* no. 227. Perhaps Dio of Prusa.

194. On Characters (*or* Styles).
195. City Foundations.
196. A Collection of Scientific Opinions.[a]
197. What was the Basis of the Athenians' Renown ? (iv)
198. On Advocates.
199. What is the best Way of Life ?
200. On Dates.[b] *Cf.* no. 150.
200a. A Collection of Scientific Lectures and Public Addresses.
201. On the Festival of Wooden Images at Plataea. Frags. 157-158.
202. A Collection of Introductions to Literary Problems.
203. On Nobility of Birth. Frags. 139-141.
204. The Reply to Dio delivered at Olympia.[c]
205. On the Question of Heraclitus' Beliefs.
206. Whether Fire or Water is the more useful. (xii)
207. An Exhortation to Philosophy, addressed to a Rich Young Man.[d]
208. Whether the Affections of the Soul or the Body are the worse. (vi)
209. On the Soul. Frags. 173-178.
210. Whether Reserving Judgement on Everything involves Inaction.
211. On Love of Wealth. (vii)
212. On Earthquakes.
213. How a Spartan should fight.
214. An Exhortation to Philosophy, addressed to Asclepiades of Pergamum.[e]

[d] Identified by Wegehaupt (*Berl. phil. Woch.* xxxiii (1913), p. 1316) with Menemachus, to whom *Praecepta Gerendae Reipublicae* and perhaps *De Exilio* are addressed.

[e] Probably the Asclepiades of no. 111, but otherwise unknown.

¹ τί τὸ Ven.: τί Neap.
² Ven. omits ἐρωτικαὶ . . . ἄλλῳ.
³ κρινοῦμεν Ven.: κρίνομεν Volkmann.

ᵃ Some think that this is referred to in *De Soll. Anim.* 959 B-D, where they believe the anonymous author of " an

215. On the Disadvantages of Borrowing. (x)
216. On Hunting.[a]
217. A Reply to those who attempt Deception.
218. Explanations of Natural Phenomena. (xi)
219. An Attack on those who do not engage in Philosophy because they practise Rhetoric.
220. What Attention is to be paid to Poetry?
221. What in Plato's view is the End of Life?
222. Love Stories (x); in another copy, To (or Against) Men in Love.[b]
223. A Book of Exercises introductory to Philosophy.
224. On Euripides.
225. How shall we determine Truth? [c]
226. That the Soul is Imperishable.
227. A Discourse in Reply to Dio.[d]

[a] encomium on hunting " to be Plutarch himself; see Helmbold's note *ad loc.* I side with those who find this incredible, since Autobulus speaks of this person as a dangerous influence, but at 964 D holds up Plutarch's teaching as a safe guide to follow in the treatment of animals.

[b] This is impossible as an alternative title and may really be that of another book, possibly that from which frags. 134-138 are derived.

[c] *Cf.* no. 124.   [d] *Cf.* no. 204.

TYRWHITT'S FRAGMENTS

DESIRE AND GRIEF — PSYCHICAL OR BODILY PHENOMENA?
(DE LIBIDINE ET AEGRITUDINE)

THE AFFECTIVE ELEMENT IN MAN— IS IT A PART OR A FACULTY OF HIS SOUL?
(UTRUM PARS AN FACULTAS ANIMI AFFECTIBUS SUBIECTA SIT)

THESE two works, both incomplete, are sometimes known as Tyrwhitt's Fragments, since they were first published in 1773 by Thomas Tyrwhitt,[a] who had discovered them in a MS. in London, Harleianus 5612. Tyrwhitt had heard that they were also in a Laurentianus, which Duebner later identified as Laur 56. 4; another Laurentianus, 80. 28, contains *De Libidine et Aegritudine*. All three MSS. are of the fifteenth century, and exhibit closely similar texts [b]; all three contain in addition only items from the *Moralia* as known to Planudes. The fact that the Harleianus prefixes to the title of the first fragment the words Πλουτάρχου φιλοσόφου was used by Volkmann, i. 105, and Treu (*Zur Geschichte d. Überlieferung*

---

[a] *Fragmenta duo Plutarchi*, London, 1773.

[b] I have collated Harl. 5612 (h), and finding Pohlenz's record in the Teubner edition trustworthy, have relied on him for knowledge of Laur. 56. 4 (i) and 80. 28 (k).

von Plutarchs Moralia, iii. 32) as an argument that they were by Plutarch the son of Nestorius, the neo-Platonist.[a] The argument is worthless, since the very next item to follow them in the manuscript, *De Sera Numinis Vindicta*, is similarly headed Πλουτάρχου φιλοσόφου.

Nevertheless there is general agreement to-day that neither work can be by Plutarch of Chaeronea. Ziegler in Pauly-Wissowa, *Realencyclopädie*, xxi. 751, put in a plea for the genuineness of the first, which he thought to be an unfinished sketch, but later withdrew it.[b] I have shown that neither has the metrical clausulae characteristic of Plutarch's authentic works.[c] Pohlenz[d] assigned the first to *c.* A.D. 400, on the authority of Wilamowitz, who claimed that it exhibited accentual clausulae, following Meyer's law. Meyer's "law," although historically important, is now recognized to be of little use in its original formulation, according to which there was, from the fourth century A.D., a tendency in some authors to write clausulae such that at least two unaccented syllables intervened between the ultimate and penultimate accents (which by then indicated stress). It has been shown that chance will secure a large majority (80%) of clausulae of this sort : samples from Polybius and Plutarch have even yielded 85%. To prove an author to have used accentual clausulae he must be shown either to have a *very* high percentage that

---

[a] Against this view see Zeller, *Phil. d. Griechen*, iii. 2. 808[3].

[b] *Studi in onore L. Castiglioni*, p. 1135 (1960).

[c] *Class. Quart.* xxxiii (1939), p. 197. This argument would be weakened if there were any reason for accepting Wehrli's assertion (*Die Schule des Aristoteles, Herakleides*, p. 83) that the first work has been abbreviated.

[d] *Fleckeisens Jahrbuch*, Suppl. xxiv, p. 593[3].

accord with Meyer's " law," or to seek or avoid
particular accentual forms. For example, many By-
zantine authors avoid juxtaposition of accents, or an
interval of an *odd* number of unaccented syllables,
and in others more individual predilections have been
discovered. The fragment under consideration is so
short that it barely allows of useful statistical treatment, especially as there is some uncertainty about
what words, when stress had been introduced, carried
a written accent without having a stressed syllable.
Nevertheless a count, necessarily making some arbitrary decisions, did not reveal a tendency to any of
the recognized accentual patterns ; about 80% of
the clausulae conform to Meyer's " law," and that
is merely the average figure for post-Hellenistic pre-
accentual prose (C. Litzica, *Das Meyersche Gesetz*, p.
12). Hence there is no reason for supposing the fragment to be written with any regard to accents.[a]

The two works differ in character. The second is a
competent and methodical academic exercise, whose
author makes no attempt to render palatable the
severity of his logic. Nothing in Plutarch's surviving
works remotely resembles it. It clearly belongs to
the time of revived Aristotelianism, and I should
guess to the third or fourth century A.D.[b] But I can
find nothing to rule out an earlier date. The other
work is more of a sophistical nature, using various
devices of rhetoric to adorn a superficial treatment of
its subject. The author appears to be showing off to
an audience of no great learning. His language is

[a] A good account of the principles to be followed in in-
vestigating accentual prose is to be found in S. Skimina, *État
actuel des études sur le rythme de la prose grecque*, ii, Eus
Suppl. 11 (Lwów, 1930).
[b] *Cf.* M. Pohlenz, *Die Stoa*, ii. 175.

heavily coloured by Stoicism, but he does not reveal his own position, at least in what survives. There is a *terminus post quem* in the mention of Posidonius, and of Diodotus, if he is one of two philosophers who bore that name in the first century B.C. I see no reason why the work should not have been composed in the first century A.D., while suspecting it may be later. It is notable that there are many parallels with the genuine Plutarch : the report about Demo-critus and Theophrastus (chap. 2), the unfamiliar story of the dismemberment of Horus (chap. 6), a simile (chap. 7), a verse quotation (chap. 8), and much in chap. 9. These similarities are too striking to be due to chance, and some may think that, in spite of the differences from Plutarch's usual style and man-ner, they make it probable that he was in fact the author. Certainly the case is much stronger than that for *Aquane an ignis* (see L.C.L., vol. xii, p. 288). Another possibility is that the work was written by someone closely associated with him, perhaps a mem-ber of the group of friends and younger men with whom he pursued his philosophical studies.

The first fragment is easily summarized. The ques-tion whether body or soul is responsible for the affec-tions of desire, grief,[a] pleasure, and fear [the cardinal " passions " of the Stoics] is an old and important one (chaps. 1-3). Strato assigned them to the soul (chap. 4), Heraclides (?) to the body ; Posidonius ascribed some to the soul, some to the body, but thought that others belonged to one but involved the other ; Diodotus also tried to divide them, but body

---

[a] No English word adequately translates λύπη, which covers sorrow, pity, envy, remorse, depression, and annoy-ance.

and soul are not easily distinguished (chaps. 5-6). Other philosophers [Peripatetics] said that affection belonged to the whole man (chap. 7); but this dodges the issue, which is, does the whole man make use of his body or of his soul when he suffers an affection? (chap. 8). To come to grips with the subject, there are good arguments for finding a bodily origin for the affections. [No more is preserved, if it ever existed.]

The second fragment is more technical. The question is whether the affective aspect of the soul, *i.e.*, that which experiences fear, desire, etc. is to be regarded as a specific irrational part of the soul, or as a faculty of the whole soul (chap. 1).[a] Both alternatives appear to have absurd consequences. The first implies that irrational animals have something less than soul, and therefore as not possessing soul are not alive [a purely verbal and sophistical argument]; the latter that opposites (reason and unreason) can co-exist. But perhaps opposites can co-exist if they are opposite *potentialities*: unreason in animals is always actualized, in man it sometimes remains a potentiality (chap. 2). Yet the concept of potentiality

---

[a] In *De Anima* Aristotle speaks indifferently of " parts " (which he usually calls μόρια, not μέρη, the word frequently used by Plato) or of " faculties " of the soul, and at *Juv.* 467 b 17 he writes τῆς ψυχῆς ἢ μόρια ἢ δυνάμεις, ὁποτέρως ποτὲ δεῖ καλεῖν. The Aristotelian commentators incline to the word δυνάμεις, and Galen, *Hipp. et Plat.* 493 (p. 476 Müller), promises to show against Aristotle and Posidonius that the soul has parts, not merely faculties. Whether one should speak of parts or faculties is a topic mentioned by Themistius, *De Anima*, p. 117. 1 Heinze. Further references to the controversy are preserved from Porphyry (Stobaeus, i. 49. 25, p. 351 Wachsmuth) and Iamblichus (*ibid.* i. 49. 33, p. 369 Wachsmuth), passages translated with a commentary by Festugière, *La Révélation d'Hermès Trismégiste*, iii, pp. 190-193.

brings difficulties. The soul becomes a mere substratum for its potentialities and so will not in itself
have life. Indeed even if regarded as substratum *plus*
potentiality, it is only *potentially* alive (chap. 3). But
if this potentiality is a *state*, it may be a state of *life*,
which can be actualized as a different sort of life, that
of the reason. If we thus explain the soul's life it
follows that soul is not a composite thing : there is
no substratum for the potentiality (chap. 4). If soul
is defined as a vital potentiality, the affections that
hinder its actualization cannot belong to it, in the
sense of arising from it, although they involve it.
They must arise from the body (chap. 5). But if affections *involve* the soul, there must be something in it
that can be affected. We cannot explain this being-
affected simply as a cessation of rational activity,
because when a human animal suffers an affection
arising in the body and involving the soul, sometimes
the extent of the affection is limited by the action of
reason (chap. 6). Yet the affection and the activity of
the reason are not simultaneous : reason follows the
affection, to give it shape. What is affected in the
soul is identical with the rational soul : its affection
is the intermittency of its activity in contemplating
the truth, and when it ceases to contemplate the
truth it falls into delusion (chap. 7).

ΠΟΤΕΡΟΝ[1] ΨΥΧΗΣ Η ΣΩΜΑΤΟΣ
ΕΠΙΘΥΜΙΑ ΚΑΙ ΛΥΠΗ

1. Ἡ μὲν πρόθεσις περὶ ἐπιθυμίας γέγονε καὶ
λύπης, πότερον σώματος πάθος ἐστὶν ἢ ἐπὶ σώματι
ψυχῆς· καὶ γὰρ εἰ τὴν αὐτοπάθειαν ἀπολύσεται τὸ
σῶμα τούτων, οὐ διαφεύξεται τὴν αἰτίαν, ἀλλὰ διὰ
σώματος πάθη φαίνεται, καὶ ἂν ἐλέγχηται[2] περὶ
ψυχήν. ἡ δὲ κοινότης τοῦ λόγου καὶ τὰ λοιπὰ πάθη
τῇ[3] ζητήσει συνυποβάλλει,[4] φόβον[5] καὶ ἡδονήν, ὧν
τὸ μὲν λύπῃ τὸ δ᾽ ἐπιθυμίᾳ συμπέφυκεν, εἴ γε πᾶς
ἄνθρωπος ὢν μὲν λυπεῖται παρόντων, δέδιε μελλόντων,[6] ὧν δ᾽ ὀρέγεται[7] μὴ παρόντων,[8] ἥδεται δεδο-
μένοις.[9] τὸν μὲν γὰρ κόσμον οἱ φυσικοὶ λέγουσιν
ἐκ τεττάρων σωμάτων πρώτων καὶ μεγίστων συν-
ηρμόσθαι[10] κατ᾽ ἀντίθεσιν καὶ ἀντίταξιν ἀλλήλοις
ἄνω καὶ κάτω φύσει ῥεπόντων, τὴν δὲ κακίαν καὶ
ἀκοσμίαν τὴν ἐν ἡμῖν τέσσαρα πάθη τὰ πρῶτα

---

[1] Πλουτάρχου φιλοσόφου πότερον h.
[2] F. H. S. : καὶ ἀπελέγχηται π. ψ. hk. καὶ π. ψ. ἐλέγχηται i.
κἂν π. ψ. ἀπελέγχηται Pohlenz.
[3] τῇ added by Wyttenbach (ζητεῖ i).
[4] Wyttenbach : συναποβάλλει. [5] Tyrwhitt : φθόνον.
[6] δέδιε μελλόντων F. H. S. : ὧνδε διαμελλόντων. ὧν δὲ δέδιε
μελλόντων Wyttenbach.
[7] καὶ deleted after ὀρέγεται by Pohlenz.
[8] οἷς δὲ deleted after παρόντων by F. H. S.
[9] Pohlenz : δεομένοις. γενομένοις Tyrwhitt.

DESIRE AND GRIEF—PSYCHICAL OR
BODILY PHENOMENA?

1. THE subject before us is whether desire and grief are an affection of the body or an affection of the soul, occasioned by the body ; for even if the body shows that it is innocent of experiencing these affections itself, it will not be acquitted of responsibility for them ; they are affections that clearly arise through the body, even should they be proved to belong to the soul. The other affections, too, namely fear and pleasure, have a similarity of definition which requires them to be treated in this discussion along with desire and grief. Fear is cognate with grief, and pleasure with desire, if it is true that every human being feels fear at the prospect of those things whose presence causes him grief, whereas he feels pleasure on obtaining the things that he desires when he is without them. Scientists tell us that the world is a harmonious combination of four primary principal bodies, which have natural inclinations upwards and downwards in antithesis or opposition to one another.[a] But the four basic affections give rise to the bad-

---

[a] That fire and air move upwards, water and earth downwards (*i.e.*, towards the centre of the universe) is common ground to Stoics and Peripatetics.

---

[10] Pohlenz (*cf. Mor.* 943 F): συνηρῆσθαι. συνηρτῆσθαι Tyrwhitt.

κινεῖ καὶ διαφέρει πρὸς τοὐναντίον ἀτάκτως καὶ
ἀλόγως τὴν ψυχήν,[1] ἄνω μὲν ἡδονὴ καὶ κάτω λύπη,
πρόσω δ' ἐπιθυμία καὶ ὀπίσω φόβος,[2] ὥσπερ ἐξ ὁρμῶν ἀσυμμέτρων μετασχηματιζομένην.[3] ἔπαρσις
γὰρ αὐτῆς ἡδονή,[4] συστολὴ δὲ[5] λύπη· τείνεται[6] δ'
εἰς ἐπιθυμίαν, φεύγει δ' ὃ δέδιεν. ὅ γε μὴν θυμός,
εἴτε τῆς ἐπιθυμίας ἐστὶν εἶδος κατ' ὄρεξιν ἀντι-
λυπήσεως ὑφιστάμενος εἴτε ἕτερόν τι καὶ διάφορον
πολλάκις δὲ καὶ μαχόμενον πρὸς ἐπιθυμίαν πάθος,
ὡς ὑπενόει Πλάτων, οὐκ ἄδηλον ὅτι καὶ αὐτὸς
παρέξει ζήτησιν, εἴτε τῆς ψυχῆς αὐτῆς κινουμένης[7]
εἴτε τοῦ σώματος ἐκριπιζόμενος[8] χειμάζει τὸν ἄνθρωπον.

2. Ἔοικε παλαιά τις αὕτη τῷ σώματι διαδικασία
πρὸς τὴν ψυχὴν περὶ τῶν παθῶν εἶναι. καὶ Δημόκριτος μὲν ἐπὶ τὴν ψυχὴν ἀναφέρων τὴν κακοδαιμονίαν[9] φησίν, εἰ τοῦ σώματος αὐτῇ[10] δίκην λαχόντος
παρὰ πάντα τὸν βίον ὧν ὠδύνηται καὶ[11] κακῶς
πέπονθεν αὐτὸς γένοιτο τοῦ ἐγκλήματος δικαστής,[12]
ἡδέως ἂν καταψηφίσασθαι τῆς ψυχῆς, ἐφ' οἷς τὰ
μὲν ἀπώλεσε[13] τοῦ σώματος ταῖς ἀμελείαις καὶ ἐξ-
έλυσε ταῖς μέθαις, τὰ δὲ κατέφθειρε καὶ διέσπασε

---

[1] τὴν ψυχήν added here by F. H. S., after μετασχηματιζομένη
by Pohlenz (μετασχηματιζομένης τῆς ψυχῆς Ziegler).

[2] Tyrwhitt : φθόνος.

[3] F. H. S., cf. S. V.F. iii. 462, φυσικὴν τῶν ὁρμῶν συμμετρίαν
ὑπερβαίνειν : ἐξ ὀργάνων ἀμέτρων (ἀσυμμέτρων Pohlenz) μετασχηματιζομένη.

[4] Tyrwhitt : ἡδονῆς.   [5] δὲ omitted by hk.

[6] τείνεται i in margin : γίγνεται. ἐκτείνεται Wyttenbach.

[7] εἴτε . . . κινουμένης added by Pohlenz.

[8] Hartman : ἐκριπτούμενος.

[9] τὴν κακοδαιμονίαν Patzig : κακοδαίμων. τὴν τοῦ κακῶσαι δύναμιν Pohlenz.

[10] εἰ . . . αὐτῇ Wyttenbach : ἡ . . . αὕτη.

ness and disorderliness in us, as they drive the soul chaotically and irrationally in opposite directions, to rise in pleasure and to sink in pain, to advance in desire, and to draw back in fear, being given its successive shapes so to speak in consequence of disproportionate impulses [a]; for its swelling is pleasure, and its contraction grief, it stretches out towards its desire and retreats from what it fears. Anger, moreover, whether a species of desire, its essence being a longing to inflict pain in reprisal,[b] or something different and distinct, an affection that, as Plato supposed,[c] often positively conflicts with desire, will obviously also provide a subject for inquiry : ⟨is it by a disturbance of soul⟩ or of body that anger is fanned to fire and drives the man in its tempest ?

2. This claim and counterclaim in the suit of body versus soul over the affections is, it seems, of long standing. Democritus, ascribing unhappiness to the soul's account, says that if the body were to bring an action against the soul for all the torment and ill-treatment it had suffered throughout its life, and if he were a member of the jury trying the charge, he would be glad to cast his vote against the soul, for the reason that it had destroyed some parts of the body by neglect, or weakened them by drunken carousals, while others it had ruined and ravaged in its pur-

---

[a] According to the Stoics a passion is an " excessive impulse " ; it oversteps " the natural proportion of the impulses," *i.e.*, is a reaction disproportionate to the stimulus. But " impulses " are introduced into the text only by an uncertain emendation.

[b] Aristotle, *De Anima*, 403 a 30, so defines ὀργή.

[c] *Republic*, 440 A.

---

[11] καί added by Tyrwhitt.   [12] Tyrwhitt : δι and lacuna.
     [13] Wyttenbach : ἀπέλυσε.

ταῖς φιληδονίαις, ὥσπερ ὀργάνου τινὸς ἢ σκεύους
κακῶς ἔχοντος τὸν χρώμενον ἀφειδῶς αἰτιασάμενος.
Θεόφραστος δὲ τοὐναντίον ἔφη τῷ σώματι πολλοῦ[1]
τὴν ψυχὴν ἐνοικεῖν, ὀλίγου χρόνου βαρεῖς μισθοὺς
ὑποτελοῦσαν, τὰς λύπας τοὺς φόβους τὰς ἐπιθυμίας
τὰς ζηλοτυπίας, αἷς συμφερομένη περὶ τὸ σῶμα
δικαιότερον ἂν αὐτῷ[2] δικάζοιτο πηρώσεως ὧν ἐπι-
λέλησται, καὶ βιαίων ἐφ᾽ οἷς κατέχεται, καὶ ὕβρεως[3]
ὧν ἀδοξεῖ καὶ λοιδορεῖται τῶν ἐκείνου κακῶν ἀνα-
δεχομένη τὰς αἰτίας οὐ προσηκόντως.

3. Ἀγωνιστέον οὖν ὑπὲρ τῆς ἀληθείας. καλὸς
γὰρ ὁ ἀγών, καὶ τῇ ψυχῇ[4] ὁ λόγος πάντως χρήσιμος, εἰ μὲν οὐκ αὐτῆς τὰ πάθη φαίνεται, πρὸς
ἀπολογίαν, εἰ δ᾽ αὐτῆς, πρὸς ἀπαλλαγήν· ὥστ᾽ ἢ
φυλάξασθαι τὸ ἑκούσιον ἢ μὴ λοιδορεῖσθαι τὸ ἀλλότριον.

4. Ἔδει μὲν τοὺς δογματικοὺς καὶ καταληπτι-
κοὺς εἶναι φιλοσόφους φάσκοντας εἰ μὴ περὶ ἄλλο
τι τήν γε τῶν παθῶν ἐνέργειαν[5] ὁμολογεῖν ἀλλήλοις
καὶ συμφέρεσθαι· πολὺς δ᾽ αὐτῶν ὁ παράλογός
ἐστιν. οἱ μὲν γὰρ ἅπαντα συλλήβδην ταῦτα τῇ
ψυχῇ φέροντες ἀνέθεσαν, ὥσπερ Στράτων ὁ φυσι-
κός, οὐ μόνον τὰς ἐπιθυμίας ἀλλὰ καὶ τὰς λύπας,

---

[1] Tyrwhitt: πολλῶ.
[2] Wyttenbach: αὑτοῦ.
[3] Ziegler: ὕβρεων.
[4] Tyrwhitt: τῆς ψυχῆς.
[5] ἐνάργειαν Pohlenz.

---

[a] Diels-Kranz, *Frag. d. Vorsokratiker*, 68 в 159 ; more
briefly cited, *De Tuenda Sanitate*, 135 ε.

[b] Porphyry, *De Abstinentia*, iv. 20, p. 266 Nauck, πολὺ τὸ
ἐνοίκιον, ὥς φησί που Θεόφραστος, διδούσης τῆς ψυχῆς, *De Tuenda
Sanitate*, loc. cit.

[c] Strato, frag. 111 Wehrli, cf. frag. 110 (*De Plac. Phil.* iv.

suit of pleasure ; he might be laying the blame for the bad condition of some tool or utensil on the person who had used it without care.[a] Theophrastus, on the contrary, said that the soul's lodging in the body was an expensive one [b] ; that for a short tenancy it paid a heavy price in its pains and fears, desires and jealousies ; and that its involvement with these emotions in the body gave it a better case to take to court, since it could accuse the body of mayhem for all it had been caused to forget, of forcible seizure for its detention, and of outrage for the ill-fame and vituperation it suffers through being undeservedly held responsible for the evils that befall the body.

3. We must enter the lists then as champions of the truth. The contest is an honourable one, and the soul will in any event profit by the discussion. If the affections prove not to belong to it, that answers the charge ; if they are found to belong, it will be helped to be rid of them. The result will be either that it is on its guard against voluntary misdeeds, or that it is not reproached for another's acts.

4. Whatever else they may disagree about, it might be expected of philosophers who have a positive creed and claim to apprehend reality, that they would at least concur and agree with one another on the action of the affections. They are, however, far from meeting our expectations. Some have ascribed all affections indiscriminately to the soul, like the scientist Strato,[c] who declared that not only our desires but also our griefs, not only our fears and

23). Wehrli, like W. Capelle, *R.E.* 2. Reihe, iv. 303, *cf.* 310, thinks it unlikely that Strato used the Stoic term ἡγεμονικόν, " centre of command," since he appears to have held a unitary view of the soul. But he localized thought and sensation between the eyebrows (see below).

οὐδὲ τοὺς φόβους καὶ τοὺς φθόνους καὶ τὰς ἐπι-
χαιρεκακίας ἀλλὰ καὶ πόνους καὶ ἡδονὰς καὶ ἀλγη-
δόνας καὶ ὅλως πᾶσαν αἴσθησιν ἐν τῇ ψυχῇ συνίστα-
σθαι φάμενος καὶ τῆς ψυχῆς τὰ τοιαῦτα πάντ'
εἶναι, μὴ τὸν πόδα πονούντων ἡμῶν ὅταν προσ-
κρούσωμεν μηδὲ τὴν κεφαλὴν ὅταν κατάξωμεν μηδὲ[1] τὸν δάκτυλον ὅταν ἐκτέμωμεν· ἀναίσθητα γὰρ
τὰ λοιπὰ πλὴν τοῦ ἡγεμονικοῦ, πρὸς ὃ τῆς πληγῆς
ὀξέως ἀναφερομένης τὴν αἴσθησιν ἀλγηδόνα καλοῦμεν. ὡς δὲ τὴν φωνὴν τοῖς ὠσὶν αὐτοῖς ἐνηχοῦσαν
ἔξω δοκοῦμεν εἶναι τὸ ἀπὸ τῆς ἀρχῆς ἐπὶ τὸ ἡγε-
μονικὸν διάστημα τῇ αἰσθήσει προσλογιζόμενοι,
παραπλησίως τὸν ἐκ τοῦ τραύματος πόνον οὐχ ὅπου
τὴν αἴσθησιν εἴληφεν ἀλλ' ὅθεν ἔσχε τὴν ἀρχὴν
εἶναι δοκοῦμεν, ἑλκομένης ἐπ' ἐκεῖνο τῆς ψυχῆς ἀφ'
οὗ πέπονθε. διὸ καὶ προσκόψαντες αὐτίκα τὰς
ὀφρῦς συνηγάγομεν,[2] τῷ πληγέντι μορίῳ τοῦ ἡγεμονικοῦ τὴν αἴσθησιν ὀξέως ἀποδιδόντος, καὶ παρ-
εγκάπτομεν[3] ἔσθ' ὅτε τὸ πνεῦμα, κἂν τὰ μέρη δεσμοῖς διαλαμβάνηται, ἀναίσθητα γίγνεται τὰ ἄκρα·
τραῦμα δὲ λαβόντες ταῖς[4] χερσὶ σφόδρα πιέζομεν,
ἐνιστάμενοι[5] πρὸς τὴν διάδοσιν τοῦ πάθους καὶ τὴν
πληγὴν ἐν τοῖς ἀναισθήτοις θλίβοντες,[6] ἵνα μὴ τῷ[7]

[1] Bernardakis : μὴ.
[2] Bernardakis : συνήγαγον ἐν. συνάγομεν Duebner.
[3] Madvig : παρεγκόπτομεν.
[4] ἀναίσθητα . . . ἄκρα added by Pohlenz, τραῦμα . . . ταῖς
by F. H. S. after Pohlenz.
[5] Bernardakis : ἱστάμενοι.
[6] ἀποθλίβοντες Pohlenz. πλήττοντες hk.

envies and malicious pleasures at others' misfortune but also our physical hurts and pleasures and pains and in general all sensations come about in the soul. According to him, everything of this sort is a psychical event ; we do not have a pain in the foot when we stub our toe, nor in the head when we crack it, nor in the finger when we gash it. Nothing has any sensation except the soul's centre of command ; any blow is quickly relayed to this centre,[a] and its sensation is what we call pain. One may compare the way we think that a noise which in fact sounds in our ears is outside us ; we add to the sensation an estimate of the distance between the origin of the noise and the centre of command.[b] Similarly we think that the pain resulting from a wound is, not where it is sensed, but where it originated, as the soul is drawn towards the source that has affected it. Hence, when we bump into something, we often instantly contract our eyebrows, and sometimes catch our breath,[c] while the centre of command rapidly refers the sensation to the part which received the knock. Again, if our limbs are secured by bonds ⟨there is no feeling in our extremities, and if we are wounded,⟩ we press hard with our hands, resisting the transmission of the injury and squeezing the blow to keep it in the parts that have no feeling, so that it does not become

[a] Plotinus, iv. 7. 7 and 2. 2, polemizes against a similar, Stoic, view of transmission.

[b] H. Poppelreuter, *Zur Psychologie des Aristoteles, Theophrastos, Straton*, p. 51, thinks that the distance involved is really that from source of noise to the *ear* : but on Strato's theory the perceiving centre has to add to *that* the distance from the ear to itself. *Cf.* [Arist.], *Aud.* 801 a 23.

[c] The *hegemonikon* is situated either in the head or in the chest.

---

[7] τῷ added by Pohlenz.

συνάψαι πρὸς τὸ φρονοῦν ἀλγηδὼν γένηται. ταῦτα
μὲν οὖν ὁ Στράτων ἐπὶ πολλοῖς ὡς εἰκὸς τοιούτοις.

5. Ἔνιοι δ' ἄντικρυς καὶ δόξαν καὶ διαλογισμὸν
εἰς τὸ σῶμα κατατείνουσιν, οὐδ' εἶναι οὐσίαν τὸ[1]
παράπαν ψυχῆς λέγοντες ἀλλὰ τῇ τοῦ σώματος δια-
φορᾷ καὶ ποιότητι καὶ δυνάμει συντελεῖσθαι τὰ
τοιαῦτα. τὸ μὲν γὰρ Περὶ τῶν ἐν Ἅιδου βιβλίον
ἐπιγραφόμενον, ἐν ᾧ τὴν ψυχὴν τῇ οὐσίᾳ παρυπάρ-
χειν ἀποφαίνεται[2] ὁ λόγος, οἱ μὲν οὐδ' εἶναι[3] τὸ
παράπαν Ἡρακλείδου νομίζουσιν οἱ δὲ πρὸς ἀντι-
παρεξαγωγὴν συντετάχθαι[4] τῶν εἰρημένων ἑτέροις
περὶ οὐσίας ψυχῆς· ὅτῳ δ' οὖν[5] γεγραμμένον ἄντικρυς ἀναιρεῖ τὴν οὐσίαν αὐτῆς, ὡς τοῦ σώματος
ἔχοντος ἐν αὑτῷ[6] τὰς εἰρημένας δυνάμεις πάσας.

Οἱ δ' ὥσπερ διὰ μέσου τῶν λόγων ἐπεχείρησαν
ἀφορίζειν τῆς ψυχῆς ἴδια πάθη καὶ[7] τοῦ σώματος,
ἐν κοινῷ καὶ πλάτος οὐκ ἔχοντι φερόμενοι τόπῳ
συνεχύθησαν. (6.) ὅ γέ τοι Ποσειδώνιος τὰ μὲν

---

[1] οὐσίαν Pohlenz : αἰτίαν. τὸ added by Bernardakis.
[2] Wyttenbach : αὐτὸ (or αὐτὸς) φαίνεται.
[3] Wyttenbach : οὖν δεινοί.
[4] Wyttenbach : τετάχθαι.
[5] ὅτῳ δ' οὖν Pohlenz : οὕτω.   [6] Ziegler : αὐτῷ.
[7] τὰ deleted before τοῦ by F. H. S. : καὶ ἴδια τοῦ Ziegler.

---

[a] Strato connected sensation and thought, arguing that
there was no sensation without mental attention, cf. De Soll.
Anim. 961 A-B.
[b] And hence also, a fortiori, the affections.
[c] Heraclides " Ponticus " (c. 390–310), a member of Plato's
Academy from Heraclea on the Black Sea ; frag. 72 Wehrli.
Nowhere else is the suggestion made that the book was not
by Heraclides, and Plutarch, Adv. Colotem, 1115 A, refers to
it as if it were genuine.   The account given here is puzzling ;
since Heraclides believed the soul to be constituted of light
or something similar and to have had an existence before

a pain by making contact with the part of us that has understanding.[a] This is the explanation given by Strato for many similar cases, as might be expected.

5. Some, however, go so far as to restrict even opinion and calculation [b] to the body. They deny the very existence of a substantive soul, and say that such mental activities are the result of bodily differences, qualities, or properties. It is true that the book entitled *On the Underworld*, the argument of which is that the soul exists as a concomitant of what is substantial, is thought by some not to be by Heraclides at all, while others say that it was composed as a controversial attack on what other authors had written about the substance of soul. But whoever the writer may have been, it completely does away with the substantial existence of soul, by maintaining that the body has in itself all the aforesaid capacities.[c]

As for those who, mediating as it were between these two positions, have tried to draw a line between the affections proper to the soul and those that belong to the body, they have landed in confusion as they wander in a no-man's-land too narrow to divide. 6. Posidonius, for instance, divided affections into those

and after its incorporation (frags. 97-100 Wehrli), he cannot have thought it to have no substantial existence. Wehrli suggests that this view may have been advanced by a character in a dialogue (if the work was a dialogue), and mistaken for Heraclides' own ; since the book was directed against Democritus' ridicule of the idea that the soul survives death, this would be a strange mistake. If there is any profit in speculation, Heraclides may have reverted to the primitive psychology which divorced the principle of life (ψυχή) from consciousness ; if he did this, and maintained that sensation, thought, and feeling were functions of the body, a later critic might argue that by robbing ψυχή (animal life) of those activities that distinguish it, in the Stoic view, from φύσις (vegetative life) Heraclides had robbed it of its being.

εἶναι ψυχικὰ τὰ δὲ σωματικά, καὶ τὰ μὲν οὐ ψυχῆς
περὶ ψυχὴν δὲ σωματικά, τὰ δ' οὐ σώματος περὶ
σῶμα δὲ ψυχικά φησι· ψυχικὰ μὲν[1] ἁπλῶς λέγων[2]
τὰ ἐν κρίσεσι[3] καὶ ὑπολήψεσιν, οἷον ἐπιθυμίας φόβους ὀργάς, σωματικὰ δ' ἁπλῶς πυρετοὺς περιψύ-
ξεις πυκνώσεις ἀραιώσεις, περὶ ψυχὴν δὲ σωματικὰ[4]
ληθάργους μελαγχολίας δηγμοὺς φαντασίας δια-
χύσεις, ἀνάπαλιν δὲ περὶ σῶμα ψυχικὰ τρόμους καὶ
ὠχριάσεις καὶ μεταβολὰς τοῦ εἴδους κατὰ φόβον ἢ
λύπην. Διόδοτος[5] πάλιν ἴδια μέν τινα τοῦ λογικοῦ
φησι[6] τῆς ψυχῆς πάθη ἴδια δὲ τοῦ συμφυοῦς καὶ
ἀλόγου εἶναι, ῥιπταζόμενος ἐπὶ πάντα καὶ ψηλα-
φῶντι προσεοικὼς τὰς διαφοράς. ὅπου γὰρ ἐπὶ τῶν
ἀγγείων ἔργον ἐστὶ διακρῖναι, πότε τῇ περὶ αὐτὰ
κακίᾳ τὸ ἐγκεχυμένον[7] διέφθαρκε, καὶ πάλιν πότε
τῶν ὑγρῶν νοσησάντων[8] διαβέβρωται,[9] ἦπού γε[10]
τῆς ψυχῆς ἀναμεμιγμένης εἰς τὸ σῶμα καὶ κατὰ
σύγκρασιν[11] ἑνωτικὴν συμπεφυκυίας[12] εὔπορόν ἐστιν
ἐκκαθᾶραι τὴν διαφοράν; ὅρους ψυχῆς καὶ σώ-

---

[1] σωματικά, τὰ δ' . . . ψυχικά and ψυχικὰ μὲν added by
Wyttenbach, φησι by Ziegler.
[2] λέγων transferred here by F. H. S. from before φόβους.
[3] Wyttenbach: τὸ ἐκρίσεσι (or τὸ κρίσεσι). ? τὰ ἐπὶ κρίσεσι,
cf. S.V.F. i. 209.
[4] Tyrwhitt: σωματικὰς or σωματικαί.
[5] Tyrwhitt: δι' ὀδόντος.   [6] Tyrwhitt: φημι.
[7] Wyttenbach: ἐκκεχυμένον.
[8] Wyttenbach: νοσῆσαν.
[9] κέκρυπται deleted after διαβέβρωται by Duebner.
[10] Wyttenbach: τε.   [11] Duebner: κατ' ἐγκράτησιν.
[12] Wyttenbach: συμπεφυκυῖαν.

---

[a] K. Reinhardt, *Poseidonios*, p. 313[1], thinks this was a
provisional distinction in orthodox language, preparatory to
a fully psychosomatic account.
[b] διάχυσις is a species of ἡδονή, being ἀνάλυσις ἀρετῆς, S.V.F.

(*a*) of the soul, (*b*) of the body, (*c*) of the body and manifested in, although not proceeding from, the soul, (*d*) of the soul and manifested in, although not proceeding from, the body. Of the soul without qualifications are those connected with judgements and suppositions, *e.g.*, desires, fears, angers ; of the body without qualification are fevers, chills, contractions and expansions ; of the body but manifested in the soul are lethargies, atrabilious derangements of mind, reactions to hurts, sense-presentations, and feelings of relaxation [a] ; of the soul, on the other hand, but manifested in the body, are tremors, pallors, and other changes of appearance related to fear or grief.[b] Diodotus,[c] again, says that some of the soul's affections are peculiar to the rational element of the soul, and others peculiar to the conjunct irrational element ; he blunders about among them all and guesses which is which, as if playing blind man's buff.[d] In the case of jars or other vessels it is hard to determine when it is through some fault of their own that they have spoiled their contents, and when on the other hand they have been eaten away because the liquids in them became unhealthy. That being so, can we suppose that, when the soul has been intermingled with the body and integrated with it in a unifying blend, it is a simple matter to make the distinction between them clear-cut ? You are looking

iii. 400. δηγμός is a natural involuntary experience at a painful stimulus, *S.V.F.* iii. 439 ; Cicero, *Tusc. Disp.* iii. 83.

[c] Perhaps the brother of Boethus of Sidon, who was Strabo's fellow-pupil in Aristotelianism ; less probably Cicero's Stoic house-philosopher. The author appears not to observe that the doctrine he ascribes to Diodotus is not relevant to his present topic, the distribution of the affections, some to the body, some to the soul.

[d] *Cf.* Plato, *Phaedo*, 99 B.

ματος ἐπιζητεῖς, οὓς ἡ φύσις ἀνεῖλεν ἐκ δυοῖν μίαν
οὐσίαν[1] γενέσθαι σοφιζομένη, καὶ τῷ λόγῳ παρεν-
δῦναι[2] γλιχόμενος[3] διαστέλλεις[4] κοινωνίαν οὐδενὶ
λυτὴν[5] οὐδὲ χωριστὴν ἢ μόνῳ θανάτῳ. ἐκεῖνος δὲ
τὰ πρὸς ἄλληλα συμπλακέντα[6] διακόψας[7] ἢ ἀπο-
κρίνας θάτερον ἐξελέγξει τὴν ἑκατέρου φύσιν ὅσον
εἶχεν ἀλλότριον· μέχρι δὲ τούτου τὸ συγκεκραμένον
ἡ κοινωνία δείκνυσιν ἀρνουμένη ἐκ[8] δυοῖν εἶναι καὶ
ἀποκρύπτουσα τὰς ἀμφοῖν εἰς κοινωνίαν[9] ἀρχὰς καὶ
ἀναπιμπλᾶσα θατέρου θάτερον, ὡς μήτε ψυχῆς εἶναι
πάθος ὃ σώματος οὐ καθάπτεται, μήτε σώματος
μεταβολὴν ἢ[10] διὰ ψυχῆς οὐ κεχώρηκε. κινδυνεύο-
μεν ὅμοιόν τι ποιεῖν τῇ περὶ τὸν Ὧρον[11] ὑπ' Αἰγυπτίων μυθολογουμένῃ διανομῇ, δικάσαντός τινος
τῶν παλαιοτέρων θεῶν, ἐπεὶ[12] τῷ πατρὶ τιμωρῶν
ἀπέκτεινε τὴν μητέρα, καὶ τὸ αἷμα αὐτοῦ καὶ τὸν
μυελὸν καταλιπεῖν, περιελεῖν δὲ τὴν πιμελὴν καὶ
τὰς σάρκας, ὡς τούτων ἐν τῇ μητρὶ τὴν σύστασιν
λαβόντων, ἐκείνων δ' ἀπὸ τοῦ πατρὸς κατὰ[13] τὴν

---

[1] οὐσίαν added by F. H. S.
[2] Wyttenbach : παρενδοῦναι.
[3] Pohlenz : ἀρχόμενος.
[4] Wyttenbach : διαστέλλει.
[5] Tyrwhitt : οὐδ' ἐνὶ αὐτὴν or οὐδ' ἐνιαυτήν.
[6] συμπλακέντα added by F. H. S. (συνδεθέντα Wyttenbach, συμπαγέντα Pohlenz, συγκραθέντα Ziegler) to fill a lacuna in mss.
[7] Wyttenbach : κόψας.   [8] Tyrwhitt : ἀρνουμένην ἐν.
[9] Pohlenz : κοινῶν.   [10] Wyttenbach : ὅ.
[11] Tyrwhitt : ὅρον.   [12] Tyrwhitt : ἐπί.
[13] κατὰ added by Tyrwhitt.

---

[a] Osiris having been killed by his own brother Set, Horus overthrew his usurping uncle and restored his father to life. An unusual story (Roeder, R.E. viii. 2449, T. Hopfner, Plutarch über Isis und Osiris, i. 123, 139) represents Horus as

for boundary marks between body and soul; but nature has removed them, using all her skill to make one substance out of two. When you crave to introduce a theoretical division between them you are trying to break up a partnership to which only death can bring dissolution or divorce. Death, indeed, when it severs or disentangles these things that are there intertwined one with the other, will prove how much there was in the very being of each that was not its own. But until that time, the partnership exhibits a complete blending; it refuses to admit that it has two constituents, it conceals the original contribution of the pair to the common stock, and so impregnates each with the other, that there is no affection of the soul that does not attack the body, and no change in the body that does not permeate the soul. We are in danger of trying to effect something like the division of Horus in Egyptian mythology [a] : when he had killed his mother to avenge his father, one of the older gods gave as his judgement that they should remove his fat and flesh but leave his blood and his marrow, because the two former had been formed in his mother, while the latter had passed into him from his father at his begetting.[b]

---

having beheaded his mother Isis because she protected Set; she was then given a cow's head by Thoth. Plutarch has a milder version of the story, *De Iside*, 358 D, in which Isis loses her headdress, not her head; but at 358 E he mentions that he has suppressed the worst features, "the dismemberment of Horus and decapitation of Isis." The tale of the dismemberment of Horus has recently been found for the first time in an Egyptian source (Pap. Jumilhac), which differs in its details from what is said here; see J. Hani, *Revue des Études Grecques*, lxxvi (1963), p. 111.

[b] Cf. *De Animae Procr.* 1026 c, where "breath" replaces "marrow."

γένεσιν ῥυέντων αὐτῷ. καθάπερ γὰρ οὗτοι τῶν
σπερμάτων τὴν¹ ἄνωθεν κατὰ φύσιν κρᾶσιν ἀχώριστον ἐπιχειροῦντες διαιρεῖν ἄχρι λόγου μυθώδους
καὶ ἀπίστου προέρχονται,² τὸν αὐτὸν τρόπον ἡμεῖς³
σώματος καὶ ψυχῆς εὐθὺς ἐν πρώτῃ καταβολῇ συγ-
χυθέντων πάθη διαλαβεῖν καὶ χωρίσαι ζητοῦντες
ἀκριβοῦς σφόδρα λόγου καθάπερ ὀργάνου λεπτοῦ
πρὸς τὴν διαίρεσιν δεόμεθα.

7. Οἱ δὲ⁴ ταύτην ἀπογνόντες⁵ φιλόσοφοί φασι
μήτε σώματος εἶναί τι μήτε ψυχῆς ἴδιον πάθος ἀλλὰ
τοῦ κοινοῦ· τὸν γὰρ ἄνθρωπον ἥδεσθαι καὶ λυπεῖσθαι καὶ φοβεῖσθαι, τὸν⁶ ἄνθρωπον, οὐχὶ τὴν ψυχήν,
ὥσπερ γε πάλιν οὐ τὸ σῶμα βάλλειν καὶ ὀρχεῖσθαι
καὶ περιπατεῖν, ἀλλὰ τὸν ἄνθρωπον ἀμφοτέροις
χρώμενον, ὥσπερ ἐξ ἀμφοῖν συνέστηκε. καὶ οὐκ
ἂν θαυμάσαιμι, εἰ⁷ τούτοις μάλιστά πως⁸ τὸ ἀληθὲς
συμφέρεται. κρίσις γὰρ ἡ λύπη κακοῦ τινος αὐτῷ
παρόντος ἐφ' ᾧ⁹ συστέλλεσθαι καθήκει, καὶ ὁ φόβος
κακοῦ¹⁰ μέλλοντος ἀφ' οὗ φεύγειν καθήκει καὶ ἀνα-
χωρεῖν· ὥστε τὸν λυπούμενον αὐτὸν αὑτῷ λέγειν
ὅτι μοι κακὸν πάρεστι, καὶ τὸν φοβούμενον ὁμοίως
ὅτι μοι κακὸν ἔσται.¹¹ "ἐγὼ" δ' οὐκ εἰμὶ ἡ ψυχὴ
ἀλλ' ὁ ἄνθρωπος, καὶ τὸ κακὸν οὐκ ἔστι τῆς ψυχῆς
ἀλλὰ τοῦ ἀνθρώπου, πενία νόσος ἀδοξία θάνατος.
διὸ τήν τε λύπην¹² καὶ τὸν φόβον ἀναγκαῖον εἶναι
πάθη τοῦ ἀνθρώπου καὶ οὐχὶ τῆς ψυχῆς.

¹ Wyttenbach : οὗτοι ὥσπερ τῶν. Post suggests omitting
ὥσπερ.
² Wyttenbach : προερρύονται. ³ Tyrwhitt : ἡμῖν.
⁴ οἱ δὲ added by Duebner. ⁵ Tyrwhitt : ἀνοίγοντες.
⁶ Wyttenbach : τινὰ. Ziegler keeps τινὰ and omits ἄνθρωπον.
⁷ εἰ added by Wyttenbach. ⁸ Wyttenbach : ὡς.
⁹ Pohlenz : οὗ. ¹⁰ Tyrwhitt : καὶ οὐ.

The Egyptians go so far as to invent an incredible fairy-tale in their attempt to divide the inseparable natural blend of inherited elements.[a] In the same way when we seek to distinguish and separate the affections of soul and body, which were immediately confused at their first nativity, we stand in need of a delicate tool, in the shape of an extremely accurate formula, to effect the division.[b]

7. The philosophers who despair of such a division say that an affection belongs peculiarly neither to the body nor to the soul, but to the combination of the two : it is the man who feels pleasure and grief and fear, the man not the soul,[c] and this exactly corresponds to the fact that it is not the body that throws or dances or walks about, but the man, who uses both body and soul together, just as he is composed of both. I should not be surprised if the truth perhaps most closely coincides with this view. For grief is a judgement of the presence of some harm, on account of which it is proper to become depressed, and fear is a judgement of impending harm from which it is proper to take flight and retreat. Therefore one who feels grief says to himself, " Harm is upon me," and similarly one who feels fear says, " There is harm coming to me." " I," however, am not the soul, but the man ; and the harm is harm, not of the soul, but of the man—poverty, disease, disgrace, or death. It follows that grief and fear must be affections of the man, not of the soul.

[a] Text uncertain.
[b] Cf. Life of Phocion, chap. 3, ὥστε λεπτοῦ πάνυ λόγου δεῖσθαι καθάπερ ὀργάνου πρὸς διάκρισιν.
[c] Cf. Aristotle, De Anima, 408 b 13.

[11] Tyrwhitt : ἐστιν or ἐστίν.   [12] Tyrwhitt : τελευτήν.

Καὶ γὰρ ἄλλως ὁρμὴ[1] μὲν πλεονάζουσα[2] τὸ πάθος,
τῷ ἀλόγῳ τὸ[3] σφοδρὸν ἔχουσα καὶ ἀπειθές· ὁρμᾷ
δὲ τὸ ζῷον, οὐχ ἡ ψυχή, πρὸς τὸ κείρασθαι πρὸς τὸ
ὁπλίσασθαι πρὸς τὸ λούσασθαι καὶ[4] κατακλιθῆναι·
ταῦτα γάρ ἐστι[5] τῷ ἀνθρώπῳ πρακτά, τῇ ψυχῇ δ᾽
ἀσύμπτωτα. οἷς καὶ πιθανὸν ὁρμᾶν τὸν ἄνθρωπον,
οὐχὶ τὴν ψυχήν· εἰ δ᾽ ὁρμᾶν, καὶ ὀρέγεσθαι· οὐκοῦν
καὶ ἀλόγως ὀρέγεσθαι, τουτέστιν ἐπιθυμεῖν[6]· εἰ δ᾽
ἐπιθυμεῖν,[7] καὶ ἥδεσθαι· εἰ δ᾽ ἥδεσθαι, καὶ λυπεῖσθαι
καὶ φοβεῖσθαι· ταῦτα γὰρ ἐκείνοις[8] ἐξ ἀνάγκης ἔπε-
σθαι[9] συμβέβηκεν· ὥστε μηδὲν[10] εἶναι ψυχῆς ἴδιον,
ἀλλὰ καὶ χαίρειν[11] καὶ ἄχθεσθαι καὶ ὀρέγεσθαι καὶ
φοβεῖσθαι τὸν ἄνθρωπον.

8. Ταῦτα δ᾽ ἐστὶν οὐ λυόντων τὴν ἀπορίαν ἀλλ᾽
ἀποδιδρασκόντων. καὶ γὰρ εἰ τὰ μάλιστα φαίη τις
εἶναι τοῦ ἀνθρώπου ταῦτα πάθη, μένει τὸ ἀπορεῖν
τίνι καὶ κατὰ τί ταῦτα πάσχει, πότερον κατὰ τὴν
ψυχὴν ἢ κατὰ τὸ σῶμα. καὶ γὰρ[12] ὀρχεῖται ὁ ἄνθρωπος ἀλλὰ ταῖς χερσί, καὶ λακτίζει ὁ ἄνθρωπος ἀλλὰ
τοῖς σκέλεσι, καὶ βλέπει κατὰ τὴν ὄψιν, καὶ ἀκούει
κατὰ τὰ ὦτα· καὶ ὅλως τὸ μὲν ἔργον ἐστὶ κοινὸν
τοῦ ἐκ τούτων[13] πάντων συνεστῶτος, τὴν δ᾽ αἰτίαν
τῆς συμπράξεως ἔχει τὸ μέρος ᾧ προσχρώμενος
ἐνεργεῖ ὁ[14] ἄνθρωπος. '' ἀλλὰ τὸ μὲν πλεῖον πολυάι-
κος πολέμοιο,'' φησὶν Ἀχιλλεύς, '' χεῖρες ἐμαὶ δι-

---

[1] Wyttenbach : ὁρμεῖ.   [2] Pohlenz : προσπλεονάζουσα.
[3] τὸ added by Duebner.   [4] καὶ added by Duebner.
[5] Tyrwhitt : ἐπὶ.   [6] ἐπιθυμεῖν added by Tyrwhitt.
[7] Duebner : ἐπιθυμεῖ or ἐπιθυμῶ.
[8] Tyrwhitt : ἐκεῖνοι or ἐκείνη.
[9] Tyrwhitt : ἔσεσθαι.   [10] Tyrwhitt : μηδ᾽.
[11] Tyrwhitt : ἀναιρεῖν.   [12] γὰρ added by Ziegler.
[13] Pohlenz : τοῦ or τῶν.   [14] ὁ added by Pohlenz.

There is also another line of argument. An affection is an excessive impulse towards something, and one that gets its violent and disobedient nature from the irrational element in the soul.[a] Now it is the living being and not the soul that has an impulse to get its hair cut or to arm itself or to take a bath and go to bed ; for these are actions that the man performs, not things that happen to the soul. These instances make it plausible that it is always the man, not the soul, that has impulses. But if impulse is his, he also has appetency, including irrational appetency, *i.e.*, desire.[b] But if he has desire, he also feels pleasure, and if pleasure, grief and fear too, since they necessarily go with pleasure and desire. So there is no affection peculiar to the soul, but it is the man who is glad and sorry and appetent and fearful.

8. But to argue thus is to run away from the difficulty, not to solve it. However much one may agree that these affections are affections of the man, the question remains by what means and in what respect he is affected ; is it in respect of his soul or of his body ? It is the man that dances ; yes, but by using his arms. It is the man that kicks ; yes, but by using his legs. Again, he sees by means of his organs of sight, and hears by means of his ears. To put it generally, the act is shared by that which is composed of all these bodily parts, but the responsibility for this joint action lies with the part utilized by the whole man in his activity.

> But in tumultuous war the greater part
> My hands perform,[c]

---

[a] Arnim, *Stoicorum Veterum Fragmenta*, iii. 468, τὸ ἄλογον καθ᾿ ὅ φασι γίγνεσθαι τὸ πάθος σφοδρότερον. *Cf. ibid.* 386, 459, 475.   [b] This is a Stoic definition of desire, *S.V.F.* iii. 463.
[c] *Iliad*, i. 165.

ἔπουσιν,'' οὐκ ἀποστερῶν ἑαυτὸν τῶν πολεμικῶν
ἔργων ὅτι ταῖς χερσὶν ἐπέγραψε τὴν αἰτίαν, ἀλλὰ
δηλονότι[1] ταῖς μὲν χερσὶ κατειργάζετο τοὺς πολε-
μίους καὶ τῷ ξίφει, αὐτὸς μέντοι ἦν ὁ διεργαζό-
μενος. καὶ ὁ λέγων

δεινὸς κολαστὴς πέλεκυς αὐχένος τομεὺς[2]

οὐ τὸ[3] ὃ κολάζει[4] εἴρηκεν ἀλλ' ᾧ[5] κολάζουσιν.
οὕτως οὖν ὁ τὴν λύπην καὶ[6] τὴν ἐπιθυμίαν ἐπιζητῶν
πότερον τοῦ σώματός ἐστιν ἢ τῆς ψυχῆς οὐκ ἀγνοεῖ
ὅτι τὸ λυπούμενον καὶ ἐπιθυμοῦν ἄνθρωπός ἐστι,
πότερον δὲ[7] τῇ ψυχῇ προσχρώμενος ἢ τῷ σώματι
καὶ κατὰ τὴν ψυχὴν ἢ[8] κατὰ τὸ σῶμα τοῦτο πάσχει,[9]
διηπόρηκεν. ὥστε τὰς προφάσεις ἐάσαντες ἀψώ-
μεθα τοῦ λόγου κατὰ[10] τὴν ζήτησιν ἤδη.

9. Ὅσοι τοίνυν τὴν ψυχὴν[11] οὐκ ἄφθαρτον οὐδ'
ἀθάνατον μόνον ἀλλὰ καὶ ἀπαθῆ πειρῶνται δια-
φυλάττειν, ῥώμην τινὰ τὴν ἀπάθειαν τῇ ἀφθαρσίᾳ[12]
προβαλλόμενοι καὶ τὸ πάσχον ἀμωσγέπως[13] ἤδη
φθορᾶς ἀναδέχεσθαι πεῖραν οἰόμενοι, τὰ δὲ πάθη
πάντα καὶ τὰς ἀσθενείας ὥσπερ ἐκ ῥίζης τῆς σαρκὸς ἀναβλαστάνειν ἐπὶ τὸν ἄνθρωπον, τῶν διαφορῶν
πρῶτον ἕξονται τῶν περὶ τὰ σώματα φαινομένων

---

[1] Post: δῆλον ὅτι. δηλῶν ὅτι Bernardakis.
[2] τομεὺς F. H. S. from 813 F: τεμεῖν or τρεμεῖν.
[3] οὐ τὸ Tyrwhitt: αὐτό.
[4] ὃ κολάζει Nauck: κολάζει ὅ.   [5] Tyrwhitt: ὡς.
[6] τὴν λύπην καὶ added by Wyttenbach.
[7] δὲ added by Tyrwhitt.
[8] κατὰ τὴν ψυχὴν ἢ added by Pohlenz, after Hartman.
[9] Tyrwhitt: πάσχειν.
[10] κατὰ before κατὰ deleted by F. H. S.; Wyttenbach added
τραπώμεθα, Ziegler γενώμεθα, after ἤδη.
[11] Tyrwhitt: τῆς ψυχῆς.

says Achilles ; but does not mean thereby to rob
himself of his deeds in war by ascribing the responsibility to his hands ; obviously, although it was by
employing his hands and his sword that he used to
kill the enemy, it was he himself who took their lives.[a]
The character who speaks of

> The dread chastising axe, that cleaves the neck [b]

denotes the instrument of punishment, not the agent.
Similarly the man who inquires whether grief and
desire belong to the body or to the soul knows quite
well that it is the man that feels grief and desire ;
his problem is whether in this experience the man is
using his soul or his body, and whether his soul or his
body is affected. So let us dismiss these shifts, and
lose no time in getting to grips with the argument as
the question requires.

9. Well then, there are those who try to maintain
that the soul is not only indestructible and immortal
but also impassive, putting forward its impassivity as
a line of defence to strengthen its indestructibility,[c]
and supposing that anything that is affected in any
way whatsoever thereby undergoes an experience of
destruction, and that all affections and weaknesses
are rooted, as it were, in the flesh, and grow out of
it to extend to the man.[d] These thinkers will seize
in the first place on the noticeable physical differences
which are related to various times of life, natural

---

[a] Cf. De Genio Socratis, 582 c.
[b] Nauck, Frag. Trag. Graec., Adespota 412, quoted again
at Moralia, 813 f.   [c] Cf. Plotinus, iii. 6.
[d] Cf. De Virtute Morali, 450 f—451 a, to which all that
follows has a close likeness.

---

[12] Hartman : τῇ ἀπαθείᾳ τὴν ἀφθαρσίαν.
[13] Tyrwhitt : ἀλλ' ὡς γέ πως.

κατὰ χρόνους καὶ φύσεις καὶ μεταβολάς. οἷον
εὐθὺς ἐν νέοις ἀκμάζει τὸ ἐπιθυμητικόν, ἐν πρεσβύ-
ταις τὸ περίλυπον· τοῖς μὲν γὰρ αἷμά τε θερμὸν
ἐγκέκραται[1] καὶ πνεῦμα ῥαγδαῖον ἐπὶ τὰς πράξεις,
παρέστηκε δὲ[2] καὶ τὸ σῶμα τοῖς ὀργάνοις καθαροῖς
καὶ ἀκραιφνέσιν ἐμμελὲς ἀεί, καὶ τὸ[3] πολύσφυκτον[4]
ἀνακινεῖ καὶ ἀναρριπίζει τὰς ἐπιθυμίας ὥσπερ ἐξ ὕλης
νεαρᾶς ἀναπτομένας τοῦ ἐπιφερομένου[5] αἵματος, ἐξ
ὧν[6] μεταβαλλόμενον ἐπὶ πολλὰ ταῖς ὁρμαῖς τὸν νέον
ὁρῶμεν.[7] ὁ δὲ[8] πρέσβυς τοῦ τε[9] θερμοῦ προλιπόντος
ἤδη, ᾧ τὸ ἐπιθυμητικὸν ἀνεζωπυρεῖτο,[10] καὶ τῷ
πνεύματι χαλῶν καὶ κατατετριμμένος τῷ σώματι
περὶ τὰς ἡδονάς, ἀμβλὺ ταῖς ἐπιθυμίαις καὶ δυσ-
κίνητον * *[11]

[1] Wyttenbach : αἷμα τὸ θερμαῖνον κέκραται.
[2] δὲ added by F. H. S.
[3] τὸ added by F. H. S.
[4] Bernardakis : πολύσφακτον.
[5] τοῦ ἐπιφερομένου Post : περιφέρειν. περιφορᾷ Wyttenbach
περισσεύοντος (or περιζέοντος) φύσει τοῦ Pohlenz. None of these

characters, and psychological changes. To take an
immediate example, desire is at its height in the
young, dejection in old men. The reason is that the
former have a hot composition of their blood, and a
tempestuous spirit for their actions, and a body, too,
to serve them that is always in tune, with organs un-
blemished and uncontaminated; their strong pulse
excites and fans their desires, which take fire from
the flow of blood as it were from fresh fuel. As a result we see the young man subject to many a change
in his impulses. The old man, however, now aban-
doned by the heat that formerly re-kindled his power
of desire, relaxed in spirit, his body worn out in
pleasures, ⟨his pulse⟩ sluggish and slow to be moved
by desires . . .

---

suggestions is convincing. Post notes that his own involves
an unusual hiatus.

[6] ἐξ ὧν Wyttenbach : ἐξὸν.
[7] ὁρῶμεν added by Wyttenbach.
[8] δὲ added by Bernardakis.
[9] τοῦ τε Tyrwhitt : τοῦτο.
[10] Tyrwhitt : ὥστε ἐπιθυμητὸν ἀναζωπυρεῖ τό.
[11] ἔχει τὸ σφύγμα would complete the sense. h leaves half a
line blank.

ΕΙ ΜΕΡΟΣ ΤΟ ΠΑΘΗΤΙΚΟΝ ΤΗΣ ΑΝΘΡΩΠΟΥ ΨΥΧΗΣ Η ΔΥΝΑΜΙΣ

1. Περὶ τῆς παθητικῆς καὶ ἀλόγου ζωῆς, πότερα μέρος ἐστὶ τῆς ἀνθρώπου ψυχῆς ἢ δύναμις, ἐπισκεπτέον. ἐοίκασι γὰρ καὶ τῶν ἀρχαίων οἱ μὲν οὕτως οἱ δ᾽ ἐκείνως ἀποφηνάμενοι περὶ αὐτῆς. ἄξιον οὖν καὶ ἡμᾶς ἀπορήσαντας καὶ ἐπὶ ζήτησιν τραπομένους ταύτῃ δοξάσαι, ᾗπερ[1] δὴ[2] καὶ ζητοῦσι φανεῖται πιθανώτερον.

2. Ὅσοι μὲν οὖν μέρος ἀποδιδόασιν αὐτήν, δόξαιεν ἂν οὐκ εἶναι[3] λέγειν ἔμψυχα τὰ ἄλογα τῶν ζῴων οὐδὲ ψυχὴν ἔχοντα, ἀλλά τι μόριον ψυχῆς, εἴ γε τοῖς ἀλόγοις ἡ παθητικὴ μέν ἐστιν, ἡ λογικὴ δ᾽ οὐδαμῶς[4]· ὅσοι δ᾽ αὖ[5] δύναμιν, πρῶτον μὲν ἄτοπον ὅτι τῷ τόπῳ διαχωρίζουσιν ἀπὸ τῆς ἀντιδιαιρουμένης αὐτῇ δυνάμεως, τῆς λογικῆς· οὐ γὰρ διαιροῦνται ἀπ᾽ ἀλλήλων αἱ δυνάμεις, ὅσαι τοῦ αὐτοῦ τυγχάνουσιν οὖσαι· ἔπειτα[6] καὶ συνυπάρχειν ποιοῦσι τἀναντία κατὰ ταὐτό· αἱ γὰρ δυνάμεις τοιαῦται, ὥστε ἑκάστην, κἂν ὁποσαιοῦν ὦσι, περὶ

---

[1] Tyrwhitt : εἴπερ.   [2] Bernardakis : ἄν.
[3] οὐκ εἶναι Wyttenbach : ἐκεῖναι or ἐκεῖνα.
[4] εἴ γε (δὲ h) . . . οὐδαμῶς transposed here by Wyttenbach from before ἔπειτα below (i omits entirely).
[5] Wyttenbach : ἄν.   [6] ἔπειτα ὅτι Ziegler.

---

[a] That is, they do so if they follow Aristotle in suspecting

60

THE AFFECTIVE ELEMENT IN MAN—
IS IT A PART OR A FACULTY
OF HIS SOUL?

1. It is necessary to examine whether affective and irrational life is a part or a faculty of the human soul, since it appears that even among the earlier philosophers there was a division of opinion. It is proper, therefore, that we too should pose the question and turn to its investigation. We shall then adopt whichever view in fact appears the more probable in the course of that inquiry.

2. Those who regard it as a *part* might be thought to maintain that irrational animals are inanimate and not possessed of soul, but of some fraction of soul; this follows if they have affective life but absolutely no rational life. As for those who regard it as a *faculty*, there is in the first place the absurdity that they separate it spatially from the contrasted faculty, that of reason.[a] This is absurd because faculties that are faculties of the same thing are not so separated. In the second place they actually make opposites coexist with respect to the same thing. For it is a characteristic of faculties that, however many there may be of them, each and every one is to be regarded

that νοῦς is spatially separable from the rest of soul, *De Anima*, 413 b 14-27. The writer also holds that the soul's reason can exist outside the body (chap. 5).

ὅλον¹ θεωρεῖσθαι τὸ ὑποκείμενον. τὸ δὲ λογικὸν
καὶ τὸ ἄλογον οὐχ οὕτω περὶ ψυχήν· ἀποτέμνεσθαι
γὰρ δοκεῖ τῆς ὅλης καὶ ποιεῖν περὶ² αὐτὴν τὸ μὲν
ἄλλο τὸ δ' ἄλλο. καὶ τοῦτ' εἰκότως· ἐναντία γάρ,
τὰ δ' ἐναντία καθ' ἑνὸς³ κατὰ⁴ τὸ αὐτὸ συνυπάρχειν
⟨ἀδύνατον, . . .⟩⁵ ἀληθές. οὐδὲν γὰρ ἴσως κωλύει
καὶ τἀναντία συνυπάρξαι τὸν εἰρημένον τρόπον, ἐὰν
δυνάμεις ὦσι καὶ μὴ ἐνέργειαι λαμβάνωνται.⁶ λογίζεσθαι μὲν γὰρ καὶ ἀλογιστεῖν ἢ ὑγιάζειν καὶ κακοῦν
ἅμ'⁷ ἄμφω ἀδύνατον· ἡ μέντοι δύναμις τοῦ ὑγιάζειν
καὶ τοῦ⁸ κακοῦν ἅμα περὶ τὸ αὐτό, ἥ τε τοῦ λογίζεσθαι καὶ τοῦ⁹ ἀλογιστεῖν περὶ τὴν ψυχὴν ἅμα, οὐ
μέντοι καὶ αἱ κατὰ ταύτας ἐνέργειαι. καὶ πλείω
δὴ τὸ αὐτὸ δύνασθαι οὐθὲν κωλύει, οἷον τὸ ἀλη-
θεύειν τόν τε ἐπιστήμονα καὶ τὸν διαλεκτικόν·
οὕτω δὴ καὶ ἀλογιστεῖν τήν τε τῶν ἀλόγων ζῴων
ψυχὴν καὶ τὴν ἀνθρώπου, ἀλλὰ τὴν μὲν τῶν ἀλόγων
ἐν τῷ εἶναι αὐτῆς τὸ ἀλογιστεῖν ἔχειν (διὸ καὶ ἀεὶ
ἀλογιστεῖ καὶ οὐχ ὁτὲ μὲν τοῦτο ὁτὲ δὲ τὸ ἐναντίον)·
τὴν δὲ τοῦ ἀνθρώπου τὸ μὲν ἀλογιστεῖν οὐκ ἐν τῷ
εἶναι ἔχειν αὐτῆς¹⁰ (οὐ γὰρ ἂν καὶ ἐλογίζετο), τὸ
δύνασθαι μέντοι ἀλογιστεῖν καὶ τὸ δύνασθαι λογίζεσθαι. ἐνεργεῖ δὲ κατ' ἄμφω· κατὰ λόγον μέν,
ὁπηνίκ' ἂν βλέψῃ πρὸς τὴν ἑαυτῆς οὐσίαν, αὕτη δ'

¹ ὅλον Tyrwhitt: ὅλην.
² περὶ added by Ziegler. ? ποιεῖν αὐτῶν.
³ ἑνός i: ἓν h. ⁴ Pohlenz: καί.
⁵ ἀδύνατον νομίζεται· ἀλλὰ τοῦτο ἐπισκεπτέον εἰ ἔστιν Wyttenbach.
⁶ Tyrwhitt: λαμβάνονται.
⁷ ἅμ' added by Duebner.
⁸ ὑγιάζειν καὶ τοῦ added by Wyttenbach.
⁹ τε . . . τοῦ added by Pohlenz, after Wyttenbach.

as belonging to the *whole* underlying substance. This is not the relation of the rational and irrational to the soul. They are considered to be sections of the whole and to have different activities.

And reasonably so, since they are opposites and ⟨it is believed to be impossible that⟩ opposites should co-exist in a single thing in the same respect. ⟨But we must examine whether this is⟩ true. There is no reason, perhaps, why opposites should not co-exist in the said manner, if they are *potentialities* and are not understood as being actualities. It is impossible simultaneously to exercise reason and show unreason, or to heal and to harm ; but the potentiality of healing and that of harming may simultaneously belong to the same thing, and similarly the potentiality of exercising reason and of showing unreason may belong simultaneously to the soul. The corresponding actualities, however, cannot occur together. Again there is no reason why several things should not have the same potentiality, *e.g.*, both exact sciences and dialectical reasoning are potentially able to yield the truth. Similarly, then, both the soul of irrational animals and that of man are potentially able to show unreason. But whereas the soul of irrational animals has the exercise of unreason as part of its being, so that it always shows unreason, without any alternation with the opposite, the soul of a man has as part of its being, not the exercise of unreason—for in that case it would not also exercise reason—but the *potentiality* for exercising unreason and the *potentiality* for exercising reason ; and the activity of a human soul is an activity in both respects, in respect of reason whenever it looks to its own essential being, which is

---

[10] Tyrwhitt : αὐτήν.

ἐστὶν ὁ ἐν αὐτῇ νοῦς, κατὰ δὲ τὴν ἀλογίαν, ὁπόταν
νεύσῃ πρὸς τὰ ἔξω αὐτῆς, ταῦτα δ' ἐστὶ τὰ αἰσθητά.
ἄλλο οὖν τὸ ἐν ἀνθρώπῳ ἄλογον καὶ ἄλλο τὸ ἐν τοῖς
ζῴοις· τὸ μὲν γὰρ ἐν τούτοις ψυχή, τὸ δ' ἐν ἀνθρώπῳ δύναμις· καὶ τοῦτ' ἂν εἴη τῆς τοῦ λογίζεσθαι
δυνάμεως ἀχώριστον. ὀρθῶς ἄρα καὶ Ἀριστοτέλης,
τὴν ἀνθρώπου ψυχὴν δύναμιν συναποκαλῶν ὅτι
ποτὲ μὲν λογίζεται ποτὲ δ' οὔ.

3. Ὅταν οὖν μὴ λογίζηται, ἄλλο τι ἢ ἀλογιστεῖ;
ἆρ' οὖν ἡ κατὰ τὸ λογίζεσθαι δύναμις καὶ αὐτὸ τὸ[1]
λογίζεσθαι ψυχῆς ἐστι, ψυχὴ δ' οὔχ, ὥσπερ τὸ
γράφειν περὶ χάρτην ἐστὶ[2] καὶ ἐν χάρτῃ, χάρτης δ'
οὔ; ἀλλ' εἰ τοῦτο, ἑτέρα ἔσται αὐτῆς οὐσία παρὰ
τὸ ἔργον καὶ τὴν πρὸς τοῦτο δύναμιν, καὶ ἕξει τι[3]
ὑποκείμενον περὶ ὃ θεωρηθήσεται ἡ δύναμις αὐτῆς,
καὶ ἔσται τὸ ὄνομα τοῦτο "ψυχὴ" τὸ ὑποκείμενον
μετὰ τῶν περὶ αὐτὸ θεωρουμένων δυνάμεων· καὶ
ζωὴν ἕξει οὐ διὰ πάσης ἑαυτῆς· κατὰ γὰρ τὸ ὑποκείμενον ἄζωος ἔσται, τάχα δὲ καὶ παντάπασιν.
οὐδεμία γὰρ αὐτῆς ἐν τῇ φύσει ἐνέργεια ζωτική,
ἀλλὰ πάντα δύναμις. δυνάμει οὖν ἔσται ζῷα.

4. Ἡ τὸ δυνάμει τὸ καθ' ἕξιν ῥητέον, ἵνα πῶς[4]
μὲν ἔχῃ ζωὴν πῶς[4] δ' οὐκ ἔχῃ; δύο γὰρ ζωαί, ἡ
μὲν ὡς ἕξις ἡ δ' ὡς τὸ ἐνεργοῦν· καὶ ἡ μὲν ὡς ἕξις
ψυχή, ἡ δ' ὡς τὸ ἐνεργοῦν ὁ νοῦς. εἰ οὖν ἡ ὡς
ἕξις ζωὴ ἡ ψυχή, ἁπλῆ ἂν εἴη χωρὶς ὑποκειμένου.

---

[1] τὸ Wyttenbach : ζῇ i, omitted by h.
[2] ψυχὴ . . . ἐστι added by F. H. S.
[3] Pohlenz : τό.
[4] Duebner : πῶς.

---

[a] De Anima, 412 a 22-27, may be intended.

the mind that is in it, and in respect of unreason whenever it inclines towards the exterior world, that is towards sensible things. The upshot is that the irrational in man is not the same as that in animals ; in animals it constitutes the soul, in man a potentiality of the soul, and thus something inseparable from the potentiality of exercising reason. It seems then that Aristotle was right in including " potentiality " among the words he applies to the human soul, because it exercises reason intermittently.[a]

3. Now when the soul is not using reason, must it not be actively unreasoning ? Then are not the potentialities concerned with reasoning and the actual act of reasoning functions of soul ⟨but not soul itself, just as writing is concerned with paper⟩ and on paper, but is not paper ? But if this is true, the substance of soul will be something other than its function and its potentiality to perform that function, and it will have a substrate in relation to which its potentiality will be considered. And the word " soul " will mean the substrate together with the potentialities that are considered in relation to that substrate. And it will not have life throughout itself, but will be lifeless so far as its substrate is concerned—perhaps it will even be completely lifeless ; for there is no actuality of life in its *nature* : it is all potentiality. So it will be only potentially living.

4. Or should we interpret this word " potentially " as referring to the potentiality that belongs to a state of being, so that in one sense the soul will have life, in another not, since there are two senses of life, life as a state, and life as an activity ? Life as a state is soul, life as an activity is mind. Now if soul is life as a state, it follows that it is a simple thing without

τοιοῦτον γάρ τι τὴν ψυχὴν ὑπολαμβάνομεν, ὃ τὴν
ζωὴν ἔχει σύμφυτον καὶ οὐ παρ' ἄλλου ἀλλὰ παρ'
αὑτῆς.[1] σωμάτων γὰρ τὸ παρ' ἄλλου τὴν ζωὴν
μεταλαγχάνειν. εἰ δ' ἦν τι σύνθετον ἡ ψυχή, ἐξ
ὑποκειμένου καὶ εἴδους συγκειμένη, οὐκ ἂν ἔσχε
παρ' αὑτῆς ἀλλὰ παρ' ἄλλου τὴν ζωήν· παρὰ γὰρ
τοῦ εἴδους, ὥσπερ καὶ τῷ πυρὶ τὸ[2] θερμῷ εἶναι παρὰ
τῆς θερμότητος καὶ οὐ παρὰ τῆς ὕλης. ἔπειτα κἂν
σῶμα ἦν· τὸ γὰρ ἐξ ὑποκειμένου καὶ εἴδους συν-
εστηκὸς σῶμα.

5. Δύναμις οὖν ζωτικὴ ἡ ψυχή, δύναμις δ' ἡ ὡς
ἕξις. διὰ τοῦτο καὶ ἐλευθέρα καὶ πρὸς τὰς ἐνεργείας
ἀκώλυτος. ἔχουσα γὰρ ζωήν, μᾶλλον δ' οὖσα ζωή,
κινεῖται καθ' ἑαυτὴν ὁπότε βούλεται. τοῦτο δὲ
περὶ τῆς ἔξω σωμάτων ψυχῆς ὑποληπτέον· ἡ γὰρ
κρατηθεῖσα σώματι καὶ τοῖς ἐκ τούτου πάθεσιν
ἀπόλλυσι τὸ ἐλεύθερον, καὶ οὐχ ὁπότε βούλεται
κινεῖσθαι ἐᾶται, ἀλλὰ δεδουλωμένη πέπαυται τῆς
ἐνεργείας, καὶ εἴ τις ἐπὶ ψυχῆς ὄλεθρος εἴη, οὗτος[3]
ἂν εἴη· οἷον γὰρ ἀπόλλυται σβεννυμένης ἐν αὐτῇ
τῆς κατὰ νοῦν ἐνεργείας. ἃ δὲ δοκεῖ ἐνέργειαν
ἀποστρέφειν,[4] ταῦτα παθήματα ἂν εἴη μᾶλλον, οὐκ
ἐνεργήματα, καὶ οὐκ αὐτῆς ταῦτα, ἀλλὰ τοῦ ζῴου,
κατ' αὐτὴν μέντοι. τὸ γὰρ λογίζεσθαι καὶ θεωρεῖν
μόνον αὐτῆς, καὶ τοῦθ' ἡ κυρίως ἐνέργεια, τὰ δὲ
παρὰ τοῦτο τοῦ ζῴου πάντα, καὶ πάθη μᾶλλον, οὐκ
ἐνέργειαι.

6. Ἀλλὰ πῶς, εἰ κατ' αὐτὴν[5] πάσχει τὰ ζῷα,

---

[1] αὑτῆς Ziegler : αὐτῆς. αὐτοῦ Pohlenz.
[2] Wyttenbach : τῷ.   [3] Wyttenbach : οὕτως.

substrate. For we suppose the soul to be a thing that has an inherent life, derived from the soul itself and not from any other source. It is only bodies that acquire life from some source outside themselves. But if the soul were something composite, being compounded of substrate and form, it would not derive its life from itself but from something else, namely its form, just as fire is essentially hot from its heat and not from its material. Secondly, the soul would in fact be a body, as any combination of substrate and form constitutes a body.

5. Soul is, then, a vital potentiality, but a potentiality in the form of a state of being. For this reason it is also free and unimpeded in its activities, since having life, or rather being life, it moves of itself whenever it wishes. But we must be understood to be speaking now of soul outside bodies. Soul that is mastered by a body and the affections that come from the body loses its freedom and is not allowed to move whenever it wishes, but is enslaved and made to cease its activity ; if there were any kind of destruction that affected soul, this is what it would be. For it is in a sense destroyed when the activity of the mind in it is extinguished. But the things that are recognized as distracting it from this activity will be affections rather than activities and, although they involve it, not its own affections but the affections of the living animal. Reason and contemplation alone belong to soul and constitute its proper activity ; all other functions belong to the living animal, and are affections rather than activities.

6. Yet if the affections of living beings involve the

---

[4] Wyttenbach : ἐνεργεῖν ἀποστρέφει.
[5] Duebner : αὐτό. Pohlenz deleted εὖ after this word.

67

οὐκ αὐτὴ παθητική; πάσχειν γὰρ κατὰ τὴν παθη-
τικὴν εὔλογον ψυχὴν ὥσπερ καὶ ὑφαίνειν κατὰ τὴν
ὑφαντικήν. ἢ τοῦτο μὲν ἀληθὲς καὶ διδόναι χρή,
ἀπορητέον δὲ περὶ τῆς καλουμένης παθητικῆς καὶ
περὶ τοῦ πάσχειν ὅλως πῶς γίνεται, πότερα τῷ[1]
μὴ ἐνεργεῖν τὴν ψυχὴν κατὰ λόγον ἢ ἄλλως; εἰ
γὰρ τῷ[2] μὴ ἐνεργεῖν, οὐθέν ἐστι πάθος ἐπαινετόν.
φαίνεται δ' ἐπαινετὰ[3] πάντα ὁπόσα μετρεῖται ὑπὸ
τοῦ λόγου, χρήσιμα ὄντα (ἀρετὰς γὰρ αὐτὰ καλοῦμεν πολιτικὰς καὶ ἐπαινοῦμεν τὸν ἔχοντα αὐτάς)·
μετρεῖσθαι δ' οὐκ ἂν ἠδύνατο μὴ ἐφορῶντος αὐτὰ
νοῦ καὶ ἐνδιδόντος αὐτοῖς ἀφ' αὐτοῦ μέτρον καὶ
ὅρον, τοῦτο δ' οὐθὲν ἀλλ' ἢ ἐνεργοῦντος περὶ αὐτά.
ἐνεργεῖ τε[4] οὖν ἅμα ὁ λόγος καὶ πάσχει τὸ ζῷον,
καὶ τῷ αὐτῷ[5] καὶ λογιζόμεθα ἅμα καὶ πάσχομεν·
ἓν γὰρ εἶδος[6] ἔχει, δυνάμεις δ' ἦσαν πλείους, ἥ τε
τοῦ ἐνεργεῖν καὶ μή, μᾶλλον δὲ μία δύναμις· τὸ γὰρ
μὴ ἐνεργεῖν ἀδυναμίας ἂν εἴη, καθ' ὃ καὶ ἀλογιστεῖν
ἐλέγετο τὸ ζῷον.

7. Ἀλλὰ τῇ τε ὑποθέσει ταύτῃ φαίνεται πλείω
τὰ ἑπόμενα ἄτοπα, καὶ ἄλλως ἀποδοῦναι τὰ πάθη
τοῖς ἀνθρώποις οὐκ εὔπορον. ἐπισκεπτέον δ' ἔτι,
πῶς ἔφαμεν ἐνεργεῖν τε ἅμα τὸν λόγον καὶ πάσχειν
τὸ ζῷον[7] καὶ εἶναι τὰ πάθη περὶ τὸ συναμφότερον.

[1] Wyttenbach : τό.
[2] Apelt, after Patzig : εἴτε γὰρ τό.
[3] ἐπαινετὰ added by Pohlenz.
[4] Wyttenbach : ἐνεργεῖται.
[5] Wyttenbach : τὸ αὐτό.   [6] Duebner : ἤδη.
[7] καὶ πάσχειν τὸ ζῷον added by Wyttenbach.

---

[a] Plato, *Phaedo*, 82 A, *Republic*, 430 c ; they are based
on training, not knowledge ; but the author seems to have
also in mind the Aristotelian definition of *moral* virtue.

soul, why is it not itself affective? It seems logical that to be affected should involve an affective aspect of the soul, just as to weave involves the knowledge of weaving in the soul. Yet, even if this is true and must be granted, is not the nature of the so-called affective aspect still a problem, as indeed is the very causation of affection? Does it come about by the mere absence of rational activity on the part of the soul or in some other way? If it is the result of the absence of such activity, no affection is praiseworthy. But it is clear that praise is due to all affections to which due measure is given by reason, since they are useful. We give them the name of social virtues [a] and praise their possessor. But they could not be given due measure of mind did not supervise them and afford them a measure and limit of its own determination, and what is this but to display an activity concerning them? So the activity of reason and the affection of the living being are simultaneous, and it is the same instrument by which we simultaneously reason and are affected. It has one form, but its potentialities turn out to be more than one, namely the potentiality of activity, and that of non-activity. Or rather there is only one potentiality; for non-activity would seem to belong to a lack of potentiality, in respect of which the living being was also said to show a failure to reason.

7. Now it is clear that there are a number of odd consequences of this hypothesis; at the same time it is not easy to explain men's affections in any other way. We have also still to consider in what sense we said that there is simultaneous activity of the reason and presence of the affections in the compound of body and soul, the animal. It is clear that activity

φαίνεται γὰρ οὐχ ἅμα ταῦτα γινόμενα ἄμφω, ἀλλὰ[1]
μεινάσης μὲν ἀργῆς τῆς διανοίας ἐπεισελθόντα τὰ
πάθη περὶ τὸ συναμφότερον, γενομένων δὲ τῶν
παθῶν παρελθὼν αὖθις ὁ λόγος καὶ διακοσμήσας
αὐτά. τίς οὖν ἡ καλουμένη παθητικὴ ψυχή; ἡ
αὐτὴ ἥπερ καὶ λογιστική. πάθος γάρ τι αὐτῆς τὸ
μὴ ἀπαύστως ἐνεργεῖν, καὶ παθητικὴ ὅτι θεωρεῖν
ἀεί τε καὶ συνεχῶς ἀδύνατος. ὅταν οὖν μὴ θεωρῇ,
πρὸς τὸ σῶμα ἐπέστραπται καὶ ἀπόστροφός ἐστι
τοῦ νοῦ· τοῦ νοῦ[2] δ' οὖσα ἀπόστροφος ἀνοηταίνειν
εἰκότως λέγοιτ' ἂν καὶ οὐθὲν ὑγιὲς βλέπειν οὐδὲ
κρίνειν ὀρθῶς, ἀλλὰ δοξάζειν[3] τά τε μὴ ἀγαθὰ ὡς
ὄντα ἀγαθὰ[4] καὶ τοὐναντίον, ἐκ δὲ τῆς τοιαύτης
δόξης καὶ κρίσεως ἀποτελεῖσθαι τὰ πάθη περὶ τὸ
σύνθετον, σύνθετον δ'[5] ἔκ τε τοῦ σώματος καὶ τῆς
ἐν αὐτῷ ζωῆς, ἣν ἐνδίδωσιν ἡ ψυχή. ἐνδίδωσι γὰρ
ἅπασα δύναμίς τινα ἀφ' αὑτῆς ἀπόρροιαν τῷ[6]

[1] ἀλλὰ added by Bernardakis.
[2] τοῦ νοῦ added by Tyrwhitt.
[3] Wyttenbach : δοξάζει.
[4] ὡς ὄντα ἀγαθὰ added by Wyttenbach.

and affection do not arise simultaneously ; when thought stops and is inactive, the affections enter the compound, and when they have come into being in it, reason subsequently comes forward to bring them into order. What then is the so-called affective soul ? It is the same soul as has the power of reasoning. It is an affection of the reasoning soul not to be in ceaseless activity and it is affective because it is unable to contemplate reality permanently and continuously. Now when it is not contemplating reality it is directed towards the body and averted from the intuitive mind ; and being averted it may properly be said to be devoid of intelligence and unsound of vision and to judge nothing correctly, but to deem what is not good to be good and vice versa ; upon this way of thinking and judging there follows the completion of the affections in the composite thing that is compounded of the body and the life in the body, life afforded it by the soul. For every potentiality provides a kind of emanation from itself . . .

---

[5] Duebner : τε.
[6] h leaves a page and a half blank.

FRAGMENTS FROM
LOST *LIVES*

ΕΠΑΜΕΙΝΩΝΔΑΣ ΚΑΙ ΣΚΙΠΙΩΝ

Besides the parallel Lives *Epaminondas and Scipio* Plutarch *wrote a single* Life *of Scipio Africanus (Lamprias 28). It is disputed whether it was the elder or the younger Scipio Africanus who was paired with Epaminondas, since both have clear points of resemblance. The elder is favoured by L. Peper, De Plutarchi Epaminonda (1912), and Ziegler in R.E. xxi. 895-896, as the victor over his country's hereditary enemy, the younger by Wilamowitz, Reden und Vorträge, ii. 269, and K. Herbert, A.J.P. lxxviii (1957), p. 83, as a type of the scholar-statesman. An argument that supports the elder Scipio is that Plutarch himself compares his prosecution to that of Epaminondas (Mor. 540 D 541 A), a comparison also made in more detail by Appian, Bell. Syr. 40-41 ; a passage which Hirzel, Plutarch, p. 77, guesses to be based on Epaminondas and Scipio. Epaminondas and the elder Scipio are paired also by Cicero, Tusc. v. 49, and Gregory Nazianzenus, Migne, xxxv. 593 A. Plutarch himself uses the simple " Scipio " and " Scipio Africanus " indifferently for either man. The words ἐν τοῖς περὶ Σκιπίωνος refer to his Life of the elder (Pyrrh. 8), but ἐν τῷ Σκιπίωνος βίῳ (Gracch. 21) refers to that of the younger. I adopt the view of Peper and Ziegler, while recognizing that it may be wrong.*

A careful attempt to reconstruct the Life *of Epaminondas is made by L. Peper, op. cit. Its outline is to be found, as was*

1

Plutarch, *Life of Agesilaüs*, c. 28.

Πολλῶν δὲ σημείων μοχθηρῶν γενομένων, ὡς ἐν τῷ περὶ Ἐπαμεινώνδου γέγραπται, καὶ Προθόου

EPAMINONDAS AND SCIPIO

(*Lamprias Catalogue* 7)

noted by Wilamowitz, *Hermes*, viii (1874), p. 439[2] and
Comm. gram. i. 11, in Pausanias, viii and ix. Peper regards
viii. 11. 7-9 and 10 in part, and ix. 13-15 as of Plutarchean
origin ; he would add a few sentences from other places,
viz.: viii. 8. 10, Μαντινέας . . . Λεύκτροις, 27. 8, συνωκίσθη
. . . στάδιον, and perhaps the references to Arcadians in
viii. 6. 2 aud 52. 4. Many of the anecdotes collected in
Reg. et Imp. Apophthegm. 192 c—194 o and scattered
about the Moralia and Life of Pelopidas probably had a
place in Epaminondas. To reprint all this material here
would take too much space, and I confine myself to a single
sentence which specifically mentions the Life.

P. L. Courier, in a letter dated 20 Sept. 1810 (Œuvres
complètes [1851], p. 371), alleges that in 1806 he and a M.
Akerblad saw in the library of the abbey at Florence, among
other 9th- and 10th-century mss., one which seemed to contain
the Life of Epaminondas ; that it was, along with others,
improperly sold before it could be transferred to the Lauren-
tian library, and that the same authorities who hounded him
for spreading ink on a ms. of Longus took no steps to recover
their lost property. Courier may have mistaken a Life of
Pelopidas for that of Epaminondas (? Laur. conv. soppr.
206 ; so R. Schöll, *Hermes*, v (1871), p. 114).

1

Many evil omens occurred, as I have recorded in
the *Life of Epaminondas*, and the Spartan Prothoüs

τοῦ Λάκωνος ἐναντιουμένου πρὸς τὴν στρατείαν,
οὐκ ἀνῆκεν ὁ Ἀγησίλαος ἀλλ' ἐξέπραξε τὸν πόλε-
μον.

2

Plutarch, *Life of Pyrrhus*, c. 8.

Ἀννίβας δὲ συμπάντων ἀπέφαινε τῶν στρατηγῶν
πρῶτον μὲν ἐμπειρίᾳ καὶ δεινότητι Πύρρον, Σκι-
πίωνα δὲ δεύτερον, ἑαυτὸν δὲ τρίτον, ὡς ἐν τοῖς
περὶ Σκιπίωνος γέγραπται.

ΣΚΙΠΙΩΝ ΑΦΡΙΚΑΝΟΣ

3

Plutarch, *Life of Tiberius Gracchus*, c. 21.

Σκιπίων ὁ Ἀφρικανός, οὗ δοκοῦσι Ῥωμαῖοι μηδένα δικαιότερον μηδὲ μᾶλλον ἀγαπῆσαι, παρὰ
μικρὸν ἦλθεν ἐκπεσεῖν καὶ στερέσθαι τῆς πρὸς τὸν
δῆμον εὐνοίας, ὅτι πρῶτον μὲν ἐν Νομαντίᾳ τὴν
τελευτὴν τοῦ Τιβερίου πυθόμενος ἀνεφώνησεν ἐκ
τῶν Ὁμηρικῶν

ὣς ἀπόλοιτο καὶ ἄλλος ὅ τις τοιαῦτά γε ῥέζοι·

ἔπειτα τῶν περὶ Γάιον καὶ Φούλβιον αὐτοῦ δι' ἐκ-
κλησίας πυνθανομένων τί φρονοίη περὶ τῆς Τιβερίου
τελευτῆς οὐκ ἀρεσκομένην τοῖς ὑπ' ἐκείνου πεπολι-
τευμένοις ἀπόκρισιν ἔδωκεν. ἐκ τούτου γὰρ ὁ μὲν
δῆμος ἀντέκρουσεν αὐτῷ λέγοντι, μηδέπω τοῦτο
ποιήσας πρότερον, αὐτὸς δὲ τὸν δῆμον εἰπεῖν κακῶς
προήχθη. περὶ μὲν οὖν τούτων ἐν τῷ Σκιπίωνος
βίῳ τὰ καθ' ἕκαστα γέγραπται.

opposed the expedition ; nevertheless Agesilaüs did not desist, but prosecuted the war.

2 *a*

Hannibal used to declare that of all generals Pyrrhus was the first in experience and cleverness, Scipio second, and himself third, as I have recorded in the *Life of Scipio*.

SCIPIO AFRICANUS

(? *Lamprias Catalogue* 28)

3 *a*

Scipio Africanus, whom the Romans are thought to have loved with more and with better cause than any other man, very nearly fell out of favour and lost the goodwill of the people. The first reason of this was that when he heard at Numantia of the death of Tiberius Gracchus, he exclaimed in the words of Homer

So perish any man who does the like.[b]

Then when C. Gracchus and Fulvius asked him at an assembly of the people what he thought of Tiberius' death, he returned an answer that showed his disapproval of the dead man's politics. After this the people heckled him when he was speaking, a thing they had never done before, and he was himself moved to use hard words of them. The details I have recorded in the *Life of Scipio*.

[a] It is possible that frag. 2 belongs to *Scipio Africanus* and frags. 3 and 4 to *Epaminondas and Scipio* ; see the note preceding frag. 1.   [b] *Odyssey*, i. 47.

4

Plutarch, *Life of Gaius Gracchus*, c. 10.

Καὶ ὅτε Σκιπίων ὁ 'Αφρικανὸς ἐξ οὐδενὸς αἰτίου
προφανοῦς ἐτελεύτησε καὶ σημεῖά τινα τῷ νεκρῷ
πληγῶν καὶ βίας ἐπιδραμεῖν ἔδοξεν, ὡς ἐν τοῖς περὶ
ἐκείνου γέγραπται, τὸ μὲν πλεῖστον ἐπὶ τὸν Φούλβιον ἦλθε τῆς διαβολῆς, ἐχθρὸν ὄντα καὶ τὴν ἡμέραν
ἐκείνην ἐπὶ τοῦ βήματος τῷ Σκιπίωνι λελοιδορη-
μένον, ἥψατο δὲ καὶ τοῦ Γαΐου ἡ ὑπόνοια.

ΝΕΡΩΝΟΣ ΒΙΟΣ

5

Plutarch, *Life of Galba*, c. 2.

Νυμφίδιος γὰρ Σαβῖνος ὢν ἔπαρχος, ὥσπερ εἴρηται, μετὰ Τιγελλίνου τῆς αὐλῆς . . .

ΗΡΑΚΛΕΟΥΣ ΒΙΟΣ

6

Plutarch, *Life of Theseus*, c. 29.

Ὅτι δ' Ἡρακλῆς πρῶτος ἀπέδωκε νεκροὺς τοῖς
πολεμίοις ἐν τοῖς περὶ Ἡρακλέους γέγραπται.

7

Aulus Gellius, i. 1.

Plutarchus in libro quem de Herculis, quantum[1]
inter homines fuit,[2] animi corporisque ingenio et

[1] *quamdiu* Klotz, *quali* β (cod. Buslidianus).   [2] *fuerit* β.

78

4 [a]

And when Scipio Africanus died with no obvious
cause of death, and it was thought that his corpse was
covered with bruises and other signs of violence, as is
recorded in my work about him, accusations were
mainly directed at Fulvius, who was his enemy and
had that very day made him the target of invective
from the rostra ; but some suspicion attached to C.
Gracchus too.

LIFE OF NERO

(Lamprias Catalogue 30)

5

Nymphidius Sabinus, being (as I have said) prefect
of the Praetorians along with Tigellinus . .

LIFE OF HERACLES

(Lamprias Catalogue 34)

6

It has been recorded in my work on Heracles that
he was the first man to surrender the corpses of the
slain to the enemy.[b]

7

In the book which he wrote on the mental and
physical endowments and achievements of Heracles

[a] It is possible that frag. 2 belongs to *Scipio Africanus*
and frags. 3 and 4 to *Epaminondas and Scipio* ; see the note
preceding frag. 1.
[b] Jacoby, *F.Gr.Hist.* iii в 328, F 112, regards this, without
reason given, as interpolated.

virtutibus conscripsit scite subtiliterque ratiocinatum
Pythagoram philosophum dicit in reperienda modu-
landaque status longitudinisque eius praestantia.
nam cum fere constaret curriculum stadii quod est
Pisis apud Iovem Olympium Herculem pedibus suis
metatum idque fecisse longum pedes sescentos, cetera
quoque stadia in terra Graecia ab aliis postea instituta
pedum quidem esse numero sescentum sed tamen
esse aliquantulum breviora, facile intellexit modum
spatiumque plantae Herculis, ratione proportionis
habita, tanto fuisse quam aliorum procerius quanto
Olympicum stadium longius esset quam cetera. com-
prehensa autem mensura Herculani pedis,[1] secundum
naturalem membrorum omnium inter se competen-
tiam modificatus est atque ita id collegit quod erat
consequens, tanto fuisse Herculem corpore excelsi-
orem quam alios quanto Olympicum stadium ceteris
pari numero factis anteiret.

8

Arnobius, *Contra Gentes*, iv, p. 144.

Chaeroneus Plutarchus nostrarum esse partium
comprobatur, qui in Oetaeis verticibus Herculem post
morborum comitialium ruinas dissolutum in cinerem
prodidit.

ΗΣΙΟΔΟΥ ΒΙΟΣ

[1] After *pedis* β adds *quanta longinquitas corporis ei men-
surae conveniret.*

[a] The length (192·27 m.) makes Heracles' foot 32·1 cm.,
compared with the English foot of 30·5 cm., and the most
usual Greek foot of 29·6 cm. : but the Athenians used a foot
of 32·8 cm.

during his life on earth Plutarch says that the philosopher Pythagoras made a clever and acute calculation to determine the extent by which that hero exceeded normal human height and stature. There was general agreement that Heracles had measured out the running-track at Pisa that adjoins the temple of Olympian Zeus, making its length 600 of his own feet.[a] It was also agreed that the other tracks in Greece, laid out later by other men, were 600 feet long but somewhat shorter than that at Pisa. From these data he had no difficulty in concluding by attention to proportionality, that Heracles' foot was larger than that of other men in the same ratio as the course at Olympia was longer than the rest. Having thus ascertained the size of Heracles' foot, he calculated what would, following the natural relation of the parts of the body to one another, be the bodily height appropriate to that size, and so arrived at the consequence that Heracles was taller than other men by the same factor as that by which the running track at Olympia exceeded all the others that had been laid out to have the same number of feet.

8

Plutarch of Chaeronea is acknowledged to be on our side ; he reported that Heracles was reduced to ashes on the summit of Mt. Oeta after collapsing in epileptic fits.

LIFE OF HESIOD

(*Lamprias Catalogue* 35)

(*Material to be found in* Moralia, *153* F, *162* D, *674* F, *969* E, *may have been used in the* Life.)

ΠΙΝΔΑΡΟΥ ΒΙΟΣ

It is probable that material from this has entered the anonymous biographies of the poet and also Eustathius' Prooemium ; it is also likely that Pausanias, ix. 23. 2-4, is

9

Eustathius, *Prooemium Commentariorum Pindaricorum*, c. 25.

Ἐπιμεμέληται ὑπὸ τῶν παλαιῶν καὶ εἰς γένους ἀναγραφὴν τὴν κατά τε Πλούταρχον καὶ ἑτέρους, παρ᾽ οἷς φέρεται ὅτι κώμη Θηβαίων οἱ Κυνοσκέφαλοι.[1]

ΚΡΑΤΗΤΟΣ ΒΙΟΣ

10

Julian, *Orat.* vii, p. 200 b.

Ἐντυχὼν δὲ τῷ Χαιρωνεῖ Πλουτάρχῳ τὸν Κράτητος ἀναγράψαντι βίον οὐδὲν ἐκ παρέργου[2] μανθάνειν δεήσῃ τὸν ἄνδρα.

ΔΑΪΦΑΝΤΟΣ

11

Plutarch, *Mulierum Virtutes*, 244 B.

Τὸ δὲ τῶν Φωκίδων ἐνδόξου μὲν οὐ τετύχηκε συγγραφέως, οὐδενὸς δὲ τῶν γυναικείων ἔλαττον

---

[1] κυνοκέφαλοι MS.
[2] τοῦ after παρέργου deleted by Cobet.

LIFE OF PINDAR

(Lamprias Catalogue 36)

based on Plutarch (Wilamowitz, Pindaros, p. 58). In Plutarch's own work stories told at Moralia, 347 F, 536 B, 557 F, 717 D, may have found a place in the Life also.

9

The old authors have taken care to make a record also of his origins, a record they found in Plutarch and others, who report that his birthplace was a Theban village called Cynoscephali.

LIFE OF CRATES [a]

(Lamprias Catalogue 37)

10

If you get hold of the biography of Crates by Plutarch of Chaeronea, you will not have any need to make a cursory study of the man.

DAÏPHANTUS

(Lamprias Catalogue 38)

11

The deed of the women of Phocis has found no famous authority to record it, but is the equal for bravery of anything ever done by women. It is

[a] The follower of Diogenes the Cynic. His Boeotian origin, as a native of Thebes, will account for Plutarch's interest. Compare the General Index.

εἰς ἀρετήν ἐστι, μαρτυρούμενον ἱεροῖς τε μεγάλοις,
ἃ δρῶσι Φωκεῖς ἔτι νῦν περὶ Ὕαμπολιν, καὶ δόγ-
μασι παλαιοῖς, ὧν τὸ μὲν καθ' ἕκαστον τῆς πράξεως
ἐν τῷ Δαϊφάντου βίῳ γέγραπται. τὸ δὲ τῶν γυναικῶν τοιοῦτόν ἐστιν.

ΑΡΙΣΤΟΜΕΝΗΣ

*12

Stephanus of Byzantium, *s.v.* Ἀνδανία.

Ἐκ ταύτης Ἀριστομένης ἐγένετο ἐπιφανέστατος
στρατηγός. τοῦτον οἱ Λακεδαιμόνιοι πολλάκις
αὐτοὺς νικήσαντα θαυμάσαντες, ὡς μόλις ἐκράτησαν ἐν τοῖς Μεσσηνιακοῖς, ἀνατεμόντες ἐσκόπουν
εἰ παρὰ τοὺς λοιποὺς ἔστι τι· καὶ εὗρον σπλάγχνον
ἐξηλλαγμένον καὶ τὴν καρδίαν δασεῖαν, ὡς Ἡρόδοτος καὶ Πλούταρχος καὶ Ῥιανός.

---

[a] Aristomenes, a Messenian hero, is usually regarded by
writers in antiquity, following Callisthenes, as a figure of the
Second Messenian War in the earlier half of the 7th century
B.C. : but the Alexandrian Rhianus (iii B.C.), in an epic poem,
dated him to a war *c.* 490 B.C., and this is accepted as probable
by G. L. Huxley, *Early Sparta*, pp. 56, 88, 92. F. Jacoby,
however, *F. Gr. Hist.* iii a, pp. 120-190, is sceptical about all the
evidence, and is tempted to see in him an imaginary figure of
propaganda of the time of Epaminondas ; see also L. Pearson, " The Pseudo-History of Messenia," *Historia*, xi (1962),
p. 409. Theban interest in him may account for Plutarch's
interest.

[b] In N.E. Messenia.

[c] *Cf.* Dio Chrys. xxxv. 3, Pliny, *N.H.* xi. 70, " pectus dis-
secuere viventi, hirsutumque cor repertum est." The Greek
is ambiguous and might possibly mean " an organ out of the

attested by important sacrifices, still performed by the Phocians at Hyampolis, and by ancient decrees. What these decrees say of the details of the action is recorded in my Life of Daïphantus, but the women's part in it is as follows.

LIFE OF ARISTOMENES [a]

(*Lamprias Catalogue* 39)

*12

From this town of Andania [b] came Aristomenes, a most eminent general. He defeated the Spartans on many occasions to their great wonder, and so when they had with difficulty overcome him in the Messenian wars, they cut him open to discover whether there was anything abnormal about him. They discovered that there was an organ displaced and that the heart was hairy,[c] as is recorded by Herodotus, Plutarch, and Rhianus.[d]

Ascribed to the *Life of Aristomenes* by Wyttenbach, but see note d.

ordinary, namely that the heart was hairy." One may compare the hairy heart of Leonidas, *Parallela Minora*, 306 D. Such stories may have been suggested by the Homeric λάσιον κῆρ.

[d] *Collectanea Alexandrina*, frag. 53; Jacoby, *F.Gr.Hist.* iii A 265, F 46. In his note Jacoby points out that Rhianus made Aristomenes die in Rhodes ; he considers the whole passage interpolated into Stephanus, and that the reference to Plutarch is to *De Herod. Malignitate*, 856 F, where Herodotus is, as here, falsely quoted as an authority for the capture of Aristomenes by the Spartans. No mention is made there, however, of the hairy heart, and Plutarch might have repeated the false citation of Herodotus in his *Life of Aristomenes*.

FRAGMENTS FROM OTHER
NAMED WORKS

ΑΙΤΙΑΙ ΤΩΝ ΑΡΑΤΟΥ ΔΙΟΣΗΜΙΩΝ

Some material from Plutarch's work on Aratus' Dio-
semiae found its way into the scholia on that poem, perhaps
more than they explicitly acknowledge. But there is no
justification for printing as fragments of Plutarch anything
beyond the notes to which his name is attached. Previous
editors could not isolate these, since they only knew the scholia
in a confused form. A great advance was made by E. Maass,
Commentariorum in Aratum Reliquiae (1898). *He based*
his text on two of the 20 mss. that contain the scholia, namely
Marcianus 476 (M), of the eleventh or twelfth century A.D.,
and Parisinus 2403 (A), to which he added the Aldine edition,
taken from a ms. that has not been identified. The evidence
of M enabled him to distinguish between the individual
scholia. His text, however, is not satisfactory, since he mis-
takenly allowed some authority to A and the Aldine edition.
J. Martin in his excellent Histoire du texte des Phénomènes
d'Arate (1956) *shows that (so far as the scholia are concerned)*
all mss. descend from M, with the one exception of Scoria-
lensis Σ III. 3 (S, c. 1490 A.D.*) ; variants in other mss. are*

13

Schol. Aratus, *Diosemiae*, 88 = *Phaenomena* 820.

ἡελίῳ καὶ μᾶλλον ἐοικότα σήματα κεῖται.

Αἱ τοῦ ἡλίου πρὸς[1] τὸν ἀέρα διαφοραὶ κυριώτεραι
τῶν τῆς σελήνης εἰσί· δυναστεύων γὰρ ἡμέρας
σαφέστερα δείκνυσι τὰ τεκμήρια.[2] δεύτερον δὲ ὅτι[3]

[1] πρὸς M : κατὰ S.   [2] τεκμήρια M : σημεῖα S.
     [3] δεύτερον δὲ ὅτι M : καὶ S.

EXPLANATIONS OF ARATUS'
WEATHERLORE

(*Lamprias Catalogue* 119)

due to error or deliberate alteration, but they include some plausible emendations. The text here presented is based on M and S ; I am indebted to the authorities of the Monasterio Real de S. Laurenzo de el Escorial for a microfilm of the relevant part of the latter. S, which is very corrupt, has many fewer scholia than M ; it entirely omits frags. 15-20. But it appears to retain some words and phrases omitted by the other ; it also confirms the lines of division between individual scholia.

Plutarch's concern seems to have been to find in each case a single natural cause that would account both for the weather-sign and for the weather it was supposed to foretell. He was thus in the tradition of, but not necessarily dependent on, the Stoic Boethus, who in the latter half of the second century B.C. wrote a four-volume commentary on the Diosemiae, giving such explanations of the weather-signs (Geminus, Elements of Astronomy, 17. 14 Petau ; Pohlenz, Die Stoa, ii. 94).

I disregard the scholiasts' lemmata, substituting enough of Aratus' text to explain the comment.

13

In the case of the sun even more likely signs are established.

Conflicts of the sun with the air are more important than those of the moon. Being dominant by day, it provides evidence that is plainer. A second reason

λαμπρότερός ἐστι, καὶ εἰ μὴ μεγάλη καὶ ἰσχυρὰ
τοῦ ἀέρος εἴη[1] μεταβολή, οὐκ ἂν κρατηθείη· τὰς
γὰρ μικρὰς καὶ ἐλαφρὰς ἀναστέλλει καὶ σκεδάννυ-
σιν· οὕτω Πλούταρχος.[2]

14

Ibid. Dios. 96 = *Phaen.* 828.

ἀλλ' οὐχ ὁππότε κοῖλος ἐειδόμενος περιτέλλῃ.

Αἱ ἐν τῷ ἡλίῳ κοιλότητες οὔκ εἰσιν αὐτοῦ, φαν-
τασίαι δ' εἰσὶ τῆς ὄψεως κατ' ἐπιπρόσθεσιν ζοφεροῦ
ἀέρος. οὐ γὰρ τὸ μέσον ὁρᾶται ἀλλ' ἡ κύκλῳ ἁψίς.
λαμπρὰ δὲ οὖσα καὶ περιφέγγουσα[3] τὸ ἐκλιπὲς[4]
ἔμφασιν κοιλότητος παρέχει.[5] ὃν τρόπον γὰρ οἱ
ζωγράφοι ἀντρώδεις τόπους γράφοντες φωτὶ τρα-
χύνουσι τὴν ὄψιν, ἅτε τῇ φύσει τοῦ μὲν λαμπροῦ
προβάλλοντος[6] ἔξω καὶ διωθοῦντος τὴν φαντασίαν
τοῦ δὲ μέλανος ὑποσκιάζειν[7] καὶ βαθύνεσθαι δοκοῦν-
τος, οὕτω καὶ περὶ τὸν ἥλιον τὸ[8] φαινόμενον τῇ
ὄψει κατὰ ἀντίφραξιν τοῦ ἀέρος ἐκκοπὴν τοῦ μέσου
λαμπροῦ διὰ τὴν σκιὰν ποιεῖ[9] ὑποφαίνεσθαι. ὃ ὅλην
ποιεῖ τὴν ἀντίφραξιν· ὁ ἀὴρ σφόδρα πιληθεὶς καὶ
παχύς, ζοφωθεὶς διὰ χειμέριον τὸ ζῴδιον. Πλούταρχος.[10]

[1] εἴη Μ : εἴη ἡ S.
[2] μικρὰς καὶ and οὕτω Πλούταρχος omitted by S, καὶ σκεδάν-
νυσιν by Μ.
[3] F. H. S.: λαμπρὰ οὖσα δοκεῖ περιφεύγειν (περιφέγγειν Wyttenbach) εἰς.
[4] καὶ εἰς τὸ ἐκλεῖπον S. Bekker added καὶ, the Aldine edition
ὡς, after ἐκλιπὲς.   [5] παρέχει S : παρέχειν Μ.
[6] Aldine edition : προσβάλλοντα MS.
[7] Suspected by Wyttenbach. ? πρὸς τὴν . . . ὑπὸ σκιᾶς εἶναι.
[8] Aldine edition : τὸ μὴ Μ : τὸν μὴ (φ. περὶ τὴν ὄψιν) S.

is that the sun is brighter, and could not be mastered unless there were a great and violent change in the air. For it brushes small, slight changes aside and disperses them. Thus Plutarch.

14

But not when it looks hollow as it rises.

" Hollows " in the sun are not real features of the sun, but optical illusions due to the interposition of dark air. What is seen is not the centre, but the circular rim ; that rim, however, being bright and shining all round the part that is invisible, gives it an appearance of concavity. For as artists, when painting cavernous places, use light to affect the eye by contrast, since a bright colour naturally gives the impression of jutting out and pushing forward, while a dark one seems to be overshadowed and to lie in a deeper plane,[a] similarly in the case of the sun what appears to our sight when air is interposed suggests, because of the shadow cast, the hollowing out of the centre of the bright disc . . .[b]

[a] Plutarch not infrequently has similes from painters or painting, e.g., Moralia, 53 D, 64 A, 452 F, 575 A, 725 C. At 57 C and 863 E he notes the effect of contrasted light and shade.

[b] The Greek text is uncertain and not readily intelligible in detail. I have given what I think may be its intended meaning. At the end S adds : " What makes the interposition complete. The air very closely packed and thick, made dark through the storminess of the zodiacal sign. Plutarch." This is probably garbled, but may be evidence that the note as a whole contains Plutarchean material.

---

[9] ἐκκοπὴν . . . ποιεῖ Aldine edition : ἡ ἐκκοπὴ . . . σκιὰν MS. The correct wording appears to be lost.

[10] ὃ ὅλην . . . Πλούταρχος in S only.

15

Ibid. Dios. 97-98 = *Phaen.* 829-830.

οὐδ' ὁπότ' ἀκτίνων αἱ μὲν νότον αἱ δὲ βορῆα
σχιζόμεναι βάλλωσι, τὰ δ' αὖ περὶ μέσσα φα-
εἴνῃ.

Ὥσπερ ἐπὶ τῶν ὀφθαλμικῶν,[1] ὅταν συμβαίνῃ
κοιλαίνεσθαι τοὺς ὀφθαλμούς, δηλονότι ἐξασθενή-
σαντος τοῦ σώματος, ἢ ὥσπερ ὅταν βλέφαρον κατ-
αγαγόντες[2] ἢ περιθλίψαντες τῷ λύχνῳ τὴν ὄψιν
προσβάλλωμεν, οὐ φαίνεται συνεχὲς τὸ φῶς ἀλλὰ
πλάγιαι καὶ σποράδες αἱ αὐγαί· οὕτως ὅταν ἀχλὺς
ἢ νέφωσις ἀνώμαλος πρὸ τοῦ ἡλίου στᾶσα περι-
θλίψῃ καὶ σείσῃ τὸν τῆς ὄψεως κῶνον εἰς λεπτὰς
ἀκτῖνας καὶ ῥαβδοειδεῖς, ὃ πάσχομεν αὐτοὶ τῇ
αἰσθήσει, τοῦτο περὶ τὸν ἥλιον εἶναι δοκοῦμεν.
οὕτω Πλούταρχος.

16

Ibid. Dios. 301-304 = *Phaen.* 1033-1036.

μηδ' ὅτε . . .
. . . πῦρ αὔηται σπουδῇ καὶ ὑπεύδια λύχνα
πιστεύειν χειμῶνι.

Τὰ καυστὰ βραδέως ἐξάπτεται παχυμεροῦς τοὺς
πόρους ἐπιφράττοντος τοῦ ἀέρος· διόπερ οἱ τὰς δᾷ-
δας ἅπτοντες προτρίβουσιν[3] ἐν τῇ τέφρᾳ, ἵνα ἀπο-
κρουσθῇ εἴ τι ἔνικμον,[4] καὶ τὸ πῦρ τῆς ὕλης μᾶλλον
ἅψηται. οὕτω Πλούταρχος.

15

Nor when its rays are split and strike some to the south, some to the north, but its centre is bright.

We may compare the experience of those who suffer from eye-trouble, when it results in their becoming hollow-eyed (through physical weakness of course),[1] or what happens when we direct our vision towards a lamp after pulling down the eyelid or pressing round the eye. The light does not appear continuous, but in scattered, slanting[2] rays. Similarly, when a mist or uneven cloud-formation, stationed in front of the sun, presses round[3] the cone of vision and disturbs it so as to produce narrow rod-like beams, we attribute to the sun what is really an effect upon ourselves in the act of sensation.[4] Thus Plutarch.

16

If fire is hard to light, or lamps, although the weather is fine, beware of storms.

Combustibles are slow to take fire when the air is composed of large particles and blocks their pores. Hence when people are lighting torches they first rub them in the ashes, to brush off any moisture there may be, so that the fire may take a better hold of the wood. Thus Plutarch.

---

[1] ? ὀφθαλμιώντων.
[2] Maass : κατάγοντες.
[3] Maass ; προστρίβουσι.
[4] ᾖ after ἔνικμον deleted by Maass. Perhaps τὸ should also be read for εἴ τι.

17

Ibid. Dios. 312-316 = *Phaen.* 1044-1048.

πρῖνοι δ' αὖ καρποῖο καταχθέες οὐδὲ μέλαιναι
σχῖνοι ἀπείρητοι . . .
πρῖνοι μὲν θαμινῆς ἀκύλου κατὰ μέτρον ἔχουσαι
χειμῶνός κε λέγοιεν ἐπὶ πλέον ἰσχύσοντος.

Φησὶν οὖν ὁ Θεόφραστος ὅτι ὁ πρῖνος καὶ ἡ σχῖνος
αὐχμηρὰ τῇ κράσει καὶ ξηρότερα τῶν ἄλλων πε-
φυκότα πολὺν καρπὸν οὐ φέρει, ἐὰν μὴ εἰς βάθος
ὑγρανθῇ. εἰκότως οὖν τῇ τούτων εὐφορίᾳ[1] καταμαν-
τεύονται περὶ τῶν σπερμάτων οἱ γεωργοί, μιᾶς
αἰτίας οὔσης δι' ἣν ἀμφοτέροις ἡ πολυκαρπία· εἰ
δ' ὑπερβάλλει τοῦ καρποῦ τὸ πλῆθος, οὐκ ἀγαθὸν
σημεῖον· ἄμετρον γὰρ ἐπομβρίαν καὶ πλεονασμὸν
ὑγρότητος ἡ περὶ τὸν ἀέρα ἄνεσις καὶ θηλύτης δηλοῖ. οὕτω Πλούταρχος.

18

Ibid. Dios. 319-321 = *Phaen.* 1051-1053.

τριπλόα δὲ σχῖνος κυέει, τρισσαὶ δέ οἱ αὖξαι
γίνονται καρποῖο, φέρει δέ τε σήμαθ' ἑκάστη
ἐξείης ἀρότῳ.

Ὅσα γὰρ τὴν σχῖνον ἐκ τοῦ ἀέρος ὠφελεῖ, ταῦτα
καὶ τὸν σῖτον· ὁμοίως καὶ τὰ βλάπτοντα. δείγματα
οὖν τῶν σπόρων ὁ πρῶτος ἐν τῇ σχίνῳ ἐστὶ τῶν
πρώτων, καὶ τῶν μέσων ὁ μέσος, καὶ ὁ τρίτος τῶν
τελευταίων.[2] οὕτω Πλούταρχος.

---

[1] εὐφορίᾳ F. H. S.: ἀφορίᾳ.
[2] Aldine edition : τοῦ τελευταίου M.

---

[a] This is not to be found in an extant work. On the other

17

> Holm-oaks and dark mastichs burdened with fruit are not without meaning. . . . Holm-oaks holding a full measure of crowded acorns would tell of stormy weather that will greatly prevail.

Now Theophrastus says that holm-oaks and mastichs, being arid in their temperament and naturally drier than other trees, do not bear much fruit unless deeply penetrated by moisture.[a] It is with good reason, therefore, that farmers use their productivity to make a forecast about the crops they have sown, since one and the same cause brings about a high yield in both cases. But if the quantity of fruit is very great, it is not a good sign : the relaxation and softness of the air indicate an immoderate rainfall and excessive wetness. Thus Plutarch.

18

> Three times does the mastich [b] flower and three times increase with fruit, and each crop in succession gives a sign for the cornfield.

All atmospheric conditions that favour the mastich also favour wheat, and similarly with everything harmful. Thus the first crop in the mastich is an indication of the prospects of the first crop of wheat, the middle one of the middle one, and the third of the last.[c] Thus Plutarch.

hand at *Caus. Plant.* v. 6. 10, Theophrastus speaks of the mastich as having warmth and moisture.

[b] *Pistacia Lentiscus.*

[c] Cicero may have understood Aratus better, when he translated *tria tempora monstrat arandi* : the flowering of the mastich indicates the times for ploughing, of which there were three (note *d* on frag. 60).

19

Ibid. Dios. 325-326 = *Phaen.* 1057-1058.

ὅντινα γὰρ κάλλιστα λοχαίη σχῖνος ἄρηται,
κείνῳ γ᾽ ἐξ ἄλλων ἄροσις πολυλήιος εἴη.

Οὐ μόνον ἐν τοῖς ζῴοις συμπάθειά ἐστι ἀλλὰ
καὶ ἐν τοῖς φυτοῖς. ὁσαοῦν[1] κεκραμένην ὑγρότητι
ἢ ψυχρότητι παραπλησίως ἔχει τὴν ἕξιν, καὶ[2] τρέφεται ἀπὸ τῶν ὁμοίων καὶ τοῖς αὐτοῖς εὐθηνεῖ καὶ
μαραίνεται. διὸ πολλὰ μετ᾽ ἀλλήλων συνακμάζει
καὶ καρποφορεῖ, τὰ μὲν θέρει τὰ δὲ χειμῶνι τινὰ
δὲ καὶ ἔαρι. τῶν μὲν οὖν αἱ κράσεις διάφοροι, τῶν
δ᾽ ὅμοιαι καὶ συγγενεῖς σφόδρα· τῶν οὖν τὴν
ὁμοίαν κρᾶσιν ἐχόντων[3] εἰσὶ πρῖνος, σχῖνος, σκίλλα,
πυρός. οὕτω Πλούταρχος.

20

Ibid. Dios. 362-364 = *Phaen.* 1094-1096.

οὐδὲ μὲν ὀρνίθων ἀγέλαις ἠπειρόθεν ἀνήρ,
ἐκ νήσων ὅτε πολλαὶ ἐπιπλήσσωσιν ἀρούραις
ἐρχομένου θέρεος, χαίρει.

Ξηρότεραι γὰρ αἱ νῆσοι τῶν ἠπείρων ὑπάρχουσαι,
ὥς φησι Πλούταρχος, θᾶττον καὶ ῥᾷον τοῦ αὐχμη-
ροῦ καταστήματος ἀντιλαμβάνονται. διὸ καὶ τὰ
ὄρνεα φεύγει καὶ ταῖς ἠπείροις ἐπιπελάζει.

ΕΙ Η ΤΩΝ ΜΕΛΛΟΝΤΩΝ ΠΡΟΓΝΩΣΙΣ
ΩΦΕΛΙΜΟΣ

There is no such title in the *Lamprias Catalogue.* The
possibility cannot be excluded that it indicates not a book,

19

When the heavily laden mastich yields its finest crop, then
most of all will the ploughland bear a great harvest.

Sympathy occurs not only among animals, but also
among plants and trees. All such as have constitu-
tions with a similar blend of moistness or coldness
also have the same sources of nourishment and
flourish and wither in the same conditions. Hence
there are many which mature and bear fruit at the
same time as one another, some in the summer,
others in the winter, some even in the spring. Some
plants, then, differ in their composition, while others
are similar and closely related. Among plants with
a similar composition are the holm-oak, the mastich,
the squill, and wheat. Thus Plutarch.

20

Nor does a mainland man rejoice when flocks of birds at
the beginning of summer descend in great numbers from
the islands upon his fields.

Islands, being drier than the mainland, as Plutarch
says, more quickly and easily take on a condition of
drought. That is why the birds leave them and fly to
the mainland.

IS FOREKNOWLEDGE OF FUTURE
EVENTS USEFUL ?

*but a part of a book. The fragments could, for example, have
found a place in no. 71, περὶ μαντικῆς ὅτι σῴζεται κατὰ τοὺς
Ἀκαδημαϊκούς.*

---

[1] ὁσαοῦν F. H. S.: ὅταν οὖν. ὅσ᾽ ἂν οὖν (with ἔχῃ) Duebner.
[2] Aldine edition : ἤ.   [3] Aldine edition : συνεχόντων.

The Stoics argued that the reality of prophecy proved the existence of Fate, and that in turn the Providence of God guaranteed the reality of prophecy, since it is to our advantage to know the future. This utility was denied by Epicureans

21

Stobaeus, i. 5. 19 (i, p. 81 Wachsmuth).

Πλουτάρχου ἐκ τοῦ εἰ ἡ τῶν μελλόντων πρόγνωσις ὠφέλιμος·

Τὸ γὰρ εἱμαρμένον ἄτρεπτον καὶ ἀπαράβατον,
  χὦπερ¹ μόνον ὀφρύσι νεύσῃ,²
  καρτερὰ τούτῳ κέκλωστ'² ἀνάγκα.

διὰ τοῦτο τὴν εἱμαρμένην καὶ Πεπρωμένην³ καὶ Ἀδράστειαν καλοῦσιν, ὅτι πέρας ταῖς αἰτίαις ἠναγκασμένον ἐπιτίθησιν ἀνέκφευκτος οὖσα καὶ ἀναπόδραστος.

22

Stobaeus, ii. 8. 25 (ii, p. 158 Wachsmuth).

Ἐκ τοῦ Πλουτάρχου εἰ ἡ τῶν μελλόντων πρόγνωσις ὠφέλιμος.

"Ὁ δὲ Νέστωρ οὐκ ἀβέλτερος, ὕπνου φθονῶν τοῖς τὰς ναῦς φυλάσσουσι καὶ διακελευόμενος

---

¹ χὦπερ Gaisford.
² Meineke : νεύσει . . . κέκλωτ'.
³ καὶ Πεπρωμένην inserted here by Wyttenbach, deleting καὶ πεπρωμένη after ἀνάγκα.

ᵃ *Frag. adesp.* 19 Diehl, 99 Page.
ᵇ For these Stoic etymologies compare *De Stoic. Repugn.*

FRAGMENTS : OTHER NAMED WORKS

(*Diogenianus, frag. 4 = Eusebius,* Praep. Ev. *iv. 3,* cf. *Schol. on Aeschylus,* P.V. *624*) *and by the New Academy* (*Cicero,* De Divinatione, *ii. 22-24*).

The first two of the following fragments give unadulterated Stoic doctrine. This suggests the possibility that Plutarch's work was a dialogue ; but as a priest of Apollo at Delphi he was bound to defend the usefulness of prophecy, and may have adapted Stoic arguments for the purpose.

21

Plutarch, from the work *Is Foreknowledge of Future Events Useful?*

What is fated is not to be averted or evaded :

> And by the mere nodding of his brow
> Strong necessity is spun.[a]

For this reason they give Fate the names of Peprômenê (Destiny) and Adrasteia because, being a power unavoidable and inescapable (*anapodrastos*),[b] she attaches to causes a final necessitated result (*peras*).

22

From Plutarch, *Is Foreknowledge of Future Events Useful?*

"And was it not fatuous of Nestor to begrudge the ships' sentries their sleep and exhort them with the words

1056 c (*S.V.F.* ii. 997), τὴν δ' εἱμαρμένην . . . αὐτὸς (sc. Χρύσιππος) Ἄτροπον καλεῖ καὶ Ἀδράστειαν καὶ Ἀνάγκην καὶ Πεπρωμένην, ὡς πέρας ἅπασιν ἐπιτιθεῖσαν ; Arius Didymus, frag. 29 fin. (Diels, *Doxogr. Graeci*, p. 465. 2, *S.V.F.* ii. 528) ; Ps.-Aristotle, *De Mundo*, 401 b 11 ; Schol. *Iliad*, xx. 127 ; Diogenianus, frag. 2 (Eusebius, *Praep. Ev.* vi. 8).

' οὕτω νῦν φίλα τέκνα φυλάσσετε, μηδέ τιν' ὕπνος
αἱρείτω, μὴ χάρμα γενώμεθα δυσμενέεσσιν ';
οὐ γενησόμεθα, φησί τις, οὐδ' ἂν καθεύδωμεν, εἰ
πεπρωμένον ἐστὶ μὴ ἁλῶναι τὸν ναύσταθμον.''[1] τίς
οὐκ ἂν εἴποι πρὸς τοὺς ταῦτα ληροῦντας, ὅτι καθεί-
μαρται μὲν ἴσως ἅπαντα ταῦτα, συγκαθείμαρται δ'
ἑκάστῳ τὸ διὰ τούτων καὶ τὸ ἐν τούτοις καὶ[2] οὕτω
καὶ τὸ μὴ ἄλλως[3] συντελεῖσθαι δίχα τούτων; οὐ
γάρ ἐστι φυλακὴ καθευδόντων οὐδὲ νίκη φευγόντων
οὐδὲ θερίσαι μὴ σπειράντων γῆν ἀγαθὴν[4] καὶ καθα-
ράν, οὐδὲ γεννῆσαι μὴ συγγενόμενον γυναικὶ ἡλικίαν
ἐχούσῃ καὶ σώματος φύσιν γόνιμον, οὐδ' ἄγρας
τυχεῖν ἐν ἀθήροις χωρίοις.

23

Stobaeus, iii. 3. 41 (iii, p. 207 Hense).

Ἐκ τοῦ Πλουτάρχου[5] εἰ ἡ τῶν μελλόντων πρόγνωσις ὠφέλιμος.

Ἀλλὰ μὴν ἡ φρόνησις οὐ σωμάτων ἀλλὰ πραγμάτων ὄψις ἐστί, πρὶν ἐν αὐτοῖς γενέσθαι τὸν ἄνθρωπον, ὅπως ἄριστα χρήσεται τοῖς ἀπαντῶσι καὶ προσ-
τυγχάνουσι παρέχουσα διασκοπεῖν τὸ μέλλον. τὸ
μὲν οὖν σῶμα πρόσω μόνον ὠμμάτωται τοῖς δ'
ὄπισθεν τυφλόν ἐστιν ἀτεχνῶς,[6] ἡ δὲ διάνοια καὶ τὰ
παρῳχημένα βλέπειν τῇ μνήμῃ πέφυκεν· ὁ γὰρ

---

[1] Canter : δύσταθμον.
[2] καὶ τὸ Usener.   [3] ? μηδαμῶς.
[4] Gercke : τὴν ἀγαθὴν γῆν.
[5] ? Πλουτάρχου, ἐκ τοῦ Hense.
[6] ἀτεχνῶς Tr. ; other mss. omit.

So now, dear children, watch, and let not sleep
Take you, lest we become the foemen's joy ? [a]

We shall not become his joy, is the answer, even
should we go to sleep, if it is destined that the ships'
station shall not be captured." Who would not reply
to such nonsense that, although all these things [b]
may be fated, it is jointly fated with each of them that
it must be achieved by such-and-such means and in
such-and-such circumstances and such a way, but
not in any other manner without these concomitants ?
There is no keeping guard by men who sleep, no
victory for those who run away, no harvesting for
those who have not sown good, cleared ground : one
cannot beget a child without intercourse with a
woman of the right age and a fertile body, nor catch
game in districts where there are no animals.

23

From Plutarch, *Is Foreknowledge of Future Events
Useful ?*

Well now, prudence is a vision not of persons, but
of events, before a man is involved in them, giving
him the opportunity to examine the future to see
how he may best deal with what meets and befalls
him. Now whereas the body has eyes in front only,
and is quite blind to the rear, the mind is so constituted as to see things past as well, by the use of

---

[a] *Iliad*, x. 192-193.
[b] Nestor will have been the last of a number of examples
adduced by the imaginary opponent, who uses the so-called
ἀργὸς λόγος, according to which, if everything is fated, all
exertion is unnecessary ; *cf.* Cicero, *De Fato*, 30 (*S.V.F.* ii.
956), who gives the same answer as that of Chrysippus.

ἐγκαθήμενος ἀεὶ καὶ οἰκουρῶν γραμματεὺς ἐν ἡμῖν,[1]
ὡς φησιν ὁ Πλάτων, οὗτός ἐστι καὶ προγεγονὼς
τῶν[2] ἐνταῦθα, τῆς ψυχῆς εἴτε μέρος εἴτε ὄργανον,
ᾧ[3] τῶν πραγμάτων ἀντιλαμβάνεται φερομένων[4] καὶ
φυλάττει καὶ ἵστησι καὶ κύκλον ποιεῖ, τὸ παρῳχη-
μένον ἐπιστρέφουσα καὶ συνάπτουσα τῷ παρόντι
καὶ παραρρεῖν εἰς τὸ ἄπειρον οὐκ ἐῶσα καὶ ἀνύπ-
αρκτον καὶ ἄγνωστον.

ΕΙΣ ΕΜΠΕΔΟΚΛΕΑ

Diels, Frag. d. Vorsokratiker, 31 A 33, guesses (quite
speculatively) that Plutarch's commentary was the ultimate
source of what Hippolytus says of Empedocles, Refutatio,
vii. 29. 5. Ibid. 20, αὕτη ἐστὶν ἡ κόλασις ἣν κολάζει ὁ δημιουρ-

24

Hippolytus, Refutatio, v. 20. 5.

Τετέλεσται δὲ ταῦτα (sc. Orphica quaedam) καὶ
παραδέδοται ἀνθρώποις πρὸ τῆς Κελεοῦ καὶ Τρι-
πτολέμου καὶ Δήμητρος καὶ Κόρης καὶ Διονύσου ἐν
Ἐλευσῖνι τελετῆς ἐν Φλιοῦντι[5] τῆς Ἀττικῆς· πρὸ
γὰρ τῶν Ἐλευσινίων μυστηρίων ἔστιν ἐν τῇ Φλιοῦντι[6] ⟨τῆς⟩ λεγομένης Μεγάλης ὄργια.[7] ἔστι δὲ

[1] ἡμῖν Cobet : μίνω.
[2] προγεγονὼς τῶν Wyttenbach : προγέγονας. προγεγονὸς Madvig.   [3] ᾧ Madvig : ὁ. καὶ Duebner.
[4] Gesner : φερόμενον.
[5] Φλυῇ Schneidewin ('Αχαῖας for 'Αττικῆς Meineke).
[6] Φλυέων Diels.
[7] τῆς . . . ὄργια F. G. Welcker, Göttingen edition : λεγομένη μεγαληγορία.

---

[a] Philebus, 39 A.
[b] If the emendation is right, this is an allusion to the Pla-

memory. Memory is the clerk, as Plato says,[a] who
always sits within us and never leaves his post, born
before this life,[b] either a part of the soul or the tool
by which the soul lays hold on events as they pass
by, preserves them, arrests their course, and forms a
circle by turning back the past and joining it to the
present, not allowing it to slip away to be lost in the
infinite, where it would neither exist nor be known.[c]

NOTES ON EMPEDOCLES

(Lamprias Catalogue 43)

γός, καθάπερ χαλκεύς τις μετακοσμῶν σίδηρον καὶ ἐκ πυρὸς εἰς
ὕδωρ μεταβάπτων, has *a faint resemblance to* De Sera Numinis Vindicta, *567 c, but the chance of a Plutarchean origin is minimal.*

24

These (Orphic) doctrines have been made the subject of initiation and were revealed to men at Phlius [d]
in Attica at a date earlier than the initiation at
Eleusis that belongs to Celeüs, Triptolemus, Demeter,
the Maiden, and Dionysus. For the rites of the so-
called Great Goddess at Phlius are earlier than the
Eleusinian mysteries. There is in that place a colon-

tonic doctrine of ἀνάμνησις, by which we are born with latent
memories.
  [c] In view of the Stoic elements in frags. 21, 22 it is worth
noting that the non-existence of the past was emphasized by
the Stoics (*S. V.F.* ii. 509, 518). How the non-existent could
be known would be a problem, to which an answer is here
given.
  [d] Hippolytus made a mistake ; he should have said *Phlyê*,
cf. Pausanias, i. 31. 4, Φλυεῦσι δέ εἰσι . . . βωμοί . . . Γῆς,
ἣν Μεγάλην θεὸν ὀνομάζουσι.

παστὰς ἐν αὐτῇ, ἐπὶ δὲ τῆς παστάδος ἐγγέγραπται
μέχρι σήμερον ἡ πάντων¹ τῶν εἰρημένων λόγων
ἰδέα. πολλὰ μὲν οὖν ἐστι τὰ ἐπὶ τῆς παστάδος ἐκείνης ἐγγεγραμμένα, περὶ ὧν καὶ Πλούταρχος ποιεῖται
λόγους ἐν ταῖς πρὸς Ἐμπεδοκλέα δέκα βίβλοις· ἔστι
δὲ τοῖς πλείοσι² καὶ πρεσβύτης τις ἐγγεγραμμένος
πολιὸς πτερωτὸς³ ἐντεταμένην ἔχων τὴν αἰσχύνην
γυναῖκα ἀποφεύγουσαν διώκων κυανοειδῆ.⁴ ἐπι-
γέγραπται δὲ ἐπὶ τοῦ πρεσβύτου φάος ῥυέντης,⁵
ἐπὶ δὲ τῆς γυναικὸς περεηφικόλα.⁶

ΕΙΣ ΤΑ ΗΣΙΟΔΟΥ ΕΡΓΑ

*The commentary on Hesiod's Works and Days, which
was written earlier than De Fraterno Amore (see note on
frag. 86) and perhaps earlier than the Life of Camillus (see
frag. 100), is not listed in the Lamprias Catalogue, and is
known mainly from the use made of it by Proclus, the neo-
Platonist (412–486 A.D.). It was probably in four books,
since Gellius quotes a comment on v. 765 as being from the
fourth book (frag. 102). The commentary of Proclus itself
does not survive in its original form, but was excerpted and
modified to provide material for the so-called " old scholia "
to Hesiod (ed. Pertusi, Milan, 1955). Other remnants of
Proclus are to be found in the commentaries of Tzetzes and
Moschopulus.*

It cannot be known whether Proclus himself always ac-

¹ τὰ τῶν before πάντων deleted by Miller.
² ἐν τοῖς πυλεῶσι Miller : ταῖς παστάσι Wendland : τοῖς κειόσι
Maass.
³ Miller : πετρωτὸς.
⁴ κυανοειδῆ Göttingen edition : κυνοειδῆ.
⁵ Φάνης ῥυείς ten Brink : Φάνης ἐριέντης (?) Maass.
⁶ Περσεφόνη Φλυά ten Brink : ἐριέντου κόρη (?) Maass.

nade (*or* a room) and on this colonnade is painted a
representation, preserved to our own day, of all the
doctrines [a] I have expounded. There are many
paintings on this colonnade, and Plutarch describes
them in his ten-volume work, *Notes on Empedocles*.
In the majority of them [b] is included a grey-haired
old man with wings, his pudendum erected, chasing a
woman of blue colour, who runs away. The old man
is inscribed " Light, flowing (?)," [c] and the woman
" Pereêphikola." [c]

COMMENTARY ON HESIOD'S WORKS
AND DAYS

*knowledged indebtedness to Plutarch, but it is certain that in
the form to which his work has been reduced acknowledgement
is at times omitted. The problem of deciding what parts of
the old scholia derive from Plutarch is not an easy one, and
it seems to be impossible to identify otherwise unknown
Plutarchean elements in Tzetzes or Moschopulus. But to
confine a collection of fragments to those passages where he is
mentioned by name would result in the omission of much that
is virtually certain to be his. Unfortunately either Proclus,*

[a] Those of the Gnostics who called themselves " followers
of Seth."
[b] Again Hippolytus has probably misread his source.
[c] The woman is later said to symbolize water. Ten Brink
supposed the old man to be the Orphic god Phanes, quoting
Orphic Hymn, v. 7, πάντη δινηθεὶς πτερύγων ῥιπαῖς κατὰ κόσμον,
λαμπρὸν ἄγων φάος ἁγνόν, ἀφ' οὗ σε Φάνητα κικλήσκω ἠδὲ Πρίη-
πον ἄνακτα. In *Life of Themistocles*, chap. 1, Plutarch mentions paintings at Phlyê, and the hereditary priesthood of the
Lycomidae, who are otherwise known to have had connec-
tions with Orphism, see J. Toepfner, *Attische Genealogie*,
p. 209.

who " *seems to have had a positive distaste for quoting
textually* " (*T. L.* Heath, *Euclid's* Elements, *i, p. 34*), *or his
abbreviators altered the wording of his source enough to make
rare the occasions on which Plutarch's style can be confidently
detected. The surest guide is the occurrence of matter that
is paralleled in his surviving works. There is also some nega-
tive evidence. Pertusi has shown that the oldest* MS. (*A, see
below*) *distinguishes by prefixed marks scholia drawn from
Proclus and those that come from other sources : the latter
are unlikely to contain Plutarchean material. Accordingly
I have omitted, following Pertusi, fragments 5, 6, 9, 41, and
48 of Bernardakis' edition, and similarly not accepted ascriptions of scholia to Plutarch made by R. Reitzenstein,* Nach.
Gött. Gesell. Wiss., *1906, p. 40 and Wilamowitz,* Ilias und
Homer, *p. 406. Eight other of Bernardakis' fragments have
been omitted : no. 8 had already been identified by Patzig as
drawn from Procopius,* Bellum Gothicum, *iv. 20 (the reference to Plutarch is to the myth of* De Facie) ; *16, 67, 68, 69,
74, and 75 seem to me to have been claimed for Plutarch by
Westerwick on quite inadequate grounds ; and 87, added by
Bernardakis himself, breathes the authentic spirit of Proclus.*

*In an attempt to distinguish what is of Plutarchean origin
in these scholia I have marked with an asterisk fragments or
parts of fragments whenever I feel uncertain whether they
are in any way based on him, and have placed within brackets
sentences which, although they may lead up to Plutarchean
material, contain no more than the usual scholiast's paraphrase of Hesiod. At the end of any fragment that does not
mention Plutarch I have appended the name of the scholar
who claimed it as derived from him.*

*The extracts from the scholia have been introduced, not by
the lemmata of the manuscripts, but by so much of Hesiod's
text as is necessary to make them intelligible. The tradition
of the scholia themselves is such that Pertusi's apparatus
criticus occupies little less space than his text. It would be
impossible to present here the evidence on which that text is
established, and I have confined myself to recording variants
where the reading remains uncertain or is due to conjecture.
It may briefly be said that there are two branches of the*

tradition. One is headed by A, which needs however to be supplemented by other and on the whole inferior manuscripts, PZBT. The other is represented by L and R, which, though they have suffered much modification, preserve a certain amount that is not in the first branch. QUO belong to a mixed tradition. The manuscripts denoted by these sigla are as follows :

A   *Paris. gr. 2771, x cent.*

Z   *Vat. gr. 38, A.D. 1323.*

B   *Paris. gr. 2708, xv cent.*

T   *Marc. gr. 464, A.D. 1316–1320, an arbitrarily revised version, written by Demetrius Triclinius.*

P   *Paris. suppl. gr. 679, xii cent.*

Q   *Vat. gr. 904, xiv cent., full of conjectures.*

U   *Neapol. Borb. gr. II F 9, xiv cent.*

O   *Bodl. Dorv. gr. 71, xiv/xv cent.*

L   *Laur. gr. 31, 23, xv cent.*

R   *Rom. Casan. gr. 306, A.D. 1413.*

The principal modern works that deal with Plutarch's commentary are :

H. Usener, Rh. Mus. *xxii (1867), p. 587 (Kl. Schr. i, p. 119).*

E. Scheer, De Plutarchi commentario in Hesiodi Opera et Dies, *Rendsburg, 1870.*

H. Patzig, Quaestiones Plutarcheae, *Berlin, 1876.*

O. Westerwick, De Plutarchi studiis Hesiodeis, *Munster, 1893.*

M. R. Dimitrijevič, Studia Hesiodea, *Leipzig, 1899.*

H. Schultz, Abh. Gesell. Wiss. Göttingen, *1910.*

M. Maes, Contribution à l'étude du commentaire de Plutarque aux Travaux et jours d'Hésiode, *Univ. de Liège, 1939. This I only know at second-hand from Pertusi.*

A. Pertusi, Aevum, *xxv (1951), pp. 147 ff.*

I refer by the name of the author to the following editions, the first two of which also contain many of the scholia :

D. Heinsius, Hesiodi Ascraei quae extant cum Graecis scholiis, *1603.*

T. Gaisford, Poetae Minores Graeci, *1814–1820.*

K. Sittl, Ἡσιόδου τὰ ἅπαντα, *1889*.
P. Mazon, Hésiode, Les Travaux et les jours, *1914*.

*25

Schol. Hesiod, *Works and Days*, 7.

ῥεῖα δέ τ' ἰθύνει σκολιὸν καὶ ἀγήνορα κάρφει.

Τὸν ποικίλον τὸ ἦθος διὰ πανουργίαν " σκολιὸν "
ὀνομάζει. τοῦτον οὖν ἰθύνειν λέγει τὸν Δία, πάλιν
εἰς τὸ ἁπλοῦν ἐπανάγοντα ἦθος διὰ τὸ κολάζειν αὐτὸν ἐπὶ τῇ πανουργίᾳ. τὸν αὐθάδη καὶ ὑπερόπτην
εὐτελῆ ποιεῖ καὶ ταπεινόν. ἡ γὰρ αὐθάδεια πρὸς
καταφρόνησιν ἐγείρει τῶν ἄλλων ἁπάντων, ἡ δὲ
ταπείνωσις εἰς ἔννοιαν ἄγει τοῦ μηδὲν ἡμᾶς δια-
φέρειν τῶν ὁμοίων καὶ μετρίους ποιεῖ τὸ ἦθος.

26

Ibid. 41.

οὐδ' ὅσον ἐν μαλάχῃ τε καὶ ἀσφοδέλῳ μέγ'
ὄνειαρ.

Ἴσως δὲ καὶ ἀφ' ἱστορίας τοῦτο λέγει. Ἕρμιπ-
πος γὰρ ἐν τῷ περὶ[1] τῶν ἑπτὰ σοφῶν περὶ τῆς
ἁλίμου βρώσεως[2] λέγει· [μέμνηται δὲ τῆς ἁλίμου
καὶ Ἡρόδωρος[3] ἐν τῷ πέμπτῳ[4] τοῦ καθ' Ἡρακλέα

---

[1] περὶ added by Jacoby.   [2] R alone has βρώσεως.
[3] Casaubon : Ἡρόδοτος.   [4] πέμπτῳ] ιε' Jacoby.

---

[a] *F.H.G.* iii. 37, 40. Athenaeus, 58 f, quotes him as
saying that mallow is an excellent ingredient for the so-called
ἄλιμος or anti-hunger food. Plutarch used this work of Hermippus for his *Life of Solon* (see most recently M. L. Paladini,
R.E.G. lxix (1956), pp. 377 ff.) and mentions this anti-hunger

FRAGMENTS : OTHER NAMED WORKS

U. von Wilamowitz Moellendorf, Hesiodos Erga, *1928.*
T. A. Sinclair, Hesiod, Works and Days, *1932.*

*25

With ease makes straight the crooked, withers the proud.

He calls crooked the man whose character is wily through being unscrupulous. Zeus, then, he says, " straightens " him when he restores his character to straightforwardness by punishing him when he is unscrupulous. He makes the self-willed and arrogant man of no account and brings him low ; self-will encourages contempt for all other men, but to be humbled leads to the thought that we are no better than our fellows and makes us modest in character.

Westerwick, claiming perhaps over-confidently to detect Plutarchean diction. It is not even certain that Plutarch included vv. 1-10 in his text ; at *Quaest. Conv.* 736 E, he speaks in his own person of vv. 11 ff. as τὰ πρῶτα τῶν Ἔργων. It is true that the scholia do not mention him as being among those who rejected the lines, but that does not justify Westerwick and Sinclair in their inference that he thought them authentic. On the whole subject see Mazon, pp. 37-41.

26

They do not know
The sustenance in mallow and asphodel.

This may in fact be based on an item of learning. Hermippus in his work *On the Seven Sages* speaks about the " anti-hunger " food [a] [it is mentioned also by Herodorus in the 5th book of his account of

diet of Epimenides in his *Banquet of the Seven Sages*, 157 D ff., as well as *De Facie*, 940 C ; in both places this line of Hesiod is said to have given him a hint for it.

λόγου, καὶ¹ Πλάτων ἐν τῷ τρίτῳ τῶν Νόμων.]
Ἐπιμενίδην φησὶ μικρόν τι ἐδεσμάτιον προσφερό-
μενον ὧδε ὅλην διατελεῖν² τὴν ἡμέραν ἄσιτον καὶ
ἄποτον.³ ἦν δ᾽ ἐξ ἀσφοδέλου καὶ μαλάχης, ὅπερ
αὐτὸν ἄλιμον καὶ ἄδιψον ἐποίει.

27

Ibid. 48.

ἐξαπάτησε Προμηθεὺς ἀγκυλομήτης.

Εἰ δὲ ἀγκυλομήτης ὁ Προμηθεύς (οὕτω γὰρ
γράφειν δεῖ καθ᾽ ἃ καὶ Πλούταρχος) . . .

*28

Ibid. 126.

πλουτοδόται, καὶ τοῦτο γέρας βασιλήϊον ἔσχον.

Καὶ πλουτοδότας εἶναι δεῖ τοὺς βασιλικοὺς ἄνδρας
καὶ⁴ καθαρεύειν πάσης τῆς⁵ κακουργίας καὶ τῆς τῶν
χρημάτων ἐπιθυμίας, ὧν εἰσιν ἄλλοις χορηγοὶ κατὰ
βούλησιν τῶν θεῶν.

¹ τῷ added by Bernardakis.
² ὅλην διατελεῖν R : τελεῖν or διὰ ὅλην τελεῖν.
³ ἄσιτον καὶ ἄποτον Pertusi : ἄσιτος καὶ ἄποτος R ; the other
mss. omit, perhaps rightly.
⁴ Omitted by all mss. but L.
⁵ Pertusi : πάσης τε (except πάσης L and τε πάσης T). Perhaps T should be followed, with Gaisford.

---

a *F.Gr.Hist.* i. 31, F 1.
b 677 D-E : Epimenides gave a practical demonstration of
Hesiod's theory.

Heracles [a] and by Plato in the 3rd book of the *Laws* [b]], saying that Epimenides would take a small morsel and so remain the whole day without food or drink ; it was of asphodel and mallow, and made him free of hunger and thirst.[c]

D. Heinsius (according to Bernardakis : I have not found where).

27

Prometheus, crooked of counsel, cheated him.

If Prometheus is crooked of counsel—this is the right reading, as Plutarch also holds [d]— . . .

*28

Givers of wealth ;
They had this privilege of kings as well.

Kingly men should both be givers of wealth and keep themselves uncontaminated by any wrong-doing and covetousness of property, with which they supply others according to the will of the gods.

Pertusi : since the line is quoted at *Moralia*, 417 B, with the comment ὡς βασιλικοῦ τοῦ εὖ ποιεῖν ὄντος.

[c] Diog. Laert. i. 114, also knows of Epimenides' magic food, but does not mention its ingredients. Porphyry, *Vit. Pyth.* 34, gives an elaborate recipe, said to have been used by Pythagoras, including mallow and asphodel. Pliny, *N.H.* xxii. 73, thinks that *alimus* is a specific plant, and has nothing to do with asphodel.

[d] It is the reading of our mss. of Hesiod : Proclus recorded an alternative ποικιλομήτης, " varied in counsel." The rest of the scholion has nothing to do with Plutarch, but is typical of Proclus, *cf. In Rempublicam*, ii. 75. 9 Kroll, *In Crat.* 66. 20 Pasquali.

*29

Ibid. 127-128.

δεύτερον αὖτε γένος πολὺ χειρότερον μετόπισθεν
ἀργύρεον ποίησαν 'Ολύμπια δώματ' ἔχοντες.

῝Οτι δὲ ἄργυρος ἰοῦ δεκτικός, ὡς[1] καὶ διῆσιν ἔξω
τεγγόμενος ὑπὸ τῶν ὑγρῶν τὴν θερμότητα[2] καὶ
ψυχρότητα παντὸς μᾶλλον κεράμου καὶ χαλκοῦ,
δῆλον. . . . ψύχεται γὰρ τὸ ὕδωρ ἐν αὐτῷ ῥᾳδίως καὶ
θερμαίνεται περιτιθεμένων ψυχρῶν ἢ θερμῶν, ὥστε
διὰ τῶν πόρων τούτων καὶ ἰὸν δέχεσθαι, τοῦ χρυσοῦ
πυκνοτάτου ὄντος.

30

Ibid. 143-145.

Ζεὺς δὲ πατὴρ τρίτον ἄλλο γένος μερόπων ἀνθρώπων
χάλκειον ποίησ', οὐκ ἀργυρέῳ οὐδὲν ὁμοῖον,
ἐκ μελιᾶν, δεινόν τε καὶ ὄβριμον.

*Τοῦτο τὸ γένος εἰκότως τρίτον οὔτε νοερὸν[3] ὂν
οὔτε πανοῦργον, ἀλλὰ δεινὸν ὄντως καὶ εἰς τυραν-
νικὴν δυναστείαν ἐκλακτίσαν καὶ φονικόν, τῶν σωμάτων μόνων ἐπιμελές. διὸ φησιν

" ἄπλατοι, μεγάλη δὲ βίη καὶ χεῖρες ἄαπτοι
ἐξ ὤμων ἐπέφυκον."*

δηλοῖ γὰρ ὅτι τῶν σωμάτων τὴν ῥώμην ἤσκουν οἱ
ἐν τούτῳ τῷ γένει, τῶν δ' ἄλλων ἀμελοῦντες περὶ
τὴν τῶν ὅπλων κατασκευὴν διέτριβον καὶ τῷ χαλκῷ
πρὸς τοῦτο ἐχρῶντο, ὡς τῷ σιδήρῳ πρὸς γεωργίαν,

*29

A second race thereafter, one far worse,
The dwellers in Olympus made, of silver.

It is clear that silver will admit tarnish, just as that
when it is moistened by liquids it transmits their
warmth or chill ^{a} to its exterior more than any
earthenware or bronze jar does. . . . For water in
a silver vessel is easily chilled or warmed if cold or
hot things are placed around it. Consequently it will
also admit tarnish through these pores, whereas gold
is very compact.

Sandbach, as suitable to Plutarch's interest in physics.

30

Then Zeus the father made a third new race
Of men unlike the silver ; these of bronze,
From ash-trees, dread and mighty.

*This race is with good reason put third, being of
men neither rational nor cunning, but truly terrible,
who ran riot in a tyrannical and murderous exercise of
power, caring only for their bodies : hence the poet
writes :

That could not be approached : great was their strength,
And arms invincible grew on their shoulders.*

For he makes it clear that the men of this generation
trained for physical strength, and neglecting all else
spent their energies in the manufacture of arms, and
employed bronze for this, as they employed iron for

^{a} Cf. Lucretius, i. 494.

---

[1] ὅς Z, Gaisford.   [2] F. H. S. : ὑγρότητα.
[3] νοερὸν QOL : νωθρὸν AZBT.

διά τινος βαφῆς τὸν χαλκὸν στερροποιοῦντες ὄντα
φύσει μαλακόν. ἐκλιπούσης δὲ τῆς βαφῆς ἦλθον
ἐπὶ τὴν τοῦ σιδήρου καὶ ἐν τοῖς πολέμοις χρῆσιν.

*Τοῦτο δὴ τὸ χαλκοῦν γένος " ἐκ μελίαν " εἶπε
φῦναι δωρικῶς, ἀντὶ τοῦ ἐκ τῶν μελιῶν τῶν δένδρων, οὐχὶ ἐκ τῶν Μελιῶν τῶν¹ Νυμφῶν· (καὶ γὰρ
Μελίας Νύμφας εἶναί φασιν)· ἄτοπον γὰρ τοὺς ἐκ
τοῦ θείου γένους ὄντας θηριώδεις φῦναι—ἀλλ' ὡς ἐκ
δένδρων στερεῶν καὶ δυσσήπτων γεγονότας τά τε
σώματα γενέσθαι ἰσχύοντας καὶ τὰ ἤθη ἀτεράμονας
καὶ βιαίους.*

31

Ibid. 199-200.

ἀθανάτων μετὰ φῦλον ἴτον προλιπόντ' ἀνθρώπους
Αἰδὼς καὶ Νέμεσις.

[Τουτέστι τὸ τῶν κακῶν ἔσχατον. ἀναιδείας γὰρ
κρατησάσης καὶ φθόνου τῶν ἀνθρώπων, πάντῃ τὸ
γένος ἡμῶν ἀπολιπεῖν αἰδῶ καὶ νέμεσιν. τούτων
γὰρ ἀπόπτωσίς ἐστιν ἡ ἀναίδεια καὶ ὁ φθόνος.]

'Αλλ' οὗτος μὲν εἴδωλον ὢν νεμέσεως (δοκεῖ γὰρ
καὶ² αὐτὸς ἐπὶ τοῖς παρ' ἀξίαν εὐτυχοῦσιν ἀγανα-
κτεῖν), ἡ δ' ἀναίδεια οὐχὶ εἴδωλον τῆς αἰδοῦς ἀλλὰ
τὸ ἐναντιώτατον πρὸς αὐτὴν ὑποκρινόμενον τὴν
παρρησίαν. . . .

Καλῶς οὖν καὶ Πλάτων ἐρωτηθεὶς τί ποτε προσ-
γέγονε τοῖς κατ' αὐτὸν ἀνθρώποις, ἀπεκρίνατο μὴ

¹ τῶν added by F. H. S.
² καὶ QUOL : omitted by AZBTR.

ᵃ Cf. Pyth. Orac. 395 в. This note has suffered some
mutilation, since Hesiod clearly states that the Bronze Men
had *no* iron and used bronze for agriculture (v. 151). Perhaps

farming. They hardened bronze, which is naturally soft, by some form of tempering. But when this method of tempering fell out of use they came to employ iron in war as well.[a]

*Now the poet using the Doric genitive *melian* said that this bronze race sprang from ash-trees (*meliai*), not from the Meliai, the Nymphs [b] (they say that there were Nymphs called Meliai) ; for it would be odd for men of divine race to be born brutal—but as being sprung from hard trees that are little liable to decay they had powerful bodies and stubborn violent characters.*

Westerwick.

31

Then Shame and Indignation will forsake
Mankind, and seek the nation of the gods.

[This is the extremity of evil. For when shamelessness and jealousy rule men, shame and indignation leave our race altogether, since shamelessness and jealousy are the negation of these things.]

Jealousy, however, is a counterfeit of indignation (for it too appears to show anger at undeserved goodfortune [c]), whereas shamelessness is not a counterfeit of shame, but its extreme opposite, masquerading as frankness of speech . . .[d]

So Plato,[e] too, when asked what conceivable progress his contemporaries had made, returned a good

---

it originally said something like : "Our ancestors, too, originally used bronze for arms, as they used iron for farming, etc."
  [b] *Theogony*, 187.   [c] Cf. *De Virtute Morali*, 451 E.
  [d] The sentences here omitted are, as Westerwick observed, characteristic of Proclus, not of Plutarch.
  [e] Plato the comic poet. Arist. *Rhet.* 1376 a 11, has a slightly different wording; Kock, *C.A.F.* i, p. 660.

αἰσχύνεσθαι κακοὺς ὄντας. ὅτι δὲ θεῖον πρᾶγμα
καὶ ἡ νέμεσις δηλοῖ τὸ καὶ θεοῖς αὐτὴν ὑπάρχειν·
" νεμέσησε δὲ πότνια Ἥρη," φησὶν ἡ ποίησις. φθόνος δ' ἔξωθεν θείου χοροῦ παντός.

32

Ibid. 214-215.

ὕβρις γάρ τε κακὴ δειλῷ βροτῷ· οὐδέ μιν ἐσθλὸς
ῥηϊδίως φερέμεν δύναται βαρύθει δέ θ' ὑπ' αὐτῆς.

Λέγει δὲ ἐσθλοὺς οὐ τοὺς τῇ τύχῃ καὶ τῇ δυνάμει
προέχοντας, ὥς φησι Πλούταρχος, ἀλλὰ τοὺς κατ'
ἀρετὴν προέχοντας, ἐκ τούτου μᾶλλον δεικνὺς τὴν
ὕβριν ἀφόρητον. οἱ μὲν γὰρ ἐν δυνάμει καὶ σφόδρα
δυσχεραίνουσιν ἐπὶ ταῖς ἐκ τῶν ἀσθενεστέρων εἰς
αὐτοὺς ὕβρεσιν· οἱ δὲ κατ' ἀρετὴν ζῶντες καὶ ταύτας τὰς ὕβρεις διαπτύουσιν. οὐδὲ γὰρ χείρων ἐγώ,
φησὶν ὁ Σωκράτης, ἂν ὁ δεῖνα ἐπὶ κόρρης πατάξῃ
με ἀδίκως.

*33

Ibid. 219.

ἅμα σκολιῇσι δίκῃσιν.

Τῆς δὲ δίκης δύο δηλούσης ἢ τὴν θεὸν αὐτὴν ἢ

---

^a *Iliad*, viii. 198, quoted, *Moralia*, 19 D.
^b Plato, *Phaedrus*, 247 A, also quoted, *Moralia*, 679 E.
^c *Hubris* is for Hesiod the use of force or violence in con-
tempt of right ; he meant that neither a great (or rich or
well-born) man nor a lowly (or poor) man would profit by
his own *hubris* or outrageous behaviour. The scholiast mis-
interprets the poet, making him mean that neither can
tolerate being treated with *hubris*. Such misunderstandings,

answer : " To have no shame in being wicked." And that indignation is a divine thing is shown by its being felt even by the gods. " And divine Hera was indignant," says the poem.[a] But " Jealousy has no part in all the divine choir." [b]

Patzig.

32

> Hubris [c] is bad for poor men ; even the noble
> Cannot bear it with ease but sink beneath it.

By " noble " he does not mean, as Plutarch says, those eminent in fortune and power, but those eminent in virtue,[d] thereby indicating more forcibly how unbearable outrageous behaviour is. For while men in positions of power greatly resent outrageous treatment from inferiors, those whose lives are ordered by virtue meet even this outrageous treatment with contempt. I am no worse after all, says Socrates, if someone or other slaps my face without justification.[e]

*33

> Along with crooked justice.

Justice means two things, either the goddess her-

due to neglect of the context, occur elsewhere, cf. frags. 60, 76, 105. Here the misinterpretation was made easier by the fact that Hesiod's words for great (rich, well-born) and lowly (poor) had later come to mean morally good and cowardly (or wretched).

[d] The Greek, like the version, leaves it ambiguous which view Plutarch took. Westerwick thought he believed Hesiod to have meant the eminent in virtue, but cf. frag. 41, and Sittl ad loc. ; it seems to me more likely that this is Proclus' opinion and that Plutarch correctly understood the " noble " to be the rich.   [e] Cf. Plato, Gorgias, 508 D.

τὸ ἀπ' αὐτῆς ἔργον, τότε μὲν τὴν θεὸν καλεῖ Δίκην, ἣν καὶ παρθένον ὀνομάζει, τότε δὲ τὴν κρίσιν καὶ τὴν ποινήν, ὡς ὅταν λέγῃ, "τοῖς δὲ δίκην τεκμαίρεται εὐρύοπα Ζεύς." σκολιὰς δὲ δίκας λέγει νῦν τὰς κακῶς δεδικασμένας διὰ τὸ μηδὲν ὑγιὲς φρονεῖν τοὺς δικάζοντας ἀλλ' ἐμπαθῶς δικάζειν· πᾶν γὰρ πάθος σκολιόν, ὡς ἁπλοῦν τὸ ἀπαθές.

34

Ibid. 220.

τῆς δὲ Δίκης ῥόθος ἑλκομένης.

Τὸν ῥόθον οἱ μὲν ἤκουσαν τὸν ψόφον . . . Πλούταρχος δὲ βοιωτιάζων (οὕτω γὰρ καλεῖν φασι[1] Βοιωτούς) τὰς[2] ὀρεινὰς ὁδοὺς τὰς στενὰς καὶ δυσάντεις ῥόθους ὀνομάζεσθαί φησιν. εἰ οὖν τοῦτο κρατοίη, λέγοι ἂν ὅτι, τῆς δίκης ἑλκομένης ὑπὸ τῶν ἐπὶ δώροις τὰς δίκας κρινόντων σκολιῶς, ῥόθος ἐστί, τουτέστι δυσάντης ἡ ὁδὸς καὶ τραχεῖα, δι' ἧς ἕλκεται ὑπὸ τῶν δικαστῶν.

*35

Ibid. 230.

οὐδέ ποτ' ἰθυδίκῃσι μετ' ἀνδράσι λιμὸς ὀπηδεῖ.

Οὔκουν οὐδὲ οἱ Λακεδαιμόνιοι λιμὸν εὐλαβοῦντο δι' εὐτέλειαν διαίτης, ἣν ἔχοντες τῶν ἀδικιῶν ἑκα-

---

[1] φησι R.

[2] Βοιωτοὺς τοὺς τὰς A. Βοιωτοὺς τοὺς ῥόθους—τὰς Pertusi.

[a] There is much about such distinctions in *De Aud. Poet.* 22 D—25 B.

self, or the act that proceeds from her [a] ; the poet sometimes calls the goddess Justice (he also names her the Maiden), sometimes he uses the word of the verdict and the penalty, as when he says, " Justice for them far-seeing Zeus provides." And here by " crooked justice " he means verdicts that are badly judged because the judges are not right-minded but give their decisions as their passions dictate : all passion is crooked, as dispassionateness is straight-forward.

Westerwick : comparing slight verbal similarities at *Moralia*, 25 D, 468 c.

34

A tumult (*rhothos*) there is as Justice is dragged off.

By *rhothos* some have understood the noise . . . but Plutarch, following the Boeotian dialect (they say the Boeotians use the word in this sense) says that mountain tracks, if steep and narrow, are called *rhothoi*. If this is the best interpretation, the poet would mean that when Justice is dragged away by those who decide trials crookedly for bribes the track on which the judges drag her is a *rhothos*, *i.e.*, steep and rough.

*35

Famine is never the companion
Of men among whom Justice goeth straight.

So even the Spartans did not avoid famine through simplicity of their way of life (so long as they kept to

θάρευον· ταῖς γὰρ πολυτελείαις ἡ πλεονεξία συνεισ-
ελθοῦσα λιμοῦ γίνεται πρόξενος.

36

Ibid. 240.

πολλάκι καὶ ξύμπασα πόλις κακοῦ ἀνδρὸς ἀπηύρα.[1]

Τοῦτο δοκεῖ μὲν οὐκ εἶναι κατὰ δίκην, τὸ ἑνὸς
ἕνεκα πονηροῦ πόλιν ὅλην διδόναι ποινήν.* δύναται
δὲ λέγειν ὅτι μοχθηροῦ ἑνὸς ὄντος ὥσπερ νοσή-
ματος ἡ πόλις παραπολαύουσα πολλάκις εἰς ὅλην
ἑαυτὴν ἀναμάττεται τὴν πονηρίαν ἐξομοιουμένη τῷ
ἑνί.* δύναται δὲ κἀκεῖνο σημαίνειν ὅτι ἑνὸς ὄντος
πονηροῦ δίδωσιν ἡ πᾶσα πόλις δίκην, ὡς ἐξὸν κωλύειν μὴ κωλύουσα τὴν τοῦ ἑνὸς πονηρίαν. οὕτω
καὶ τοῦ Ἀγαμέμνονος αὐθαδῶς τῷ ἱερεῖ προσενεχ-
θέντος, εἰς πάντας Ἕλληνας διέτεινεν ὁ λοιμός, ὡς
παρέντας βοηθῆσαι τῷ ἱερεῖ· καὶ τοῦ Αἴαντος ἀσε-
βήσαντος περὶ τὸ τῆς Ἀθηνᾶς ἱερόν, πάντες ἔνοχοι
τῇ δίκῃ γεγόνασιν, ὡς μὴ ἀγανακτήσαντες ἐπὶ τῷ
ἀσεβήματι. δεῖ γὰρ μὴ ἐπιτρέπειν τοῖς ὑβρισταῖς
μηδὲ συνεπινεύειν τοῖς ἀδίκοις, δυναμένους μὲν
παῦσαι περιορῶντας δὲ τοῦ παῦσαι[2] τὴν ἐξουσίαν
τῶν πονηρῶν.

37

Ibid. 244.

Δεῖ δὲ συνάπτειν τῷ

λιμὸν ὁμοῦ καὶ λοιμόν, ἀποφθινύθουσι δὲ λαοί,

---

[1] ἐπηύρεν Rzach : ἐπαυρεῖ late mss.
[2] Patzig would omit τοῦ παῦσαι.

it they were free from injustice), for greed coming in with luxurious living is the sponsor of famine.

Pertusi doubtfully.

36

Often a whole city suffers for a sinner.

This is taken to be unjust—that a whole city should be punished for one bad man. *But it may mean that if there is one bad man in it the city often becomes like that individual and is contagiously affected throughout by his wickedness, as if catching a disease.* It may also mean that if there is one bad man the whole city is punished because it does not restrain his wickedness, although it could do so. Thus when Agamemnon had dealt with the priest as he pleased, the plague spread to all the Greeks, because they had failed to support the priest, and when Ajax committed an act of impiety at Athenê's shrine, they were all liable to punishment because they had expressed no indignation at the act. We ought not to let outrage have its way, nor connive at wrong-doers, omitting to put a stop to the licence of the wicked, although it is in our power to do so.

Patzig, thinking it in Plutarch's manner to adduce the example of Agamemnon.

37

One should continue after

Famine and plague at once, the death of the people [a]

[a] Quoted again, *Moralia*, 1040 c.

τοὺς ἐν τοῖς[1] πολλοῖς φερομένους[2] ὑπερβάντα δύο
στίχους, τὸ[3]

ἢ τῶν γε στρατὸν εὐρὺν[4] ἀπώλεσεν
καὶ τὰ ἑξῆς. οὕτω Πλούταρχος.

38

Ibid. 270-272.

νῦν δὴ ἐγὼ μήτ' αὐτὸς ἐν ἀνθρώποισι δίκαιος
εἴην μήτ' ἐμὸς υἱός· ἐπεὶ κακὸν ἄνδρα δίκαιον
ἔμμεναι, εἰ μείζω γε δίκην ἀδικώτερος ἕξει.

[Τὸ μὲν λεγόμενον φανερόν· εἰ μὴ ἔστι δίκη καὶ
τιμωρία κατὰ τῶν ἀδίκων, μηδ' ἕξουσί τι πλέον οἱ
δίκαιοι τῶν ἀδίκων ἐν τῷδε τῷ παρόντι ὃ ἐφορᾷ ὁ
Ζεύς, μήτ' αὐτὸς εἴην δίκαιος μήτε παῖς ἐμός·
δίκης γὰρ οὐκ οὔσης, ὄνομα μόνον ἔσται τὸ δίκαιον.]
Εἰ δὲ δὴ τὸ[5] δίκαιον αἱρετόν, κἂν μὴ ᾖ πρόνοια,
καὶ φευκτὸν τὸ ἄδικον, δῆλον ὅτι πᾶς οὗτος ὁ λόγος περιττός. διόπερ ὁ Πλούταρχος τοὺς ἑπτὰ τούτους στίχους ἐκβάλλει ἀπὸ τοῦ

πάντα ἰδὼν Διὸς ὀφθαλμός
ἕως τοῦ

ἀλλὰ τά γ' οὔπω ἔολπα τελεῖν Δία μητιόεντα,
ὡς ἀναξίους τῆς Ἡσιόδου περὶ δικαίων καὶ ἀδίκων
κρίσεως.

---

[1] τοῖς omitted by all mss. but A.
[2] οὐ φερομένους Koechly.
[3] τὸ added by Duebner.
[4] εὐρὺν added by Rzach.
[5] δὴ τὸ Wyttenbach : διὰ τὸ A : τὸ Q : κατὰ LR.

with

> He may destroy a great army, etc.

omitting the two intermediate verses that are found in most copies.[a]

Thus Plutarch.[b]

38

> So now may neither I nor son of mine
> Do right on earth, since to do right is bad
> If the wrong-doer wins the greater rights.

[The meaning is plain : if there is no justice and punishment for the wicked, and the just are not going to have any advantage over the wicked in this world that Zeus watches over, may neither I nor son of mine be just, for if there is no Justice, to be just is no more than a word.]

But if justice ought to be chosen, even if there is no such thing as Providence, and injustice avoided, it is clear that all this argument is beside the point. Hence Plutarch expels these seven lines (267-273) from

> the all-seeing eye of Zeus

to

> Yet I do not expect
> That all-wise Zeus will bring such things to pass,

as being unworthy of Hesiod's views on justice and injustice.

---

[a]   And women bear no children, families
        Decay by Zeus's will : another time . . .

They are absent from a quotation by Aeschines, *In Ctes.* 134, but present in Pap. Rainer of 4th cent. A.D.

[b] Mazon, p. 82, suggests that Plutarch found it absurd to oppose private misfortunes to public calamities, not understanding that sterility prevents the people's recovery.

39

Ibid. 282-284.

ὃς δέ κε μαρτυρίῃσι ἑκὼν ἐπίορκον ὀμόσσας
ψεύσεται, ἐν δὲ δίκην βλάψας νήκεστον ἀασθῇ,
τοῦ δέ τ᾽ ἀμαυροτέρη γενεὴ μετόπισθε λέλειπται.

*Τὰ γὰρ τῶν πατέρων ἀδικήματα χραίνει καὶ τοὺς
ἐκγόνους αὐτῶν καὶ ἐνόχους ἀποφαίνει ταῖς τιμω-
ρίαις· καὶ γὰρ ὀνείδη καὶ ἀδοξίαι αὐτοῖς ἐκ τῶν
ἀδικιῶν συμβαίνουσι, καὶ τίσεις ἐκ τῶν ἁμαρτη-
μάτων ἀπολαμβάνοντες, ὧν ἔσχον ἀδικήσαντες οἱ
πατέρες αὐτῶν, συναπολαύουσι τῶν ὀφειλομένων
ἐκείνοις κολάσεων.*

Ἄλλως δὲ γινώσκει τὸ θεῖον ὡς τοῖς ἤθεσιν
αὐτῶν ἐμπέφυκέ τι τῆς ἀδίκου τῶν γεννησάντων
προαιρέσεως κἂν ἡμᾶς λανθάνωσι, καὶ εἰκότως ταύτην ἐν αὐτοῖς ὁρῶντες τὴν ῥίζαν ἐκκόπτουσι διὰ
τῶν τιμωριῶν καὶ τοῦ μὴ ἐνεργῆσαι κωλύουσιν ὡς
ἰατροὶ προκαθαίροντές τινας ὧν ὑφορῶνται νόσους.[1]

40

Ibid. 286.

σοὶ δ᾽ ἐγὼ ἐσθλὰ νοέων ἐρέω.

Κάλλιστα τὸ φιλόσοφον ἦθος οἷόν ἐστιν εἶπε διὰ
τούτων ὁ Πλούταρχος δηλοῦσθαι. τὸν μὲν γὰρ
Ἀρχίλοχον καὶ τὸν Ἱππώνακτα βλασφημίας συγ-
γράψαι κατὰ τῶν λυπησάντων· Τιμοκράτην δὲ καὶ
Μητρόδωρον τοὺς Ἐπικουρείους, ἀδελφοὺς ὄντας
καὶ προσκρούσαντας ἀλλήλοις, ἐκδοῦναι κατ᾽ ἀλλήλων συγγράμματα. καὶ τί δεῖ τούτους λέγειν, ὅπου

---

[1] νόσων Bernardakis.

39

> And if a man shall wittingly swear false,
> Defeating justice with a sin past cure,
> Feebler is his posterity thereafter.

For the sins of the fathers stain their offspring and make them liable to punishment ; reproach and disgrace attach to them for their wrong-doing, and being repaid for the crimes their fathers have committed, they share the punishments due to their fathers.

Alternatively divine Providence recognizes that some part of the immoral tendency of the fathers has been implanted in the characters of the sons, even if we do not see it, and so the gods, observing the presence in them of this root of evil, quite properly excise it by the punishments they inflict, and prevent it from becoming active, like doctors who take the initiative in purging some persons of the diseases they suspect them of harbouring.[a]

Westerwick.

40

> I've good advice for you.

Plutarch said that these lines excellently demonstrate what sort of thing a philosophic character is. Archilochus and Hipponax, he said, composed slanderous attacks on those who had hurt them, while the Epicureans Timocrates and Metrodorus, being brothers who had fallen foul of one another, published writings against each other.[b] Why mention

---

[a] Cf. De Sera Numinis Vindicta, 562 D.
[b] Cf. Adv. Colotem, 1126 c, Cicero, Nat. Deor. i. 93, Metrodorus, frag. 30 Koerte (Jahrb. Klass. Phil., Suppl. 17).

γε καὶ Ξενοφάνην[1] διὰ δή τινα πρὸς τοὺς κατ᾽ αὐτὸν φιλοσόφους καὶ ποιητὰς μικροψυχίαν σίλλους ἀτόπους συνθεῖναι κατὰ πάντων φιλοσόφων καὶ ποιητῶν· ἀλλὰ τὸν ὄντως μουσικὸν ʽΗσίοδον μηδὲν τοιοῦτο παθεῖν· οὐ γὰρ μουσικοῦ τὸ μελαγχολᾶν· λυπηθέντα δὲ πρὸς τὸν ἀδελφὸν ἀντὶ τοῦ βλασφημεῖν νουθετεῖν, *εἰδότα τοῦτο δὴ τὸ τοῦ Σωκράτους, ὅτι πᾶς ὁ κακὸς ἄκων ἐστὶ κακός· δεῖται οὖν νουθεσίας, καὶ ἴσως ἐπιγνώσεται ἑαυτὸν ὄντα κακόν.*

41

Ibid. 287.

τὴν μέν τοι κακότητα καὶ ἰλαδὸν ἔστιν ἑλέσθαι.

Οὐκ ἀποδεκτέον τὸ ἰλαδόν, ὡς Πλούταρχος ἐξηγήσατο, τὸ πᾶσαν ἐγκολπίσασθαι κακίαν ὁμοῦ δηλοῦν.

42

Ibid. 293, 295.

οὗτος μὲν πανάριστος ὃς αὐτῷ πάντα νοήσῃ.
ἐσθλὸς δ᾽ αὖ κἀκεῖνος ὃς εὖ εἰπόντι πίθηται.

Ζήνων μὲν ὁ Στωικὸς ἐνήλλαττε τοὺς στίχους, λέγων

οὗτος μὲν πανάριστος ὃς εὖ εἰπόντι πίθηται·
ἐσθλὸς δ᾽ αὖ κἀκεῖνος ὃς αὐτῷ[2] πάντα νοήσῃ[3].
τῇ εὐπειθείᾳ τὰ πρωτεῖα διδούς, τῇ φρονήσει δὲ τὰ

---

[1] Pertusi : Ξενοφάνης.
[2] αὐτὸς R (the correct text of Hesiod).
[3] νοήσῃ edd. : νοήσει.

these persons, when even Xenophanes through some petty feeling towards contemporary philosophers and poets composed nasty lampoons on all philosophers and poets ? But Hesiod, who was really cultured, did not react in that way, since it is not in the nature of the cultured to fall into a violent passion. Although he had been hurt by his brother he did not slander, but admonished him, *knowing the maxim of Socrates that every bad man is unwillingly bad, and consequently needs admonition and may come to realize his own badness.*

41

Your bad life can be got in companies.

" In companies " is not be understood, as Plutarch explained it, to denote embracing all vices simultaneously.[a]

42

Far best the man who sees all for himself,
Yet good the one who follows good advice.

Zeno the Stoic interchanged the lines to run

Far best the man who follows good advice,
Yet good the one who sees all for himself,[b]

giving first place to docility and second to wisdom.

[a] Proclus objects that whereas the virtues imply one another, the vices do not. For the true meaning of the line see Wilamowitz.
[b] S.V.F. i. 235, where add references to Julian, Or. viii. 245 A and Suidas, s.v. ὀρθῶς. Diog. Laert. vii. 25 explains that Zeno meant that action is superior to theoretical knowledge.

δευτερεῖα. Ἀρίστιππος δ' ἀπ' ἐναντίας ὁ Σωκρατι-
κὸς ἔλεγε τὸ συμβούλου δεῖσθαι χεῖρον εἶναι τοῦ
προσαιτεῖν. ὁ δ' Ἡσίοδος τοῦ μέτρου μάλιστα
τυγχάνει, τρεῖς[1] ἕξεις διελών, τὴν ἔμφρονα τὴν
ἀνόητον τὴν μέσην· ὧν ἡ μὲν ἀρίστη καὶ τῷ θείῳ
παραπλησία· καὶ γὰρ τὸ θεῖον αὔταρκες, ὥσπερ[2]
καὶ ὁ ἑαυτῷ πάντα νοῶν καὶ προορῶν ὅσα ἂν ᾖ καὶ
εἰς τὸν ἔπειτα χρόνον ἀμείνω. ἡ δὲ φευκτοτάτη τὸ
μήθ' ἑαυτῷ δύνασθαι τὰ ὀρθὰ λογίζεσθαι μήτ'
ἄλλοις ἕπεσθαι συμβούλοις ἐθέλειν. μέση δὲ τούτων ἡ τοῦ συνορατικοῦ μὲν τῶν ἀμεινόνων οὐκ
ἔχουσα δύναμιν,[3] ἐπακολουθητικὴ δὲ τοῦ συνορῶν-
τος. *καὶ ταῦτα μὲν οὕτως ἔχει· μάλιστα δὲ ἄξιον
ἐπαίνου τὸ εἰπεῖν τί τοῦ ἔμφρονος ἴδιον· οὐ γὰρ τὸ
τὰ παρόντα ὁρᾶν καὶ τὰ ἐγγύς, ἀλλὰ καὶ τὸ τὰ
ἐσόμενα προορᾶν· τοῦτο γὰρ δηλοῖ τὸ φράσασθαι
ἅπερ ἂν εἴη ἐπὶ τὰ[4] ἀμείνω.*

*43

Ibid. 313.

πλούτῳ δ' ἀρετὴ καὶ κῦδος ὀπηδεῖ.

Μηδεὶς λοιδορείτω τὸν στίχον εἰς τὸν πολυάρατον
πλοῦτον ὁρῶν τὸν[5] πόρρω τῆς ἀρετῆς ἐσκηνημένον,
ἀλλὰ πλοῦτον οἰέσθω νῦν λέγεσθαι τὴν ἀπὸ τῶν
ἔργων πορισθεῖσαν ἀφθονίαν τοῖς ἐργαζομένοις δι-
καίαν οὖσαν καὶ ἀπὸ τῶν οἰκείων πόνων ἠθροι-
σμένην. εἴρηται γὰρ ἐν τοῖς ἔμπροσθεν ἐκ τῶν

---

[1] εἰς τρεῖς LR.   [2] ὥσπερ F. H. S. : ὥστε. ὥς τε Pertusi.
[3] Duebner : οὖσα δύναμις.   [4] Pertusi : τοῦ.
[5] τὸν added by Schultz.

Aristippus the Socratic went to the opposite extreme by saying that to need an adviser was worse than begging.[a] Hesiod strikes a happy mean by distinguishing three conditions, that of wisdom, that of folly, and their intermediate. The first of these is the best and similar to the condition of the divine—for the divine is self-sufficient, just as is the man who sees and foresees everything that will be advantageous for himself in the future as well as the present ; the condition most to be avoided is inability to calculate the right course for oneself along with unwillingness to follow the advice of others ; the intermediate condition is one that lacks the ability of a man who can discover the right course, but is capable of following one who does discover it. *So much for that ; but Hesiod is particularly deserving of praise for giving the characteristic feature of wisdom—not to see just what is present and at hand, but to foresee the future as well ; that is what is meant by " discerning " what would be for the better.* [b]

Wyttenbach.

*43

And wealth has fame and virtue in its train.

Let no one speak ill of this line through envisaging that cursed wealth that camps far from virtue, but let him think that " wealth " here means the plenty that workers get by their work, a just plenty garnered from their own toil. It has been said earlier

---

[a] Frag. i. 55 Giannantoni, frag. 17 Mannebach, cf. frag. 16 = Diog. Laert. ii. 70, Mullach, ii, p. 406.

[b] This refers to v. 294, φρασσάμενος τά κ' ἔπειτα καὶ ἐς τέλος ᾖσιν ἀμείνω, which seems to have been unknown to Zeno, as to Aristotle and others in antiquity.

ἔργων τοὺς ἀνθρώπους γίνεσθαι πολυμήλους καὶ
ἀφθόνους καὶ ἀφνειούς. τῷ δὲ τοιούτῳ πλούτῳ
ἕπεσθαι πάντως τὴν ἀρετὴν καὶ τὴν δόξαν· ἕπεσθαι
δ᾿ οὐχ ὡς παρακολουθήματα ὄντα ταῦτα τῆς εὐ-
πορίας ἀλλ᾿ ὡς συνυπάρχοντα τῷ τοιούτῳ πλούτῳ·
καὶ ὡς παντός, ὃς ἂν οὕτω πλουτῇ, καὶ δόξαν
ἀγαθὴν κεκτημένου καὶ δηλοῦντος ὅτι ἀρετὴν ἔχει,
δι᾿ ἣν προσκαρτερεῖ τοῖς οἰκείοις ἔργοις.

44

Ibid. 314.

δαίμονι δ᾿ οἷος ἔησθα, τὸ ἐργάζεσθαι ἄμεινον.

Δαίμων οὐ μόνον ὁ ἀπονέμων ἡμῖν τὸν βίον καὶ
διοικῶν τὰ ἡμέτερα κρείττων[1] ἡμῶν καλεῖται, ἀλλὰ
καὶ αὐτὸς ὁ ἀπ᾿ ἐκείνου βίος ἑκάστοις[2] ἀπονεμό-
μενος, εἰς ὃν βλέποντες τοὺς μὲν εὐδαιμονεῖν φαμεν
τοὺς δὲ κακοδαιμονεῖν· ὡς καὶ τύχη λέγεται ἥ τε
ἐπιτροπεύουσα τοὺς βίους ἡμῶν καὶ τὸ ἀποδιδόμενον
ἑκάστοις[3] παρ᾿ αὐτῆς· ὅθεν καὶ εὐτυχεῖν τινας καὶ
δυστυχεῖν λέγομεν. *τοῦτο οὖν φησιν ὁ Ἡσίοδος
προτρέπων εἰς τὸ μὴ ζῆν ἀργόν, ὅτι ὁποῖος ἂν
ἑκάστῳ τυγχάνῃ βίος ἀποδεδομένος, τούτῳ ἄμεινον
ἐργάζεσθαι, εἴτε ἀμείνων εἴτε χείρων· καὶ μὴ ποιεῖσθαι πρόφασιν ἀργίας ἡλικίαν ἢ τύχην ἢ ἄλλο τι
τοιοῦτον, ἀλλὰ πάντως ἔργον τι ζητεῖν ἢ γεωργικὸν
ἢ τεκτονικὸν ἢ ἐμπορικὸν ἢ ἄλλ᾿ ὁτιοῦν.*

[1] ὁ κρείττων D. Heinsius : κρεῖττον Bernardakis.
[2] ἑκάστῳ TLR.   [3] ἑκάστῳ TL.

that it is from their labours that men become rich in flocks and have plenty and wealth. He means that virtue and good-repute necessarily follow wealth of that kind, and they they follow not as subsequent to, but as co-existent with, such wealth, for the reason that anyone who is wealthy in this way also has a good repute and shows that he possesses virtue, which is the cause of his perseverance in his own labours.

Scheer, but although the method of interpretation is Plutarchean, it is applied at *Moralia*, 24 E in a different way, by giving ἀρετή the sense not of " virtue " but of " renown " or " power."

44

Whatever your fortune be, to work is best.

" Fortune (*daimon*) " is the name given not only to the power which allots our way of life and controls our affairs as our superior, but also to the way of life itself that is allotted to each of us by that power, and in respect of which we say that some men are fortunate and others unfortunate. Similarly " luck " means both the luck that controls our lives and what each of us gets from it ; hence we say that certain people are lucky or unlucky. *Hesiod's intention is to exhort us not to live in idleness, since work is best for whatever sort of way of life, better or worse, may happen to be given to each of us, and not to find an excuse for laziness in our years or our luck or anything like that, but to look without fail for *some* work—in farming, or building, or trading, or anything.*

Westerwick, on the ground that θείης τύχης ἐπιτροπευούσης occurs at *Moralia*, 322 A.

45

Ibid. 317.

αἰδὼς δ' οὐκ ἀγαθὴ κεχρημένον ἄνδρα κομίζει.

Καὶ τοῦτον καὶ τὸν ἐξῆς στίχον παρεμβεβλῆσθαι, ληφθέντας ἀπὸ τοῦ Ὁμήρου, καὶ Πλούταρχος εἶπε.

46

Ibid. 327-334.

ἶσον δ' ὅς θ' ἱκέτην ὅς τε ξεῖνον κακὸν ἔρξῃ
ὅς τε κασιγνήτοιο ἑοῦ ἀνὰ δέμνια βαίνῃ
κρυπταδίης εὐνῆς ἀλόχου, παρακαίρια ῥέζων,
ὅς τέ τευ ἀφραδίης ἀλιταίνεται ὀρφανὰ τέκνα
ὅς τε γονῆα γέροντα κακῷ ἐπὶ γήραος οὐδῷ
νεικείῃ χαλεποῖσι καθαπτόμενος ἐπέεσσιν,
τῷ δ' ἦ τοι Ζεὺς αὐτὸς ἀγαίεται, ἐς δὲ τελευτὴν
ἔργων ἀντ' ἀδίκων χαλεπὴν ἐπέθηκεν ἀμοιβήν.

Διαφερόντως δὲ τοῦ Διὸς ἐμνημόνευσεν, ἐπειδὴ πάσας εἰς τὸν θεὸν τοῦτον ἀνῆγον τὰς τοιαύτας προσηγορίας, Ἱκέσιον καλοῦντες ὡς ἔφορον τῶν ἱκετῶν καὶ Ξένιον ὡς τῶν ξένων προστάτην καὶ[1] Ὁμόγνιον ὡς τῶν συγγενῶν μάλιστα φύλακα καὶ τῶν πρὸς τοὺς ὁμογνίους καθηκόντων. οὕτω γὰρ καὶ τῶν ἐν ὀρφανίᾳ ζώντων αὐτὸν ἔλεγον κηδεμόνα, πατέρα νομίζοντες πάντων καὶ ὧν οὔκ εἰσιν ἄνθρωποι πατέρες, καὶ βοηθὸν τῶν ἀδικουμένων πατέρων ὑπὸ τῶν παίδων. ἀγάλματα γάρ εἰσιν οἱ πατέρες τοῦ πάντων πατρός, τοῦ Διός· οἱ δ' εἰς τὰ ἀγάλ-

---

[1] καὶ added by Bernardakis.

45

A sense of shame ill suits a needy man.

Plutarch, too, said that this and the following line were interpolated, being taken from Homer.[a]

46

To harm the stranger or the suppliant,
To climb into a brother's bed and lie
Stealthily with his wife, working him wrong,
Senselessly to offend against the orphan,
To taunt with bitter speech an aged parent
On eld's grim threshold, all these things alike
Arouse the wrath of Zeus, who in the end
Imposes a hard repayment for wrong deeds.

He made especial mention of Zeus because he was the god to whom men applied all titles such as the following, calling him Hikesios as guardian of suppliants (*hiketōn*) and Xenios, as protector of strangers (*xenōn*) and Homognios as keeping particular watch and ward over relatives and over duties towards those of the same parentage (*homogniōn*). In the same way they also used to say that he was guardian of those who lived an orphaned life, thinking him to be the father of all and in particular of those who have no human fathers, and that he came to the aid of fathers who were injured by their children. For human fathers are the images of the universal father, Zeus [b];

[a] *Odyssey*, xvii. 347 (but κεχρημένῳ ἀνδρὶ παρεῖναι) and *Iliad*, xxiv. 45 ; the latter is quoted by Plutarch at *Moralia*, 529 D as Homer's. Others held that the line was interpolated into the *Iliad* from Hesiod, see Schol. A *ad loc.*
[b] Plato, *Laws* 931 A, cited also with the same inaccuracy (ἄγαλμα for ἵδρυμα), frag. 86.

ματα τῶν θεῶν δυσσεβεῖς, εἰς αὐτοὺς ἀναφέρουσι
τοὺς θεούς, ὧν τὰ ἀγάλματα, τὴν δυσσέβειαν· ὥστε
εἰκότως ἔφη τὸν Δία καὶ νεμεσᾶν τούτοις καὶ πᾶσιν
ὁμοῦ τῶν ἀδίκων ἔργων, ἅπερ διηριθμήσατο, χαλεπὴν ἀποδιδόναι ἔκτισιν. αὕτη γὰρ ἡ ἀμοιβὴ τῶν
ἀδικημάτων τιμωρία τις οὖσα τῆς ἀδικίας ἀκόλ-
ουθος.

47

Ibid. 336.

κὰδ δύναμιν δ' ἔρδειν ἱέρ' ἀθανάτοισι θεοῖσιν.

*Τὸ μὲν θύειν, ὅπερ εἰώθασιν οἱ νεώτεροι λέγειν,
ἔρδειν ὠνόμαζον οἱ παλαιοὶ καὶ ῥέζειν. τὸ δ'
ἀπάρχεσθαι τῶν παρόντων διὰ τοῦ θύειν ἐδήλουν
καὶ θυηλὰς τὰς ἀπαρχὰς ἐκάλουν· " ὁ δ' ἐν πυρὶ
βάλλε θυηλάς," φησὶν Ὅμηρος . . .*

Τὸ μὲν οὖν κατὰ δύναμιν ἔρδειν ἀφαιρεῖται πᾶσαν
τὴν πολυτέλειαν ἐπὶ τῇ προφάσει τῆς εὐσεβείας ἡδυ-
πάθειαν εἰσάγουσαν, καλῶς οὖν τοῦ Λάκωνος εἰπόντος, ὃς ἐρωτηθεὶς διὰ τί εὐτελῆ θύουσιν ἔφη ὅτι ἵνα
πολλάκις θύωσιν. οὕτω γὰρ καὶ Νουμᾶς Ῥωμαίοις,
ὡς Λυκοῦργος Λακεδαιμονίοις, προσέταξεν ἀπὸ τῶν
εὐτελεστάτων θύειν. τὸ γοῦν μὴ ὑπερβάλλειν τὴν
περιουσίαν ἐν τῇ θεραπείᾳ τῶν θεῶν πρεπωδέστατόν
ἐστι παράγγελμα τοῖς εἰς αὐτὸ μόνον βλέπουσι τὸ
ὅσιον· τὴν δ' ἁγνείαν καὶ καθαρότητα μάλιστα προ-
ηγουμένως δεῖ σπουδάζεσθαι τοῖς ἱερουργεῖν μέλ-

---

[a] Plato, *Laws*, 728 c, quoted also in connexion with the
Works and Days at *Mor.* 553 f.

[b] *Cf. Quaest. Conv.* 729 f, but this is a grammarian's

and those who do not respect the images of the gods show their disrespect for the very gods whose images they are. So that he was right to say that Zeus is indignant with them and imposes on all alike for the unjust deeds he enumerated a retribution that is a hard one. For this is the repayment of wrong-doing, being a " punishment that follows the heels of injustice." [a]

Westerwick.

47

Do offering to the gods to suit your means.

*What more recent generations are accustomed to call *thyein* (to sacrifice an animal), the men of old used to name *erdein* (to do) or *rhezein* (to perform) [b] ; by the word *thyein* they indicated the offering of a portion from the food before one, and they called such offerings *thyelai*. " He cast *thyelai* on the fire," says Homer [c] . . . *

" To sacrifice according to one's means " excludes all extravagance that might introduce high living under the pretence of piety. The Spartan who was asked why they made simple sacrifices returned a good reply by answering " so that they may sacrifice frequently." [d] Similarly Numa enjoined the Romans, and Lycurgus the Spartans, to make sacrifices of the simplest offerings.[e] Not to exceed one's means in the cult of the gods is a most suitable maxim for those whose sole concern is piety. And those who intend to perform holy rites should take particular care of purity

commonplace, *cf.* Schol. ABT on *Iliad*, ix. 219, *Etym. Magn.* 701. 36, *Etym. Gud.* 491. 38.
  [c] *Iliad*, ix. 220.
  [d] *Cf. Apophthegmata Laconica*, 228 c ; *Life of Lycurgus*, chap. 19.
  [e] *Life of Numa*, chap. 8.

λουσι, τὴν μὲν ἐν αὐτῇ τῇ ζωῇ—τοιαύτη δ' ἐστὶν
ὅση ἂν ἐξάντης ᾖ πάσης ἀσελγείας πάσης ἀδικίας
πάσης ἐμπαθείας· ταύτην γὰρ ἂν εἴποιμεν κυρίως
ἁγνεύειν, καὶ μετὰ ταύτην τὴν ἀποχὴν τῶν βρωτῶν
καὶ τῶν ποτῶν κατὰ τὰ πάτρια ἤθη· καὶ γὰρ ἄλλα
ἄλλοις ἔστιν, ὧν ὁ μετασχὼν εἴργεται τῶν νομίμων
θυσιῶν—τὴν δὲ ἐν τοῖς ὀργάνοις πᾶσι τοῖς ἱεροῖς,
τοῖς[1] τόποις ἐν οἷς δεῖ θύειν, τοῖς περὶ τὸ σῶμα
ἡμῶν κόσμοις. γελοῖον γὰρ τοῖς καθαρωτάτοις
προσιόντας οἷς θύουσιν ἀκαθάρτοις χρῆσθαί τισιν,
ἢ ἐν τοῖς μεμολυσμένοις οἴκοις τοῦτο πράττοντας
ἢ μοῖραν τῷ ἱερῷ προσάγοντας ἔκ τινος μεμια-
σμένης ἐνεργείας ἢ ἐσθῆτα φέροντας ἀκάθαρτον,
ὅπου γε καὶ τῷ πάντα[2] καθαίροντι πυρὶ παρήγ-
γελται χρῆσθαι μὴ ἐξ ἀκαθάρτου οἰκίας ληφθέντι.
τὸ δ'[3] αὖ ἱλάσκεσθαι τοὺς θεοὺς ταῖς ἀπαραλείπτοις
σπονδαῖς καὶ τοῖς μετὰ τούτων θυέσσιν, ἀρχομένης
ἡμέρας ἢ νυκτός, οἷον ψαιστοῖς ἢ ἄλλοις τισὶ τοιούτοις, ἐνδείκνυται· καὶ ὅτι χρὴ ταῖς τοιαύταις ἀπαρ-
χαῖς ταῖς εὐπορίστοις ἀπάρχεσθαι τῶν προσόδων[4]
αὐτοῖς, διὰ τῆς συνεχείας τηροῦντας αὐτῶν τὸ πρὸς
ἡμᾶς εὐμενές· ἡ γὰρ ἱλέωσις οὐκ ἐκείνοις προστίθη-
σιν ὃ μὴ εἶχον, ἀλλ' ἡμᾶς ἐπιτηδειοτέρους ποιήσει
πρὸς τὸ μενόντων αὐτῶν ἀεὶ τοιούτων οἷοί πέρ εἰσι
μετέχειν ἀκωλύτως· καὶ τοῦτο δηλοῖ τὸ εὐμενές, τὸ
μένειν ἡμῖν τὸ εὖ ἀεὶ παρὰ τῶν θεῶν, καὶ ὡς ἐκεῖνοι
διαμένουσιν ἀεὶ ὅμοιοι ὄντες.

---

[1] τοῖς added by F. H. S. καὶ added by Gaisford after πᾶσι
and after θύειν.
[2] Gaisford : τῷ παντὶ all mss. save T (τὰ πάντα).
[3] δ' added by Bernardakis.
[4] Gaisford : περιόδων.

and cleanness, first in their own life—such a life is one free from all indecency, all wrong-doing, all yielding to passion, for this is what is primarily to be meant by " being pure " ; secondarily we mean abstention from certain foods and drinks according to the customs of the country ; among different peoples there are different things that it involves exclusion from the customary sacrifices to partake of—and then we must look to the purity of all the sacred instruments, of the places where we have to sacrifice, of whatever we wear on our persons. It is ridiculous when approaching the purest beings to use any impure means of sacrifice, either by doing so in polluted rooms or by bringing to a shrine a share in the profits of some tainted activity, or by wearing a dirty garment. Why, we are enjoined to use fire taken from a house that is not unclean, although fire purifies everything. Again, the poet indicates that one should never omit to placate the gods with libations, at daybreak and nightfall, and with the associated offerings, such as cakes or such-like ; and that one ought to begin one's approaches to them with such easily-provided first offerings, retaining their goodwill by the regularity of our observances. Propitiation of the gods does not give them anything they had not got, but will make us fitter for unhindered communion with them, while they remain always exactly what they are. And this is the meaning of the word " good-will " (*eumenes*), that good (*eu*) at the hands of the gods always remains (*menei*) with us, and that they remain (*menousi*) always the same.[a]

Wyttenbach.

[a] The word *eumenes* is often used of the gods, derived from *menos*, " disposition," not *menein*, " remain.' Ancient

PLUTARCH'S MORALIA

48

Ibid. 342-343.

τὸν φιλέοντ᾽ ἐπὶ δαῖτα καλεῖν, τὸν δ᾽ ἐχθρὸν ἐᾶ-
σαι·
τὸν δὲ μάλιστα καλεῖν ὅς τις σέθεν ἐγγύθι ναίει.

Ταῦτα καὶ τὰ ἑπόμενα τούτοις περὶ τῶν πρὸς
τοὺς φίλους καὶ γείτονας¹ καθηκόντων ἔχει τὴν
παραίνεσιν, οὐκ ὄντα εὐηθικὰ² ὥς τισιν ἔδοξεν, ἀλλ᾽
εἰς εὐγενὲς ἦθος καὶ δεξιὸν προσάγοντα τὸν πειθό-
μενον. οὐ γὰρ δεῖ τὰ αὐτὰ φίλοις καὶ ἐχθροῖς ἀποδιδόναι οὐδ᾽ ὁμοίως ἑκατέρους ὁμοτραπέζους ποιεῖσθαι καὶ ὁμοσπόνδους, ἡγουμένους καὶ τράπεζαν
βωμὸν εἶναι τῆς Ἑστίας καὶ θεῶν³ πάντων τῶν τὴν
τροφὴν δωρησαμένων. θύειν μὲν οὖν καὶ ὑμνεῖν⁴
νόμος πρὸ τοῦ τῆς τροφῆς ἅψασθαι· δεῖ οὖν μὴ τοὺς
ἐχθροὺς ἄγειν ἐπὶ δαῖτα φιλίαν δὴ ὑποκρινομένους,
ἀλλὰ τοὺς ὄντως φίλους, οἷς καὶ κοινωνεῖν ὅσιον ὡς
τῆς ἄλλης φιλίας οὕτω καὶ ἁλῶν καὶ σπονδῶν καὶ
ἑστίας καὶ φιλοφροσύνης. καὶ γὰρ εἰ ὡς ἔτυχε καὶ
τοὺς ἐχθροὺς ἑστιῶμεν, τί ποιήσομεν ἐκείνων ἡμᾶς
ἐν μέρει καλούντων ἐπὶ τὰ ὅμοια; μὴ ὑπακούοντες
γὰρ ἀδικήσομεν τοὺς ὑπακούσαντας, ὑπακούοντες
δὲ προησόμεθα ἑαυτοὺς ἀνθρώποις ἀπεχθῶς δια-
κειμένοις.

¹ Westerwick : γονέας.
² F. H. S., *cf.* ἀβέλτερον, *Moralia*, 530 D : ἠθικά.
³ θεῶν transferred here by F. H. S. from after ἑστίας six
lines below.
⁴ ὑμνεῖν QLR : ὑμῖν A : ἡμῖν ZB.

etymology is concerned not with the history of words, but
with finding hidden " truths " in them.

138

FRAGMENTS : OTHER NAMED WORKS

48

> Invite your friend to dinner, leave out your foe ;
> Above all ask the man who lives near by.

This and the succeeding lines give advice on duties to friends and neighbours, and are not silly, as some have thought,[a] but tend to bring the man who follows them to gentlemanly and courteous conduct. It would be wrong to treat friends and enemies in the same way, or to invite both on an equal footing to share our board and our libations, since we believe that the table too is an altar of Hestia and of all the gods by whose gift we have our food. It is indeed the custom to sacrifice and sing a hymn before touching food. One should not, therefore, bring one's enemies to a feast under a mask of friendship, but one's real friends, who may lawfully share one's salt, one's libations, one's hearth, and one's hospitality, just as they share all else that friendship offers.[b] And indeed, if we indiscriminately entertain our enemies, as well as our friends, what shall we do when they in their turn invite us to similar occasions ? If we decline, we shall be unfair to them, since they did not decline our invitation ; if we accept, we shall abandon ourselves to the mercy of persons who are ill-disposed towards us.

Westerwick, who would extend the extract further.

[a] Cf. De Vitioso Pudore, 530 D.
[b] Cf. Quaest. Conv. 707 c.

49

Ibid. 346, 348.

πῆμα κακὸς γείτων, ὅσσον τ' ἀγαθὸς μέγ' ὄν-
εἰαρ . . .
οὐδ' ἂν βοῦς ἀπόλοιτ' εἰ μὴ γείτων κακὸς εἴη.

Ταῦτα καὶ διὰ τῆς ἱστορίας ὁ Πλούταρχος ἐπι-
στώσατο· καὶ γὰρ Αἰτωλοὺς καὶ 'Ακαρνᾶνας, "Ελ-
ληνας ὄντας καὶ γείτονας, ἐκτρῖψαι διὰ πλεονεξίαν
ἀλλήλους, καὶ Χαλκηδονίους καὶ Βυζαντίους διὰ
τὴν ἔμφυτον δυσμένειαν περὶ σκαλμοῦ[1] διενεχθέντας
ἐν τῷ Βοσπόρῳ ναυμαχῆσαι[2]· καὶ ἐπὶ τῶν ἰδιωτικῶν
γειτνιάσεων πολλὰ μὲν ἀγαθὰ συμβαίνειν διὰ ταύτας, ὡς ἐπὶ Φλάκκου[3] καὶ Κάτωνος, πολλὰ δὲ τὰ
ἐναντία· τὰς γὰρ γειτνιάσεις ἀφορμὰς προξενεῖν
ἐνίοτε πολλῶν ἐπηρειῶν.

Αὐτὸς μὲν οὖν τὸν βοῦν εἰς παράδειγμα παρέλαβε·
δεῖ δ' ἐκτείνειν ἐπὶ τὰ ὅμοια τὸν λόγον, ὡς οὐκ ἂν
οὐδὲν[4] ἀπόλοιτο εἰ μὴ[5] διὰ τὸν γείτονα. πρὸς ἃ
καὶ οἱ παλαιοὶ νόμοι βλέποντες ἐδικαίωσαν τῶν
ἀπολλυμένων τοὺς γείτονας τὴν τιμὴν συνεισάγειν.[6]

50

(*a*) Tzetzes on 346.
(*b*) Scholia on 347.

(*a*) Δείκνυσι τοῦτο Πλούταρχος.   Θεμιστοκλέα

---

[1] Hemsterhuys added πλοιαρίου τινὸς after Tzetzes.
[2] Duebner : ναυμαχήσαντας.
[3] Gaisford : φυλάκου.
[4] ὡς οὐκ ἂν οὐδὲν] ὁσαοῦν ἂν Duebner.
[5] εἰ μὴ added by F. H. S.
[6] τὴν τιμὴν συνεισάγειν QR : συναλλαγμάτων AZB.

49

Bad neighbours are a curse, and good as great a boon ...
You'd lose no ox, were your neighbour not a knave.

Plutarch confirmed this by historical examples. The
Aetolians and the Acarnanians, neighbouring Greek
peoples, ruined one another by their aggressiveness,[a]
and the inhabitants of Chalcedon and Byzantium
were led by their innate enmity to fight a battle in
the Bosporus over a quarrel about a thole.[b] And in the
case of private neighbours many advantages may arise,
as with Flaccus and Cato,[c] and many disadvantages
too : proximity sometimes provides the occasions for
many affronts.

Hesiod took the ox as an example ; but we should
extend what he says to cover anything similar, as
nothing would be lost except through a neighbour's
action.[d] With such things in view old laws condemned the neighbours to contribute among them
the value of lost property.[e]

50

(a) Plutarch demonstrates this. He records that

[a] B.C. 330–270 and 230–205, Pauly-Wissowa, *R.E.* i. 1154.
[b] I cannot identify this battle. According to Tzetzes, who
may have drawn on a fuller form of Proclus' note, the thole
belonged to a small boat.
[c] Cato was launched in politics by his neighbour, L.
Valerius Flaccus, *Life of Cato*, chap. 3, 337 D.
[d] *Cf. De Audiendis Poetis*, 34 B.
[e] Said by Heraclides (Aristotle, frag. 611. 38) to have
been a custom among the Cumaeans ; Hesiod's line is quoted
by him.

γάρ φησιν ἢ Κάτωνα πιπράσκοντα τὸν ἀγρὸν λέγειν
ὅτι ἀγαθὸν ἔχει γείτονα.

(b) Λέγεται ὅτι Θεμιστοκλῆς χωρίον πιπράσκων
ἐκέλευσε κηρύττεσθαι ὅτι ἀγαθὸν ἔχει γείτονα.

51

(a) Scholia on 353-354.
(b) Tzetzes on 353-354.

τὸν φιλέοντα φιλεῖν καὶ τῷ προσιόντι προσεῖναι,
καὶ δόμεν, ὅς κεν δῷ, καὶ μὴ δόμεν, ὅς κεν μὴ
δῷ.

(a) Τούτους ὁ Πλούταρχος ἐκβάλλει τοὺς στίχους. ὁ γὰρ μέλλων λέγειν ὅτι τοῖς ἀγαθοῖς τὸ
διδόναι προσήκει καὶ ὡς χαίρουσι διδόντες, ἄτοπος
ἂν εἴη λέγων καὶ διδόναι τῷ διδόντι καὶ μὴ διδόναι
τῷ μὴ διδόντι· οὕτω γὰρ ἂν τὰς δόσεις ἀναγκαίας
ἐποίει, τὰς δὲ προκαθηγουμένας τῶν εὐεργεσιῶν
ἐξέκοψεν.

(b) Ὁ μὲν Πλούταρχος τούτους ὀβελίζει τοὺς
στίχους, λέγων οὐδέποτε ἂν γενέσθαι φίλον, εἰ τῶν
φιλιωθησομένων ἑκάτερος ἀναμένει παρὰ τοῦ ἑτέρου
προφιλιωθῆναι.[1]

52

Scholia on 355.

δώτῃ μέν τις ἔδωκεν, ἀδώτῃ δ᾽ οὔ τις ἔδωκεν.

Τὸν δώτην καὶ ἀδώτην οὐ λέγει τὸν δεδωκότα
πρότερον ἢ μὴ δεδωκότα—καὶ γὰρ ἂν καὶ τοῦτο
ὑπεναντίως ἔλεγε τοῖς περὶ τῶν ἀγαθῶν δόγμασιν—

Themistocles or Cato, when selling his farm, said
that it had a good neighbour.

(b) It is said that Themistocles, when selling a
piece of land, caused it to be advertised as having a
good neighbour.[a]

51

> Love him who loves, and him who helps you, help ;
> To him who gives, not him who gives not, give.

(a) Plutarch excises these lines, on the ground that
it would be absurd if a man, who is going to say that
it is fitting for the good to give and that they enjoy
giving, should say that they give to him who gives
and give not to him who gives not. He would thereby
be making their gifts compulsory, and would have
eliminated initiative in conferring benefits.

(b) Plutarch obelizes these lines, saying that no-one
would ever become a friend, if each of two persons
who might act in a friendly way waits for the other
to make the first move.

52

> A giver gifts, no gifts the giftless wins.

By " giver " and " giftless " he does not mean the
man who has or has not previously made a gift—that,
too, would of course have been inconsistent with his

---

[a] *Life of Themistocles*, chap. 18, *Reg. et Imp. Apophthegm.*
185 D. A. Pertusi, *Aevum*, xxv (1951), p. 152, argues that
Tzetzes wrongly ascribed this anecdote to Plutarch.

---

[1] Bernardakis : προσφιλιωθῆναι.

ἀλλὰ τὸν δωρητικὸν καὶ μὴ δωρητικὸν χαρίτων
ἐμμελῶν καὶ χαριέντων. ὁ Πλούταρχος εἰκάζει
τοὺς τοιούτους, ὅσοι προαίρεσιν δωρητικὴν ἔχουσι,
τοῖς σφαιρίζουσιν, οἳ λαβόντες τὴν ὑπ' ἀλλήλων[1]
ῥιφεῖσαν σφαῖραν οὔτε κατέχουσιν οὔτε ἀντιπέμ-
πουσι τοῖς μὴ εἰδόσι σφαιρίζειν, ἀλλὰ τοῖς ἀντιπέμψαι δυναμένοις.

53

Ibid. 359-362.

ὃς δέ κεν αὐτὸς ἕληται ἀναιδείηφι πιθήσας,
καί τε σμικρὸν ἐόν, τό γ' ἐπάχνωσεν φίλον ἦτορ,
εἰ γάρ κεν καὶ σμικρὸν ἐπὶ σμικρῷ καταθεῖο
καὶ θάμα τοῦτ' ἔρδοις, τάχα κεν μέγα καὶ τὸ
    γένοιτο.

Δοκεῖ μὲν ἀπηρτῆσθαι τοῦτο τοῦ προρρηθέντος·
ἔχει δὲ καὶ συνέχειαν. ἐπειδὴ γὰρ εἶπεν ὅτι, κἂν
ᾖ σμικρὸν τὸ ἀφαιρεθέν, παχνοῖ τὸν ἀφαιρεθέντα
διὰ τὴν ἀκούσιον ἀφαίρεσιν, ἐπήγαγεν ὅτι τὸ σμικρὸν ἐπισωρευόμενον μὲν μέγα τι γίνεται, ἀφαιρούμενον δ' εἰς μηδὲν καταλήγει· ὥστε εἰκότως λυπεῖ
καὶ τὸ σμικρὸν ἀφαιρούμενον. καὶ εἰ τοῦτο ἀληθές,
ὀρθῶς Ἀριστοτέλης ἔλεγεν ὅτι χείριστον τῶν ἐν
τῷ βίῳ τὸ μὴ παρὰ τοῦτο λεγόμενον· εἰ γὰρ κατα-
φρονοῖτο ὡς μικρὸν ἕκαστον καὶ ἐπιλέγοιμεν, " μὴ
παρὰ τοῦτο," κακῶς πράξομεν.[2] ἐν μὲν οὖν οἰκο-

---

[1] ἀλλήλων AZBR : ἀλλοτρίων Q. ἄλλων Bernardakis.
[2] Duebner : πράξοιμεν.

---

[a] A similar use of this image, *De Genio Socratis,* 582 F;
it may have originated with Chrysippus, *S.V.F.* iii. 725.

opinions about goodness—but those who are or are
not of the sort to give tasteful and charming favours.
Plutarch compares persons of this kind, who have an
inclination for giving, to ball-players [a]; they, on
catching the ball that they throw to one another,
neither keep it nor pass it on to others who do not
know how to play the game, but pass it to players who
can send it on.

53

> Whatever a man may seize in shamelessness,
> However small it be, it chills the heart.
> For set aside a little on a little,
> And do it often ; that soon grows to much.

This is thought to have no connection with what
has gone before ; there is, however, in fact a continuous thread. For after saying that even if what is
taken is small, it " chills " him from whom it is taken [b]
(since it is taken against his will), the poet added that
an accumulation of small things constitutes a large
thing, and that to go on losing small things ends in
having nothing, so that a man who loses even a small
thing quite reasonably feels hurt. And if this is true,
Aristotle was right to say [c] that there is no worse
phrase in life than " Not enough to matter " : if each
item is disregarded, as of little importance, and we
dismiss it with a " Not enough to matter," we shall
come to grief [d] ; we shall go hungry if we are always

[b] This interpretation of Hesiod's line is defended by Wilamowitz, although others think the meaning to be that the
taker loses his peace of mind.
[c] Perhaps in a lost exoteric work ; the fragment is omitted
by Rose.
[d] Cf. *Moralia*, 85 E, and Wyttenbach's note there.

PLUTARCH'S MORALIA

νομίαις λιμώξομεν τοῦτο ἀεὶ ἐπᾴδοντες· ἐν δὲ τῇ
διαίτῃ νοσήσομεν πολλάκις μὲν παρορῶντες τὸ ὀρθόν, λέγοντες δὲ ταύτην τὴν φωνήν· ἡ γὰρ καθ' ἓν
ἕκαστον ἔλλειψις μεγάλην ἀθροίζει τοῖς παρορῶσι
τὴν βλάβην.

54

Ibid. 368-369.

ἀρχομένου δὲ πίθου καὶ λήγοντος κορέσασθαι,
μεσσόθι φείδεσθαι· δειλὴ δ' ἐν πυθμένι φειδώ.

Καὶ ἐν τοῖς πατρίοις[1] ἐστὶν ἑορτὴ Πιθοιγία,[2] καθ'
ἣν οὔτε οἰκέτην οὔτε μισθωτὸν εἴργειν τῆς ἀπολαύ-
σεως τοῦ οἴνου θεμιτὸν ἦν, ἀλλὰ θύσαντας πᾶσι
μεταδιδόναι τοῦ δώρου τοῦ Διονύσου. καλῶς οὖν
εἴρηται δεῖν " ἀρχομένου πίθου κορέσασθαι," καὶ τῇ
ἑορτῇ συμφώνως[3]· δεῖ[4] δὲ καὶ φειδοῦς ταμιευομένοις[5] τὴν ἀπόλαυσιν, ὥστε καὶ εἰσαῦθις ἡμῖν γενέσθαι καὶ αὖθις. εἰ δ' ἀπαναλωθέντος τοῦ πλείστου
τὸ λειπόμενον ὀλίγον εἴη, χαλεπὴν εἶναι τὴν φειδώ.
τοῦτο[6] γάρ, φησί, τάχα ἂν καὶ τραπείη καὶ ἄχρη-
στον γένοιτο τοῖς φεισαμένοις.

---

[1] ἐνίοις πάτριος Bernardakis. ἐν τ. Ἀθηναίων πατρίοις Westerwick.
[2] Πιθοίγια Duebner.
[3] συμφώνως AZBQR : συμφωνεῖν TL.
[4] δεῖν Pertusi.
[5] Wyttenbach : φειδοῦς ταμιευομένους. φειδοῦς (or φείδεσθαι)

146

using this incantation in our housekeeping, and our way of life will result in illness if we often disregard the rules of health with this remark. A deficiency item by item piles up a mass of harm for the careless.

Wyttenbach.

54

> Starting the jar and finishing, drink your fill,
> Go slow between : no good to spare at the bottom.

Among our ancestral customs is a festival called Pithoigia [a] (opening of the jar), at which it was forbidden to bar either a slave or a hired man from enjoying the wine. The rule was to sacrifice and then give everyone a share of Dionysus' gift. So it is well said, and accords with the festival, that one should take one's fill when the jar is started. But we also need thrift, husbanding our enjoyment, so that we may have it again and again. But if most of the wine has been consumed and there should be little left, then it is " hard to be sparing " [b]; the poet means that this little might well go sour [c] and become useless to those who had been sparing of it.

Wyttenbach, Patzig.

---

[a] Plutarch may not have said exactly this, since the festival at Chaeronea that corresponded to the Athenian Pithoigia was called the " Festival of the Good Spirit," *Quaest. Conv.* 735 D, 655 E.

[b] The text commented on may have had χαλεπή for δειλή.

[c] Cf. *Quaest. Conv.* 701 D-F ; *Geoponica*, vii. 6.

μεσοῦντος ταμιευομένοις Gaisford. φείδεσθαι τοῦ μέσου τοὺς τ. Pertusi.

[6] τοῦτο AQLR : τότε ZB.

55

Ibid. 370-372.

μισθὸς δ' ἀνδρὶ φίλῳ εἰρημένος ἄρκιος ἔστω.
καί τε κασιγνήτῳ γελάσας ἐπὶ μάρτυρα θέσθαι.
πίστιες ἄρ τοι ὁμῶς καὶ ἀπιστίαι ὤλεσαν ἄνδρας.

Τούτους δέ τινες τοὺς στίχους ἐξέβαλον, ὁ δὲ
Πλούταρχος ἐγκρίνει· δεῖν γὰρ καὶ τὸν φίλον συνερ-
γὸν παραλαμβάνειν ἐπὶ ὡρισμένῳ μισθῷ· ἔχθραν
γὰρ προξενεῖ τὸ τῆς ἀμοιβῆς μετὰ τὸ ἔργον ἐλλιπὲς
ἀδοκήτως[1] ὑπάρξαν. τούτῳ δ' ὅμοιον καὶ τὸ τὰ
πρὸς τοὺς ἀδελφοὺς συναλλάγματα μὴ ἀμάρτυρα
ποιεῖσθαι· τὸ δ' ἐπαχθὲς ἀφαιρῶν εἶπεν ὅτι γελάσας,
τουτέστιν ὡς παίζοντας καὶ μὴ σπουδάζοντας.[2]
πολλοὺς γὰρ ἀπολέσθαι διὰ τὸ πιστεῦσαί τισιν οἷς
ἀπιστεῖν δέον, ἀπιστῆσαι δὲ πάλιν οἷς πιστεῦσαι
δέον.

56

Ibid. 375.

ὃς δὲ γυναικὶ πέποιθε, πέποιθ' ὅ γε φηλήτῃσι.

Τοῦτον ὁ Πλούταρχος χαράττει τὸν στίχον.

---

[1] Wyttenbach : ἀδόκητον.
[2] See Schwyzer, *Griech. Gramm.* i. 811[3], but some words
may be lost, as Dr. Dawe suggests. παίζων . . . σπουδάζων
Pertusi.

---

[a] W. J. Verdenius, *R.E.G.* lxiii (1960), p. 350, notes that
Aristotle, *E.N.* 1164 a 25, explains in the same way, but
does not explicitly ascribe the lines to Hesiod : they are
absent from most MSS. and P. Oxy. 2091.   Plutarch, *Life of*

55

Promise a friend his wage, and see you pay him :
Laugh at your act, but bring a witness in
Even when doing a deal with your own brother.
Trust and mistrust alike have ruined men.

Some have excised these lines, but Plutarch includes them, because it is right that even a friend
ought to be engaged as an assistant at a definite
wage, since it causes bad blood if, when the work is
over,[a] the reward turns out to be short of his expectations. The injunction not to make unwitnessed
agreements with one's brothers is of the same sort.
To remove the invidiousness of this the poet said
that a man should do it with a laugh, that is as if in
jest and not in earnest. Many people have been
ruined by misplaced trust or distrust.[b]

56

Who trusts a woman, puts his trust in thieves.

Plutarch expunges this line.[c]

Theseus, chap. 3, says that some ascribe v. 370 to Pittheus, a
view for which he cites Aristotle (frag. 598) ; he quotes 371
as Hesiod's in *De Vitioso Pudore*, 533 B.

[b] One can do nothing but translate this scholion as it
stands, but note that it must be a distortion. What it puts
forward as Plutarch's reason for including the disputed lines
is merely an explanatory paraphrase of them, in typical
scholiast's style, but no-one can have condemned the lines
on the ground that they were not intelligible.

[c] Perhaps because he had a better opinion of women ;
other guesses about his reason can be found in Wilamowitz's
commentary.

57

Ibid. 376.

μουνογενὴς δὲ πάις σῴζοι πατρώιον οἶκον.[1]

Δόξειεν ἂν ἄτοπος ὁ στίχος εἶναι καὶ ἀγανακτοῦν-
τος ὅτι γέγονεν οὐ μόνος τῷ πατρί. μήποτε, φησὶν ὁ Πλούταρχος, καὶ Πλάτων ἕπεται τῷ Ἡσιόδῳ
καὶ Ξενοκράτης, καὶ Λυκοῦργος πρὸ τούτων· οἳ
πάντες ᾤοντο δεῖν ἕνα κληρονόμον καταλιπεῖν· καὶ
τοῦτο ἦν τὸ ὑπὸ Ἡσιόδου λεγόμενον.

58

Tzetzes on 378.

γηραιὸς δὲ θάνοις[2] ἕτερον παῖδ᾽ ἐγκαταλείπων.

Οἱ περὶ Πρόκλον καὶ Πλούταρχον ἀδιανόητον
τοῦτό φασιν εἶναι καὶ περισσόν.

59

Scholia on 380.

πλείων μὲν πλεόνων μελέτη, μείζων δ᾽ ἐπιθήκη.

Μήποτε δέ, φησὶν ὁ Πλούταρχος, ἐκεῖνο λέγει τὸ

[1] There are old variants σῴζοι and εἴη, the latter requiring
v. 377 to complete the sense. Since the scholiast speaks of
one line, he must have read σῴζοι.   [2] θάνοι Hermann.

[a] *Laws*, 923.
[b] Frag. 97 Heinze.
[c] Elsewhere Plutarch condemns Hesiod's sentiment, *De
Fraterno Amore*, 480 E.

57

And may there be an only son, to preserve
His father's house.

This might be thought an extraordinary line,
written by a man who was repining that he had not
been his father's only son. May it not be, says Plutarch, that Plato [a] and Xenocrates [b] follow Hesiod,
and Lycurgus before them ? All these men thought
that one should leave one's property to a single heir ;
and this is what Hesiod meant.[c]

58

May you die old and leave a second son.

Proclus and Plutarch say that this is unintelligible
and could be dispensed with.[d]

59

More goods, more cares ; but greater is the gain. [e]

May it not be, says Plutarch, that his meaning is

[d] Translated as above the line is not intelligible after v.
376, " May you have only one son to keep his father's
estate." Some suppose Hesiod to have meant, " if you have
a second son, may you die old, having had time to accumu-
late wealth enough for both." More probable is Hermann's
emendation, which gives the sense, "And may he (sc. your
only son) die an old man, leaving another son in his turn."
[e] So Plutarch seems to have understood the text. But he
must have neglected the previous line, which requires a
different interpretation, viz., " Yet easily could Zeus give
untold wealth to a numerous family : the more they are, the
more trouble they take, and greater is their gain."

τοῦ Λάμπιδος, ὅτι πλείων μὲν ἡ φροντὶς ἐπὶ τοῦ
πλείονος πλούτου, μείζων δ' ἡ ἐπίδοσις, ἣν '' ἐπιθή-
κην '' εἶπεν, αὐτοῦ συναύξοντος ἑαυτὸν τοῦ πλούτου
διὰ τὴν τῶν ὀργάνων εὐπορίαν καὶ τῶν ὑπηρετῶν.
ὃ καὶ ὁ Λάμπις εἴρηκεν ἐρωτηθεὶς πῶς ἐκτήσατο τὸν
πλοῦτον· τὸν¹ μὲν γὰρ² ὀλίγον ἔφη χαλεπῶς, τὸν δὲ
πολὺν ῥᾳδίως, πολλῶν ὄντων ἤδη τῶν ὑπουργούν-
των.

60

Ibid. 391.

γυμνὸν σπείρειν.

Κάλλιον δέ φησιν ὁ Πλούταρχος μετὰ τὸν σπόρον
ὑετὸν συμβῆναι ἢ πρὸ σπόρου· δῆλον δέ· τὰ γὰρ
μετὰ Πλειάδα σπαρέντα καὶ πρὸ τροπῶν φύεσθαι
ἑβδομαῖα—ἐν Αἰγύπτῳ δὲ καὶ τριταῖα—τὰ³ δὲ μετὰ
τροπὰς μόλις ἐν τριπλασίῳ τούτου τοῦ χρόνου.
οὕτως τὸ ἐπιγενέσθαι ὑετὸν ἀγαθὸν μᾶλλον ἢ τὸ
προγενέσθαι. οἱ δ' ἀρχαῖοι καὶ πρωϊαίτερον ἔσπει-
ρον, ὡς δῆλον ἐκ τῶν Ἐλευσινίων τελετῶν, ἐν αἷς⁴
ἐλέγετο, ''πάριθι⁵ κόρη γέφυραν· ὅσον οὔπω τρίπολον
δή.''⁶

---

¹ πλοῦτον τὸν added by Bernadakis.
² γὰρ omitted by LR.   ³ τὰ TL : τὸν AZBQR.
⁴ Bergk : οἷς.

⁵ Bergk : ͘πθι.
⁶ Wilamowitz : τριπόλεον δέ QR, and probably A.

ᵃ *An Seni Sit Gerenda Res Publica*, 787 ᴀ ; Lampis was a
merchant operating in Aegina, and according to Demosthenes, xxiii. 211, the greatest ship-owner of that time.

ᵇ This is a misinterpretation of Hesiod, according to which
he meant, not '' prepare for hard work when you set out to
sow,'' but '' sow while it is still warm enough to need few or

that of Lampis' aphorism, namely that although more wealth involves more anxiety, its increase, which Hesiod calls " gain," is greater, because such wealth multiplies of itself through making it easy to procure tools and servants ? That is what Lampis said when asked how he had got his riches : " I made my little competence," he answered, " with difficulty, and my fortune easily,[a] as by then I had many men to serve me."

60

Strip to sow.

It is better, says Plutarch, for rain to occur after sowing rather than before.[b] Clearly so, for seed sown after the setting of the Pleiads [c] and before the winter solstice sprouts after six days, and even after two days in Egypt, whereas seed sown after the solstice takes at best three times as long to sprout. It is so much better for rain to come after the sowing than before. But the ancients sowed even earlier, as is shown by the rites of Eleusis, in which they used to say : " Come forth, O Maid, to the bridge : they have all but done the third ploughing." [d]

no clothes," cf. Virgil, Georgics, i. 299, " nudus ara, sere nudus : hiems ignava colono."
[c] Hesiod has just said that ploughing should begin at the setting (at sunrise) of the Pleiads, early November in his time.
[d] Carmina Popularia, fr. 50 Diehl, 9 Bergk, 31 Page. Text and meaning are uncertain. The Eleusinian mysteries took place in mid-Boëdromiôn, corresponding roughly to September. The bridge may be that over the Attic Cephisos, which is mentioned in connexion with these rites, Wilamowitz, Griechische Verskunst, 286. The first ploughing is in the spring, the second in the summer, the third at seed-time, to cover the seed : Varro, Res Rusticae, i. 29, " tertio arant iacto semine " (Mazon, pp. 111-112).

61

Ibid. 414-421.

ἦμος δὴ λήγει μένος ὀξέος ἠελίοιο
καύματος ἰδαλίμου μετοπωρινὸν ὀμβρήσαντος
Ζηνός . . .
τῆμος ἀδηκτοτάτη πέλεται τμηθεῖσα σιδήρῳ
ὕλη.

Λέγοι δ' ἂν καὶ τὴν[1] ἄβρωτον ὑπὸ τῶν ἐγγινο-
μένων θηριδίων τοῖς φυτοῖς, ὡς ἀδηκτοτάτην οὖσαν,
οἷον θριπῶν καὶ τερηδόνων, ἃ διεμφύεται τοῖς
δένδρεσι σηπομένης τῆς ἐν αὐτοῖς ὑγρότητος. τὸ
δ' ἐν τούτῳ ὑλοτομεῖν ὀρθόν, ὅτε ξηρὰ μέν ἐστι τὰ
δένδρα, ἀποδεδωκότα τὸν οἰκεῖον καρπόν, καὶ
οὐκέτι κάμνει περὶ τὴν ἐκτροφὴν αὐτοῦ, μετρίας δὲ
ἔτυχεν ὑγρότητος ἀλλ' οὐ πολλῆς ἤδη πρὸς τὸ
οἰκεῖον, τοῖς[2] τέμνουσιν ὥστε[3] μὴ σήπεσθαι μετὰ
τὴν τομήν· εἰς ὅ τινας βλέποντας καὶ φθινούσης
τέμνειν τῆς σελήνης ἀλλὰ μὴ πανσελήνου μηδ'
αὐξανομένης· ἡ γὰρ τοῦ φωτὸς ἐπίδοσις ὑγρότερα
ποιεῖ τὰ δένδρα καὶ εὐεπίφορα τεμνόμενα πρὸς τὴν
σῆψιν.

62

Ibid. 423.

ὅλμον μὲν τριπόδην.

Πολὺς ἐν τούτοις ὁ Πλούταρχος ἀμυνόμενος τοὺς
γελῶντας τὸν Ἡσίοδον τῆς σμικρολογίας, καὶ Πλάτωνα λέγων περὶ τῆς τῶν σκευῶν ἐν οἴκοις διειλεχ-

---

[1] τὴν] αὐτὴν Pertusi.   [2] τότε Pertusi ; TL omit.
[3] T : ὥστε γε.

61

But when the fierce sun's might desists at last
From sweaty scorching heat, once Zeus has sent
The autumn rains . . .
Then iron tools fell timber that's least gnawn.

But he may also mean, as being " least gnawn,"
the wood which has not been eaten by the little
creatures that occur in growing things, like wood-
worms and borers, which are generated in trees when
the moisture in them putrefies.[a] It is the right thing
to cut timber at this time, when the trees are dry,
having yielded their proper fruit, and are no longer
burdened with the nourishment of that fruit. At the
same time they have been given only a moderate
access of moisture,[b] not a great deal yet, in addition
to their own—right, that is, for men who are cutting
so that the timber shall not rot after they have cut
it. With an eye on this some people are said to cut
when the moon is waning, not at full moon or waxing.
The reason is that the increase of light makes the
trees moister and so prone to decay when cut.[c]

Pertusi.

62

A three-foot mortar.

Plutarch strongly rebuts those critics who make fun
of Hesiod for his petty detail ; he says that Plato
discoursed on the proper size of domestic utensils,[d]

[a] Cf. Quaest. Conv. 636 D, where σκνῖπες (insects that live
under the bark) take the place of θρῖπες.
[b] i.e., from the first autumn rain.
[c] Cf. Quaest. Conv. 659 A, and frag. 109. Athen. 276 e,
Theophrastus, Hist. Plant. v. i. 3, Geoponica, iii. 1.
[d] Laws, 746 E.

155

θαι συμμετρίας καὶ Λυκοῦργον περὶ τῆς τῶν θυρῶν
κατασκευῆς, ἵν' ἀπὸ πρίονος ὦσι καὶ πελέκεως
μόνον ἀποίκιλοι. δεῖν[1] οὖν ἀποδέχεσθαι καὶ τὸν
Ἡσίοδον μέτρα παραδόντα καὶ ὅλμου καὶ ὑπέρου
καὶ ἄξονος καὶ σφύρας. καὶ τοὺς ἀρχαίους δὲ πολὺν
καὶ τούτων ποιεῖσθαι λόγον καὶ τῶν εὑρετῶν Πάμ-
φων μὲν τιμᾶν διότι τὸν λύχνον πρῶτος εὗρε καὶ τὸ
ἐκ τούτου φῶς εἰσήγαγεν εἴς τε τὰ ἱερὰ καὶ τὴν
ἰδίαν χρῆσιν, τὸν δὲ τῶν Πιτθέων[2] δῆμον διὰ τοῦτο
οὕτως[3] ὀνομάσαι,[4] διότι τῶν πίθων ἐπενοήσαντο τὴν
πλάσιν· ὥστε μὴ τὴν πολυτέλειαν προσήκειν θαυμά-
ζειν ἀλλὰ τὴν τῶν χρειωδῶν, κἂν εὐτελῆ τυγχάνῃ,
περιποίησιν.

63

(a) Scholia, 426.
(b) Hesychius, s.v. δεκαδώρῳ ἁμάξῃ.

τρισπίθαμον δ' ἀψῖν τάμνειν δεκαδώρῳ ἁμάξῃ.

(a) Σπιθαμὴ μέν ἐστιν ἁπλωθείσης τῆς χειρὸς
ἀπὸ τοῦ ἀντίχειρος[5] ἐπὶ τὸ ἄκρον τοῦ σμικροτάτου
δακτύλου διάστημα . . . δῶρον δὲ τὸ αὐτό πως
καὶ παλαιστή, ἀλλ' αὕτη[6] μὲν ἐκ τῶν τεσσάρων
δακτύλων ὀρθῶς συντεθέντων, δῶρον δὲ τούτων
συστραφέντων καὶ τοῦ ἀντίχειρος ἐγερθέντος.

(b) Δεκαδώρῳ ἁμάξῃ· ἧς ἡ διάμετρος τῶν τρο-
χῶν δέκα δώρων.[7] δῶρον δέ, ὡς μέν τινες, ἡ

---

[1] Wyttenbach : δεῖ.   [2] Πιθέων Z, Lenschau.
[3] διὰ τοῦτο οὕτως added by ZB. οὕτως alone would have
sufficed.   [4] ὀνομάσθαι Fischer.
[5] ἀπὸ τοῦ ἀντίχειρος added by Schultz.
[6] αὕτη Pertusi : οὕτως. οὗτος (with παλαιστής) Gaisford.

and Lycurgus on the making of doors, to ensure that they should be unornamented and made by saw and axe alone.[a] We should therefore welcome Hesiod's instructions about the measurements of mortar, pestle, axle, and wedge. Moreover, the ancients attached much importance to these things : among other inventors, they honoured Pamphôs because he was the original inventor of the lamp and introduced lamp-light into temples and into private use, and they gave the deme of Pithos [b] its name because its members conceived the idea of moulding jars (*pithoi*).[c] So it is not costly elaboration that we should admire, but the procuring of useful objects, cheap and simple though they may be.

63

Cut a three-span rim for a ten-palm waggon.

(*a*) A span is the distance from the thumb to the tip of the little finger when the hand is spread open. . . . A palm and a hand's breadth are much the same, but the latter is obtained by placing the straightened fingers side by side, whereas the palm is got by closing the fingers and extending the thumb.[d]

(*b*) Ten-palm waggon : one of which the diameter of the wheels is ten palms. According to some

[a] *Cf. Life of Lycurgus*, chap. 13.
[b] An attic deme in the upper Cephisus-valley. The demotic is normally Πιθεύς, but Πιτθεύς is found in one inscription (ii cent. A.D.) and in Harpocration's lexicon.
[c] Stephanus of Byzantium, *s.v.* Πίθος.
[d] The extended thumb must be placed alongside the bent fingers.

[7] δεκάδωρος Musurus.

παλαιστή· ὡς δ' ἕτεροι, ὅταν τοὺς τέσσαρας δακτύ-
λους συστρέψας ἐγείρῃς τὸν ἀντίχειρα, ὡς Πλούταρχος.

64

Scholia, 427.

φέρειν δὲ γύην.

[Τὸν μὲν οὖν γύην εἶναι κελεύει πρίνινον, προσθείς,
" ἢ κατ' ἄρουραν εἰ εὕροις, ἢ κατ' ὄρος, πρίνινον.'']
οὐ γὰρ εὔπορος Βοιωτοῖς ἡ πρῖνος, φησὶν ὁ Πλούταρχος, ἀλλὰ τοῖς πτελεΐνοις ἀντὶ τῶν πρινίνων
χρῶνται τοὺς γύας κατασκευάζοντες.

65

Ibid. 435.

δάφνης δ' ἢ πτελέης ἀκιώτατοι ἱστοβοῆες.

Τὸ δ' ἄσηπτον ἐδήλωσεν εἰπὼν ἀκιώτατον· ὁ δὲ
Πλούταρχος ἐξηγήσατο τὴν αἰτίαν, λέγων εἶναί τι
θηρίδιον, ὃ καλεῖται κίς, διεσθίον τὰ ξύλα· τοῦτο
καὶ Πίνδαρον οὕτω καλεῖν περὶ τοῦ χρυσοῦ λέγοντα,

κεῖνον οὐ[1] σῆς, οὐ κὶς δάμναται,[2]

[1] κεῖνον οὐ Pindar : κείνου.
[2] οὐδὲ κὶς δάπτει Pindar.

---

[a] Latte thinks that this note was transmitted by Diogenianus.   A span is reckoned as three παλαισταί or hand's
breadths.   Rightly or wrongly, the scholiasts suppose that by

" palm " means the hand's breadth, but according to others, including Plutarch, it is measured by closing the fingers and extending the thumb.[a]

64

And carry a plough-beam.

[Now he tells us that the plough-beam should be of holm-oak, adding, " of holm-oak, if you should find one in your field or on the mountain."] For the Boeotians, says Plutarch, do not easily come by holm-oaks, but use elm instead when fashioning their plough-beams.

65

Poles of bay or elm are *akiôtatoi*.

By *akiôtatos* he means " uncorrupted." Plutarch explained the reason, saying that there is a small creature named *kis* (beetle), which eats through wood, and that Pindar gives it this name, saying of gold as being incorruptible :

This neither moth nor beetle can subdue.[b]

rim (ἁψίς) is meant one quarter of the wheel's whole circumference, which will therefore be of 36 hand's breadths, too great for a diameter of ten hand's breadths. On the approximation that the circumference is three times the diameter, the diameter should be twelve hand's breadths (Mazon, p. 103). Plutarch, by supposing that the δῶρον is almost five fingers wide, not four, obtains nearly the right diameter. Another explanation given in the scholia is that the ἁψῖδες would overlap, being joined by tenons and mortices.
[b] Frag. 261 Turyn, 222 Bergk.

ὡς ἄσηπτον· ἐγγίνεται δ' οὖν τὰ τοιαῦτα θηρίδια
τοῖς γλυκέσι καὶ μαλακοῖς ξύλοις, δάφνη δὲ καὶ
πτελέα δριμύτατα.

66

Ibid. 453-454.

ῥηίδιον γὰρ ἔπος εἰπεῖν· βόε δὸς καὶ ἄμαξαν.
ῥηίδιον δ' ἀπανήνασθαι· πάρα ἔργα βόεσσιν.

[Τούτων τὸ μὲν ὁ " ἀβούτης " εἴποι ἂν ὁ αἰτῶν
βόας ἵν' ἀρόσῃ τοῦ καιροῦ καλοῦντος, τὸ δ' ὁ
εὐπορῶν βοῶν ἀποκρίναιτο[1] ἄν, ὅτι καὶ οἱ παρ'
αὐτῷ βόες ἔργα ἔχουσι, καὶ διὰ τοῦτο οὐκ ἂν
αἰτούμενος δοίη.] ὃ καὶ ὁ Λάκων[2] τὴν κυνῆν[3]
αἰτούμενος εἰπεῖν λέγεται πρὸς τὸν αἰτοῦντα, " εἰ
μὲν εὐδία, ἔσται καὶ σοὶ ἄχρηστος· εἰ δὲ χειμών,
καὶ ἐμοὶ χρήσιμος." καὶ γὰρ καὶ περὶ τῶν βοῶν
ἐρεῖ ταὐτὸν ὁ αἰτηθείς, " εἰ μὲν μὴ καιρὸς τοῦ ἀροῦν,
καὶ σοὶ ἄχρηστοι· εἰ δὲ καιρός, κἀμοὶ χρήσιμοι."

67

Ibid. 465.

εὔχεσθαι δὲ Διὶ χθονίῳ Δημήτερί θ' ἁγνῇ.

Ταῦτα καὶ θεοσεβείας ἐστὶ δόγματα,[4] τρέποντα
τοὺς ἔργων ἁπτομένους ἐπὶ τὰς παρακλήσεις τῶν
τὰ ἔργα ταῦτα ἐφορώντων καὶ τελειοῦν δυναμένων
θεῶν· καὶ οὐδὲν ἀπολείπει πρὸς τέρψιν, εἰ ἐννοήσο-
μεν τὸν ἀροῦν μέλλοντα λαβόμενον τῆς ἐχέτλης (ἣν

---

[1] Gaisford : ἀποκρίνετο LR : -ηται Q : -εται ZB.
[2] ὃ . . . Λάκων Gaisford : ὃν (or ἣν) . . . λάβων.

Now such creatures are found in sweet soft timber,
whereas bay and elm are very acrid.

66

> Easy to say : lend me a team and a cart ;
> Easy to answer : I have work for my oxen.

[The former sentence would be spoken by the " ox-
less " man, asking for oxen to plough with when the
time calls, the latter would be the answer of the man
with plenty of oxen, namely that his oxen have their
work to do and that he would therefore not lend
them.] This is the same answer that the Spartan is
said to have given when asked for the loan of a cap :
" If the weather is fine, it will be no good to you
either ; if there is a storm, I shall need it too."
And in fact the man who is asked for a loan will say
the same thing about his oxen also : " If it is not a
suitable time for ploughing, they will be no good to
you either ; if it is suitable, I shall need them too."

Gaisford, Westerwick.

67

Pray to Zeus of the Earth and holy Demeter.

These are also precepts of piety, directing men as
they begin their tasks to call upon the gods who
watch over those tasks and can bring them to success.
What a delightful picture it is, if we imagine the man
who is about to plough as laying hold of the handle

---

³ κυνῆν Scaliger : κοινῆν.
⁴ διδάγματα L.

προείπομεν ὅ τι ποτὲ δηλοῖ τοῦ ἀρότρου μέρος)
πρὶν ἐλάσῃ τοὺς βόας, μάρτυρα καλοῦντα τοῦ ἔργου
τὸν Δία καὶ τὴν Δήμητραν, τὸν μὲν ὡς τελεσιουργὸν
διὰ τῶν ὄμβρων τῆς σπορᾶς, τὴν δ' ὡς προστάτιν
τῶν γονίμων δυνάμεων τῆς γῆς. ὁ γοῦν πάντα τὰ
παρ' ἑαυτοῦ¹ ποιήσας οὐχ ἁπλῶς αἰτεῖ τοὺς θεοὺς
ἀλλ' ὥσπερ ἀπαιτεῖ τὸ τέλος. ὡς οὖν ἔλεγε
Σωκράτης εὔχεσθαι δεῖν μουσικὴν τὸν μανθάνοντα
καὶ γονὴν παίδων τὸν γαμοῦντα, οὕτω καὶ Ἡσίοδος
καρπῶν γονὴν τὸν τῆς ἐχέτλης ἤδη λαμβανόμενον
καὶ ὄρπηκα φέροντα καὶ ἐπάγοντα τοῖς νώτοις τῶν
βοῶν ὥστε κινηθῆναι καὶ ἑλκύσαι τὸ ἄροτρον.

68

Ibid. 486-489.

ἦμος κόκκυξ κοκκύζει δρυὸς ἐν πετάλοισι
τὸ πρῶτον, τέρπει δὲ βροτοὺς ἐπ' ἀπείρονα γαῖαν,
τῆμος Ζεὺς ὕοι τρίτῳ ἤματι μηδ' ἀπολήγοι,
μήτ' ἂρ ὑπερβάλλων βοὸς ὁπλὴν μήτ' ἀπολείπων.

Ὅτι δ' ὁ τοιοῦτος ὄμβρος χρήσιμος, πιστοῦνται²
ἀπὸ τοῦ τὴν Σικελίαν εὐκαρπεῖν πολλοὺς δεχο-
μένην ἐαρινοὺς ὄμβρους· καὶ ἀπὸ τοῦ προσηνὲς
εἶναι τῇ γῇ τότε τὸ ὕδωρ³ ὑποθερμαινόμενον καὶ
νηπίοις οὖσι τοῖς καρποῖς συμφέρον· καὶ ἀπὸ τοῦ
τινας καὶ ἐν ἰσημερίᾳ σπείραντας ἐαρινῇ πολλοὺς
θερίσαι καρπούς· καὶ γὰρ ὁ τριμηνιαῖος λεγόμενος

¹ ἑαυτὸν Bernardakis.
² πιστοῦται ZBLR.
³ τὸ ὕδωρ τότε τῇ γῇ ZB : τῇ γῇ τὸ ὕδωρ τότε Bernardakis.

(we have already explained which part of the plough
that means) before he drives his oxen forward, and
calling Zeus and Demeter to witness his work, the
former as effecting the growth of the seed by his rains,
the latter as presiding over the fruitful powers of the
earth. Certainly the man who has done all he can
does not simply make a request of the gods, but as it
were claims the fulfilment that is his due. Socrates
said that the pupil should pray that he might acquire
the art of music and the bridegroom that he might
beget children ; just so Hesiod meant that the farmer
should pray for fruitful crops at the moment when
he lays his hand on the plough-handle and brings his
goad to lay it on the backs of his oxen, so that they
shall move and draw the plough.

Westerwick, comparing *De Superstitione*, 169 B, where
vv. 465-468 are referred to, with the same interpretation that
God may be expected to help those who help themselves.
Plutarch is also a likely source for the apocryphal statement
of Socrates.

68

When in the oak-tree's leaves the cuckoo first
Shall cry, and gladden men the wide world over,
May Zeus send rain on three days and not cease,
To fill an ox's hoof-mark, no more, no less.

They prove that such rain is useful from the good
crops grown in Sicily, which receives much spring
rain [a] ; and from the fact that the water being then
slightly warm is agreeable to the earth and beneficial
to the tender young crops ; and from the fact that
some people who have sown as late as the spring
equinox have harvested heavy crops ; indeed the so-

[a] Cf. *Quaest. Nat.* 913 A.

πυρὸς ὑπὸ τοιούτων ὄμβρων ἐκτρέφεσθαι ἔοικε τῶν
ἐαρινῶν.

69

Ibid. 496-497.

μή σε κακοῦ χειμῶνος ἀμηχανίη καταμάρψῃ
σὺν πενίῃ, λεπτῇ δὲ παχὺν πόδα χειρὶ πιέζῃς.

*Τῶν λιμωττόντων τοὺς πόδας παχύνεσθαί φησι
τὸ δ' ἄλλο σῶμα λεπτύνεσθαι. καὶ εἷς νόμος ἦν Ἐφε-
σίων, μὴ ἐξεῖναι πατρὶ παῖδας ἀποθέσθαι ἕως ἂν διὰ
λιμὸν παχυνθῇ τοὺς πόδας. ἴσως δὲ καὶ τὴν ἀπὸ καθ-
ίσεως καὶ ἀργίας πάχυνσιν δηλοῖ τῶν ποδῶν* . . .
ἔοικε δὲ καὶ ἡ ἐν τοῖς λιμοῖς πάχυνσις εἶναι κατὰ
φύσιν, ὡς ὁ Πλούταρχος· δεῖται γὰρ τὸ ἐν ἡμῖν
θερμόν, ἵνα μένῃ, τῆς ἔξωθεν τροφῆς, ἣν οὐ δεχό-
μενον δαπανᾷ τὸ σῶμα καὶ αὐτοῦ τι ἀποσπᾷ· δι'
ἀσθένειαν δ' ἀδυνατοῦν ἀλλοιῶσαι τὸ ἀποσπώμενον
ἄπεπτον[1] ἀφίησι· καὶ αὐτὸ μὲν τὰ μέσα καὶ τὰ ἄνω
λεπτύνει τοῦ σώματος, ἐν οἷς ἐστι πλεῖον· ἐκεῖνο δ'
ἄρα τὸ ἄπεπτον εἰς τὸ κάτω φέρεται καὶ οὕτω δὴ
παχύνει τοὺς πόδας.

70

Ibid. 502-503.

δείκνυε δὲ δμώεσσι θέρευς ἔτι μέσσου ἐόντος·
οὐκ αἰεὶ θέρος ἐσσεῖται, ποιεῖσθε καλιάς.

Διὰ τούτου τοῦ παραγγέλματος καὶ τὰ ὅμοια νο-
ητέον. οὐκ ἀεὶ εὐτυχήσομεν· παρασκευαστέον οὖν

---

[1] ὂν after ἄπεπτον AQUL ; omitted by ZBT.

called three-month wheat [a] seems to owe its growth to such spring rains.

Wyttenbach.

69

> Lest in grim winter helplessness seize thee
> And poverty, and thin hand squeeze swollen foot.

He says that starving men's feet swell, while the rest of their body shrinks. And it was a law of the Ephesians that a father might not abandon his children before his feet had swollen through hunger. But perhaps he indicates a swelling of the feet through sitting in idleness . . . But it seems that the swelling in times of starvation is due to a natural process, as Plutarch says. For the heat in us needs external nourishment for its maintenance,[b] and if it does not get it, consumes the body and abstracts something from it. But if through weakness it is unable to convert what it abstracts, it lets it go unconcocted ; and although its own action on the middle and upper parts of the body, where it mainly is, is to make them thin, that unconcocted matter sinks, sure enough, to the lower parts and so causes the feet to swell.

70

> When summer's at its height remind your servants :
> " It won't be summer always ; make your huts."

This precept should lead us to think of other similar things,[c] e.g., " we shall not always be fortunate, so

---

[a] *Quaest. Nat.* 915 D with note. " Three-month " wheat was spring-sown and harvested three months after sowing.
[b] *Cf. Quaest. Conv.* 686 E, 687 A.
[c] *Cf.* frag. 49.

καὶ πρὸς τὰς περιστάσεις. οὐδ' ἀεὶ ὑγιανοῦμεν·
φροντιστέον οὖν καὶ τῶν ταῖς νόσοις ἐπιτηδείων.

71

(a) *Ibid.* 504.
(b) Hesychius, *s.v.* Ληναιών.

μῆνα δὲ Ληναιῶνα, κάκ' ἤματα, βούδορα πάντα.

(a) Πλούταρχος οὐδένα φησὶ μῆνα Ληναιῶνα Βοιωτοὺς καλεῖν· ὑποπτεύει δ' ἢ τὸν Βουκάτιον[1] αὐτὸν
λέγειν, ὅς ἐστιν ἡλίου τὸν αἰγόκερων διόντος (καὶ
τοῦ[2] βούδορα τῷ Βουκατίῳ[3] συνᾴδοντος διὰ τὸ πλείστους ἐν αὐτῷ διαφθείρεσθαι βόας) ἢ τὸν Ἑρμᾶϊον,
ὅς ἐστι μετὰ τὸν Βουκάτιον[4] καὶ εἰς ταῦτόν ἐρχό-
μενος τῷ Γαμηλιῶνι, καθ' ὃν καὶ τὰ Ληναῖα παρ'
Ἀθηναίοις· Ἴωνας[5] δὲ τοῦτον οὐδ' ἄλλως, ἀλλὰ Ληναιῶνα καλεῖν.[6]

(b) Οὐδένα τῶν μηνῶν Βοιωτοὶ οὕτω καλοῦσιν·
εἰκάζει δὲ ὁ Πλούταρχος Βουκάτιον· καὶ γὰρ ψυχρός
ἐστιν. ἔνιοι δὲ τὸν Ἑρμᾶϊον, ὃς κατὰ τὸν Βου-
κάτιόν ἐστιν· καὶ γὰρ Ἀθηναῖοι τὴν τῶν Ληναίων
ἑορτὴν ἐν αὐτῷ ἄγουσιν.

[1] Wyttenbach : βούκαιρον (-κερον, -καρον).
[2] τοῦ Q : τὸν AZBR. τὸ Duebner (with συνᾴδειν).
[3] Wyttenbach : βουκαίρῳ (-κέρῳ, -κάρῳ).
[4] Wyttenbach : βούκαιον AQ βουκάρῳ R βούδορα ZB.
[5] Pertusi : Ἴωνες.
[6] Q : καλεῖ A : καλοῦσι ZBR.

---

[a] Lenaion was an Ionic month.
[b] Wilamowitz remarks that the traditional accent of βούδορα (not βουδόρα) suggests that βου- is the intensive prefix,
and the word has nothing to do with oxen ; see, however,

we must prepare for changes of circumstance ; nor shall we always be in good health, so we must take thought for what is useful in disease."

Westerwick.

71

Lênaiôn, month of wretched days, all fit to skin an ox.

(a) Plutarch says that there is no month named Lênaiôn by the Boeotians,[a] but he suspects that the poet means either Bucatios, which is at the time when the sun is passing through the zodiacal sign of Capricorn—the phrase " to skin an ox " agrees with Bucatios, as the greatest mortality among cattle takes place then [b]—or Hermaïos, which comes after Bucatios and at the same time as Gamêliôn,[c] the month in which the Athenians celebrate the Lenaia ; and this month has exactly that name among the Ionians, who call it Lenaion.

(b) The Boeotians do not give this name to any month, but Plutarch guesses Bucatios to be meant : for it is a cold month. Some people think Hermaïos, which is about the time of Bucatios, to be intended, as the Athenians celebrate their festival of the Lenaia during it.

L. J. D. Richardson, *Hermathena*, xcv (1961), p. 53. But Plutarch may well have been right in deriving βουκάτιος from βοῦς and καίνω ; it was a name in use in Central Greece, the first month of the year in Boeotia, *Life of Pelopidas*, chap. 25.

[c] Hermaïos was an Aeolian and Dorian month, not everywhere at the same time of year, but in Boeotia coincident with the Athenian Gamêliôn, roughly January. It is to be noticed that according to Hesychius it was not Plutarch, but others, who identified Lenaion with Hermaïos.

72

Ibid. 524.

ὅτ' ἀνόστεος ὃν πόδα τένδει.

᾿Αριστοτέλης δέ φησι ψεῦδος εἶναι τὸ κατὰ τοὺς
πολύποδας· αὐτοὺς γὰρ ἑαυτοὺς μὴ κατεσθίειν ἀλλ'
ὑπὸ τῶν παγούρων[1] κατεσθίεσθαι.

*73

Ibid. 539-540.

τὴν περιέσσασθαι, ἵνα τοι τρίχες ἀτρεμέωσι,
μηδ' ὀρθαὶ φρίσσωσιν ἀειρόμεναι κατὰ σῶμα.

Τοῦτο συμβαίνει τοῖς ῥιγῶσι· πιεζομένων γὰρ τῶν
τριχῶν κατὰ τὰς ῥίζας ὑπὸ τῆς ψυχρότητος καὶ πυκνώσεως[2] περὶ αὐτὰς γινομένης αἴρονται ὀρθαί.

74

Ibid. 541-542.

ἀμφὶ δὲ ποσσὶ πέδιλα βοὸς ἶφι κταμένοιο
ἄρμενα δήσασθαι, πίλοις ἔντοσθε πυκάσσας.

᾿Εκ βοείων δερμάτων εἶναι κελεύει τὰ ὑποδήματα,
καὶ τούτων τῶν[3] ἰσχυρῶν· τοιαῦτα δ' εἶναι τὰ τῶν
σφαγέντων βοῶν, ἀλλ' οὐ τὰ τῶν αὐτομάτως ἀπο-
θανόντων. εἰκότως· ἀποθνήσκουσι μὲν γὰρ ἢ νοσή-
σαντες ἢ γηράσαντες ὥστε ἠσθενηκότες, τῶν δὲ

---

[1] παγούρων also in Tzetzes : γόγγρων Aristotle.
[2] Pertusi : πυκνώσεως AZBL : πύκνωσιν QR.
[3] τῶν AZBQ, omitted by LR.

72

When No-Bones gnaws his foot.

Aristotle says this about the cuttle-fish is untrue : they do not devour themselves but are devoured by crabs.[a]

Patzig.

*73

Put on this cloak, that your hairs may stay in place,
Not rise and stand up straight upon your body.

This happens to people who are cold. Their hairs are pressed at the roots by the cold, and contraction taking place around them, they stand up straight.

Sandbach. The interest in physical explanation is characteristic of Plutarch.

74

Around the feet fasten well-fitting shoes
From slaughtered ox, padded with slippers of felt.

He tells us that the footwear should be of oxhide, and strong hide too ; such is the hide of slaughtered oxen, but not that of those that have died a natural death. This might be expected since they die either of disease or of old age, and therefore in a weak condition.[b] But if they are slaughtered, the strength

[a] *History of Animals*, 591 a-b ; Plutarch, *De Soll. Animalium*, 978 F, where, as in Aristotle, Athenaeus, 316 e, Antigonus, 92 (99), and Pliny, *N.H.* ix. 87, the damage to the cuttle-fish's tentacles is ascribed to congers (γόγγροι). It is likely, but not certain, that this is what Plutarch wrote in his commentary, and that the word has been corrupted.

[b] *Cf. Quaest. Conv.* 642 E.

σφαγέντων ἢ ἐν τοῖς δέρμασιν ἐνοῦσα δύναμις μένει. δεῖν οὖν ἐκ τούτων εἶναι τὰ ὑποδήματα· δεῖν
δὲ καὶ πίλοις ἔνδοθεν χρῆσθαι συμφύεσθαι τοῖς
ποσὶ δυναμένοις καὶ μειζόνως ἀλεαίνειν· τὰ γὰρ
ἄκρα μείζονος δεῖται βοηθείας ὡς πορρώτερον ὄντα
τοῦ μέσου, ἐν ᾧ τὸ ἔμφυτον θερμόν.

75

Ibid. 548-553.

ἠῷος δ' ἐπὶ γαῖαν ἀπ' οὐρανοῦ ἀστεροέντος
ἀὴρ πυροφόρος τέταται μακάρων ἐπὶ ἔργοις·
ὅς τε ἀρυσσάμενος ποταμῶν ἄπο αἰεναόντων,
ὑψοῦ ὑπὲρ γαίης ἀρθεὶς ἀνέμοιο θυέλλῃ,
ἄλλοτε μέν θ' ὕει ποτὶ ἕσπερον, ἄλλοτ' ἄησι
πυκνὰ Θρηϊκίου Βορέω νέφεα κλονέοντος.

*Ταῦτα λέγεται φυσικῶς περὶ τῶν εἰς τὸν ἀέρα
φερομένων ἐκ τῶν ὑγρῶν τῶν ἐπὶ γῆς οἷον ποταμῶν ἢ λιμνῶν ἀναθυμιάσεων . . . τὴν δὲ θέσιν
αὐτοῦ μεταξὺ[1] γῆς καὶ οὐρανοῦ τάσιν ἐκάλεσεν ὡς
καὶ εἰς ὕψος χωροῦντος καὶ εἰς τὰ κοῖλα καταδυο-
μένου τῆς γῆς. τοῦτον δέ φησιν ἀπὸ τῶν ποταμῶν
ἀρυσάμενον τὰς ἀτμίδας αἴρεσθαι ὑπὲρ τὴν γῆν
ἀνάγοντα ταύτας.* διὰ γὰρ τὴν ψῦξιν τὸ θερμὸν
εἴσω τῆς γῆς εἰργόμενον ἀναπέμπει τὰς ἀτμίδας
καὶ ἐκ τῶν ποταμῶν τῶν ἐν αὐτῇ καὶ ἐκ τῶν
φρεάτων· καὶ ἔστιν ἰδεῖν τοῦτο ἐναργῶς ἀποτελού-
μενον ἀπὸ τῶν ἁλυκῶν[2] καὶ φρεατίων ἀνάδοσιν
ἔωθεν τοιαύτην ἀτμώδη. ὁ οὖν ἀὴρ δεχόμενος
ταύτας ὑψοῖ διὰ τῆς τῶν ἀνέμων συστροφῆς, καὶ

[1] αὐτοῦ μεταξὺ F. H. S. after Pertusi: μεταξὺ αὐτήν.

contained in their hides is preserved. So footwear should be made from them. And we should use felt inside, that can mould itself to the feet and give greater warmth ; this is because the extremities need more help to resist the cold, being further from the centre of the body where the innate heat is.

Wyttenbach.

75

At dawn upon the earth from starry heaven
Stretches a mist, wheat-bringing for the fields
Of rich men ; drawing from ever-flowing rivers,
Raised high above the earth by swirling wind,
Sometimes it rains at evening, sometimes blows
When Thracian Boreas drives the thickening clouds.

This is an account, based on natural science, of the exhalations which are carried into the air from wet places on the earth, e.g., rivers and marshes. . . . He used the word " stretching " of its position between earth and heaven because it finds its way to a great height and also sinks into the hollows of the earth. And he says that it draws vapours from rivers and then rises above the earth taking them with it. Owing to the cooling effect (sc., of the north wind at dawn) the heat of the earth is confined in its interior, and causes vapours to rise from its rivers and wells.[a] It is possible to see how this heat clearly effects a vaporous exhalation of this sort at dawn from the water of salt-pans and of wells. The air receives these vapours and carries them up high · by wind-

[a] Cf. Quaest. Nat. 915 B. We have here, as in frag. 76, an example of the widespread view that in the face of cold heat may concentrate itself and so gain in effectiveness.

___

[2] Pertusi : ἁλικῶν.

ὅταν τοῦτο γένηται τοτὲ μὲν ὡς πρὸς ἑσπέραν ὕει, ψυχθείσης[1] τῆς ἀτμίδος, τοτὲ δὲ εἰς πνευμάτων μεταβάλλει συστάσεις.

76

Ibid. 559.

τῆμος τώμισυ βουσίν, ἐπ᾽ ἀνέρι δὲ πλέον εἴη ἁρμαλιῆς· μακραὶ γὰρ ἐπίρροθοι εὐφρόναι εἰσίν.

Διὰ τὸν χειμέριον μῆνα τροφὴν πλείονα κελεύει διδόναι, ταῖς μὲν βουσὶ τὸ ἥμισυ τῆς εἰωθυίας προστιθέντα, τοῖς δ᾽ ἀνθρώποις πλέον ἢ τὸ ἥμισυ· εἰ μὴ ἄρα τὸ ἥμισυ καὶ τὸ πλέον δεῖ συντάττειν, ἵν᾽ ἀμφοτέροις πλέον ἢ τὸ ἥμισυ διδῷ[2] τις τοῦ ἔθους· πέττεται γὰρ χειμῶνος ὄντος ἡ τροφὴ μᾶλλον ἐν μήκει τῶν νυκτῶν· ἥ τε γὰρ θερμότης εἴσω καθειργμένη διὰ τὴν ἔξωθεν πύκνωσιν πλείονα δαπανᾷ· καὶ μῆκος αἱ νύκτες ἔχουσαι πλείονα πέττουσι τροφήν,[3] ἣν "ἁρμαλιὰν" εἶπεν ὡς προσφιλῆ τοῖς τρεφομένοις καὶ εὐάρμοστον.

77

Ibid. 561-563.

ταῦτα φυλασσόμενος . . .

Τοῦτον. καὶ τοὺς ἑξῆς δύο διαγράφει[4] Πλούταρ-

---

[1] διαχθείσης R.   [2] Bernardakis : δίδωσι.
[3] τὴν τροφήν Q.
[4] L : ἀναγράφει ΑΖΒQ : γράφει R. περιγράφει Dimitrijevič.

---

[a] *i.e.*, in addition. The author of this note has strangely

currents. When this happens, sometimes it rains at evening, when the vapour is cooled, but sometimes the vapour changes to form winds.

Sandbach.

76

> Half-rations for the oxen now, but more
> For men : the nights are long, and that's a help.

He tells us to give more food throughout the winter month, adding a half to the cattle's usual quantity, and more than half for the men—unless indeed one should take " half " and " more " together, so that one would give both more than half the normal.[a] Food is better digested in the winter, during the long nights. For not only does the bodily heat, being confined inside by the closing up of the body's surface, consume more,[b] but since the nights are long men digest more food, which the poet called *harmalia* as being welcome and well-adapted [c] (*euharmoston*) to those it nourishes.

Westerwick.

77

> Guarding against this . . .

Plutarch strikes out this verse and the two succeed.

misunderstood Hesiod, who plainly intends the cattle, with no work to do, to replace eating by sleeping, and may have meant the men to have something between half and full rations.

[b] *Cf. Quaest. Conv.* 635 c, *De Defectu Oraculorum*, 411 c.

[c] Adjectives also joined at *Moralia*, 141 A, 697 D (Westerwick).

χος. . . . τούτων δὲ διαγραφέντων ἀκόλουθα τὰ ἑξῆς.[1]

*78

Ibid. 571.

ἀλλ' ὁπόταν φερέοικος.

Ὁ μὲν Θρᾷξ Διονύσιος ἔλεγε φερέοικον τὸν κοχλίαν, ἐπιτιμῆσαι δέ φησιν ὁ Πλούταρχος[2] αὐτῷ
τινα τοῦτο λέγοντι Ἀρκάδα· εἶναι γὰρ ἐν Ἀρκαδίᾳ
τὸν φερέοικον ὁρᾶν μελίττῃ[3] ἐοικότα σμικρότατον
κάρφη καὶ συρφετὸν ἑαυτῷ συνάγοντα στεγοποιεῖ-
σθαι διὰ τοὺς χειμῶνας.[4] βαίνειν δ' ἀνὰ τὰ φυτὰ
θέρους· τὸν δὲ κοχλίαν μὴ φαίνεσθαι θέρους, ἀλλ'
ὁπόταν ὄμβρος γενήται ἀναδυόμενον[5] διὰ τῶν φυτῶν
βαίνειν ἕλκοντα τὸ κοῦφον ἐξόπισθεν ὄστρακον.

79

Ibid. 580.

ἠώς, ἥ τε φανεῖσα πολέας ἐπέβησε κελεύθου
ἀνθρώπους.

Τὸν μὲν οὖν Ὅμηρόν φησιν ὁ Πλούταρχος ἐπι-

[1] All mss. but R have ἑξῆς ᾖ.
[2] ὁ Πλούταρχος added by Maes.
[3] ὁρᾶν μελίττῃ] σκίουρον μυγαλῇ Pertusi, *cf. Et. Magn. s.v.*
φερέοικος· . . . ἔνιοι δὲ ζῷον λευκὸν ὅμοιον γαλῇ ὑπὸ δρυσὶ καὶ
ἐλαίαις (read ἐλάταις with Meineke on Hesychius) γινόμενον,
βαλανηφάγον, οὕτω καλούμενον ὑπ' Ἀρκάδων. Tzetzes found
μελίττῃ in his version of the scholia.
[4] τὸν χειμῶνα L.
[5] φαίνεσθαι after ἀναδ. deleted by F. H. S.

[a] Vv. 561-563 have obscurities and difficulties of which
174

ing ones [a] . . . If they are struck out, the next follow
consecutively.

*78

But when House-bearer . . .

Dionysius of Thrace [b] said that " House-bearer "
means the snail, but ⟨Plutarch (?)⟩[c] says that an
Arcadian criticized him for the statement, asserting
that it is possible to observe the " House-bearer "
in Arcadia—a very small animal like a bee [d] (?),
which collects fluff and rubbish to make itself a
covered nest to meet bad weather, but climbs up the
plants in summer ; the snail, on the other hand, does
not appear in summer, but whenever there is rain it
comes out and climbs about the plants drawing its
light shell behind it.

Maes.

79

The Dawn, whose coming sets upon the road
Many men's feet.

Now Plutarch says that Homer adorned the day

Mazon and Sinclair make light.   Wilamowitz follows Plutarch.
  [b] Frag. 7 (M. Schmidt, *Philologus*, vii [1852], p. 372).
  [c] The name of some authority is missing here, and Plutarch is the authority most frequently quoted in these scholia.
The guess that this note goes back to him may be wrong.
  [d] *Et. Magn.* describes this Arcadian animal as white, like
a weasel, and feeding on acorns ; but it gives another interpretation of the name φερέοικος, which makes the creature
something like a large wasp.   These two meanings are also
in Hesychius.   Photius, quoting the word from Cratinus,
gives the former and adds that the animal's nest is made
among the roots of trees.   Kock thought γαλῇ (weasel) in all
three places a mistake for γαλεώτη (gecko lizard).

175

θέτοις εἰς τέρψιν εὐδοκιμοῦσι κοσμῆσαι τὴν ἡμέ
ραν[1] " κροκόπεπλον " αὐτὴν λέγοντα καὶ " ῥοδοδά
κτυλον "· τὸν δ' Ἡσίοδον μειζόνως ἀπὸ τῶν ἔργων,
ἐφ' ἃ δὴ προϊοῦσα κινεῖ τοὺς ἀνθρώπους καὶ ἀπὸ
τῆς ἐκλύσεως εἰς τὴν ἐνεργὸν μεθίστησι ζωήν.

80

Ibid. 586.

μαχλόταται δὲ γυναῖκες ἀφαυρότατοι δέ τοι ἄν
δρες.

Μαχλόταται δὲ γυναῖκες ὡς ψυχρότεραι τὴν κρᾶ
σιν καὶ διὰ τοῦτο βράδιον[2] ὀργῶσαι ἀναθερμαι
νόμεναι. οἱ δ' ἄνδρες ἀφαυρότεροι[3] διὰ τῆς ἔξωθεν
θέρμης ἀφαυαινόμενοι,[4] φύσει θερμότεροι ὄντες καὶ
ξηρότεροι τῶν γυναικῶν. *τοιαῦτα δὲ καὶ τὸν Ἀλ
καῖον ᾄδειν·

οἴνῳ[5] πνεύμονας[6] τέγγε· τὸ γὰρ ἄστρον περιτέλ
λεται,[7]

ἁ δ' ὥρα χαλεπά,

ἀχεῖ δ' ἐκ πετάλων ἀδέα[8] τέττιξ,

ἀνθεῖ δὲ καὶ σκόλυμος· νῦν δὲ γυναῖκες μιαρώ
ταται,

λεπτοὶ δέ τοι ἄνδρες, ἐπεὶ κεφαλὴν καὶ γόνατα
Σείριος ἄζει.*

---

[1] ἠῶ Pertusi.
[2] βράδιον] ῥᾶον Coraes. Perhaps some words are lost after
ὀργῶσαι. [3] ΑΖΒL : ἀφαυρότατοι TQR.
[4] Wyttenbach : ἀναφαινόμενοι.
[5] So also Athenaeus, 22 e, Macrobius, vii. 15. 13, Eustathius,
1612. 14, Suidas, *s.v.* τέγγε : τέγγε . . . οἴνῳ Plutarch, *Moralia*, 698 Λ, Athenaeus, 430 b. [6] πνεύμονα ZBR.
[7] περιστέλλεται ΑΖΒ. [8] ἀδέα Graeve : τάδεἀν.

with epithets distinguished for their delightfulness, calling it "saffron-robed" and "rosy-fingered"; whereas Hesiod gave it greater honour by referring to the tasks to which its appearance stirs men, bringing a change from relaxation to an active life.

80

Women most lustful, but men are at their weakest.

Women most lustful as being colder in bodily temperament [a] and therefore coming to sexual heat more slowly, but now being warmed (*sc.*, by the heat of the summer). But men are weaker (*aphauroteroi*) through being desiccated (*aphauainomenoi*) by the external heat, being naturally hotter and drier [b] than women.
*Similar sentiments are expressed in Alcaeus' ode :

Wet your lungs with wine : the Dog-star comes again ;
This weather is hard to bear.
Sweetly the cicada chirps among the leaves,
And thistles flower. Women are now at their damnedest,
But men are feeble as Sirius parches
Their head and knees. [c] *

Wyttenbach.

[a] *Cf. Quaest. Conv.* 650 F, but it is the common Greek view that women are colder than men ; *cf.* G. E. R. Lloyd, *J.H.S.* lxxxiv (1964), p. 102.
[b] *Cf. Quaest. Conv.* 650 B.
[c] Frag. 39 Bergk, 94 Diehl, of which this is a somewhat abbreviated and unmetrical version, retaining few traces of the Aeolic dialect. For a full version see Page, *Sappho and Alcaeus*, 303. On the sexual significance of "head and knees" see R. B. Onians, *Origins of European Thought*, pp. 110 ff. The fact that the same unmetrical form of the first line is found also in Athenaeus and Macrobius shows that this false version was current. Neither it nor the other mistakes should be corrected, since they may have been in Pro-

Ibid. 591-596.

καὶ βοὸς ὑλοφάγοιο κρέας μήπω τετοκυίης
πρωτογόνων τ' ἐρίφων· ἐπὶ δ' αἴθοπα πινέμεν
οἶνον,
ἐν σκιῇ ἑζόμενον, κεκορημένον ἦτορ ἐδωδῆς,
ἀντίον ἀκραέος Ζεφύρου τρέψαντα πρόσωπα,
κρήνης τ' αἰενάου καὶ ἀπορρύτου, ἥ τ' ἀθόλωτος,
τρὶς ὕδατος προχέειν, τὸ δὲ τέτρατον ἱέμεν οἴνου.

*Ἐργάτῃ μὲν ἡ τροφὴ πρέπουσα πληροῦν βοείων
κρεῶν τὴν γαστέρα, καὶ ἐν σκιᾷ δὲ καθήμενον καὶ
ὑπὸ τοῦ Ζεφύρου καταπνεόμενον πίνειν ἐπὶ τῇ κρεω-
φαγίᾳ μίξαντα κρηναῖον ὕδωρ τῷ οἴνῳ, τρία μέτρα
πρὸς ἕν· οὐ γὰρ διαρρέουσιν ἀνθρώποις γράφει
δίαιταν, ἀλλ' ἐκπονοῦσι τὴν γῆν καὶ αὐτουργοῖς καὶ
βιωτικοῖς· τοῖς γὰρ τοιούτοις οὐδὲν προσφορώτερον
τῆς ἰσχυρᾶς καὶ δυσφθάρτου ταύτης τροφῆς, οὐ
χιόνων[1] δεομένοις[2] οὐδὲ ῥιπιδίων, ἀλλὰ φυσικῆς
εὐπνοίας, οἷος ὁ ἀκραὴς Ζέφυρος, καθαρὸς ὤν[3]· τὰ
γὰρ βόρεια λήγοντα συνάπτεται τοῖς δυτικοῖς πνεύ-
μασι.*

Τὸ δὲ ταύτην ἐπαινέσαι τὴν κρᾶσιν τοῦ οἴνου
καὶ τοῦ ὕδατος ἄτοπον εἶναι δοκεῖ· λέγεται γάρ,

ἢ πέντε πίνειν ἢ τρί'[4] ἢ μὴ τέσσαρα·

τὸ δὲ τρία μιγνύναι πρὸς ἕν τοιοῦτον εἶναι δοκεῖ.

---

[1] σκιάδων D. Heinsius.
[2] δεομένοις AQL : δεομένης ZBR.
[3] After ὤν AZBQ have ζέφυρος : Pertusi omits, with LR.
[4] Gaisford (as at *Moralia*, 657 c) : τρία πίνειν ἢ πέντε.

---

clus' text. Plutarch cites the first line correctly (*Moralia*,

81

And meat of a leaf-fed heifer that has not calved
And first-born kids : and fire-red wine to drink
Seated in shade, when food has sated the heart,
Facing a fresh west wind ; and draw from a spring,
That never fails but flows away unmuddied,
Three measures of water, and add a fourth of wine.

*The food suits a working man—to fill his belly
with beef and then to sit in the shade, fanned by the
west wind, and drink after his meat, mixing spring
water with his wine, three measures to one. The
poet is not writing a way of life for the dissolute, but
for tillers of the ground, working farmers with a
living to get. For such there is nothing more suitable
than this strong food that does not easily spoil ; they
need no snow [a] or fans, but only a natural pleasant
breeze, like the " fresh," [b] i.e., clean west wind. (For
north winds, as they die out, are associated with
breezes from the west.)*

But to praise these proportions of wine and water
seems to be strange. There is a saying,

Drink either five or three or else not four.[c]

But to mix three to one seems to be a drink of this

698 A), and may therefore not be responsible for the quotation here.
   [a] Used, like ice to-day, to cool drinks.
   [b] The word ἀκραής has here been understood to mean
" unmixed " ; more probably it is a compound of ἄημι
" blow " and means " blowing strongly " or " blowing on
the heights " (Frisk, Gr. Etym. Wörterbuch, s.v.).
   [c] R. Stromberg, Greek Proverbs, p. 97 ; also quoted,
Quaest. Conv. 657 c and by Athenaeus, 426 d, Plautus,
Stichus, 707 : three measures of water and two of wine make
five, or two of water and one of wine make three.

179

ἀλλ᾽ ἐκεῖναι μὲν αἱ κράσεις, δύο πρὸς ἓν καὶ τριῶν
πρὸς δύο, κατὰ λόγους διπλάσιον καὶ ἡμιόλιον, τοὺς
ἡγεμόνας τῶν πολλαπλασίων καὶ ἐπιμορίων, εἰς
μέθην εἰσὶ πινόντων· αὕτη δὲ σωφρόνως πινόντων.

Καὶ μὴν καὶ περὶ ὕδατος ἄλλοι μὲν γράφουσιν[1] εἰς
σταθμὸν ἀποβλέποντες, ἐκλεγόμενοι τὸ κουφότερον·
καί τινες καὶ ὑδροστάτας κατασκευάζουσι, δι᾽ ὧν
τὸ βαρὺ καὶ κοῦφον ὕδωρ κρίνουσι—καίτοι πολλα-
χοῦ κοῦφον μέν ἐστι πονηρὸν δέ, ὡς ἐν Χαλκίδι
Πλούταρχος ἱστορεῖ τὸ τῆς Ἀρεθούσης. οἱ δὲ καὶ
τὸ ῥαδίως οἴνῳ κεραννύμενον δοκιμάζουσιν ὕδωρ
ἄριστον, πολλῆς δεόμενον πείρας καὶ διαφόρων
οἴνων εἰς τὸ[2] φωραθῆναι τοιοῦτον ὄν. ἄλλοι δὲ
εἰς κεράμειον ποτήριον ὕδωρ ἐμβαλόντες ἐῶσι δι᾽
ὅλης μεῖναι νυκτός, εἶτα γενομένης ἡμέρας ὁρῶσιν
εἴ τινα ἐντὸς τῆς κύλικος ἔχει γεώδη περιφέρειαν
συστᾶσαν καὶ μελανίζουσαν· καὶ τοῦτο σημεῖον τίθενται τῆς τοῦ ὕδατος φαυλότητος, οὐδ᾽ οὗτοι πεῖραν παραδιδόντες εὐπόριστον. πάντων δὴ οὖν τῶν
τοιούτων ἁπλούστερον ὁ Ἡσίοδος κελεύει τῷ γεωρ-
γικῷ μιγνύναι τῷ οἴνῳ ὕδωρ ἐκ κρήνης ἀπορρύτου,
ἵν᾽ ᾖ κινούμενον καὶ λεπτὸν[3] καὶ ἀθόλωτον, ἀλλὰ
μὴ γεῶδες.

[1] γράφουσιν] κρίσιν ποιοῦσιν Pertusi doubtfully.
[2] μὴ after τὸ omitted by Wyttenbach, or placed before
τοιοῦτον. τὸ φ. τ. οὐκ ὄν Duebner.

last kind. Those other two mixtures, however, two
parts to one and three parts to two, standing in the
ratios of 2 : 1 and 1½ : 1, the first in the series of
multiples and superparticulars,[a] are suitable for men
drinking to the point of intoxication ; this of Hesiod's
is for sober drinkers.

Again with regard to water one set of people write
with an eye on the scales, choosing the lightest, and
some even construct hydrostatic balances [b] which
they use to determine what water is heavy and what
light—yet in many places the water, though light, is
bad, as Plutarch records of the water of Arethusa
in Chalcis. Others adjudge best the water that
readily mixes with wine, a thing needing much ex-
periment with different wines, before a water can
be detected as being such. Others again put water
into an earthenware cup and let it stand over-
night ; then they look the next day to see whether
any earthy blackish ring has formed inside the cup ;
they count this a sign of the water's inferiority. They
too enjoin a test that is not easy to carry out.
Hesiod's advice is simpler than all tests of this sort :
he tells the farmer to mix with his wine water from
a spring that flows freely away,[c] so that its movement
will make it light and unmuddied, without earthiness.

---

[a] 1½, 1⅓, 1¼ . . .
[b] According to the dictionaries the Greek word does not occur elsewhere in this sense. The instrument meant is perhaps
the hydrometer described under the name of ὑδροσκόπιον by
Synesius, *Epist.* 15, *cf.* A. Fitzgerald, *Letters of Synesius*,
p. 99.
[c] Line 595 is also quoted at *Quaest. Conv.* 725 D, where a
spring that flows easily away is said to be free of earthiness.

---

[3] καὶ λεπτὸν ZBQ : χαλεπὸν R λεπτὸν ATL.

82

Ibid. 639-640.

οἰζυρῇ ἐνὶ κώμῃ,
"Ἀσκρῃ.

Κεῖται μὲν οὖν ὑπὲρ τὴν ὁδὸν ἣν βαδίζουσιν οἱ ἐπὶ τὸ Μουσεῖον ἀπιόντες ἡ "Ἀσκρη. τοῦ δ' Ἑλικῶνος ἐκκειμένου τοῖς ἀνέμοις, καὶ θαυμαστὰς μὲν ἀναπαύλας ἔχοντος ἐν θέρει δυσηνέμου δ' ὄντος ἐν χειμῶνι, τὴν "Ἀσκρην ἐν τῷ μεσημβρινῷ κειμένην τοῦ ὄρους τῆς μὲν ἐκ τῶν ἀνέμων ἀπολαύειν βίας ἐν δὲ τῷ θέρει τὸ εὔπνουν μὴ ἔχειν. ἀοίκητον δ' αὐτὴν¹ ὁ Πλούταρχος ἱστορεῖ καὶ τότε εἶναι, Θεσπιέων ἀνελόντων τοὺς οἰκοῦντας, Ὀρχομενίων δὲ τοὺς σωθέντας δεξαμένων· ὅθεν καὶ τὸν θεὸν Ὀρχομενίοις προστάξαι τὰ Ἡσιόδου λείψανα λαβεῖν καὶ θάψαι παρ' αὐτοῖς, ὡς καὶ Ἀριστοτέλης φησὶ γράφων τὴν Ὀρχομενίων πολιτείαν.

*83

(a) *Ibid.* 643.
(b) Plutarch, *De Audiendis Poetis,* 22 f.

νῇ' ὀλίγην αἰνεῖν.

(a) "Αἰνεῖν" δέ τινες ἀντὶ τοῦ παραιτεῖσθαι παρέλαβον, τοῦ χαίρειν λέγειν ἢ παρέρχεσθαι ἢ οὐκ αἰνεῖν ὡς δεινήν, ὥσπερ " ἐπαινὴν Περσεφόνειαν."

¹ αὐτὴν Q : αὐτὸ all other mss.

ª Aristotle, frag. 565 Rose ; see a fuller account in *Septem Sapientium Convivium,* 162 c–e.

82

In a wretched village,
Ascra.

Now Ascra lies above the road followed by those
going to the temple of the Muses. Helicon is exposed
to the winds and has some remarkably fine summer-
resorts, but is unpleasantly windy in winter ; Ascra,
lying on the southern side of the mountain, gets all
the violence of the gales, but does not enjoy pleasant
breezes in summer. Plutarch records that it was
uninhabited even in those days, the Thespians having
destroyed the inhabitants ; the survivors found refuge
at Orchomenos. Hence the god ordered the men of
Orchomenos to take Hesiod's remains and bury them
in their own territory, as Aristotle says in his book
on the Constitution of Orchomenos.[a]

*83

Praise a small ship.

(a) Some took " praise " in the sense of " decline,"
i.e., say good-bye to or pass over or *not* praise, as being
dreadful, as in " commendable (*epainê*) Persephonê."[b]

D. Heinsius. A dubious fragment : the sign prefixed to
the scholion in A indicates that it is not derived from Proclus,
and the passage printed as frag. 83 (*b*) shows that its matter
falls in the category of " what every schoolboy knows." It
may be, however, that Plutarch's commentary, although
not the source of the scholion, nevertheless expressed the
same views.

[b] An example of etymology from an opposite, as in *lucus
a non lucendo*. The true meaning of the traditional epithet
ἐπαινή is uncertain ; ancient guesses connected it with ἔπαινος
(praise) and αἰνός (dreadful).

(b) Χάριεν δὲ καὶ τὸ τὴν χρείαν τὴν τῶν ὀνομάτων συνοικειοῦν τοῖς ὑποκειμένοις πράγμασιν,
ὡς οἱ γραμματικοὶ διδάσκουσιν, ἄλλην πρὸς ἄλλα
δύναμιν λαμβανόντων, οἷόν ἐστι

νῆ᾽ ὀλίγην αἰνεῖν, μεγάλῃ δ᾽ ἔνι φορτία θέσθαι.

τῷ[1] μὲν γὰρ αἰνεῖν σημαίνεται τὸ ἐπαινεῖν, αὐτὸ δὲ
τὸ[2] ἐπαινεῖν ἀντὶ τοῦ παραιτεῖσθαι νῦν κέχρη-
ται, καθάπερ ἐν τῇ συνηθείᾳ καλῶς φαμὲν ἔχειν
καὶ χαίρειν κελεύομεν ὅταν μὴ δεώμεθα μηδὲ λαμ-
βάνωμεν. οὕτω δὲ καὶ τὴν "ἐπαινὴν Περσεφόνειαν" ἔνιοί φασιν ὡς παραιτητὴν εἰρῆσθαι.

84

Ibid. 651-662.

ἔνθα δ᾽ ἐγὼν ἐπ᾽ ἄεθλα δαΐφρονος Ἀμφιδάμαν-
τος, κτλ.

Ταῦτα πάντα περὶ τῆς Χαλκίδος καὶ[3] τοῦ Ἀμφι-
δάμαντος καὶ τοῦ ἄθλου καὶ τοῦ τρίποδος ἐμβεβλῆ-
σθαί φησιν ὁ Πλούταρχος οὐδὲν ἔχοντα χρηστόν.
τὸν μὲν οὖν Ἀμφιδάμαντα ναυμαχοῦντα[4] πρὸς
Ἐρετριέας ὑπὲρ τοῦ Ληλάντου ἀποθανεῖν· ἆθλα δ᾽
ἐπ᾽ αὐτῷ καὶ ἀγῶνας θεῖναι τελευτήσαντι τοὺς
παῖδας[5]· νικῆσαι δ᾽ ἀγωνιζόμενον τὸν Ἡσίοδον καὶ
ἆθλον μουσικὸν τρίποδα λαβεῖν καὶ ἀναθεῖναι τοῦτον
ἐν τῷ Ἑλικῶνι, ὅπου καὶ κάτοχος ἐγεγόνει ταῖς

---

[1] τό most mss.
[2] αὐτῷ δὲ τῷ some mss. Paton suggested the omission of
the seven words from σημαίνεται to ἐπαινεῖν.
[3] καὶ added by Pertusi.

(b) It is also an admirable procedure to relate the use of words to the subject-matter, as the teachers of literature instruct us to do, when these words take on different meanings in different connexions, as with

> Praise a small ship, put your goods in a large one.

By the word " praise " (*ainein*) is meant " commend " (*epainein*), and " commend " is itself here used as the equivalent of " decline," [a] just as in our everyday language, when we do not need something or do not accept it, we say " that's very nice " or " good-bye to that." Similarly some people say that " commendable Persephonê " is so called because we should decline her invitation.[b]

84

> There to the games of wise Amphidamas, etc.

Plutarch says that all this about Chalcis, Amphidamas, the games, and the tripod has been interpolated, and contains nothing of value. The story is that Amphidamas died in a naval battle with the Eretrians over the Lelantine Plain ; contests and games for the dead man were held by his sons ; Hesiod competed and won, and received, as a prize for poetry, a tripod which he dedicated on Helicon, where he had been possessed by the Muses ; the

[a] Text and exact meaning are uncertain. Babbitt in L.C.L. translates not " here " but " nowadays." The usage, however, was an old one, cf. Aristophanes, *Frogs*, 508, κάλλιστ', ἐπαινῶ.

[b] Not wishing to leave this life for the underworld.

---

[4] μονομαχοῦντα K. F. Hermann, but the error, if it is one, may be that of the scholiast himself.

[5] Thus QULR Trinc. : ἀγῶνες ἐγένοντο τελευτήσαντος παρὰ τῶν ἑαυτοῦ παίδων AZB.

Μούσαις, καὶ ἐπίγραμμα ἐπὶ τούτῳ θρυλοῦσι. πάντα
οὖν ταῦτα ληρώδη λέγων ἐκεῖνος ἀπ' αὐτῶν ἄρχεται
τῶν εἰς τὸν καιρὸν τοῦ πλοῦ συντεινόντων, " ἤματα
πεντήκοντα."

85

Ibid. 706.

εὖ δ' ὄπιν ἀθανάτων μακάρων πεφυλαγμένος εἶναι.

*Τοῦτο μετὰ τοὺς περὶ γάμου λόγους προοίμιόν
ἐστι τῶν ῥηθησομένων παιδευμάτων· δεῖ γὰρ πρὸ
πάντων στοχάζεσθαι τοῦ κεχαρισμένου τοῖς θεοῖς.*
καὶ γάρ, ὡς¹ Πλάτων φησίν, ὁ βλέπων εἰς τὸ θεῖον ἐξ
ἀσελγημάτων² φυλάττειν ἑαυτὸν σπουδάζει καὶ πάντων ἀσεβημάτων· καὶ γὰρ ὁ τοὺς ἀγαθοὺς ἄνδρας
αἰσχυνόμενος, παρόντων αὐτῶν ἀπέχεται τούτων,
μή τί γε ὁ³ τοὺς θεούς. καὶ τί λέγω τοὺς ἀγαθοὺς
αὐτούς; ἀλλὰ καὶ εἰκόνας ἀγαθῶν τινες σέβονται
καὶ ὑπ' αὐταῖς ὀκνοῦσί τινα πονηρὰν πρᾶξιν πρᾶξαι,
ὡς ἡ μὴ προσιεμένη τὸν ἐραστὴν ἑταίρα δρᾶσαί τι
ἄσχημον ὑπὸ τῇ τοῦ⁴ Ξενοκράτους εἰκόνι τοῦ σώ-
φρονος.

¹ F. H. S. : καί.
² αὐτοῦ deleted by Wyttenbach after ἀσελγημάτων.
³ μή τί γε Westerwick : ὁ F. H. S. : μὴ ὅτι γε.
⁴ τῇ τοῦ Pertusi : τῇ AZB : τοῦ QL.

ᵃ Dio Chrysostom, ii. 11, Proclus, *Chrestomathia* (Homer,
vol. v, p. 101 O.C.T.), *A.P.* vii. 53, Ἡσίοδος Μούσαις Ἑλικωνίσι
τόνδ᾽ ἀνέθηκεν, ὕμνῳ νικήσας ἐν Χαλκίδι θεῖον Ὅμηρον. Plutarch

inscription is constantly quoted.[a] Plutarch says that all this is silly stuff, and begins with the lines concerned with the right season for navigation, " Fifty days, etc."

85

Beware the vengeance of the blessed gods.

Following what he says about marriage, this is the introduction to the pieces of instruction he is about to give. For to aim at what is pleasing to the gods should take precedence of all else. Indeed, as Plato says, a man who has regard to the Deity takes care to keep himself from improper acts and all forms of impiety ; for one who feels shame before good men, refrains from such things in their presence, let alone one who feels shame before the gods. And why talk merely of good men themselves ? There are some who respect even the portraits of good men and are loath to commit any evil beneath them, like the hetaira who would not allow her lover to behave improperly beneath the portrait [b] of Xenocrates, who was famous for his chastity.

Westerwick : on ground of interest in Xenocrates.

will certainly have disbelieved in the possibility of a contest between Hesiod and Homer ; he may have found it impossible that Hesiod could be contemporary with an Amphidamas who died in the circumstances stated (but see J. Defradas, *Banquet des sept sages*, p. 103). Thucydides, i. 13, places the first Greek sea-battle in the early 7th century ; the Lelantine War is assigned to the late 8th century (W. G. Forrest, *Historia*, 6 (1957), pp. 160-175). Modern scholars argue that the falsity of the legend does not prove the spuriousness of the lines, which do not imply it.
    [b] Either a painting or a bust.

Ibid. 707-708.

μηδὲ κασιγνήτῳ ἶσον ποιεῖσθαι ἑταῖρον·
εἰ δέ κε ποιήσῃς, μή μιν πρότερος κακὸν ἔρξῃς.

*Τὴν κατὰ φύσιν ἡμῶν σχέσιν πρὸς ἀλλήλους τῆς
κατὰ προαίρεσιν εἶναι τιμιωτέραν φησὶν οὗτος ὁ
λόγος. καὶ γὰρ τὴν μὲν ἀποθέσθαι ἐφ' ἡμῖν· τῆς
δὲ τὸν δεσμὸν ἐπήγαγε τὸ πᾶν αὐτὴν[1] φυλάττειν
βέβαιον· δεῖν οὖν μείζονα τιμὴν νέμειν ἀδελφοῖς ἢ
ἑταίροις· καὶ γὰρ καὶ τοῖς πατράσιν οὕτω φίλα
πράξομεν, οὓς[2] δεῖ μετὰ θεοὺς τιμᾶν ὡς ἀγάλματα,
φησίν, ὄντας[3] ἑφέστια[4] θεῶν.* οὕτω δὲ καὶ τὴν
οἰκείαν πόλιν τινὲς εἶπον ἐγγυτέραν[5] τῆς μὴ οἰκείας,
κἂν μᾶλλόν τις ἐν ταύτῃ τυγχάνῃ τιμώμενος, διὰ
τὴν κατὰ φύσιν σχέσιν. καὶ ὀρθῶς ὁ Παναίτιος,
πολίτην αὐτὸν Ἀθηναίων ποιεῖσθαι σπευδόντων,
εἶπε τῷ σώφρονι μίαν πόλιν ἀρκεῖν. καὶ ὁ τῶν
Σπαρτιατῶν βασιλεὺς πρὸς τὸν Ἀρκάδα τὸν ξένον
εἰπόντα πρὸς αὐτὸν ὅτι φιλολάκων οἴκοι καλοῖτο,
"κάλλιόν τοι," εἶπεν, "εἰ φιλόπολις ἐκαλοῦ μᾶλλον
ἢ φιλολάκων." . . .

[Τούτῳ δ' ἀκόλουθον τὸ ἑξῆς, ὅτι εἴ τινα ποιησό-
μεθα φίλον, ἀπροσκρούστους εἶναι δεῖ πρὸς αὐτόν.]
*καὶ γὰρ ἡ τῶν Πυθαγορείων παραίνεσις οὐχ ὅτι
προτέρους ἁμαρτάνειν εἰς φίλον διακωλύσειεν ἄν,

---

[1] αὐτὴν AZBTL : αὐτὸν Q Pertusi.
[2] Duebner : πραξαμένοις L : -μένων Q : -μένῳ A : πράττοντας ZBT.   [3] ὄντας] ὁ Πλάτων Cobet.
[4] Gaisford : ἐφέστια or ἐφ' ἑστία.
[5] Herwerden : ἐγγιωτέραν.

86

Don't make a friend the equal of your brother.
But if you should, don't harm him unprovoked.

*This sentence says that our natural relationship
to one another is more valuable than one that is of
our own choice, since we can at will give up the latter,
whereas the bond of the former is imposed by the
Universal Power, and firmly preserves it. We ought,
then, to esteem our brothers more than our friends.
We shall thereby also do what is pleasing to our
fathers, whom we should honour next after the gods,
as being (in Plato's words) " household images of the
gods." ^{a} * Similarly some have said that a man's own
city is closer to him than that which is not his own,
even if he is more honoured in the latter, because of
the natural relation. And Panaetius was right, when
the Athenians were eager to give him their citizenship, to answer that " one city was enough for a
sensible man." ^{b} And the Spartan king replied to a
visitor from Arcadia, who told him that at home he
had the name of being a friend of Sparta, " it would
do you more credit to be called a friend of your own
country." ^{c} . . .

[The next line follows on from this, to the effect
that if we do make anyone a friend we should not
offend him.] *Indeed, the advice of the Pythagoreans
would not merely prevent us from being the first to
wrong a friend, but also encourages us to bear

---

^{a} *Laws*, 931 A, ἐφέστιον ἵδρυμα, but ἄγαλμα is in the context.
Cf. frag. 46, and F. M. Cornford, *Plato's Cosmology*, p. 100.
^{b} Frag. 27 van Straaten. As a Rhodian, he had the right
to Athenian citizenship, since the two cities had ἰσοπολιτεία,
Polybius, xvi. 26.
^{c} *Cf. Life of Lycurgus*, chap. 20, *Apophthegm. Lac.* 221 D.

PLUTARCH'S MORALIA

ἀλλὰ καὶ τὰ ἁμαρτήματα τοῦ φίλου πράως φέρειν,¹
ἕως ἂν δυνώμεθα, παρακελεύεται. καὶ ἔχει τὸ παράγγελμα πρὸς τῇ ἄλλῃ δικαιοσύνῃ καὶ τὸ ἔμφρον·
εἰκὸς γὰρ ἡμᾶς καὶ θαρρήσαντας τυγχάνειν τινὰ
τῷ φίλῳ, καὶ δεῖ μηδὲν εἰς αὐτὸν ποιεῖν λῦον τὴν
σχέσιν.*

*87

Ibid. 709.

μηδὲ ψεύδεσθαι γλώσσης χάριν.

Μὴ μόνον παραιτεῖσθαι τὸν φίλον λυπεῖν διά
τινος ἔργου προσκρούοντα, ἀλλὰ μηδὲ ψευδόμενον
πρὸς αὐτὸν φαίνεσθαι διὰ περιττὴν καὶ ἀνόνητον
τῆς γλώττης ὁρμήν· καὶ γὰρ τοῦτο λυπηρὸν καὶ
προάγον εἰς ἀπέχθειαν· ὁ γὰρ ψευδόμενος καὶ ἀπα-
τῶν οὐ φίλος· ὅθεν τοῦτο παραιτητέον. ὁ καὶ
Πλάτων εἶπε, τὸν ἑκουσίως ψευδόμενον ἄπιστον
εἰκότως εἶναι, τὸν δ' ἄπιστον ἄφιλον. μέγα οὖν
σημεῖον ἤθους οὐ φιλητικοῦ τὸ ψευδολόγον πρὸς ὃν
οἴεται φίλον εἶναι² καὶ ἐπιθολοῦν τὴν φιλίαν.

88

Ibid. 717-718.

μηδέ ποτ᾽ οὐλομένην πενίην θυμοφθόρον ἀνδρὶ
τέτλαθ᾽ ὀνειδίζειν, μακάρων δόσιν αἰὲν ἐόντων.

Τὴν πενίαν ἢ³ ἡμεῖς ἑαυτοῖς προξενοῦμεν διχῶς ἢ

¹ πράως φέρειν Bernardakis : προσφέρειν AQL ὑπομένειν καὶ
φέρειν ZB.
² εἶναι placed before πρὸς ὃν by ZB.
³ ἢν ZBR.

190

patiently the friend's faults, so long as we can.[a] And
the precept is not only one of morality ; it contains
good sense into the bargain, for we are likely to have
entrusted some of our interests to a friend, and we
should not act towards him in any way that would
make a breach in the relationship.*

Wyttenbach. Plutarch refers at *De Fraterno Amore*, 491 B,
to his discussion of v. 707 " elsewhere," presumably in this
commentary. The passage should be compared.

*87

Don't lie to please your tongue.

Not only avoid hurting a friend through offending
him by some action, but do not be discovered lying
to him either through an unnecessary and unprofi-
table impulse of the tongue. For this, too, is hurting
and leads to enmity. For the liar and cheat is no
friend. So this must be avoided. Which is what
Plato said, namely that the willing liar is naturally
not trusted, and the man who is not trusted has no
friends.[b] So it is a strong indication of a character
not made for friendship to speak untruth to another
whom he believes to be a friend and so to muddy the
waters of friendship.

Westerwick, on ground of diction.

88

Never reproach a man with poverty,
Accursed and heart-breaking gift of heaven.

Poverty is either of our own making, in one of

[a] *Carmen Aureum*, 7-8, μηδ' ἔχθαιρε φίλον σὸν ἁμαρτάδος
εἵνεκα μικρῆς, ὄφρα δύνῃ. [b] *Laws*, 730 c.

δι' ἀργίαν ἢ δι' ἀσωτίαν πενόμενοι, ἢ ἀπὸ τοῦ
παντὸς ἔχομεν ἀποκληρωθεῖσαν ἡμῖν. ταύτην οὖν
ἀξιοῖ μὴ ὀνειδίζειν, ὡς τήν γε παρ' ἡμᾶς ἀξίαν
εἶναι μυρίων ὀνειδῶν οὐ βοηθουμένην ὑφ' ἡμῶν.
οὕτω δὴ καὶ νόσον τὴν μὲν εἱμαρμένην οὐ δεῖ
ὀνειδίζειν, τὴν δ' ἀπὸ τῆς ἡμετέρας ἀκρασίας διὰ
τὴν ἀκρασίαν ὀνειδιστέον, οἷς ἐξὸν ὑγιαίνειν οὐχ
ὑπάρχει τοῦτο δι' αὐτήν.

89

Ibid. 719-721.

γλώσσης τοι θησαυρὸς ἐν ἀνθρώποισιν ἄριστος
φειδωλῆς, πλείστη δὲ χάρις κατὰ μέτρον ἰούσης.
εἰ δὲ κακὸν εἴποις, τάχα κ' αὐτὸς μεῖζον ἀκού-
σαις.

*Ὁ μὲν θησαυρὸς τῆς γλώττης ἐστὶν ἡ κρύψις τῶν
νοημάτων ἢ ἐν τῇ ψυχῇ καὶ τῶν φαντασιῶν τῶν
μὴ γενομένων ἐκφόρων ὑπὸ τῆς γλώττης προπετῶς
κινουμένης· δεῖ γὰρ τὴν κρίσιν[1] ἐπιμετρεῖν τῇ
γλώσσῃ τὸν καιρὸν τῆς κινήσεως, ἀλλ' οὐ ταύτην
κυρίαν εἶναι ἑαυτῆς. τὸ δὲ πλείστην μὲν αὐτῆς[2]
εἶναι χάριν μετρίας οὔσης, ἀρχὴν δὲ γίνεσθαι μειζό-
νων καὶ ἀλγεινοτέρων ἀκουσμάτων τὴν προπέτειαν
αὐτῆς, ἄμφω παρέστησε, καὶ ὅτι αἱρετὸν τοῦτο τὸ
μόριον καὶ ὅτι φευκτόν·* ὡς Πιττακόν φασι, πέμ-
ψαντος αὐτῷ τοῦ Ἀμάσιδος ἱερεῖον καὶ ἀξιώσαντος
ἀντιπέμψαι τῶν μορίων αὐτοῦ[3] τὸ κάλλιστον ἅμα
καὶ χείριστον, ἐξελόντα τὴν γλῶσσαν ἀποστεῖλαι.

---

[1] κίνησιν Gaisford.   [2] Duebner : ἑαυτῆς.
[3] QU : αὐτῷ AZBLR.

two ways, laziness or extravagance, or we have it allotted to us by the Universe. It is this latter kind he thinks we should not taunt a man with, since the kind that we have ourselves to thank for deserves a million reproaches, if we do nothing to relieve it. Similarly one should not make a disease for which fate is responsible a subject of reproach, but when a disease comes from our own self-indulgence, reproach is called for, because of that self-indulgence : owing to it we are not well, although we could have been.

Patzig ; *cf. De Audiendis Poetis*, 23 F.

89

A man's best treasure is a thrifty tongue ;
It earns much thanks wagging in moderation.
If you speak ill, you may hear something worse.

The tongue's treasure is the concealment in the mind of thoughts and fancies, when they are not divulged by unconsidered movements of the tongue ; for the tongue should not be its own master, but our judgement should determine the right time for it to be set in motion. To say that it earns great thanks when moderated, and that its impulsiveness is the cause of our hearing more damaging and painful things said of ourselves, shows it to be simultaneously true that this member is desirable and that it is undesirable. So they say that when Amasis sent Pittacus a sacrificial animal and asked him to return to him that part of it which was at once the finest and the worst, the latter removed the tongue and sent it back.[a]

[a] Cf. *De Audiendo*, 38 B, *Sept. Sapient. Conv.* 146 F (in these passages Bias, not Pittacus), *De Garrulitate*, 506 C ; and *Gnomologium Vaticanum*, 131.

καὶ ἔοικεν ἡ φύσις τὸ μὲν τῶν ὀδόντων ἕρκος αὐτῆς
θεῖναι[1] πρόσθεν, κατακλείουσα μαλακὴν αὐτὴν οὖσαν
καὶ εὐκίνητον, τὸν δ' ἐγκέφαλον ἄνωθεν θεῖναι, παρὰ[2]
τοῦ λόγου τὸ μέτρον αὐτῇ δεῖν ὑπάρχειν ἐνδεικνυ-
μένη.[3]

90

Ibid. 724-725.

μηδέποτ' ἐξ ἠοῦς Διὶ λείβειν αἴθοπα οἶνον
χερσὶν ἀνίπτοισιν.

Ἐν μὲν οὖν Σπάρτῃ τοῖς πολίταις οἱ[4] εἰς ἀρχὴν
καθισταμένοι[5] ἔφοροι[6] προεκήρυττον μὴ τρέφειν
μύστακας, ἵνα τοὺς τὸ φαῦλον τοῦτο καὶ εὐτελὲς
παραβάντας μειζόνως κολάζωσιν[7]· ὁ δ' Ἡσίοδος
νίπτεσθαι τὰς χεῖρας παραινῶν πρὸ τοῦ σπένδειν
ἐνδείκνυται τὸν περὶ τοῦτο μὴ πεισόμενον μείζονος
ἄξιον εἶναι καταγνώσεως, ὡς ἀνεπιτήδειον πρὸς
παιδείαν.

91

Ibid. 733-734.

μηδ' αἰδοῖα γονῇ πεπαλαγμένος ἔνδοθεν οἴκου
ἑστίῃ ἐμπελαδὸν παραφαινέμεν, ἀλλ' ἀλέασθαι.

Ταῦτα τῆς ἀπαιδευσίας ὄντα ἔκγονα, κἂν σμικρὰ

[1] Duebner : αὐτῆς (or αὐτῇ) εἶναι.
[2] F. H. S. : ἄνωθεν εἶναι παρ' οὗ (παρ' ἧς R : παρὰ U).
[3] Bernardakis : ἐνδεικνυμένην.
[4] πολίταις added by Maes, οἱ by Pertusi, *cf. Life of Cleomenes,* chap. 9.   εὖ μὲν οὖν Σπαρτιάταις Ruhnken.
[5] Ruhnken : καθισταμένοις.
[6] οἱ before ἔφοροι deleted by Pertusi.
[7] κολάζοντες παραβαίνειν μείζονα κωλύσωσιν Pertusi after Wyttenbach.

And it seems that nature has put the " fence of teeth "
in front of the tongue, shutting it up because it is
weak [a] and easily set in motion, and has placed the
brain above it to indicate that the check on it should
come from our reason.

Wyttenbach.

90

> Never at dawn pour fire-red wine to Zeus
> With unwashed hands.

In Sparta the ephors on entry into office used to
issue a proclamation against growing moustaches,
with the object of heavily punishing those who trans-
gressed in this small and insignificant matter.[b] Hesiod
in enjoining washing of the hands before libation indicates that the man who is not going to comply
with this deserves severe censure, as being unfitted
for education.[c]

Wyttenbach.

91

> And privy parts, if splashed with seed indoors,
> Disclose not near the hearth : that act avoid.

These results of lack of education, although minor

[a] The Greek word μαλακός is a kind of pun, literally
meaning " soft " and metaphorically " lacking self-control."
[b] Cf. Moralia, 550 B, Life of Agis and Cleomenes, chap.
30, 808 D, Aristotle, frag. 539 ; Annual of British School at
Athens, xii, Plate X.
[c] If this note derives from Plutarch, it must be a garbled
version of what he wrote. In the Life the object of the ban
on moustaches is said to be that of making the citizens
obedient even in small matters.

ἦ, δεῖ παραφυλάττειν, καλῶς τοῦ Πλουτάρχου λέγοντος, ὅτι καθάπερ ἐν λόγοις τὸ μὴ σολοικίζειν οὐ
θαυμαστόν, ἀλλὰ τὸ σολοικίζειν καταγέλαστον, καὶ
ἐν τοῖς ἔργοις οὐ τὸ μὴ πράττειν τὰ τοιαῦτα ἐπαινετόν, ἀλλὰ τὸ πράττειν ἐπονείδιστον· *δεῖν οὖν τὸν[1]
μεμολυσμένον ἀπὸ γονῆς ἀποκρύπτειν τὰ αἴτια τοῦ
μολυσμοῦ καὶ μὴ γυμνοῦν[2] ἐγγὺς τῆς ἑστίας· βωμὸς
γὰρ καὶ αὕτη τῶν θεῶν καὶ καθημερινῶν θυσιῶν
καὶ σπονδῶν ὑποδοχή.*

92

Ibid. 742-743.

μηδ᾽ ἀπὸ πεντόζοιο θεῶν ἐν δαιτὶ θαλείῃ
αὖον ἀπὸ χλωροῦ τάμνειν αἴθωνι σιδήρῳ.

Παρακελεύεται τοίνυν μὴ ἐν εὐωχίαις θεῶν τέμνειν τοὺς ὄνυχας· τεμόντας[3] γὰρ καὶ καθηραμένους[4]
ἐκείναις[5] δεῖ παραβάλλειν ἀλλ᾽ οὐκ ἐν αὐταῖς τοῦτο
ποιεῖν.

*Καὶ γὰρ τρόπον τινὰ νεκροῦν ἐστι τῶν ἐν ἡμῖν
τινα μορίων ἀφαιροῦντας[6] αὐτὰ τοῦ σώματος, ὡς
συμπεφυκότα ᾧ[7] ποτε τρέφεται. χρὴ οὖν, εἰ εὐσεβήσομεν,[8] μηδὲ[9] ταῦτα τὰ[10] προαποθνήσκοντα τοῦ
λοιποῦ σώματος ἀποστερεῖν ζωῆς ἐν ταῖς ἄσβεστον
ἐχόντων τὴν ζωὴν θεῶν εὐωχίαις[11]· ἀλλότριον γὰρ
ἐκείνων τὸ τοιοῦτον.*

[1] τὸν added by Pertusi.   [2] ? γυμνοῦσθαι Pertusi.
[3] Bernardakis : τέμνοντας.
[4] Bernardakis : καθ.ρ.μένους A κεκαθαρμένους ZBQL καθ-
αιρουμένους R.
[5] Bernardakis : ἐκείνῳ.
[6] QLR : ἀφαιροῦνται A. εἰ ἀφαιροῦνται Schultz.
[7] ZB : ὡς.   [8] εὐσεβήσομεν added, *e.g.*, by F. H. S.

196

matters, should be avoided. Plutarch well says that although there is nothing marvellous in not talking ungrammatically, yet ungrammatical talk is ridiculous; similarly although it is not praiseworthy *not* to do things of this kind, yet it is reprehensible to do them. *A man, then, when polluted by semen should hide the parts responsible for the pollution, and not bare them near the hearth, for the hearth, too, is an altar of the gods and the recipient of our daily offerings and libations.*

92

From five-branch at rich banquet of the gods
Do not with shining steel cut dry from quick.

So he enjoins men not to cut their nails at the festivals of the gods. For one ought to have cut them and made oneself clean before coming to those festivals, not do these things at them.[a]

* And indeed in a way it brings death to certain parts of ourselves when we remove them from the body, since they have become united with that which at one time nourishes them. So if we are to act rightly (?) even these parts, that die before the rest of the body, ought not to be deprived of life at the festivals of the gods, who have a life that cannot be extinguished. Such an action is foreign to their festivals.*

D. Heinsius and Scheer claimed the first sentence as Plutarchean, Westerwick the rest.

[a] *Cf. De Iside*, 352 E.

9 μή σε LR.   10 τὰ added by Post.
11 ZB rewrite this passage from νεκροῦν to εὐωχίας and are followed in whole or in part by editors.

*93

Ibid. 744-745.

μηδέ ποτ' οἰνοχόην τιθέμεν κρητῆρος ὕπερθε
πινόντων.

Πολλὰ τοιαῦτα καὶ τοῖς Πυθαγορείοις ἐλέγετο·
ζυγὸν μὴ ὑπερβαίνειν καὶ χελιδόνα μὴ εἰσδέχεσθαι
καὶ μαχαίρᾳ πῦρ μὴ σκαλεύειν, συμβολικῶς παραι-
νοῦντας[1] τῶν ὀργιζομένων μὴ ἐπεγείρειν διὰ λόγων
παροξυντικῶν τὸ πάθος, καὶ φλυάρους μὴ εἰσάγειν
εἰς τὸν οἶκον καὶ λάλους καὶ μὴ δεῖν τὸ δίκαιον
ὑπερβαίνειν. τοιοῦτον οὖν καὶ τὸ ἐπιτιθέναι τῷ
κρατῆρι τὴν οἰνοχόην συμβολικὸν παίδευμα· τουτέστι μὴ ἐπίπροσθεν ἄγειν τοῦ κοινοῦ τὸ ἴδιον. ὁ
μὲν γὰρ κρατὴρ προὔκειτο κοινὸς ἐν ταῖς τραπέζαις,
ἐκ δὲ τῆς οἰνοχόης ἀρυόμενοι ἔπινον οἱ συνδει-
πνοῦντες.

94

Ibid. 746-747.

μηδὲ δόμον ποιῶν ἀνεπίξεστον[2] καταλείπειν
μή τοι ἐφεζομένη κρώξῃ λακέρυζα κορώνη.

*Οἱ μὲν ὅτι δεῖ οἰκίας πρὸ χειμῶνος συντελεῖν—ὁ
γὰρ κρωγμὸς τῆς κορώνης χειμῶνος σύμβολον—οἱ

---

[1] παραινοῦντα U, Pertusi : παραινοῦνται Heinsius, but there
may be an anacoluthon.
[2] The scholia give a variant ἀνεπίρρεκτον.

---

[a] Quoted, *Moralia*, 28 β, as a line typical of those commonly thought to need explanation.
[b] *Cf. Quaest. Conv.* 727 c, where an interpretation is mentioned which made this a warning against " slanderers and
whisperers."

*93

Don't put the ladle down above the bowl
When men are drinking.[a]

Many precepts of this sort were also given by the
Pythagoreans—not to step over a yoke, and not to
receive a swallow,[b] and not to stir the fire with a
knife,[c] symbolically enjoining us not to stir up further
by exasperating words the passion of men who are
growing angry, and not to introduce into our house
drivellers and chatterboxes, and that we ought not
to transgress the right. And this matter of putting
the ladle over the bowl is a similar piece of symbolical
instruction—that is to say it means " do not put
private interest before common interest." For the
mixing-bowl used to stand among the tables for all
to share, while it was from the ladle that those who
were dining together took their wine and drank.

Wyttenbach, Westerwick. Plutarch, *Sept. Sap. Conv.*
156 D, understands Hesiod to have meant " Don't fail to
keep the cups full " ; hence Wilamowitz thinks that this
scholion does not derive from him.

94

When building, do not leave the house untrimmed,
Lest croaking rook [d] should find a perch and caw.

*Some say that one ought to finish houses before
the winter. The cawing of the rook is a sign of winter.

[c] Mentioned, *Quaest. Rom.* 281 A, *De Iside*, 354 E.
[d] The word may mean crow, but it is the rook that appears
in Greece in the winter. On the difficulties of this passage
see Sinclair's note. The true meaning of the injunction can
be gathered from Michael Glycas, *Lines written in Imprison-
ment*, 20-21, ὅταν ὁ κόραξ πούποτε καθίσῃ καὶ φωνάξῃ, ἐκεῖ σημαίνει θάνατον καὶ χωρισμὸν ἀθρόον.

δ' ὅτι μὴ ἀτελῆ δεῖ[1] τὸν οἶκον ἐᾶν, μὴ ψόγον ἐπ-
αγάγῃ παρ' ἄλλων, οὓς τῇ κορώνῃ ἀπείκασεν, ὡς
πολλὰ ἂν φθεγξαμένους νεμεσῶντας ἐπὶ τῷ ἐλλιπεῖ.[2]*
δεῖ δὲ καὶ ἐπὶ τὰ ἄλλα τὸ παράγγελμα διατείνειν
καὶ μηδὲν τῶν ἡμετέρων ἔργων ἀτελὲς περιορᾶν
φερόμενον ἀλλ' ἑκάστῳ τὸ προσῆκον ἐπάγειν τέλος.

95

Ibid. 748-749.

μηδ' ἀπὸ χυτροπόδων ἀνεπιρρέκτων ἀνελόντα
ἔσθειν μηδὲ λόεσθαι.

Θυσίαν ταύτην ὁ Πλούταρχος πρόχειρον καὶ
καθημερινὴν εἶπεν ὀρθῶς, ἀφ' ὧν μέλλομεν ἐσθίειν
ἱερὰ πάντα ποιοῦντας διὰ τοῦ ἀπάρξασθαι. καὶ γὰρ
αἱ τῶν ἱερῶν τραπεζώσεις τοῦτο εἶχον· ἀπαρξά-
μενοι γὰρ ἀπ' αὐτῶν ἐδαίνυντο. *χρῆναι δὲ καὶ
ἐπὶ τῶν λουτρῶν τὸ αὐτὸ δρᾶν· ἐλούοντο δὲ περι-
χεόμενοι " κατὰ κρατός τε καὶ ὤμων"· χρῆν οὖν
καὶ τούτου πρότερον ἀφορίσαι τι τῆς[3] ἡμετέρας
χρήσεως ἱερὸν[4] θεῶν,[5] καὶ οὕτω τὸ λοιπὸν εἰς τὴν
ἀναγκαίαν χρείαν παραλαμβάνειν.*

96

Ibid. 750-752.

μηδ' ἐπ' ἀκινήτοισι καθίζειν, οὐ γὰρ ἄμεινον,
παῖδα δυωδεκαταῖον, ὅ τ' ἀνέρ' ἀνήνορα ποιεῖ,
μηδὲ δυωδεκάμηνον· ἴσον καὶ τοῦτο τέτυκται.

[1] Westerwick : δεῖν. [2] Bernardakis : ἐλλειπεῖ.
[3] τῆς AQR : πρὸ τῆς ZBL.
[4] Duebner : ἱερῶν or τοῖς ἱεροῖς. ὡς ἱερὸν Wyttenbach.
[5] θεοῖς ZB.

Others that one ought not to leave the house unfinished for fear of attracting censure from others, whom
the poet compared to the rook, because they would
make a great noise in their indignation at your
failure to finish.* But we ought to extend the injunction to other things [a] and not suffer any of our tasks
to run on unfinished, but give everything its proper
completion.

Patzig.

95

> Don't take and eat food from the cooking-pot,
> Nor bathing-water, without a sacrifice.

Plutarch rightly called this an easy daily sacrifice,
when we render holy all we are going to eat by making
an offering from it.[b] For this was a feature of ceremonies where a table was spread for a god : the
worshippers used to make an offering from it and
then dine. *And one ought to do the same when
bathing ; of old they bathed by having water poured
" over head and shoulders." [c] We ought therefore
first to set apart from our own use a portion of the
water, too, as sacred to the gods, and then take the
rest for our necessary purposes.*

96

> Don't seat a boy of twelve days (better not !)
> On what may not be moved—it unmans the man—
> Nor yet a twelve-month old : that's just as bad.

[a] Cf. frag. 49.
[b] At Quaest. Conv. 703 D, it is explained that an offering
should be made to the fire which had heated the pot. But
Hesiod probably meant that there should be a sacrifice before
a new pot was taken into use (Mazon).   [c] Odyssey, x. 362.

Μήποτε δὲ κάλλιον Πλούταρχος,[1] ὅτι μὴ δεῖ[2] τὰ νεογνὰ ἀκίνητα ἐᾶν καὶ ἀποτίθεσθαι ἐν ἀκινήτοις· ἀσθενέστερα γὰρ γίνεται· κινεῖν δ' αὐτὰ ὅτι μάλιστα. κἂν ἐπί τινων αὐτά τις καθίζῃ,[3] ἐπὶ[4] κινουμένων καθίζειν[5] καὶ σαλεύειν διὰ τούτων, οἷά τισιν εὐκίνητα κλινίδια μεμηχάνηται πρὸς τὴν τῶν παιδίων εὐνήν.

97

Ibid. 753.

μηδὲ γυναικείῳ λουτρῷ χρόα φαιδρύνεσθαι.

Μὴ δεῖν συναπογυμνοῦσθαι ταῖς γυναιξὶ τοὺς ἄνδρας· πρὸς γὰρ τῷ ἀσχήμονι καὶ ἀπόρροιαί τινες ἐκ τῶν γυναικείων σωμάτων καὶ περιττωμάτων[6] χωροῦσιν, ὧν ἀναπίμπλασθαι τοὺς ἄνδρας μολυσματῶδές ἐστι· καὶ τοῖς εἰς τὸν αὐτὸν ἀέρα εἰσιοῦσι καὶ τοῖς εἰς τὸ αὐτὸ ὕδωρ ἀνάγκη τούτων ἀπολαύειν.

98

Ibid. 757-759.

μηδέ ποτ' ἐν προχοῆς ποταμῶν ἅλαδε προρεόντων, μηδ' ἐπὶ κρηνάων οὐρεῖν, μάλα δ' ἐξαλέασθαι, μηδ' ἐναποψύχειν. τὸ γὰρ οὔ τοι λώϊόν ἐστιν.

Ταῦτα διαγράφει Πλούταρχος, ὡς εὐτελῆ καὶ ἀν-

---

[1] ZB add φησι.   [2] D. Heinsius : δεῖν.
    [3] Pertusi : καθιζάνῃ.

But it may be that Plutarch gives a better explanation, namely that young babies should not be left unmoved or put down on something immovable,[a] since they thus become weakly. They ought to be kept on the move as much as possible, but if one does set them down on anything, they should be set on moving things and be swayed by them, as in the rocking cradles that some people have devised for children to sleep in.

97

Let men not cleanse themselves in the women's bath.

Men should not strip along with women. Besides the impropriety, there are certain effluences that proceed from the female body and its excretions with which it is a kind of defilement for men to be infected. Both those who enter into the same air and those who enter into the same water are necessarily affected by them.

Wyttenbach.

98

Never in the flow of rivers running seaward
Make water, nor at springs (but shun the act),
Nor cleanse thyself therein. 'Tis better not . . .

Plutarch strikes out these lines as being paltry and

---

[a] Cf. Plato, Laws, 789 B-E, for this advice. The other interpretation given by the scholiast, namely that the prohibition is against seating a child on a grave, is in fact correct.

---

[4] ἐπὶ added by Wyttenbach.
[5] Pertusi : καθιζάνειν. [6] περιττώματα Duebner.

ἄξια παιδευτικῆς Μούσης· *μὴ οὐρεῖν ἐν προχοαῖς
ποταμῶν ἢ ἐπὶ κρηνῶν μηδ' ἀποπατεῖν, τοῦτο γὰρ
τὸ ἀποψύχειν.*

99

Ibid. 760-764.

ὧδ' ἔρδειν· δεινὴν δὲ βροτῶν ὑπαλεύεο φήμην

. . . .

. . . . θεός νύ τίς ἐστι καὶ αὐτή.

[Τοῦτο τὸ τέλος ἐστὶ τῶν παραγγελμάτων, ἱκανὸν
εἰς τὸ παιδεῦσαι ἡμᾶς τὸ ἑαυτῶν ἦθος, εὐλαβουμέ-
νους τὴν φήμην.] *οὐ γὰρ ὅσον ἀρετῆς οἱ ἄνθρωποι
σφάλλονται, τοσοῦτον καὶ κρίσεως ἀρετῆς, φησὶν
ὁ Πλάτων . . . ἔτι δὲ καὶ ἀρξαμένην ταύτην παῦσαι χαλεπόν· εἰώθασι γὰρ οἱ ἄνθρωποι πολλαπλα-
σιάζειν ἃς ἂν παραλάβωσι φήμας καὶ ἐκ σμικρῶν
μεγάλας ποιεῖν.* καὶ τέλος προσέθηκεν ὅτι κινδυ-
νεύει καὶ ὡς ἐπὶ τὸ πλεῖστον ἀληθὴς εἶναι πᾶσα¹
φήμη " ἣν λαοὶ πολλοί² φημίξωσι," καὶ διὰ τοῦτο
ἔχειν τι καὶ αὐτὴν θεῖον· πολλάκις γοῦν ὁ μὲν ἄρ-
ξας αὐτῆς οὐκ ἐπιστήμων³ ἐστίν, εὔστοχος δ' αὐτὴ⁴
δι' αὐτῶν ἀναφαίνεται τῶν ἀποβαινόντων, ὥστε εἰκότως δεῖ φυλάττεσθαι τὴν κακὴν φήμην. κατὰ⁵
τοῦτο οὖν χρήσιμον τὸ δεῖν καὶ δόξαν ὑφορᾶσθαι
τὸν παιδευόμενον. οὐ γὰρ ἁπλῶς ἀληθὲς ὃ ἔλεγε
Γοργίας· ἔλεγε δέ, " τὸ μὲν εἶναι ἀφανὲς μὴ τυχὸν

¹ πᾶσι Q, Pertusi.
² πολλοὶ λαοὶ Q (with Hesiod).

unworthy of an educative Muse—*not to urinate in
the flowing water of rivers or at springs, and not to
defecate there ; that is what " cleanse " means.^a *

99

> So do, and so avoid an ill repute . . .
> Repute, too, is herself a goddess.

[This is the end of his maxims, and enough to
cause us to educate our characters by being careful
of our repute.] *For men, says Plato, are not as
bad at judging of virtue as they are at practising it.
. . . Further it is hard to put a stop to a reputation
once started, since men are accustomed to multiply
reports they receive and make much out of little.*
Finally the poet added that probably for the most
part every report " that many folk recount " is in
fact true, and therefore has something divine about
it. Certainly the originator of a report is often without knowledge, but the report itself proves to be
right on the mark as a result of its very consequences. There is good reason, then, why we should avoid
ill-repute. The maxim that the pupil should beware even of opinion is useful when this is considered.
What Gorgias said is not true without qualification ;
he said : " To be without seeming to be, lacks notice,

---

^a An odd mistake : ἀποψύχειν must, as in Homer, mean
"wash off sweat." For the meaning of προχοαί, not "mouths,"
but " flowing waters," see Bacchyl. 6. 3, ἐπ' Ἀλφεοῦ προχο-
αῖσ[ι νικῶν, and other passages collected by W. Bühler, Die
Europa des Moschos, p. 80.

---

³ ἐπιστήμων added, e.g., by F. H. S.
⁴ αὐτὴ Q : αὕτη.   ⁵ Duebner : καὶ.

τοῦ δοκεῖν, τὸ δὲ δοκεῖν ἀσθενὲς μὴ τυχὸν τοῦ
εἶναι." παρὰ γὰρ τοῖς πολλοῖς καὶ τὸ δοκεῖν ἰσχὺν
ἔχει καὶ τὰ ἐκ τοῦ δοκεῖν ἀποβαίνοντα δυσχερῆ
δείκνυται οὐκ ὄντα ὀλίγα. μᾶλλον οὖν, ὡς Ξενοκράτης ἔλεγε τοῦ μὲν[1] φίλον ᾿Αλέξανδρον ἔχειν
ἕνεκα μηδ' ἂν τὸν δάκτυλον κινῆσαι, τοῦ δὲ μὴ
ἐχθρὸν πάντα ἂν πρᾶξαι, οὕτω καὶ ῾Ησίοδος τῆς
μὲν παρὰ τοῖς πολλοῖς δόξης ἀξιοῖ ποιεῖσθαι λόγον
μηδένα, τῆς δ' ἀδοξίας, ἵνα μὴ συμβῇ, πάντα ποιεῖσθαι λόγον.

100

Plutarch, *Life of Camillus*, chap. 19.

Περὶ δ' ἡμερῶν ἀποφράδων εἴτε χρὴ τίθεσθαί τινας εἴτε[2] ὀρθῶς ῾Ηράκλειτος ἐπέπληξεν ῾Ησιόδῳ τὰς
μὲν ἀγαθὰς ποιουμένῳ τὰς δὲ φαύλας, ὡς ἀγνο-
οῦντι φύσιν ἡμέρας ἁπάσης μίαν οὖσαν, ἑτέρωθι δι-
ηπόρηται.

101

Scholia, 765-766.

ἤματα δ' ἐκ Διόθεν πεφυλαγμένος εὖ κατὰ μοῖραν
πεφραδέμεν δμώεσσι.

Αἱ περὶ τῆς τῶν ἡμερῶν ἐκλογῆς καὶ ἀπεκλογῆς
παραινέσεις ἔχουσι μὲν τὰς ἀρχὰς ἐκ τῶν παρα-

---

[1] οὖν after μὲν deleted by F. H. S.
[2] εἴτε Reiske : εἴτε μὴ.

to seem to be without being lacks effect." [a] That needs qualification because with the masses even seeming is powerful, and its disagreeable consequences are shown to be not a few. Better be guided by Xenocrates' remark that he would not even lift a finger to be Alexander's friend, but would do anything to avoid having him as an enemy. [b] Similarly Hesiod tells us not to pay any attention to the good opinion of the masses, but to take every care to avoid getting a bad name.

Wyttenbach.

100

I have discussed elsewhere the question whether one should reckon certain days as inauspicious, or whether Heraclitus [c] was right in reproving Hesiod for considering some days good and others bad, on the ground that he did not know that the nature of all days is one and the same.

Sandbach. Taken by Bernardakis to refer to περὶ ἡμερῶν (Lamprias Catalogue no. 150), but the discussion is as likely to have been in the commentary on Hesiod, or in both places.

101

Watching the Zeus-appointed days right well,
Reveal them to your slaves.

The injunctions given about choosing and avoiding particular days have their origin in observations that men have made, but some injunctions have prevailed

---

[a] Diels-Kranz, *Frag. d. Vorsokratiker*, 82 B 26.
[b] Frag. 105 Heinze.
[c] Diels-Kranz, *Frag. d. Vorsokr.* 22 B 106.

τηρήσεων, ἄλλαι δὲ παρ' ἄλλοις[1] ἐκράτησαν, ἐπεὶ
καὶ παρ' Ὀρφεῖ λέγονταί τινες αὐτῶν διακρίσεις
καὶ ἐν τοῖς Ἀθηναίων πατρίοις διωρίσθησαν, αἱ
μὲν ἀγαθαί τινες αἱ δὲ φαῦλαι μέσαι δέ τινες εἶναι.
καὶ οὐχ ὅλας ἡμέρας μόνον ὑπέλαβόν τινες εὐκαιρίαν ἔχειν πρὸς καταρχὰς τινων πράξεων ἀλλὰ καὶ
μόρια τῆς ἡμέρας, ὁτὲ μὲν τὰ ἑωθινὰ ἐπαινοῦντες
ὁτὲ δὲ τὰ περὶ δείλην ὀψίαν, ὅπου δὲ καὶ τοῖς μὲν
θεοῖς οἰκεῖα τὰ πρὸς μεσημβρίαν[2] εἰρήκασιν ἥρωσι
δὲ τὰ μετὰ μεσημβρίαν. ὁ γοῦν Ἡσίοδος τὰς
πολλὰς ἐν τούτοις εἰδὼς τῶν κατ' αὐτὸν παρατηρή-
σεις, εἰς τὰς ἡλίου κινήσεις καὶ σελήνης καὶ τὰς
πρὸς ἀλλήλους σχέσεις αὐτὸς ἀποβλέψας ἀνάγει τὰς
τῶν ἐπιτηδείων καὶ ἀνεπιτηδείων διαφοράς, ἀφ' ὧν
μάλιστα γίνεται πάντα μὲν τὰ θνητὰ τῶν[3] κινουμένων, ἄλλα δὲ μᾶλλον ἄλλων. πρὸς δὲ τὰς[4] περιόδους αὐτῶν οἰκείως ἢ ἀλλοτρίως ἔχει.[5]

Δηλοῖ δὲ καὶ τῶν φυτῶν τὰ μὲν σελήνῃ συγ-
κινούμενα τὰ δὲ ἡλίῳ· τὰ μὲν γὰρ ῥόδα καὶ ἴα καὶ
μετὰ τούτων τὰ ἡλιοτρόπια πρὸς ἥλιον ἀνίσχοντα
τρέπει τὰ φύλλα καὶ πρὸς καταδυόμενον ὡσαύτως
εἰς ἑσπέραν ῥέποντα, τὰ δὲ τῶν ἐλαιῶν φύλλα διδάσκει καὶ τοὺς γεωργικοὺς γεγονέναι τροπὰς ἢ
χειμερινὰς ἢ θερινὰς διὰ τῆς ἑαυτῶν περιστροφῆς,
ὁτὲ μὲν ἄνω τὸ μελάντερον ἰσχόντων, ὁτὲ δὲ τὸ

---

[1] Kern : ἄλλαις.
[2] ? πρὸ μεσημβρίας.
[3] QR omit τῶν, perhaps rightly.

among some people and others among others. We see
that distinctions between days are also recorded in the
works of Orpheus, and it was determined by the ancestral customs of the Athenians that some days were
good, some bad, and others intermediate. And certain people have supposed that not only whole days,
but also times of day were opportune for the putting
in hand of certain actions, approving sometimes the
early morning hours and sometimes those of late
evening. They have also said that the hours up to
noon are appropriate to the gods, those after noon to
the heroes.[a] Hesiod, then, knew most of the contemporary observations in this field, and himself took
the step of referring the differences between propi-
tious and unpropitious days to the movements of the
sun and moon and their mutual aspects : all mortal
things in the realm of change have in these [b] their
chief source of becoming, but some more than others ;
and having an affinity for their revolutions or being
alien to them, are favourably or unfavourably affected.

This is shown indeed by plants, some of which move
in conjunction with the moon, others with the sun.
Roses and violets and also the heliotropes turn their
leaves to the rising sun and similarly to the setting
sun, inclining towards the west. And the leaves of
the olive tell the farmers by turning over that the
winter or summer solstice has come, having the
darker side up at one time and the lighter at another.

---

[a] Diog. Laert. viii. 33. This is a Pythagorean injunction,
cf. M. P. Nilsson, *Entstehung d. griech. Kalenders*, p. 22.

[b] According to another reading, " all mortal things have
in these movements, etc."

---

[4] Post: πρὸς τὰς δὲ τὰς (T omits δὲ τὰς). πρὸς τὰς δὲ Pertusi.
[5] After ἔχει all mss. have τῶν γινομένων, perhaps a variant
for τῶν κινουμένων above.

λευκόν. τὰ δὲ τῶν αἰλούρων ὄμματά φασι καὶ τὰ
σπλάγχνα τῶν μυῶν πάντες[1] φθίνειν μὲν σελήνης
ληγούσης, αὔξεσθαι δὲ ἀκμαζούσης· . . . .[2] εἰ μὲν
περὶ πανσέληνον ἐξαιρεθείη, τὴν μὲν γόνιμον ἀρχὴν
ἔτι φυλάττει καὶ αὖθις βλαστάνει κατὰ τὴν προσήκουσαν ὥραν, εἰ δὲ φθινούσης, ἄγονον γίνεται. καὶ
ἁπλῶς τὰ μὲν πληρουμένης εὐθηνεῖται τὰ δὲ ληγούσης αὐτῆς, τοῖς μὲν ὠφελίμου τῆς ὑγρότητος
οὔσης ἣν διαχεῖ τὸ σεληναῖον φῶς αὐξανόμενον,[3]
τοῖς δὲ βλαβερᾶς.

102

Aulus Gellius, xx. 8.

Id etiam, inquit, multo mirandum est magis, quod
apud Plutarchum in quarto in Hesiodum commentario
legi : cepetum[4] revirescit et congerminat decedente
luna, contra autem inarescit adulescente ; eam cau-
sam esse dicunt sacerdotes Aegyptii cur Pelusiotae
cepe non edint,[5] quia solum olerum omnium contra
lunae augmenta[6] atque damna vices minuendi et
augendi habeat contrarias.

¹ πάντες ATQL : πάντων ZBR, Pertusi.
² Lacuna noted by Schultz.
³ ? αὐξανομένοις.
⁴ cepe tum some mss. (see Skutsch, Archiv für Lexicogra-
phie, xii, p. 199).
⁵ Hertz : edunt.
⁶ Hertz : aucta.

ᵃ Cf. De Iside, 376 ᴇ for cats' eyes. At Quaest. Conv.
670 ʙ it is not the entrails of mice, but the livers of shrews

Everybody says, too, that the eyes of cats and the entrails of mice contract as the moon wanes, and increase as it grows to the full.[a] If . . .[b] should be taken up at the full moon it still retains its principle of growth and sprouts again at the proper season, but if taken up when the moon is waning, it is sterile. And in general some things flourish when the moon is waxing, and others when it is waning, since the moisture shed by the increasing light of the moon[c] is beneficial to some things but harmful to others.

Schultz, Pertusi.

102

Much more remarkable, he said, is what I have read in the fourth book of Plutarch's commentary on Hesiod : an onion-bed grows green again and puts out shoots when the moon is waning, but shrivels when it is waxing.[d] The Egyptian priests say that this is the reason why the inhabitants of Pelusium do not eat onions : alone of all vegetables its alternations of increase and decrease are contrary to the changes of the moon.[e]

that contract with the moon, and this peculiarity of the shrew (μυγαλῆ) is alluded to also by Pliny, *Nat. Hist.* ii. 109, and Iamblichus, *De Mysteriis*, 5. 8. Probably here too Plutarch himself spoke of shrews, but it would not be right to alter the scholiast's μυῶν to μυγαλῶν.

   [b] The name of a plant is missing.
   [c] Frequently mentioned by Plutarch, *e.g.*, *Moralia*, 658 F, 917 F, and the note there.
   [d] *Cf. De Iside*, 353 E.
   [e] H. Schultz, *Die handschriftliche Überlieferung der Hesiodscholien*, p. 68, associated this passage with the scholion on 765-768.

Scholia, 770-771.

πρῶτον ἔνη τετράς τε καὶ ἑβδόμη ἱερὸν ἦμαρ·
τῇ γὰρ Ἀπόλλωνα χρυσάορα γείνατο Λητώ.

Τὴν δὲ σὺν ἀνίερον Αἰγύπτιοί φασιν, ὅτι μίξεσι
χαίρει κρυπτομένης ὑπὸ τοῦ ἡλίου τῆς σελήνης.
καὶ μήποτε καὶ τοῦτο τὸ ζῷον, ὡς χθόνιον καὶ
γεννήσεσι χαῖρον, οἰκεῖόν ἐστι πρὸς ταύτην εἰκότως
μάλιστα τῆς θεοῦ τὴν συνοδικὴν φάσιν,[1] ἣν πρὸς
ἥλιον λόγον ἔχειν ὡς θήλεος πρὸς ἄρρενά φασι.
[μετὰ δὲ ταύτην . . . ἐπαινεῖ τὰς τρεῖς· τὴν ἔνην
. . . τὴν τετράδα τὴν ἑβδόμην, καὶ πάσας ἱερὰς λέ-
γων], τὴν δὲ ἑβδόμην καὶ ὡς Ἀπόλλωνος γενέθλιον
ὑμνῶν, διὸ καὶ Ἀθηναῖοι ταύτην ὡς Ἀπολλωνιακὴν
τιμῶσι δαφνηφοροῦντες καὶ τὸ κανοῦν ἐπιστέφοντες[2]
καὶ ὑμνοῦντες τὸν θεόν.

104

Ibid. 780-781.

μηνὸς δ᾽ ἱσταμένου τρισκαιδεκάτην ἀλέασθαι
σπέρματος ἄρξασθαι· φυτὰ δ᾽ ἐνθρέψασθαι ἀρίστη.

Καλῶς ἐπέστησεν ὁ Πλούταρχος ὅτι τὸ σπεῖραι
καὶ τὸ φυτεῦσαι οὐχ ὑπὸ τῶν αὐτῶν ἔοικεν ὠφελεῖ-
σθαι. τὸ μὲν γὰρ σπέρμα δεῖ καταβληθὲν κρυφ-
θῆναι πρῶτον εἴσω τῆς γῆς καὶ σαπῆναι καὶ οὕτως
ἑαυτοῦ διαδοῦναι τὴν δύναμιν εἰς τὴν περικρύψασαν

---

[1] R : φασίν AZBL φύσιν QT.
[2] Scaliger : ἀποστρέφοντες.

*103

Holy the new moon, fourth day, and the seventh,
When Leto bore Apollo, golden-glaived.

The Egyptians say that the pig is unholy because
it enjoys copulation when the moon is hidden by the
sun. And may it not be that this animal, being of
the earth and enjoying procreation, is connected particularly with that conjunctive phase of the moon-
goddess, who they say is related to the sun as female
to male ? [After this he praises the three days, the
new moon, . . . the fourth, the seventh, calling them
all holy], and singing the praises of the seventh also
as Apollo's birthday,[a] for which reason the Athenians,
too, honour this day as Apolline by carrying branches
of bay and garlanding the sacred basket and singing
the god's praises.

Pertusi, doubtfully.

104

Avoid the thirteenth day of waxing moon
For sowing : yet it's best for making trees grow.[b]

Plutarch well observed that it seems that the same
conditions are not favourable both for sowing and
for planting. The seed, after being cast on the
ground, needs first to be hidden in the earth and to
rot and then to transfer its power into the earth

---

[a] Cf. Moralia, 292 F, 391 F, 717 D, 738 D.
[b] The meaning of this phrase is uncertain. By φυτά
Hesiod probably intended mainly fruit-trees and vines. ἐνθρέψασθαι is taken by Evelyn-White, Mair, and Sinclair to
mean " plant," but the scholiast seems to have understood
it as " cause to grow " ; Mazon believes the meaning is
" cultivate."

213

αὐτὸ γῆν, ἵν' ἐξ ἑνὸς πυροῦ τυχὸν ἢ κριθῆς γένηται
πλῆθος. διὸ καὶ ὑετοῦ δεῖσθαι καὶ πάχνης αὐτό φασι τὴν ἀρχὴν πιεζόντων ἔσω καὶ χεόντων τὰς ἐν
αὐτῷ φυσικὰς δυνάμεις. τὸ δὲ φυτὸν ῥιζωθὲν βλα-
στῆσαι χρὴ καὶ ἀναδοῦναι τὸν ἐν τῇ ῥίζῃ κρυπτό-
μενον λόγον, οἷον διοιχθείσῃ[1] διὰ φωτός· *ὥστ'
εἰκότως τὴν τρισκαιδεκάτην πρὸς μὲν τὸ σπείρειν
ἀνεπιτήδειον εἶναι, πρὸς δὲ τὸ φυτεύειν ἐπιτηδείαν·
διὸ καὶ τὸ '' ἐνθρέψασθαι '' οἰκείως ἔχει πρὸς τὴν
φυτείαν· τὸ γὰρ προκαλέσασθαι[2] τὸν ῥιζικὸν λόγον
καὶ εἰς ἐπίδοσιν ἄγειν καὶ βλάστην ἐσήμηνε διὰ τοῦ
ὀνόματος, πρὸς ἃ συντελεῖ πλεῖον ὂν τὸ ἐκ τῆς σελήνης ἐν ταύτῃ φῶς.*

105

Ibid. 782-784.

ἕκτη δ' ἡ μέσση μάλα σύμφορός[3] ἐστι φυτοῖσιν,
ἀνδρογόνος δ' ἀγαθή· κούρη δ' οὐ σύμφορός ἐστιν,
οὔτε γενέσθαι πρῶτ' οὔτ' ἂρ γάμου ἀντιβολῆσαι.

Τὴν ἐκκαιδεκάτην μέσην ἕκτην εἰπὼν ὠφέλιμον
εἶναι τοῖς φυτοῖς φησιν δι' ἣν εἴπομεν αἰτίαν· τὸ
γὰρ φῶς θερμὸν ὂν τὸ σεληναῖον καὶ ὑγρὸν προ-
καλεῖται[4] τὴν βλάστην αὐτῶν. τῶν δ' ἀνθρώπων
ἄρρεσι μὲν σπέρμασι σύμφορον θήλεσι δ' ἀσύμφο-
ρον· αἴτιον δὲ τούτων ὅτι τὸ μέν ἐστι ξηρότερον τὸ
δ' ὑγρότερον τῶν σπερμάτων, οἷς καὶ αὐτὸ τὸ
ἄρρεν διαφέρει τοῦ θήλεος· καὶ διὰ ταῦτά φασι καὶ

_____

[1] διοιχθείσῃ F. H. S. : διοικηθείσῃ (διοικηθήσῃ L). διοχευ-
θείσῃ Gaisford : διοικηθείσῃ Duebner.
[2] Wyttenbach : προσκαλέσασθαι.
[3] μάλ' ἀσύμφορός mss. of Hesiod.
[4] Gaisford : προσκαλεῖται.

that has covered it,[a] so that from a single grain of, say, wheat or of barley there may come a quantity. Hence they say it needs rain and frost at first, to exert pressure on the natural powers inside it and to cause them to flow out. A tree, on the other hand, after being set, must put out shoots and send up the principle of structure hidden in its root, when that is unlocked, so to speak, by light. *So it is reasonable that the thirteenth should be unsuitable for sowing but suitable for planting trees. It follows that the phrase " for making trees grow " is appropriate to their planting ; by it the poet meant calling forth the principle contained in the root and bringing about increase and leaf-growth, to which the brighter moonlight of this day contributes.*

105

> The middle sixth is helpful for the trees,[b]
> And good to get a man [c] : but bad for girls,
> Both to be born on, and for wedding-day.

The sixteenth day, which the poet calls the " middle sixth," he says is useful for trees,[b] for the reason we have given : the light of the moon, being warm and moist, encourages them to put out shoots. But in the case of human beings it is helpful for male seeds, the reverse for female. The reason for this is that male seeds are dryer, female moister, a characteristic difference of male and female.[d] And they

---

[a] The seed is supposed to fertilize the earth, by an analogy with the supposed fertilization of an animal's womb by the semen. [b] See note b on the previous fragment.

[c] Although the scholiast clearly thought conception to be meant, Hesiod had birth in mind.

[d] Cf. Quaest. Conv. 650 B.

τὰς συλλήψεις τὰς μὲν βορείων πνευμάτων ὄντων
γινομένας εἶναι ἀρρενογόνους τὰς δὲ νοτίων θηλυ-
γόνους. καὶ μέντοι καὶ τὰς διαρθρώσεις τῶν
θηλέων ἐμβρύων βραδυτέρας γίνεσθαι ἢ τῶν ἀρρέ-
νων διὰ τὸ πλῆθος ἐκεῖ τῆς ὑγρότητος, μὴ ῥᾳδίως
κρατουμένης ὑπὸ τῆς δημιουργούσης ἐν τῇ θερμότητι φύσεως. φυσικῶς οὖν εἴρηται τὴν ἑκκαιδεκά-
την ἀρρενογόνον μὲν ἄριστον εἶναι θήλεσι δ' ἀσύμ-
φορον· ἔχει δέ τινα καὶ πρὸς γάμους ἐναντίωσιν,
τῆς σελήνης πάμπολυ τοῦ ἡλίου διεστώσης. διὸ
καὶ Ἀθηναῖοι τὰς πρὸς σύνοδον ἡμέρας ἐξελέγοντο
πρὸς γάμους καὶ τὰ Θεογάμια ἐτέλουν τότε, φυσικῶς εἶναι πρῶτον οἰόμενοι γάμον τὴν σελήνης πρὸς
ἥλιον[1] σύνοδον.

106

Ibid. 790-791.

μηνὸς δ' ὀγδοάτῃ κάπρον καὶ βοῦν ἐρίμυκον
ταμνέμεν, οὐρῆας δὲ δυωδεκάτῃ ταλαεργούς.

Τὴν ὀγδόην τοῦ μηνὸς τοῦ Ποσειδῶνος ἱερὰν ὡς
ἐπὶ τρία διαστᾶσαν πρώτην τῷ τριαινούχῳ θεῷ
προσήκειν εἰκότως λέγουσι καὶ τρίτην χώραν λαχόντι[2] τῶν ἐν κινήσει στοιχείων. διὸ καὶ τοὺς ταύ-
ρους αὐτῷ φέροντες ἀνῆκαν ὡς ὁρμητικοὺς καὶ τοὺς

---

[1] τὴν . . . ἥλιον F. H. S.: τῆς . . . ἡλίου. After σελήνης
ZBT add οὔσης.

[2] τρίτην χώραν λαχόντι F. H. S. after Pertusi: τριχίτωνι τριῶν
ἄρχοντι. Pertusi reads τρίτην χώραν λαχόντι καὶ τριῶν ἄρχοντι,
comparing *De Iside*, 381 E, ἡ δὲ τοῦ Ποσειδῶνος τρίαινα σύμβολόν
ἐστι τῆς τρίτης χώρας ἣν θάλαττα κατέχει μετὰ τὸν οὐρανὸν καὶ
τὸν ἀέρα τεταγμένη.

say that this is why conceptions taking place when
north winds blow result in male births, while those
taking place when south winds blow result in female
births. Moreover, the articulation of female em-
bryos is slower than that of male, because the quantity of moisture in them is not easily mastered by the
formative power contained in the heat. So there is
a scientific explanation for the statement that the
sixteenth day is excellent for getting males, but unsuitable for females. It also has a certain opposition
to marriage, the moon being then very far removed
from the sun. Hence the Athenians, too, chose the
days near the conjunction of sun and moon for
marriages, and celebrated the Theogamia *a* then,
thinking that in nature the first marriage is the conjunction of the moon with the sun.

Bernardakis.

106

> Upon the eighth day boar and bellowing bull
> Castrate, laborious mules upon the twelfth.

The eighth day of the month is sacred to Posidon ;
they say that, being the first day of which the number
has three factors, it appropriately belongs to the god
of the trident,*b* who has been assigned the third
place among the three elements that are in motion.*c*
Hence they brought and dedicated to him both bulls

---

a Nothing more is known about this festival. For guesses
see Pfister, *R.E.*, *s.v.*

b *Cf. De Iside*, 354 f, and *Life of Theseus*, chap. 36 ; in
both places the first cube (8) is associated with Posidon.

c The text is uncertain. Unemended, it gives Posidon the
unique and unintelligible epithet " of the three tunics." The
three moving elements are fire, air, and water, which occupies
the lowest or third place and is Posidon's realm.

κάπρους· ἄμφω γὰρ διὰ θυμὸν ἀκάθεκτοι γίνονται,
πραΰνονται δὲ ἐκτμηθέντες. εἰκότως οὖν πρὸς[1] τὴν
τῷ κινητικῷ θεῷ προσήκουσαν ἡμέραν—ὃς καὶ τὴν
ἀκίνητον γῆν κινεῖ Ἐνοσίχθων καλούμενος—ᾠκείω-
σαν[2] ταῦτα τὰ ζῷα ὁρμητικὰ ὄντα· καὶ μήποτε τὸν
μὲν ταῦρον ὡς τῆς ὑγρᾶς οὐσίας κινητικῷ,[3] τὸν δὲ
κάπρον ὡς τῆς ξηρᾶς. τοῦ δ' αὐτοῦ ἐστι τὸ κινεῖν
καὶ ἠρεμεῖν τὰς ἀστάτους τῶν κινουμένων ὁρμάς.
διὸ καὶ ὁ θεὸς οὗτος οὐ μόνον Ἐνοσίχθων ἀλλὰ καὶ
Ἀσφάλειος ὑμνεῖται· καὶ οἱ τοὺς σεισμοὺς παύειν
ἐθέλοντες Ποσειδῶνι θύουσιν. ἔχει δ' ἄρα καὶ ἡ
πραΰνουσα διὰ τῆς τομῆς τὰ ζῷα τὰ οἰκεῖα τῷ θεῷ
πρᾶξις οἰκειότητα πρὸς τὴν ἱερὰν τοῦ Ποσειδῶνος
ταύτην ἡμέραν.

107

Ibid. 791.

Τὰς ἡμιόνους οἰκειοῦσι τῇ σελήνῃ· διὸ καί τινες
αὐτὴν φασιν ἐφ' ἡμιόνων ὀχεῖσθαι. καὶ γὰρ ὁ μὲν
ἵππος ἡλιακόν ἐστι ζῷον ὡς εὔδρομον, ὁ δ' ὄνος[4]
χθόνιον ὡς[5] Τυφῶνι φίλον καὶ συνουσιαστικόν[6]· ἡ
δὲ σελήνη μέση ἀμφοῖν, γῆς μὲν ἔχουσα τὸ σκοτί-
ζεσθαι, ἡλίου δὲ τὸ οἰκεῖον εἰληχέναι φῶς. διὰ
τοῦτο μὲν οὖν ᾠκείωται[7] πρὸς αὐτὴν ἡ ἡμίονος.

---

[1] πρὸς added by Pertusi.
[2] οἰκείωσαν Schultz.
[3] F. H. S. : κινητικόν.
[4] ὁ δ' ὄνος added by Schultz.
[5] Pertusi : καί.
[6] Τυφῶνι φίλος ὡς χθόνιος καὶ συνουσιαστικός Schultz.

and boars, as being impetuous ; both are so spirited
as to become uncontrollable, but become gentle by
castration. So they had good reason to associate
these animals that are impetuous with the day that
belongs to the god of movement—he moves even the
unmovable earth, and is called Earth-shaker. (Is it
possible that the bull was associated with him as
mover of the moist substance, and the boar as mover
of the dry ?) The same power that can set in motion
can also bring to a standstill the impetus and in-
stability of what is in motion ; hence this god is
addressed in hymns not only as " Earth-shaker " but
also as " Lord of Security," and men sacrifice to
Posidon when they wish to put a stop to earthquakes.
So the action which makes gentle, by castrating them,
the animals that are associated with the god has an
association with this day that is sacred to the god.

Pertusi.

107

They associate mules with the moon ; hence some
say that she rides in a mule cart. The reason is that
the horse is a solar animal, as being a swift runner,
whereas the donkey belongs to the earth, as being
dear to Typhon [a] and given to copulation ; the moon,
however, is intermediate between sun and earth,
having the earth's characteristic of being darkened,
and the sun's of having its own light ; so there is a
natural association between the moon and the mule.

Pertusi.

[a] Cf. Sept. Sap. Conv. 150 f, De Iside, 371 c.

[7] Pertusi : οἰκείωται AZBTL ᾠκείωτο Q.

Ibid. 797-799.

πεφύλαξο δὲ θυμῷ
τετράδ' ἀλεύασθαι φθίνοντός θ' ἱσταμένου τε
ἄλγεα θυμοβορεῖν.

Τοὺς πρὸ τούτων τέσσαρας[1] στίχους οὐδὲ μνήμης
ὁ Πλούταρχος ἠξίωσεν, ὡς ἂν μὴ φερομένους· τούτους δ' ἐξηγούμενος ἀξιοῖ μὴ ἐγκαλεῖν τῷ Ἡσιόδῳ
ὡς ἂν γελοίως εἰπόντι μὴ χρῆναι λύπας ἑαυτῷ
κινεῖν ἐν ταύταις, ὡς δέον ἐν ἄλλαις τισὶ τοῦτο
ποιεῖν· οὐ γὰρ τοῦτο λέγειν, ἀλλ' ὡς ἱεραῖς ταύταις
μάλιστα τὰς λυπηρὰς ἀποσκευάζεσθαι ἐνεργείας,
ἃς εἰ καὶ ἄλλοτε δεῖ ὡς ἀναγκαίας αἱρεῖσθαι, ἐν
ταύταις οὐ δέον.
*Τὰς δὲ τετράδας ἄμφω εἶναι ἱεράς, τὴν μὲν ὡς
μάλιστα τὸ σεληναῖον ἐκφαίνουσαν φῶς, τὴν δ' ὡς
τοῦτον ἔχουσαν πρὸς τὴν τριακάδα[2] λόγον, ὃν ἡ ἑβδόμη πρὸς τὴν νουμηνίαν· καὶ γὰρ ἡ τετάρτη καὶ
εἰκοστὴ ἑβδόμην ἔχει τάξιν πρὸς τὴν ἐσχάτην.*

109

Ibid. 805-808.

μέσση δ' ἑβδομάτη . . .
ὑλοτόμον τε ταμεῖν θαλαμήια δοῦρα.

---

[1] πέντε Pertusi.
[2] τριακάδα F. H. S. : τετράδα. πρώτην τετράδα Wyttenbach.

---

[a] Possibly meaning 3½ ; Pertusi emends " four " to
" five," supposing that Plutarch's text had lost 792-796
through the homoeoteleuton of ταλαεργούς. But although the
lemma of the scholion is πεφύλαξο δὲ θυμῷ, Plutarch may have

108

Bear in mind to shun
Fourth day of waning, or of waxing, moon
For heart-devouring sorrow.

Plutarch did not deign even to mention the previous four [a] lines, as if they were not in the text ; but in explaining these he claims that Hesiod should not be criticized, as if he had absurdly said that one should not stir up sorrow for oneself on these days, with the implication that one should do so on some others. That is not what he meant, but that on these days in particular, since they are sacred, one should eliminate painful activities ; if such activities, as being necessary, have to be undertaken at other times they should not be undertaken on *these* days.

*Both fourth days are sacred, the one because it especially displays the moon's light, the other because it has the same relation to the thirtieth day as the seventh has to the day of the new moon ; for the twenty-fourth day is seventh in order from the last day of the month.[b] *

109

On middle seventh . . .
And woodman cut the timber for a room.

taken those words as an adjunct of the previous sentence, and so passed over four complete lines, 794-797.

[b] Hesiod divides the month into three equal periods each of ten days (waxing, middle, waning) ; hence the fourth day of the waning moon is the 24th of the month, and this is (by inclusive reckoning) 7th from the 30th or last day. Hesiod states that the 7th is a sacred day (v. 770, see Sinclair's note).

The statement that the fourth day " especially displays

Τὸ μὲν οὖν ὑλοτομεῖν τηνικαῦτα συμβαίνει τοῖς
ἔμπροσθεν ἐν οἷς εἶπε τότε χρῆναι τοῦτο ποιεῖν
ὅταν ἄρχηται τὸ μετόπωρον·

τῆμος ἀδηκτοτάτη πέλεται τμηθεῖσα σιδήρῳ,

μετρίως ξηρῶν ὄντων τῶν ξύλων ὑγρότητός τέ
τινος οὐκ ἐπιδεῶν. ἡ γὰρ ἀρχή[1] τῆς ὥρας εὔκαιρος
καὶ μηνὸς ἡ ἑπτακαιδεκάτη χρήσιμος, ὅτε τὸ μὲν
φῶς τῆς σελήνης πρόσθεσιν οὐκέτ' ἔχει πανσελήνου
γεγονυίας, ἔνικμα δέ πώς ἐστι τὰ ξύλα καὶ διὰ τῆς
ἐλαττώσεως τοῦ φωτὸς ἐλαττοῦται τὸ ὑγρὸν ἀφ'
οὗ συμβαίνειν εἴωθεν ἡ σῆψις.

*110

Ibid. 809.

τετράδι δ' ἄρχεσθαι νῆας πήγνυσθαι ἀραιάς.

Καὶ τοῦτο συμβαίνει τοῖς περὶ τῆς τετράδος
ἀξιώμασιν· εἰ γὰρ στιγμῇ μὲν ἡ μονὰς ἀνάλογος
γραμμῇ δ' ἡ δυὰς ἐπιπέδῳ δ' ἡ τριάς, δῆλον ὡς τῷ
στερεῷ προσήκοι ἂν ἡ τετράς· εἰκότως οὖν ἐπιτη-
δεία πρὸς σύμπηξιν τῶν νεῶν. εἰ δὲ καὶ πρώτη τὸ
ἰσάκις ἴσον ἔχει καὶ πρώτη πάντας τοὺς ἁρμονικοὺς
περιέχει λόγους, ὡς[2] εἴπομεν, καὶ ταύτῃ πρὸς τὸ
εἰρημένον ἔργον εὐκαιρίαν[3] δίδωσιν. οὐδὲν γὰρ

[1] Post: αὐτὴ AZBQLR. ἥ τε οὖν ὥρα αὕτη μᾶλλον τῶν ἄλλων
T. ? ἡ γὰρ αὐτὴ αἰτία δι' ἧς ἡ ἀρχὴ τῆς ὥρας.
[2] Bernardakis : καί.   [3] Gaisford : εὔκαιρα ἰδίαν.

the moon's light " is surprising ; one would have expected
this to be said of the " second fourth " or 14th, the day of the
full moon. But perhaps the fourth day was thought to be
that on which the moon first gives any appreciable amount

To fell timber on that day agrees with the earlier passage in which he said that one should do it when autumn begins :

Then iron tools fell timber that's least gnawn.[a]

The wood is moderately dry at that time, while not lacking a certain moisture. The beginning of the autumn is a good time to choose [b] and the seventeenth day of the month is a useful one : at that time the light of the moon gets no more increase, since the full moon is past, while the wood has some sap in it, and with the diminution of its light comes a diminution of the moisture that is the usual cause of rotting.[c]

Pertusi.

*110

On fourth day start to build the narrow ships.

This, too, fits our propositions about the number four. If the number one is analogous to the point, two to the line, and three to the surface, it is clear that four would fit the solid [d] ; so it would be suitable for building ships. And if it is the first number to be a multiple of equal factors and the first to contain all the harmonic ratios, as we have explained,[e] in this way too it provides a good time for the aforesaid

of light : thus some people who believed in the desirability of sowing seed while the moon was waxing advised doing it from the fourth day onwards, *Geoponica*, ii. 14.

[a] V. 414.
[b] The Greek is corrupt.
[c] Compare frag. 61. *Geoponica* iii. 1 on the other hand recommends cutting at moonless times in January.
[d] Cf. *De E Apud Delphos*, 390 D, but this is a commonplace.
[e] Σ on 769-771 ; $\frac{4}{3}, \frac{4}{2}, \frac{4}{1}$.

οὕτως ἁρμονίας δεῖται τῶν ἔργων, ὡς ναῦς μέλ-
λουσα καὶ ἀέρος κινήσει μαχεῖσθαι καὶ θαλάσσῃ
πολλῇ, καὶ μόνην ἔχουσα τὴν ἀπὸ τῆς ἁρμονίας
βοήθειαν τοῦ σῴζεσθαι, τάχα καὶ Ὁμήρου διὰ
τοῦτο μόνον καλέσαντος Ἁρμονίδην τὸν ναυπηγόν·
εἰ δὲ τὰς ναῦς ὡς κούφας ἀραιὰς ἐκάλεσε (δεῖ γὰρ
αὐτὰς εἶναι κούφας ἐπιπλεῖν μελλούσας), δῆλός ἐστι
καὶ αὐτὸς τὴν μὲν πύκνωσιν βαρύτητος αἰτίαν τὴν
δὲ μάνωσιν κουφότητος ὑπολαβών.

*111

Ibid. 814-816.

παῦροι δ' αὖτ' ἴσασι τρισεινάδα μηνὸς ἀρίστην
ἄρξασθαί τε πίθου καὶ ἐπὶ ζυγὸν αὐχένι θεῖναι
βουσὶ καὶ ἡμιόνοισι καὶ ἵπποις ὠκυπόδεσσι.

[Τρίτην εἰνάδα[1] τὴν εἰκοστὴν εἶπεν ἐνάτην, ἣν
ὀλίγους εἰδέναι ἀρίστην οὖσαν ἀνοίγειν πίθους
καὶ καταζευγνύναι βόας καὶ ἡμιόνους καὶ ἵππους.]
φησὶ γὰρ[2] τῆς σελήνης ἀρχομένης ἀποκρύπτεσθαι
δοκεῖν[3] καὶ τὰ θυμοειδέστερα τῶν ἀλόγων ἀμβλύ-
νειν τὸν θυμὸν καὶ μὴ ὁμοίως ἀνθίστασθαι τοῖς
δαμάζουσιν, ἀσθενέστερα γινόμενα. καὶ τὸ περὶ
τὴν ἄνοιξιν τοῦ πίθου φυσικῶς εἴρηκε· μάλιστα γὰρ
φασι περὶ τὰς πανσελήνους ἐξίστασθαι τὸν οἶνον
διὰ τὴν ἀπὸ τῆς σελήνης ὑγρὰν θερμήν, ὥστ' εἰκό-

---

[1] τρισεινάδα L, perhaps rightly.
[2] Maes adds ὁ Πλούταρχος.
[3] Schultz : δοκεῖ.

---

[a] *harmonia* means " jointing," particularly of carpenter's
work, as well as " musical scale."

224

work. No work needs harmony [a] so much as a ship, which will have to contend with the movements of the air and great seas, and the only thing that can help it is its harmony ; perhaps it was for this reason alone that Homer called his shipwright Harmonides.[b] And if Hesiod called ships *araiai* [c] as being light (for they must be light if they are to float), it is clear that he too took denseness to be the cause of heaviness and rarefaction to be that of lightness.

Bernardakis.

*111

> Few know the triple-ninth [d] day is the best
> To start a jar, or harness to a yoke
> Oxen or mules or the fleet-footed horse.

[He called the twenty-ninth day " third ninth," saying that few know that it is best for opening jars and yoking oxen, mules, and horses.] For . . . says that it is believed that when the moon begins to be hidden even the more spirited brutes have their spirit blunted and, growing weaker, do not so much resist those who are breaking them in. And what the poet says about the opening of the wine jar has a basis in nature ; for they say that wine is most liable to spoil at the time of the full moon because of the moist heat from the moon, so that it

[b] *Iliad*, v. 60.
[c] The word *araios* has several senses : Hesiod probably meant *narrow* when he applied it to ships, but this note supposes him to have intended a later use, *loose in texture*, which would imply *light*.
[d] The scholion clearly supposes this to mean 29th, but the alternative 27th is more plausible.

τως ὅταν ἥκιστα τοῦτο προβάλῃ κελεύει τὸν πίθον
ἀνοίγειν καὶ τοῦ οἴνου πεῖραν λαμβάνειν.

112

Ibid. 819.

τετράδι δ᾽ οἶγε πίθον.

*Τὴν μέσην τετράδα ταύτην λέγων τὴν¹ τεσσαρεσ-
καιδεκάτην ἐπαινεῖ καὶ ὡς πίθοιγον καὶ ὡς πᾶσιν
ἀρίστην· καὶ γὰρ τὸ φῶς τῆς σελήνης πλούσιον
ἅμα τῷ ἡλίῳ καταδυομένῳ ἀνατελλούσης* . . .

Καί τις Αἰγύπτιος μυθολογεῖ μῦθος τὸν Ὄσιριν
τοσαῦτα ἔτη βασιλεῦσαι ὁπόσος ἐστὶν ὁ τῶν ἡμερῶν τούτων ἀριθμός, *ἐνδεικνύμενος ὡς ἐμοὶ δοκεῖ
πάντων αὐτὸν εἶναι τῶν γεννητῶν δημιουργὸν καὶ
τελεσιουργόν, μετὰ τῶν σεληνιακῶν ἀκτίνων τέχνῃ
τεύχοντα τὴν γένεσιν τῶν τε αὐξητικῶν καὶ τῶν
μειωτικῶν, ἵνα καὶ γένηται τὰ τῇδε καὶ φθείρηται.*

ΕΙΣ ΤΑ ΝΙΚΑΝΔΡΟΥ ΘΗΡΙΑΚΑ

113

Scholion on Nicander, *Theriaca*, 94.

Ἐν δὲ χεροπληθῆ καρπὸν νεοθηλέα δαύκου
λειαίνειν τριπτῆρι.

¹ τὴν LT, omitted by AZBQR.

ᵃ The 28 days of the lunar cycle, *De Iside*, 367 ꜰ.
ᵇ Gow and Schofield, ed. Nicander, prefer a variant men-
226

is reasonable for him to recommend us to open the
jar and try the wine when the moon emits this heat
least.

Maes, who would supply " Plutarch " as the subject of
' says.''

112

Open your jar upon the fourth . . .

*By this he means the " middle fourth,'' and thus
praises the fourteenth day, both for jar-opening and
as best for all purposes. And in fact the light of the
moon is rich when it rises at sunset.* . . .
And there is an Egyptian myth which relates that
Osiris was king for as many years as is the number of
these days [a] ; *it indicates, to my mind, that Osiris
is the craftsman who brings all generated things to
their completion, contriving their birth by his skill
with the aid of the rays of the moon, both those that
bring increase and those that bring decrease, so that
things on this earth may come into being and also
perish.*

Pertusi.

ON NICANDER'S *ANTIDOTES TO SNAKE-BITE*

(*Lamprias Catalogue* 120)

113

A handful of fresh-growing parsnip [b] seed
With pestle grind.

tioned by the scholiast, δαυχμοῦ, which A. S. F. Gow, *Class.
Quart.*, N.S. i (1951), p. 100, shows to mean " bay tree."

[Δαύκου· δύο γένη τῆς βοτάνης ἡ μὲν Κρητική, ἡ
δ' Ἀσιατική.] Πλούταρχος πλείονα μέν φησιν
γένη αὐτῆς εἶναι, τὸ δὲ κοινὸν τῆς δυνάμεως ἰδίωμα
δριμὺ καὶ πυρῶδες, ὡς καὶ[1] ἡ γεῦσις αἰσθάνεται
καὶ ἡ[2] ὄσφρησις, καὶ πειρώμενον[3] δῆλον εἶναι· καὶ
γὰρ ἔμμηνα κινεῖ σφόδρα καὶ διαλύει στρόφους τῇ
θερμότητι, καὶ τῶν περὶ τὸν θώρακα σπλάγχνων
καθαρτικὸν καὶ πρόσετί γε μὴν λεπτυντικὸν ἔχει
σθένος.[4]

114

Scholion (Ambr. C. 32 sup.) on Nicander, *Theriaca*, 333
(*Studi classici e orientali*, vi [1956]).

λευκαὶ δ' ἀργινόεσσαν ἐπισσεύονται ἔφηλιν.

Ὁ Πλούταρχος τὰς πικρὰς ἀμυγδάλας φησὶ τὰς
τῶν προσώπων ἐξαιρεῖν[5] ἐφήλιδας.

115

Stephanus of Byzantium, *s.v.* Κορόπη.

Νίκανδρος ἐν Θηριακοῖς·

ἦ ἐν[6] Ἀπόλλων
μαντείας[7] Κοροπαῖος ἐθήκατο καὶ θέμιν ἀνδρῶν.

Οἱ δὲ ὑπομνηματίσαντες αὐτὸν Θέων καὶ Πλούταρχος καὶ Δημήτριος ὁ Χλωρός[8] φασι· Νίκανδρος
" Ὀροπαῖος " καὶ " Κοροπαῖος Ἀπόλλων "· ἀγνοεῖ

---

[1] Keil : καὶ ὡς or ὡς.
[2] ἡ added by Bernardakis.   [3] πειρωμένῳ Warmington.
[4] θώρακα καὶ σπλάγχνα παθῶν καθαρτικὴν καὶ λεπτυντικὴν
ἔχει δύναμιν G(öttingensis).
[5] ἐξαίρειν ms., as at 624 d.   [6] Nicander : αἰέν.
[7] μαντοσύνας Nicander.   [8] Wyttenbach : Φαληρεύς.

FRAGMENTS : OTHER NAMED WORKS

[Parsnip. There are two varieties of this plant, one Cretan, the other Asiatic.] Plutarch says that there are several varieties, but that their common characteristic is to be pungent and fiery, as both taste and smell perceive ; and that if put to the test, this is clear, since by their heat they give a strong stimulus to the menstrual flow and also remove colic, and have the power to purge, and indeed also to reduce the size of, the organs situated in the chest.

114

Leprous eruptions spread a chalky rash.

Plutarch says that bitter almonds remove blotches from the face.[a]

115

Nicander in his *Theriaca* :

> . . . and there Apollo
> Of Coropê set up his oracle
> And laws for men . . . [b]

His commentators Theon,[c] Plutarch, and Demetrius " the Pale " [d] say, " Nicander : ' Oropaean ' and ' Coropaean ' Apollo. He does not know that

[a] Cf. *Quaest. Conv.* 624 D.
[b] *Theriaca*, 613-614.
[c] Theon, grammarian, perhaps of the first century B.C., wrote commentaries on several Alexandrian poets. Wendel, *R.E.* v A 2054-2059, J. Martin, *Histoire du texte des Phénomènes d'Aratos*, pp. 196-199.
[d] Not later than early first century B.C. (Susemihl, *Gr. Lit. d. Alexanderzeit*, ii. 20) ; the origin of his nickname is not known.

δ' ὅτι[1] Ἀμφιαράου ἱερόν, οὐκ[2] Ἀπόλλωνός ἐστι. λέγεται δὲ κατ' ἔλλειψιν τοῦ ι Κοροπαῖος[3]· Κορόπη δὲ Θεσσαλίας πόλις. βέλτιον δὲ ὑπονοεῖν ὅτι ἡμάρτηται.[4] καὶ γράφεται Ὀροπαῖος· Ὀρόπη[5] γὰρ πόλις Εὐβοίας, ὅπου Ἀπόλλωνος διασημότατον ἱερόν.

ΚΑΤΑ ΗΔΟΝΗΣ

Wilamowitz, Hermes, lviii (1923), p. 84, is clearly right

*116

Stobaeus, iii. 6. 49 (iii, p. 297 Hense).

Πλουτάρχου ἐκ τοῦ κατὰ ἡδονῆς·

Ὅτι τὰ σώματα ἀνίησιν ἡ ἡδονὴ καθ' ἡμέραν ἐκμαλάττουσα ταῖς τρυφαῖς, ὧν ἡ συνέχεια παραιρεῖται τὸν τόνον ἀναχαλῶσα τὴν ἰσχὺν αὐτῶν· ἐξ ὧν ῥαστώνη μὲν νόσων ῥαστώνη δὲ καμάτων, προμελετώμενον δ' ἐν νεότητι[6] γῆρας.

*117

Stobaeus, iii. 6. 50 (iii, p. 297 Hense).

Ἐν ταὐτῷ[7]·

Θηρίον ἐστὶ δουλαγωγὸν ἥ[8] ἡδονή, ἀλλ' οὐκ ἄγ-

---

[1] Salmasius : δὲ τὸ.   [2] οὐκ added by Salmasius.
[3] τοῦ κ Ὀροπαῖος Holsten.
[4] Wilamowitz places this sentence after ἐστι, and continues καὶ γραπτέον Ὀροπαῖος κατ' ἔλλειψιν τοῦ ι ἀντὶ Ὀροπαῖος· Ὀροπία γάρ, κτλ. See also I. Cazzaniga, *Maia*, N.S. 1 (1965), p. 60.
[5] γράφεται καὶ Ὀρόπειος· Ὀρόπεια scholion on this line of Nicander.   [6] Gesner : μεσότητι LA : μισότητι M.

the shrine there belongs to Amphiaraüs, not Apollo.
(The form of the word is ' Coropaean,' without an
i,[a] and Coropê is a town in Thessaly.) But it is better
to suppose that a mistake has been made.[b] There is
also a reading ' Oropaean,' Oropê being a town in
Euboea, where there is a very famous shrine of
Apollo." [c]

AGAINST PLEASURE

(Not in Lamprias Catalogue)

*in denying the authenticity of these fragments, on the grounds
of hiatus and the " nauseous affectation " of their style.*

*116

Plutarch, from the work *Against Pleasure* :

He says that pleasure relaxes our bodies, softening
them day in, day out, with luxuries which, if continued, take away their energy and relax their
strength ; there ensues an easy path for diseases,
an easy path for pains, and a rehearsal of old age in
youth.

*117

In the same work :

Pleasure is a beast that makes us its slaves, but it

[a] Possibly meaning " not ' Coropiaean.' "
[b] It is uncertain how much of this greatly confused note,
discussed by Wilamowitz, *Euripides* Herakles[1], i. 190[141]
(where he rejects the ascription in *Grammatici graeci*, iii, p.
188, to Herodian), derives from Plutarch.
[c] This town was called Orobiae. The shrine of Amphiaraüs was at Orôpus in Boeotia. On these places see *R.E.*
xi. 1436, xviii. 1133, 1175.

---

[7] ἐν ταὐτῷ omitted by L.   [8] ἡ added by Hense.

ριον· εἴθε γὰρ ἦν· φανερῶς ἂν[1] πολεμοῦσα ταχέως
ἑάλω· νῦν δὲ καὶ ταύτῃ μισητότερον, ὅτι κλέπτει
τὴν ἔχθραν ὑποδυομένη σχῆμα εὐνοίας. ὥστε διχῶς[2] ἀποτρόπαιον καὶ ὧν βλάπτει καὶ ὧν ψεύδε-
ται.

*118

Stobaeus, iii. 6. 51 (iii, p. 298 Hense).

Ἐν ταὐτῷ[3]·

Τὰς μὲν οὖν δικαίας ἡδονὰς οὐκέτ᾽ ἂν ἡδονὰς
οὔτε καλέσαιμεν οὔτε νομίσαιμεν[4] ἀλλὰ θεραπείας.
ὅσαι δὲ παρὰ ταύτας πᾶσαι ὕβρεις περιτταί[5] εἰσι
πεπληρωμένα[6] βιαζόμεναι, καὶ ταῖς ποικιλίαις κολα-
κεύουσαι λανθάνουσι βλάπτουσαι. ὁ δὲ εἰς τὰ
ἡμέτερα νόμος ὁ καὶ[7] τῶν ἀλόγων ζῴων, οἷς[8] μετὰ
τὸ ἀκέσασθαι τὰς ἐπιθυμίας οὐδενὸς ὄρεξις, ἀλλὰ
κόρος τῶν[9] ἐπειγόντων ἀβιάστοις ἡδοναῖς.

*119

Stobaeus, iii. 6. 52 (iii, p. 298 Hense).

Ἐν ταὐτῷ[10]·

Μή τις προδότας ἐπαινεῖ; τοιοῦτόν ἐστιν ἡ[11]

---

[1] ἂν L : omitted by MA γὰρ ἂν Br. γὰρ ἂν Herwerden. ἵνα φανερῶς πολεμοῦσα Cobet.
[2] διχῶς Buecheler : διχῶ L διχῇ MA.
[3] ἐν ταὐτῷ omitted by L.
[4] νομίσαιμεν F. H. S. : ἴσμεν.
[5] περιτταί should perhaps be placed after ταύτας.

232

is no savage beast. Would it were ! If it warred
upon us openly, it would quickly be detected. But
as things are, it is the more hateful for the very reason
that it hides its hostility by assuming the guise of
good will. It is therefore doubly abominable, for its
harmfulness and for its falsity.

*118

In the same work :

Legitimate pleasures we should cease to call pleasures and should not think of them as such, but as
curative processes. All others, apart from these, are
unnecessary violations of nature, that bring force to
bear on the satisfied, and are not recognized to be
harmful because they cajole us with their variety.
But the law for us should be the same as governs the
irrational animals ; with them there is no appetite for
anything, once their desires have been assuaged, but
satiety with regard to what stimulates them, since
they are not constrained by pleasures.

*119

In the same work :

Surely no one praises traitors ? But that is what

---

⁶ F. H. S. : πεπηρωμέναι. πεπληρωμέναι Gesner.
⁷ κατὰ Jacobs.
⁸ οἷς added by F. H. S. (ὧν Jacobs). μετὰ γὰρ Bernardakis.
⁹ ? ταῖς τῶν ἐπαγόντων.
¹⁰ omitted by L.
¹¹ ἡ added by A.

ἡδονή, προδίδωσι τὰ τῆς[1] ἀρετῆς. μή τις βασανι-
στάς; τοιοῦτόν ἐστι τὸ ἥδεσθαι, βασανίζει τὰ τῆς[1]
σωφροσύνης. μή τις φιλαργυρίαν; ἀπλήρωτόν
ἐστιν ἑκάτερον. τί τηλικούτῳ χαίρομεν θηρίῳ, ὃ
κολακεῦον ἡμᾶς ἀναλίσκει;

*120

Stobaeus, iii. 6. 53 (iii, p. 299 Hense).

Ἐν ταὐτῷ[2]·

Τί δ' οὐ πάντων ὁρώντων ἀρρητεύεις,[3] ἀλλὰ καὶ
σαυτὸν αἰδούμενος φεύγεις, νυκτὶ καὶ σκότῳ τοῖς
ἀμαρτύροις πιστεύων τὴν ὕβριν; οὐδεὶς γὰρ τῶν
καλῶν ἔργων σκότος προβάλλει, τὸ φῶς αὐτοῖς
μαρτυρεῖν αἰσχυνόμενος· ἀλλ' ὅλον ἅμα τὸν κόσμον
ἥλιον γενέσθαι πρὸς ἃ κατορθοῖ βούλοιτ' ἄν.
ἅπασα δὲ κακία ὁρᾶσθαι γυμνὴ φυλάττεται, σκέπην
προβαλλομένη τὰ πάθη. ἀποκόψαντες οὖν αὐτὰς[4]
γυμνὰς βλέπωμεν τὰς ἡδονάς· μεθύουσιν εἰς ἀναι-
σθησίαν, λαγνεύουσιν εἰς αἰῶνα,[5] καθεύδουσιν εἰς
ἔργα,[6] οὐκ ἐπιστρέφονται πόλεις, οὐ φροντίζουσι
γονέων, οὐκ αἰσχύνονται νόμους.

[1] τῆς added by A.
[2] Omitted by L.
[3] Bernardakis : ἀριστεύεις LM ἀρρη στεύεις A. ἀκρατεύεις
Gesner (? better ἀκρατεύει).
[4] αὐτὰ Gesner. ? Read ταῦτ', αὐτὰς and delete τὰς ἡδονάς.
[5] μωρίαν Jacobs ἀτονίαν Meineke ἄνοιαν Haupt μανίαν Hense
ἕω Usener.

234

pleasure is ; it betrays our virtue. Surely no one praises torturers ? But that is what it is to feel pleasure ; it puts our self-control to the torture. Surely no one praises avarice ? Pleasure is as insatiable. Why do we enjoy this great monster, that consumes us as it cajoles us ? [a]

*120

In the same work :

Why do you not perform your unmentionable acts for all men to see, but hide away, ashamed even of yourself, and entrust your excesses to night and darkness, where there are no witnesses ? No one makes darkness a cover for his noble deeds, ashamed that daylight should witness them ; a man would wish that the whole universe might become a sun to see what he does aright. But every vice takes care not to be seen naked, sheltering behind a screen of feelings. Let us cut them away, then, and look at pleasures in their naked selves (?).[b] Men get drunk until they are insensible, they are lecherous all their lives, they sleep when they should be at their work, they take no care of their cities, have no thought for their parents, and feel no shame before the laws.

[a] Hense suggests that this fragment preceded the previous one.
[b] The required sense seems rather to be " Vice shelters behind a screen of feelings of pleasure. Let us cut this away and look at vices in their nakedness." But I can find no plausible way of emending the Greek.

---

[6] ἀργίαν Duebner ἀγῶνας Post ἑσπέραν Usener.

ΚΑΤ' ΙΣΧΥΟΣ

121

Stobaeus, iv. 12. 14 (iv, p. 344 Hense).

Πλουτάρχου ἐκ τοῦ κατ' ἰσχύος·

Τί δέ σοι τοιοῦτον ἀγαθὸν εὐτύχηται; ἀλλ' ἠτύχηται[1] μᾶλλον, ὡς ἕνεκα τούτου μητρυιὰν μὲν
τῶν ἀνθρώπων μητέρα δὲ τῶν ἀλόγων ζῴων γεγε-
νῆσθαι τὴν φύσιν, μεγέθους καὶ ὠκύτητος[2] καὶ ὀξυ-
ωπίας χάριν; ἡ δ' ἀνθρώπων ἴδιος ἰσχὺς ὁ ψυχῆς
ἐστι λογισμός, ὃς[3] καὶ ἵππους ἐχαλίνωσε καὶ βόας
ἀρότροις ὑπέζευξε καὶ ἐλέφαντας ὑπὸ δρυμὸν εἷλε
ποδάγραις[4] καὶ τὰ ἐναέρια[5] κατέσπασε καλάμοις καὶ
τὰ βύθια δεδυκότα δικτύοις ἀνήγαγε· τοῦτ' ἔστιν
ἰσχύς. ἡ δ' ἔτι μείζων, ὅταν γῆς περιόδους καὶ
οὐρανοῦ μεγέθη καὶ ἀστέρων κύκλους διώκουσα μὴ
κάμῃ. ταῦτ' ἦν Ἡρακλέους ἄξια. τίς γὰρ οὐκ ἂν
βούλοιτο μᾶλλον Ὀδυσσεὺς εἶναι ἢ Κύκλωψ;

---

[1] εὐτύχηται; ἀλλ' ἠτύχηται F. H. S., ex. gr.: εὐτυχεῖται.
[2] Hense, as Wyttenbach translated: ὀξύτητος.
[3] ὃς Elter: ὃ. ᾧ Gesner.
[4] Gesner: ποδάγραις (ποδάγρᾳ A).
[5] Trincavelli's edition: ἐν ἀέρια S ἐν ἀέρι MA.

---

[a] Philo, Post. Cain. 162 (see also 161), puts this metaphor
down to οἱ δοκιμώτατοι τῶν πάλαι λογίων, cf. Cicero, De Re-
publica, iii. 1-2, and E. Norden, Jahrbücher für kl. Philologie,
suppl. xviii, pp. 304-306. E. Bignone, Riv. fil., N.S. 14

A DEPRECIATION OF STRENGTH

(Not in Lamprias Catalogue)

121

Plutarch, from his *Depreciation of Strength* :

What good fortune can you see in a good of that sort ? It is truer to say that you have come off badly, so that so far as this goes Nature has been a stepmother to men, but a mother to brute animals,[a] that is to say where size and speed and sharpness of vision are concerned. But the proper strength of man is his mind's power of reason, which has bridled horses and yoked cattle to his ploughs, and in the forests captured elephants in traps,[b] and fetched down the birds of the air by fowlers' rods and brought up in nets the denizens of the deep. There you have strength. But there is a strength greater still, when the mind tirelessly investigates the earth's geography, the vast distances of the heavens, or the revolutions of the stars. These were tasks worthy of Heracles ; for who would not rather be Odysseus than the Cyclops ?[c]

(1936), p. 232, suggests a source in Aristotle's *Protrepticus,* Ziegler, *R.E.* xxii. 723, in Democritus. For the passage in general *cf. De Fortuna,* 98 c–f.

[b] Perhaps, as Duebner suggested, part of a hexameter, if δρῠμόν can be so scanned on the analogy of δρῠμά : elsewhere we find δρῡμός.

[c] *i.e.*, an explorer than a giant.

ΟΜΗΡΙΚΑΙ ΜΕΛΕΤΑΙ

122

Aulus Gellius, iv. 11.

Plutarchus quoque, homo in disciplinis gravi auctoritate, in primo librorum quos de Homero composuit Aristotelem philosophum scripsit eadem ipsa de Pythagoricis scripsisse, quod non abstinuerint edundis animalibus nisi pauca carne quadam. verba ipsa Plutarchi, quoniam res inopinata est, subscripsi : Ἀριστοτέλης δὲ μήτρας καὶ καρδίας καὶ ἀκαλήφης καὶ τοιούτων τινῶν ἄλλων ἀπέχεσθαί φησι τοὺς Πυθαγορικούς, χρῆσθαι δὲ τοῖς ἄλλοις.

123

Aulus Gellius, ii. 8.

Plutarchus secundo librorum, quos de Homero composuit, imperfecte atque praepostere atque inscite syllogismo esse usum Epicurum dicit verbaque ipsa Epicuri ponit : Ὁ θάνατος οὐδὲν πρὸς ἡμᾶς· τὸ γὰρ διαλυθὲν ἀναισθητεῖ, τὸ δὲ ἀναισθητοῦν οὐδὲν πρὸς ἡμᾶς. "nam praetermisit," inquit, "quod in prima parte sumere debuit, τὸν θάνατον εἶναι ψυχῆς καὶ σώματος διάλυσιν· tunc deinde eodem ipso quod omiserat quasi posito concessoque ad confirmandum aliud utitur. progredi autem hic," inquit, "syllogismus, nisi illo prius posito, non potest."

ᵃ I have been unable to see H. Schrader, *De Plutarchi Chaeronensis* Ὁμηρικαῖς Μελέταις, Gotha, 1899.

HOMERIC STUDIES [a]

122

Plutarch, too, a weighty authority in matters of scholarship, wrote in the first of his books on Homer that the philosopher Aristotle made the same statement about the Pythagoreans, namely that they did not abstain from eating animals, except for a few particular meats. As this is unexpected, I add Plutarch's own words : "Aristotle says that the Pythagoreans abstained from the pig's paunch, the heart, the sea-nettle, and some other things of the sort, but ate everything else." [b]

123

Plutarch, in the second of his books on Homer, says that Epicurus made an imperfect, absurd, and clumsy use of the syllogism, and quotes Epicurus' own words : " Death does not concern us ; for what is dissolved is without sensation, and what is without sensation does not concern us." [c] " For he passed over," he writes, " what he ought to have posited to begin with, namely that death is a dissolution of body and soul ; then he proceeds to use this omitted premise, as if it had been stated and agreed, to establish another proposition. But unless that premise is first stated, the syllogism cannot proceed."

[b] Frag. 194 ; cf. *Quaest. Conv.* 670 c, Porphyry, *Vit. Pyth.* 45, Diog. Laert. viii. 18-19. W. K. C. Guthrie, *History of Greek Philosophy*, i. 187-191, translates and discusses the principal texts concerning Pythagorean abstention from animal food.

[c] Κυρία Δόξα 2.

124

Aulus Gellius, ii. 9.

In eodem libro idem Plutarchus eundem Epicurum reprehendit quod verbo usus sit parum proprio et alienae significationis. ita enim scripsit Epicurus : ῞Ορος τοῦ μεγέθους τῶν ἡδονῶν ἡ παντὸς τοῦ ἀλγοῦντος ὑπεξαίρεσις. " non," inquit, " παντὸς τοῦ ἀλγοῦντος sed παντὸς τοῦ ἀλγεινοῦ dicere oportuit. detractio enim significanda est doloris," inquit, " non dolentis."

125

Galen, *Hippocratis et Platonis Dogmata*, iii, p. 265 Müller (v. 300 Kühn).

᾿Εν οἷς ἐγὼ μὲν ἐκπλήττομαι τῇ μεγαλοψυχίᾳ[1] τοῦ Χρυσίππου[2]· δέον γὰρ ὡς ἄνθρωπον ἀνεγνωκότα τοσούτους ποιητὰς καὶ γινώσκοντα σαφῶς ἅπασι τοῖς δόγμασιν αὐτοῦ[3] μαρτυροῦντας ἄλλοτε κατ᾿ ἄλλα τῶν ἐπῶν, ὥσπερ καὶ Πλούταρχος ἐπέδειξεν ἐν τοῖς τῶν ῾Ομηρικῶν μελετῶν, ἐκλέγειν[4] μὲν ἐξ αὐτῶν ὅσα μαρτυρεῖ τῷ σπουδαζομένῳ πρὸς αὐτοῦ δόγματι. . . .

126

Scholion on Euripides, *Alcestis*, 1128.

Ψυχαγωγοί τινες γόητες[5] ἐν Θετταλίᾳ[6] οὕτω καλούμενοι, οἵτινες καθαρμοῖς τισι καὶ γοητείαις τὰ εἴδωλα ἐπάγουσί τε καὶ ἐξάγουσιν· οὓς καὶ Λάκωνες μετεπέμψαντο, ἡνίκα τὸ Παυσανίου εἴδωλον ἐξ-

---

[1] Müller : τῆς μεγαλοψυχίας.

FRAGMENTS : OTHER NAMED WORKS

124

In the same book the same Plutarch criticizes Epicurus again for using an unsuitable word with a meaning foreign to the context. Epicurus wrote, "The limit of quantity in pleasures is the removal of all that feels pain." [a] "He ought not," objects Plutarch, "to have said, 'of all that feels pain,' but 'of all that is painful.' For the required meaning," he says, "is the removal of pain, not of what is pained."

125

Here I am astonished at Chrysippus' magnanimity. A man who had read so many poets and knew that in various passages of their poems they clearly gave their testimony in support of all his doctrines, as Plutarch has shown in his *Homeric Studies*, should have selected such passages as support the doctrine he favours. . . .

126

Certain so-called spirit-summoning magicians in Thessaly, who by certain rites of purification [b] and magic practices both call up and banish ghosts. They were sent for by the Spartans, too, when the ghost of

---

[a] Κυρία Δόξα 3.
[b] On the blurring of the distinction between purificatory and propitiatory rites see Rohde, *Psyche*, ii. 79 ; on control of spirits, *ibid*. ii. 87[2, 3].

---

[2] Laur. lxxiv. 22 : τὸν Χρύσιππον Hamilton 270 (whose readings I owe to P. de Lacy).   [3] αὐτοῦ] αὐτοὺς Müller.
[4] Laur. lxxiv. 22 : ἐκλέγει Hamilton 270.
[5] γόητες omitted by A.   [6] ? Φιγαλία Mittelhaus.

ἐτάραξε τοὺς προσιόντας τῷ ναῷ τῆς Χαλκιοίκου,
ὡς ἱστορεῖ Πλούταρχος ἐν ταῖς Ὁμηρικαῖς μελέταις.

127

Scholion on *Iliad*, xv. 624 ; *Etymologicum Magnum*, *s.v.*
ἀνεμοτρεφές.

Τὰ γὰρ ὑπεύδια καὶ κατασκιαζόμενα τῶν δένδρων εὐγενῆ[1] μὲν καὶ λεῖον τὸν ὅρπηκα ποιεῖ, ἀ-
σθενῆ δὲ καὶ μαλακὸν καὶ ἀγύμναστον ἀναδίδωσιν·
οἷς δὲ προσπίπτει τραχὺς ἀὴρ καὶ ἀνεμώδης, ταῦτα
ταῖς τῶν πνευμάτων τριβόμενα πληγαῖς εὔτονον καὶ
δύσθρυπτον[2] ἔχει τὴν στερρότητα, ὥς φησι Πλούταρχος ἐν μελέταις Ὁμηρικαῖς.

ΟΤΙ ΚΑΙ ΓΥΝΑΙΚΑ ΠΑΙΔΕΥΤΕΟΝ

This work is not listed in the Lamprias Catalogue.
Several instances of hiatus in the fragments, and their lack
of relevance to the title, caused Ziegler to doubt whether they

128

Stobaeus, iii. 18. 27 (iii, p. 520 Hense).

Πλουτάρχου ἐκ τοῦ ὅτι καὶ γυναῖκα παιδευτέον·
Τῷ Διονύσῳ νάρθηκα καὶ λήθην συγκαθιεροῦσιν,

---

[1] εὐτενῆ Wyttenbach, but *cf. Geoponica*, v. 37. 2, Aelian,
V.H. ii. 14, Philo, *Vit. Mos.* i. 22 (and Kohn's index).
[2] δύσθραυστον Schol. Ven.

---

a Pausanias starved to death in the temple of Athêna of
the Bronze House at Sparta. At *De Sera Numinis Vindicta*,
560 E, the exorcists are said to have come from Italy. Mittelhaus, *R.E.* xix. 2084, suggests that " Thessaly " and " Italy "

Pausanias alarmed visitors to the shrine of the Lady of the Bronze House.[a] So Plutarch records in his *Homeric Studies*.

127

Trees situated in sheltered and shady places send up shoots that are well grown and smooth, but also weak, soft, and flabby ; those, however, that are exposed to a harsh, windy atmosphere have a stiffness that is elastic and resists breaking, the result of being battered by blows from the winds, as Plutarch says in his *Homeric Studies*.[b]

A WOMAN, TOO, SHOULD BE EDUCATED

come from the alleged source, or are by Plutarch at all. But the hiatus may be due to an excerptor, and four of the fragments have parallels in genuine works. For the title compare Musonius' Εἰ παραπλησίως παιδευτέον τὰς θυγατέρας τοῖς υἱοῖς.

128

Plutarch, from the work *A Woman, too, should be Educated* :

They dedicate the cane [c] to Dionysus and along

are both corruptions of Phigalia, a town in Arcadia, where Pausanias himself consulted ψυχαγωγοί (Pausanias, iii. 17. 9). See also W. Burkert, *Rh. Mus.* cv (1963), p. 49.

[b] The scholion is on the phrase " wind-bred wave," but Plutarch was commenting on the application of the same epithet (ἀνεμοτρεφές) to a spear at *Iliad*, xi. 256.

[c] Both this fragment (another version of *Quaest. Conv.* 612 c ; *cf.* also *De Cohibenda Ira*, 462 в) and the next have probably been abbreviated. The Dionysiac thyrsus was the

ὡς μὴ δέον μνημονεύειν τῶν ἐν οἴνῳ πλημμελη-
θέντων ἀλλὰ νουθεσίας παιδικῆς δεομένων. ᾧ[1]
συνᾴδει καὶ τὸ " μισέω[2] μνάμονα συμπόταν."[3] ὁ
δ᾽ Εὐριπίδης τῶν ἀτόπων τὴν λήθην σοφὴν εἴρηκε.

129

Stobaeus, iii. 18. 31 (iii, p. 521 Hense).

Πλουτάρχου ἐκ τοῦ ὅτι καὶ γυναῖκα παιδευτέον·

᾽Αμαθίην, ὥς φησιν Ἡράκλειτος, καὶ ἄλλως κρύπτειν ἔργον ἐστὶν ἐν οἴνῳ δὲ χαλεπώτερον· καὶ
Πλάτων δέ φησιν ἐν οἴνῳ τὰ ἤθη φανερὰ γίνεσθαι,
ὥσπερ καὶ Ὅμηρος·

οὐδὲ τραπέζῃ
γνώτην ἀλλήλων.

130

Stobaeus, iii. 18. 32 (iii, p. 522 Hense).

Τοῦ αὐτοῦ·

Σοφοκλῆς ἐμέμφετο Αἰσχύλῳ, ὅτι μεθύων ἔγρα-
φε· " καὶ γὰρ εἰ τὰ δέοντα ποιεῖ," φησίν, " ἀλλ᾽
οὐκ εἰδώς γε."

[1] Gesner : ὡς.
[2] Bernardakis : μισῶ.
[3] Gesner, Hense : μνημοσύναν ποτάν.

---

stalk of the giant fennel, tipped with ivy. This stalk was also
used in school as an instrument of correction : for illustra-
tions see J. D. Beazley, *Am. Journ. Arch.*, 2nd ser. xxxvii
(1933), p. 400.

with it forgetfulness, in the belief that one ought not to remember offences committed while drinking, yet needing the disciplinary action appropriate to children. Consistent with this is the phrase " I hate a boon companion with a good memory." [a] And Euripides said that forgetfulness of bad events was wise.[b]

129

Plutarch, from the work *A Woman, too, should be Educated* :

Stupidity, as Heraclitus says, is in any case difficult to hide,[c] but harder than ever over the wine. Plato also says that men's characters are brought to light over the wine,[d] and similarly Homer has : " They knew not one another at table." [e]

130

The same author :

Sophocles criticized Aeschylus for writing under the influence of wine.[f] " Even if there is nothing wrong with his poetry," he explained, " that is not because he knows what he is doing as he writes."

---

[a] Diehl, *Anthologia lyrica*, ii, p. 160 (anonymous) ; Page, *Greek Melic Poets*, adespota 1002.

[b] *Orestes*, 213.

[c] Heraclitus, frag. 95, is quoted elsewhere by Plutarch (*Mor.* 43 D, 439 D, 644 F) in the form ἀμαθίην ἄμεινον κρύπτειν, " it is better to hide stupidity."

[d] *Laws*, 650 A.

[e] *Odyssey*, xxi. 35, quoted also at *Quaest. Conv.* 645 A.

[f] *Cf. Quaest. Conv.* 622 E, 715 D ; the anecdote is due to Chamaeleon (Athenaeus, 22 b, 428 f). For the sentiment *cf.* Plato, *Rep.* 598 E.

131

Stobaeus, (a) iv. 1. 140, (b) 31. 46 (iv, p. 89, v, p. 749 Hense).

Πλουτάρχου ἐκ τοῦ ὅτι καὶ γυναῖκα παιδευτέον·

Μὴ παιδὶ μάχαιραν, ἡ παροιμία φησίν· ἐγὼ δὲ φαίην ἄν· '' μὴ παιδὶ πλοῦτον μηδὲ ἀνδρὶ ἀπαιδεύτῳ δυναστείαν.''

132

Stobaeus, iv. 32. 15 (v, p. 784 Hense).

Πλουτάρχου ἐκ τοῦ ὅτι καὶ γυναῖκα παιδευτέον·

Ἀρχύτας ἀναγνοὺς τὸν Ἐρατοσθένους Ἑρμῆν, τοῦτον ἐπήνεγκε[1] τὸν στίχον·

χρειὼ πάντ' ἐδίδαξε· τί δ' οὐ χρειώ κεν ἀνεύροι; καὶ τοῦτον[2]·

ὀρθοῦ· καὶ γὰρ[3] μᾶλλον[4] ἐπωδίνουσι μέριμναι.

133

Stobaeus, iv. 52. 43 (v, p. 1085 Hense).

Πλουτάρχου ἐκ τοῦ ὅτι καὶ γυναῖκα παιδευτέον·

Τροφώνιος καὶ Ἀγαμήδης ποιήσαντες ἐν Δελφοῖς ναὸν ᾔτουν παρὰ τοῦ Ἀπόλλωνος τὸν μισθόν· ὁ δ' αὐτοῖς ἔφη δώσειν τῇ ἑβδόμῃ ἡμέρᾳ· καὶ τῇ

[1] ἐπήνεσε Cobet.
[2] Meineke : τοῦτο.
[3] A : ὀρθοῦ γὰρ καὶ SM : ὄρθρου γὰρ καὶ Meineke.
[4] μεῖον Bergk.

131

Plutarch, from the work *A Woman, too, should be Educated* :

Don't give a child a knife, says the proverb.[a] I would say, " Don't give a child wealth, nor an un-educated man political power."

132

Plutarch, from the work *A Woman, too, should be Educated* :

Archytas,[b] having read Eratosthenes' *Hermes*, quoted the line

> Need teaches all ; what could not Need invent ?

and also

> Arise ! the birth-pangs of your problems grow.

133

Plutarch, from the work *A Woman, too, should be Educated* :

Trophonius and Agamedes, having built a temple at Delphi, asked Apollo for their reward. He replied that he would give it them six days later ; and six

---

[a] Leutsch, *Paroemiographi graeci*, i. 276, ii. 528.

[b] The poet Archytas of Amphissa ; these are frags. 3 and 4 in *Collectanea Alexandrina*, ed. J. U. Powell, who thinks, however, that they may have been quotations from Philetas' *Hermes*. Cobet's emendation (" praised " for " quoted ") would make the lines part of Eratosthenes' poem, for which see *Coll. Alex.*, p. 58. The first line is quoted again by Plutarch, frag. 147.

ἑβδόμη ἀπέθανον. ἔτι δὲ Κλέοβις καὶ Βίτων, Κυ-
δίππης τῆς μητρὸς αὐτῶν εὐξαμένης τῇ Ἥρᾳ δοῦ-
ναι τοῖς παισὶν ὅπερ ἂν εἴη κάλλιστον, ὅτι ἑαυτοὺς
ὑποζεύξαντες τὴν μητέρα εἰς τὸ ἱερὸν ἀνήγαγον, τὸν
βίον παραχρῆμα κατέστρεψαν· εἰς οὓς καὶ τοιόνδε
τις ἐπίγραμμα πεποίηκεν·

οἵδε Βίτων Κλέοβίς τ' ἐπὶ σώμασιν οἰκείοισιν
    ζεῦγλαν ζευξάμενοι μητέρα ἦν ἀγέτην
Ἥρας εἰς ἱερόν· λαοὶ δέ μιν ἐζήλωσαν
    εὐτεκνίας παίδων. ἡ δὲ χαρεῖσα θεᾷ
εὔξατο παῖδε τυχεῖν τοῦ ἀρίστου δαίμονος αἴσης,
    οὕνεκ' ἐτίμησαν μητέρα τὴν σφετέρην.
αὐτοῦ δ' εὐνηθέντε λίπον βίον ἐν νεότητι,
    ὡς τόδ' ἄριστον ἐὸν καὶ μακαριστότατον.

ΠΕΡΙ ΕΡΩΤΟΣ

134

Stobaeus, iv. 20. 34 (iv, p. 444 Hense).

Πλουτάρχου ἐκ τοῦ περὶ ἔρωτος·

Τῶν Μενάνδρου δραμάτων ὁμαλῶς ἁπάντων ἕν
συνεκτικόν ἐστιν, ὁ ἔρως, οἷον πνεῦμα κοινὸν δια-
πεφοιτηκώς.[1] ὄντ'[2] οὖν μάλιστα θιασώτην τοῦ θεοῦ
καὶ ὀργιαστὴν τὸν ἄνδρα συμπαραλαμβάνωμεν[3] εἰς
τὴν ζήτησιν, ἐπεὶ καὶ λελάληκε περὶ τοῦ πάθους
φιλοσοφώτερον. ἄξιον γὰρ εἶναι θαύματος φήσας[4]

---

[1] Bernardakis : διαπεφυκώς. διακεχυκώς Meineke.
[2] Bernardakis : ὄν. Deeper corruption is possible.
[3] Wyttenbach (-οιμεν): συμπεριλαμβάνομεν (-ωμεν Meineke).
[4] Jacobs : φῆσαι.

days later they died. Again, Cydippê, the mother of Cleobis and Biton, prayed to Hera to give her sons whatever might be her finest gift, because they had harnessed themselves and drawn their mother to the goddess's temple ; they immediately passed away.[a] Someone has composed an epigram on them as follows :

Here lie Biton and Cleobis, who placed a yoke on their own shoulders and drew their mother to the shrine of Hera. The people envied her for having such fine children for her sons, and she in her joy prayed to the goddess that her sons might be allotted the best of fortunes, since they had done this honour to their mother. And thereupon they laid them down to sleep and departed life in their youth, showing this to be the best and most blessed thing there is.

ON LOVE

(Not in Lamprias Catalogue)

134

Plutarch, from the work *On Love* :

One thing regularly gives cohesion to all Menander's plays—Love, which pervades them like a universal spirit.[b] Let us then associate with us in our inquiry this leading celebrant and devotee of the god, since he has also talked about the passion quite philosophically. Having said that the experience of

[a] Both these stories are told by Ps.-Plutarch, *Consolatio ad Apollonium*, 108 E—109 A, Cicero, *Tusc.* i. 113-114 ; the latter by Herodotus, i. 31.

[b] Plutarch uses the language (" give cohesion," " pervade," " universal spirit ") applied by the Stoics to their God, immanent in the world.

τὸ περὶ τοὺς ἐρῶντας, ὥσπερ ἐστὶν ἀμέλει,[1] εἶτ'
ἀπορεῖ καὶ ζητεῖ πρὸς ἑαυτόν,

"τίνι δεδούλωνταί ποτε;
ὄψει; φλύαρος· τῆς γὰρ αὐτῆς πάντες ἂν
ἤρων· κρίσιν γὰρ τὸ βλέπειν ἴσην ἔχει.
ἀλλ' ἡδονή τις τοὺς ἐρῶντας ἐπάγεται
συνουσίας; πῶς οὖν ἕτερος ταύτην ἔχων
οὐδὲν πέπονθεν, ἀλλ' ἀπῆλθε καταγελῶν,
ἕτερος δ'[2] ἀπόλωλε; καιρός ἐστιν ἢ[3] νόσος
ψυχῆς· ὁ πληγεὶς δ' εἰς ἀκμὴν[4] τιτρώσκεται."

ταῦτα τίν' ἐστὶ σκεψώμεθα· καὶ γὰρ ἔχει τι κρου-
στικὸν καὶ κινητικὸν αἴτιον ὁ ἔρως, εἰ καὶ μήτε τὴν
ὄψιν[5] μήτε τὴν συνουσίαν αἰτίαν εἶναι πιθανόν ἐστι·
ἀρχαὶ γὰρ αὐταί[6] τινες ἴσως, ἡ δ' ἰσχὺς καὶ ῥίζωσις
τοῦ πάθους ἐν ἑτέροις. ἡ δ' ἀπόδειξις ἐλαφρὰ καὶ
οὐδ' ἀληθής· οὐ γὰρ ἔχει κρίσιν ἴσην[7] τὸ βλέπειν,
ὥσπερ οὐδὲ τὸ γεύεσθαι. καὶ γὰρ ὄψις ὄψεως καὶ
ἀκοῆς ἀκοὴ φύσει τε μᾶλλον διήρθρωται καὶ τέχνῃ
συγγεγύμνασται πρὸς τὴν τοῦ καλοῦ διάγνωσιν,
ἐν μὲν ἁρμονίαις καὶ μέλεσιν αἱ τῶν μουσικῶν ἐν
δὲ μορφαῖς καὶ ἰδέαις αἱ τῶν ζωγράφων[8]· ὥσπερ
εἰπεῖν ποτε Νικόμαχον λέγουσι πρὸς ἄνθρωπον
ἰδιώτην φήσαντα μὴ καλὴν αὐτῷ φανῆναι τὴν

---

[1] F. H. S. : ἅμα λαλεῖ. [2] δ' added by Dobree.
[3] 763 B, and also below : ἔστη or ἐστι. ἐστιν ᾗ Post.
[4] F. H. S., cf. ἐν ἀκμῇ below : εἴσω δή. ὡς ἔδει Grotius εἰς
ὃ δεῖ Wyttenbach εἰς ἑκὼν Post (cf. Amatorius, 763 B, εἴληπται
δ' εἰς), after G. Hermann's εἰς ὁδί.
[5] εἰ μήτε τὴν ὄψιν added by Halm, ὁ ἔρως and καὶ by F. H. S.
[6] A : αὐταί S.
[7] ἴσην added by Gesner. [8] Gesner : ζῴων φρένες.

---

[a] Frag. 568 Koerte, 541 Kock. The last line and a half
are cited also at Amatorius, 763 B where there is a lacuna

those who are in love is fit matter for astonishment, as to be sure it is, he goes on to puzzle and ask himself :

> Of what are they the slaves ?
> Their eyes ? What nonsense ! All men would then love
> The same girl, since sight's judgement is impartial.
> Some pleasure then in intercourse draws men
> To love ? Then why does one, having this woman,
> Come off untouched and ridicule her charms,
> And yet another's lost ? No, this disease
> Comes when the heart is ready, and a man,
> Struck at the critical time, will get a wound.[a]

Let us see what is to be made of these lines. Love certainly has some impelling, motive cause, even if it is not plausible either that sight or that intercourse should be responsible ; although these are things that may very well be origins of a sort, the strength of the passion has its roots elsewhere. The proof here given, however, has little weight, or is even false. It is not true that " sight's judgement is impartial " any more than it is true of taste. One man's vision and one man's hearing is more developed by nature and more trained by art to recognize beauty than another's : the hearing of the musician where scales and melody are concerned, the vision of the painter where it is a matter of shape and form. For example, there is a story that when some man with no professional knowledge of art told Nicomachus that he had not thought Zeuxis's

for the corrupt words εἴσω δή. Numerous emendations have been suggested, but the cure remains doubtful. Post translates his text : " Sickness of mind makes the difference. The one man smitten is wounded of his own free will," and cites Augustine, *City of God*, xii. 6, who proves, by using the same argument as is found here, that falling in love is a matter of free will.

Ζεύξιδος Ἑλένην· "λάβε γάρ," ἔφη, "τοὺς ἐμοὺς ὀφθαλμούς, καὶ θεός σοι φανήσεται." πολὺ δὲ καὶ μυρεψοὶ περὶ τὰ ὀσφραντὰ καὶ νὴ Δί' ὀψοποιοὶ περὶ τὰ γευστὰ διατριβῇ καὶ συνηθείᾳ διαφέρουσαν ἡμῶν κρίσιν ἔχουσι. πάλιν δὲ τὸ συνουσίᾳ τὸν ἐρῶντα[1] μὴ κρατεῖσθαι, διὰ τὸ τῇ αὐτῇ συγγενό-μενον ἄλλον ἀπαλλαγῆναι καὶ καταφρονῆσαι, τοιοῦ-τόν ἐστιν, οἷον εἰ λέγοι τις μηδὲ χυμῶν ἡδονῇ δε-δουλῶσθαι Φιλόξενον τὸν ὀψοφάγον, ὅτι τῶν αὐτῶν Ἀντισθένης γευσάμενος οὐδὲν ἔπαθε τοιοῦτον, μηδ' ὑπὸ οἴνου μεθύειν Ἀλκιβιάδην, ὅτι Σωκράτης πίνων τὸν ἴσον οἶνον ἔνηφεν.

Ἀλλὰ ταῦτα μὲν ἐάσωμεν, τὰ δ' ἐφεξῆς, ἐν οἷς ἤδη τὴν αὐτοῦ[2] δόξαν ἀποφαίνεται, σκοπῶμεν. "καιρός ἐστιν ἡ νόσος ψυχῆς." εὖ καὶ ὀρθῶς. δεῖ γὰρ ἅμα τοῦ πάσχοντος εἰς ταὐτὸ καὶ τοῦ ποιοῦντος ἀπάντησιν γενέσθαι, πρὸς ἄλληλά πως ἐχόντων· ὡς ἄκυρον εἰς τὴν τοῦ τέλους ἀπεργασίαν ἡ δραστικὴ δύναμις, ἂν μὴ παθητικὴ διάθεσις ᾖ. τοῦτο δ' εὐ-στοχίας ἐστὶ καιροῦ τῷ παθεῖν ἑτοίμῳ[3] συνάπτον-τος ἐν ἀκμῇ τὸ ποιεῖν πεφυκός.[4]

135

Stobaeus, iv. 20. 67 (iv, p. 468 Hense).

Ἐκ τῶν Πλουτάρχου ὅτι οὐ κρίσις ὁ ἔρως·

Οἱ μὲν γὰρ νόσον[5] τὸν ἔρωτα οἱ δ' ἐπιθυμίαν οἱ δὲ

[1] Meineke : ἔρωτα. [2] Meineke : αὐτοῦ.
[3] Wyttenbach : ἐμοί πως S : ἔμοιγέ πως A.
[4] Trincavelli's ed. : πεφυκώς. [5] Cobet : νοῦν.

[a] The same anecdote is in Aelian, *Varia Hist.* xiv. 47. Nicomachus was a leading painter of the 4th century B.C.

Helen beautiful, the painter replied : " Take my eyes, and you will think her a goddess." [a] Perfume-makers, too, through practice and familiarity judge very much better than we do about the scent of things, and, if it comes to that, cooks about flavours. Then to argue that the lover is not mastered by the pleasure of intercourse because another man who has lain with the same woman makes off without giving her another thought, is like saying that Philoxenus [b] the gourmand was not enslaved to the pleasure of the palate because Antisthenes tasted the same food without its having any such effect on him ; or that wine did not make Alcibiades tipsy, because Socrates drank as much and remained sober.[c]

But let us drop these points and consider the following lines in which he expresses his own opinion. " This disease comes when the heart is ready." Well and truly put ! There must occur the simultaneous meeting at one point of agent and patient, related to one another in a particular way. The active power is incapable of producing the final result unless the passive condition is there ; and this is a matter of hitting the right moment that brings together at the critical time what is of the sort to act and what is ready to be acted upon.

135

From Plutarch's argument that love is not a matter of decision :

To some love seems to be a disease, to others a

[b] Identified in antiquity, perhaps mistakenly, with Philoxenus the writer of dithyrambs (c. 435–380 B.C.).

[c] Plato, *Symposium*, 213 E—214 E.

φιλίαν[1] οἱ δὲ μανίαν οἱ δὲ θεῖόν τι κίνημα τῆς ψυχῆς
καὶ δαιμόνιον, οἱ δ᾽ ἄντικρυς θεὸν ἀναγορεύουσιν.
ὅθεν ὀρθῶς ἐνίοις ἔδοξε τὸ μὲν ἀρχόμενον ἐπιθυμίαν
εἶναι τὸ δ᾽ ὑπερβάλλον μανίαν τὸ δ᾽ ἀντίστροφον
φιλίαν τὸ δὲ ταπεινότερον ἀρρωστίαν τὸ δ᾽ εὐη-
μεροῦν ἐνθουσιασμόν. διὸ καὶ πυρφόρον αὐτὸν οἵ
τε ποιηταὶ λέγουσιν οἵ τε πλάσται καὶ γραφεῖς
δημιουργοῦσιν, ὅτι καὶ τοῦ πυρὸς τὸ μὲν λαμπρὸν
ἥδιστόν ἐστιν τὸ δὲ καυστικὸν ἀλγεινότατον.

136

Stobaeus, iv. 20. 68 (iv, p. 469 Hense).

Ἐν ταὐτῷ·

Ὥσπερ γὰρ τοὺς φίλους ὑγιαίνοντας μέν, ἂν
πλημμελῶσιν, ἐξελέγχειν καὶ νουθετεῖν κράτιστόν
ἐστιν, ἐν δὲ ταῖς παρακοπαῖς καὶ τοῖς φρενιτισμοῖς
εἰώθαμεν μὴ διαμάχεσθαι μηδ᾽ ἀντιτείνειν ἀλλὰ
καὶ συμπεριφέρεσθαι καὶ συνεπινεύειν· οὕτω τοὺς
δι᾽ ὀργὴν ἢ πλεονεξίαν ἁμαρτάνοντας ἀνακόπτειν
τῇ παρρησίᾳ δεῖ καὶ κωλύειν, τοῖς δ᾽ ἐρῶσιν ὥσπερ
νοσοῦσι συγγνώμην ἔχειν. διὸ κράτιστον μὲν ἐξ
ἀρχῆς τοιούτου πάθους σπέρμα μὴ παραδέχεσθαι
μηδ᾽ ἀρχήν· ἂν δ᾽ ἐγγένηται, ἴθι ἐπὶ ἀποτροπαίων
βωμοὺς θεῶν κατὰ τὸν Πλάτωνα, ἴθι ἐπὶ τὰς τῶν
σοφῶν ἀνδρῶν συνουσίας, ἐξέλασον αὐτοῦ τὸ θηρίον
πρὶν ὄνυχας φῦσαι καὶ ὀδόντας· εἰ δὲ μή, μαχέσῃ
τελείῳ κακῷ, τὸ παιδίον τοῦτο καὶ νήπιον ἐναγκαλι-
ζόμενος. τίνες δ᾽ εἰσὶν οἱ τοῦ ἔρωτος ὄνυχες καὶ
ὀδόντες; ὑποψία, ζηλοτυπία. ἀλλ᾽ ἔχει τι πιθανὸν

[1] οἱ δὲ φιλίαν added by F. H. S.

254

desire, to others friendship, to others a madness, to others a divine or demoniac change in the soul, and yet others proclaim it a god outright. Hence there are those who have rightly thought its beginning a desire, its excess a madness, its reciprocation friendship ; in its abasement it is a malady and when it flourishes happily it is possession by a supernatural power. And so poets speak of Love, and sculptors and painters fashion him, as the bearer of fire, because fire, too, has a splendour that gives the greatest pleasure, but a power of burning that inflicts the greatest pain.

136

In the same place :

Although when our friends are in their right minds it is best to show them their errors and correct them when they make a mistake, we usually do not struggle with them or contend against them when they are mentally deranged or delirious, but humour them and agree with them. Just so, we should speak freely to check and deter those who do wrong through anger or avarice, but show forbearance towards those who are in love, as if they were sick.

And so it is best from the first not to harbour the seed or origin of such a passion. But if it is implanted, betake yourself to the altars of the averting deities as Plato advises,[a] betake yourself to the company of wise men, expel the wild beast from you before it grows teeth and claws. If you do not, you will find yourself fighting a fully-grown monster, through taking to your arms this child, this infant. And what are Love's teeth and claws ? Suspicion, jealousy.

[a] *Laws*, 854 B.

καὶ ἀνθηρόν. ἀμέλει καὶ ἡ[1] Σφὶγξ εἶχεν ἐπαγωγὸν
τὸ ποίκιλμα τοῦ πτεροῦ, καὶ

εἰ μὲν πρὸς αὐγὰς[2] ἡλίου, χρυσωπὸν ἦν
νώτισμα θηρός· εἰ δὲ πρὸς νέφη[3] βάλοι,
κυανωπὸν ὥς τις *Ἶρις ἀντηύγει[4] σέλας.

οὕτω δὴ καὶ ὁ ἔρως ἔχει τι χαρίεν καὶ οὐκ ἄμουσον
ἀλλ' αἱμύλον καὶ ἐπιτερπές· ἁρπάζει δὲ καὶ βίους
καὶ οἴκους καὶ γάμους καὶ ἡγεμονίας,[5] οὐκ αἰνίγ-
ματα προβάλλων ἀλλ' αὐτὸς αἴνιγμα δυσεύρετον
ὢν καὶ δύσλυτον, εἰ βούλοιτό τις προτείνειν τί
μισεῖ καὶ φιλεῖ, τί φεύγει καὶ διώκει, τί ἀπειλεῖ
καὶ ἱκετεύει, τί ὀργίζεται καὶ ἐλεεῖ, τί[6] βούλεται
παύσασθαι καὶ οὐ βούλεται, τί χαίρει τῷ αὐτῷ μάλιστα καὶ ἀνιᾶται, τί τὸ αὐτὸ λυπεῖ καὶ θεραπεύει.[7]
τῆς μὲν γὰρ Σφιγγὸς τὸ αἴνιγμα τὰ πλεῖστα καὶ
πεπλασμένα ἔχει· οὔτε γὰρ τρίπους ὁ γέρων ἀληθῶς, εἴ τι[8] προσείληφε τοῖς ποσὶ βοηθεῖν· οὔτε τε-
τράπους ὁ νήπιος, ἐπεὶ ταῖς χερσὶν ὑπερείδει τὴν
τῶν βάσεων ὑγρότητα καὶ ἀσθένειαν. τὰ δὲ τῶν
ἐρώντων πάθη[9] ἀληθῆ· στέργουσιν, ἐχθραίνουσι·
τὸν αὐτὸν ποθοῦσιν ἀπόντα, τρέμουσι παρόντος·
κολακεύουσι λοιδοροῦσι, προαποθνῄσκουσι φονεύου-
σιν, εὔχονται μὴ φιλεῖν καὶ παύσασθαι φιλοῦντες
οὐ θέλουσι· σωφρονίζουσι καὶ πειρῶσι,[10] παιδεύουσι
καὶ διαφθείρουσιν, ἄρχειν θέλουσι καὶ δουλεύειν

---

[1] ἡ added by second hand in A.
[2] ἱπ]πους P. Oxy. 2459.
[3] νέφος P. Oxy. 2459.
[4] ἀνταυγεῖ, corrected by second hand in A.
[5] Wyttenbach : ἡγεμόνας.
[6] τί added by Wakefield.
[7] τί . . . θεραπεύει Kronenberg : τοῦτο λῦσαι καὶ θερα-
πεῦσαι.

But he has something gay and winning about him.
No doubt the Sphinx, too, had something attractive
in the changing colours of her feathers, and

> Gold gleamed the creature's coverts, turned she them
> To face the shining sun ; but cloudwise turned,
> A dark reflection shone, hued like a rainbow.[a]

So Love, too, has something about him that is graceful
and not without elegance but full of wiles and blan-
dishment. He robs men of their livelihoods, their es-
tablishments, their marriages, their high commands,
propounding no riddles, but being himself a riddle
that would be hard to discover or solve, if one were
to propose as a puzzle " what is it that hates and
loves, flees and pursues, threatens and implores,
feels anger and pity, wishes and does not wish to
come to an end, finds the greatest joy and torment
in the same source, and hurts the very thing it
serves ? " The riddle of the Sphinx consists for
the most part of what are really fictions : an old
man is not in truth three-footed if he has taken a
stick to reinforce his feet, nor an infant four-footed
because it supports its weak and infirm steps with
its hands. But there is nothing unreal about lovers'
passions : they show affection and hate, long for the
absent one, yet tremble at his presence, flatter him,
abuse him, sacrifice their lives for him, murder him,
pray not to be fond, while unwilling to cease being
fond ; they discipline and tempt, educate and corrupt,
wish to command and endure to be slaves. There

---

[a] Nauck, *Trag. Graec. Frag.*, adespota 541, now known
to be from Euripides' *Oedipus* (P. Oxy. 2459).

---

[8] τι added by Gaisford.
[9] πάντ' added by Piccolos to remove hiatus.
[10] Wyttenbach : πηρῶσιν.

ὑπομένουσι. τοῦτ' αἴτιον γέγονε μάλιστα τοῦ μανίαν ὑποληφθῆναι τὸ πάθος·

ἥρων· τὸ μαίνεσθαι δ' ἄρ' ἦν ἔρως βροτοῖς,
ἐρωτικὸς ἀνὴρ Εὐριπίδης φησίν.

137

Stobaeus, iv. 20. 69 (iv, p. 470 Hense).

Τοῦ αὐτοῦ περὶ ἔρωτος·

Ὁ ἔρως οὔτε τὴν γένεσιν ἐξαίφνης λαμβάνει καὶ
ἀθρόαν ὡς ὁ θυμός, οὔτε παρέρχεται ταχέως καίπερ
εἶναι πτηνὸς λεγόμενος· ἀλλ' ἐξάπτεται μαλακῶς[1]
καὶ σχεδὸν οἷον ἐντήκων ἑαυτόν· ἁψάμενός τε τῆς
ψυχῆς παραμένει πολὺν χρόνον, οὐδ' ἐν γηρῶσιν
ἐνίοις ἀναπαυόμενος ἀλλ' ἐν πολιαῖς ἀκμάζων ἔτι
πρόσφατος καὶ νεαρός· ἂν δὲ καὶ λήξῃ καὶ διαλυθῇ,
χρόνῳ μαρανθεὶς ἢ λόγῳ τινὶ κατασβεσθείς, οὔπω
παντάπασιν ἐξαπήλλακται τῆς ψυχῆς ἀλλ' ἐναπο-
λείπει πυρίκαυτον ὕλην καὶ σημεῖα θερμά, καθάπερ
οἱ κεραυνοὶ οἱ[2] τυφόμενοι. λύπης μὲν γὰρ οὐδὲν
ἀπαλλαγείσης ἴχνος ἐν τῇ ψυχῇ παραμένει σύνοικον
οὐδ' ὀργῆς τραχείας πεσούσης, συστέλλεται[3] δὲ
καὶ φλεγμονὴ ἐπιθυμίας[4] παρεχούσης τραχὺ κίνημα·
τὰ δ' ἐρωτικὰ δήγματα, κἂν ἀποστῇ τὸ θηρίον, οὐκ
ἐξανίησι τὸν ἰόν, ἀλλ' ἐνοιδεῖ[5] τὰ ἐντὸς σπαράγ-

---

[1] Gesner : μαλακός.   [2] οἱ added by F. H. S.
[3] Piccolos : στέλλεται.   [4] ? ἐπιθυμίας φλεγμονή.
[5] ἐνδροῖ mss. : corrected by second hand in A.

---

[a] Nauck, *Trag. Graec. Frag.*, Euripides, frag. 161. Possibly " they loved."
[b] M. Pohlenz, *Göttinger Gelehrter Anzeiger*, 1916, p. 548,
argues that this passage has some echoes of a work on anger

you have the very reason why this passion is conceived of as a madness.

> I loved : for mortals Love is to grow mad.[a]

Those words are from a man who was susceptible to love, Euripides.

137

From the same, on Love :

Love is not born suddenly and all at once as anger is,[b] nor does it pass away quickly, for all that it is said to have wings. It takes fire gently, almost melting its way in, as it were ; and when it has taken hold of the soul it long endures—in some men it does not sleep even when they grow old, but remains in its prime, still fresh and vigorous when their hairs are grey.[c] But if it does abate and dissolve, either dying away with the passage of time or being extinguished by some rational consideration, it does not remove itself finally and completely from the soul, but leaves charred matter and a hot trail there behind it, smouldering as thunderbolts do where they have fallen. When grief has gone or savage anger subsided no trace of them remains lodging in the soul ; the inflammation of desire, too, subsides, sharp though the disturbance may be that it causes. But the bites inflicted by love[d] do not rid themselves of his venom, even if the brute leaves go ; no, the internal lacera-

by the Peripatetic philosopher Hieronymus, and that it is earlier than *De Cohibenda Ira*, where Fundanus (who may be taken as Plutarch's mouthpiece) rejects Hieronymus' view that anger is a sudden thing (454 r).

[c] *Cf. Amatorius*, 770 c.
[d] *Cf.* Xenophon, *Symposium*, iv. 28 ; Sophocles, frag. 757 Nauck.

ματα, καὶ ἀγνοεῖται τί ἦν, πῶς συνέστη, πόθεν εἰς τὴν ψυχὴν ἐνέπεσεν.

138

Stobaeus, iv. 21. 25 (iv, p. 492 Hense).

Πλουτάρχου ἐκ τοῦ περὶ ἔρωτος·

Καὶ τοὺς καλοὺς ὁρᾶν μὲν ἐπιτερπέστατον, ἅψα- σθαι δὲ καὶ λαβεῖν οὐκ ἀκίνδυνον· μᾶλλον δέ, ὥς φησιν ὁ Ξενοφῶν, τὸ μὲν πῦρ τοὺς ἁψαμένους κάει μόνον, οἱ δὲ καλοὶ καὶ τοὺς μακρὰν ἑστῶτας ὑφ- άπτουσιν· ἡ γὰρ ὄψις λαβὴ τοῦ πάθους ἐστί.

ΠΕΡΙ ΕΥΓΕΝΕΙΑΣ

The work from which Stobaeus drew these fragments may have been a dialogue, since one is for and two are against good birth. Whether it was in fact by Plutarch may be a matter for doubt [c]: the style of the latter passages is a strained

139

Stobaeus, iv. 29. 21 (v, p. 708 Hense) = Ps.-Plutarch, *De Nobilitate*, chap. 10.

Πλουτάρχου ἐκ τοῦ κατὰ εὐγενείας·

Τί γὰρ ἄλλο νομίζομεν εἶναι τὴν εὐγένειαν, εἰ μὴ παλαιὸν πλοῦτον ἢ[1] παλαιὰν δόξαν, οὐδέτερον ἐφ'

---

[1] ἢ SM : ἢ καὶ A, Ps.-Plut.

---

[a] *Cyropaedia*, v. 1. 16.
[b] ἐρᾶν is explicitly derived from ὁρᾶν by Philostratus,

260

tions swell, and no one knows what the trouble is, how it arose, or from where it came to attack the victim's soul.

138

Plutarch, from the work *On Love* :

And it is a most delightful thing to look upon the beautiful, but to touch and hold them has its dangers. Or rather, as Xenophon says,[a] whereas fire burns only those who touch it, the beautiful kindle a flame even in those who stand well away. For it is sight that allows this passion to get its grip.[b]

ON GOOD BIRTH

(*Lamprias Catalogue* 203)

one, and the construction νομίζεις ὅτι in frag. 140 unusual at the least, while in the same fragment ἄν with ἐδύνατο and ἰδίας with πατρίδος appear to be solecistic superfluities. The fragments are included in a forgery De Nobilitate, for which see Appendix A.

139

Plutarch, from the work *Against Good Birth* :

What else do we take good birth to be but ancient wealth or ancient reputation ? Neither is ours to com-

Epist. 52, but the play on words is much older, *e.g.*, Agathon, frag. 29 (Nauck, *T.G.F.*).

[c] *Cf.* Wyttenbach's edition of *De Sera Numinis Vindicta*, p. 85.

ἡμῖν ὄν, ἀλλὰ τὰ μὲν τύχης ἀδήλου τὰ δ' ἀκρισίας[1]
χάριν ἀνθρωπίνης· ὥστ' ἐκ δυεῖν ἀλλοτρίων κρέ-
μαται τὸ πεφυσημένον ὄνομ' ἡ εὐγένεια. καὶ ὁ[2]
πλοῦτος μὲν οὐχ ὁμοίους αὑτῷ τοὺς γεννηθέντας
ποιεῖ, ἀλλ' ὁ ἐξ ἀρετῆς γεννηθεὶς εἰκονίζεται, τῶν
ἐπὶ τῆς ψυχῆς δικαίων εἰς τοὺς ἐκγόνους διαχεο-
μένων. καὶ τοῦτ' ἔστιν ἡ ὄντως εὐγένεια, ὁμοίω-
σις δικαιοσύνης.

140

Stobaeus, iv. 29. 22 (v, p. 709 Hense)=Ps.-Plutarch, *De
Nobilitate*, chap. 10.

Ἐν ταὐτῷ·

Ἆρ' οὖν εὐγενέστερος ἦν ὁ Μίδου πλοῦτος τῆς
Ἀριστείδου πενίας; καίτοι ὁ μὲν[3] οὐδ' ἐντάφια
καταλιπών, τῷ δὲ Φρυγὶ πάντ' ἂν ἐδύνατο εἶναι
τάφος. ἀλλ' οὐκ ἐν πλουσίῳ[4] τὸ εὐγενές. πυρὸς
ἔχει τινὰ τρόπον πᾶσα πονηρία· ἀμφότερα χωρὶς
τροφῆς ἀφανίζεται σβεννύμενα.[5] ἡ δὲ Σωκράτους
ἀδοξία, μαίας[6] καὶ ἑρμογλύφου πατρός, οὐκ ἦν
εὐγενεστέρα τῆς Σαρδαναπάλλου δόξης; μὴ σύ γε
νομίζεις[7] ὅτι Ξέρξης εὐγενέστερος ἦν Κυνεγείρου;[8]
καίτοι ὁ μὲν ὑπὲρ τῆς ἰδίας πατρίδος ἀπεκόπη τὴν
χεῖρα, ὁ δ' ὑπὲρ τοῦ ζῆν ἔφυγεν, ἀντὶ τῆς μεγάλης
βασιλείας μεγάλην περικείμενος δειλίαν.

[1] ἀκρισίας S : ἀκρασίας MA, Tr., Ps.-Plut.
[2] ὁ Tr., Ps.-Plut. : τὸ SMA.
[3] ? add ἀπέθανεν.
[4] ? πλούτῳ or πλουσίου, or a noun may be missing.
[5] πυρὸς . . . σβεννύμενα deleted by Grammius.
[6] Bernardakis suggested adding μητρὸς.

mand, but both are in part the gift of uncertain fortune, in part that of human lack of judgement. So that this inflated name of good birth hangs on two alien pegs. And wealth does not create offspring like itself, whereas the man begotten from virtue grows in his father's image, since spiritual goods are transmitted to descendants. This is what true good birth is—assimilation to morality.

140

In the same work :

Was then Midas' wealth better-born than Aristides' poverty ? Yet the latter did not leave enough even for his funeral,[a] while the Phrygian's tomb could have been anything in the world. Nobility does not lie in wealth. All badness has a certain likeness to fire : both, if they have nothing to feed on, are extinguished and vanish.[b] And was not the obscurity of Socrates, son of a midwife and a stone-mason, nobler than the renown of Sardanapallus ? Perhaps you suppose that Xerxes was nobler than Cynegirus ?[c] Yet the latter lost his hand in his own country's cause, whereas the former fled to save his life, in the trappings of a great coward instead of those of a great kingdom.

[a] See *Life of Aristides*, chap. 27.
[b] As the text stands, this sentence is irrelevant ; the context may have been abbreviated.
[c] Sardanapallus, last king of Assyria, became a by-word among the Greeks for luxury and self-indulgence. Cynegirus, brother of the poet Aeschylus, and killed at the battle of Marathon, was a type of martial valour.

---

[7] νομίζης M before correction, Tr., Ps.-Plut.
[8] M : κυνειγείρου S. κυναιγείρου A, Ps.-Plut., κυναιγύρου Tr.

Stobaeus, iv. 29. 51 (v, p. 722 Hense) = Ps.-Plutarch, *De Nobilitate*, chap. 1.

Πλουτάρχου ὑπὲρ εὐγενείας·

Ἄπιστος ἡ τῶν σοφιστῶν συκοφαντία κατὰ τῆς εὐγενείας, εἰ μηδὲ τὰ ἐν μέσῳ καὶ πᾶσι γνώριμα σκοποῦσιν, ὅτι πρὸς τὰς ὀχείας τοὺς εὐγενεῖς ἵππους καὶ κύνας ὠνοῦνται καὶ κιχρῶνται καὶ[1] ἀμπέλων εὐγενῆ σπέρματα καὶ ἐλαιῶν καὶ τῶν ἄλλων δένδρων, ἀνθρώπου δ' οὐδὲν ὄφελος νομίζουσιν εὐγένειαν εἰς τὰς μελλούσας διαδοχάς, ἀλλὰ ταὐτὸ[2] πείθονται βάρβαρον εἶναι καὶ Ἑλληνικὸν σπέρμα καὶ οὐκ οἴονται λεληθυίας τινὰς ἀρχὰς καὶ σπέρματ' ἀρετῆς συγκαταβάλλεσθαι τοῖς γεννωμένοις, ὥσπερ τῷ Τηλεμάχῳ τοῦ Ὀδυσσέως, ἐφ' οὗ καὶ πάνυ †τῷ ὀνόματι[3] ὁ ποιητὴς εἴρηκεν

ἐνέστακται μένος ἠΰ,

ὡς ἂν ἐν ταῖς σπερμάτων ὀλίγαις σταγόσι καὶ τῶν ἀρετῆς συρρεόντων ἀγαθῶν.[4]

ΠΕΡΙ ΗΜΕΡΩΝ

It is clear that some events mentioned in chap. 19 of the Life of Camillus were dealt with in the book On Dates, *besides the two specifically referred to it. It is likely that*

141

Plutarch, in favour of good birth :

The sophists' denunciation of good birth has no plausibility ; without even considering the obvious and universally familiar facts that we buy or borrow well-bred horses and dogs for purposes of mating, and similarly seeds of good stock for vines, olives, and other trees, where man is concerned they recognize no value in good birth for future inheritance. They prefer to believe that Greek and non-Greek seed is identical and do not think that certain invisible principles or seeds of excellence are contributed to the offspring, as they were to Odysseus' son Telemachus, of whom the poet said, choosing the word most appropriately,

> good strength has been *instilled*,[a]

as if with those few drops of semen there had flowed the good qualities of excellence as well.

ON DATES

(Lamprias Catalogue 150)

some at least of those mentioned in Quaestiones Convivales, *717 B-D, also found a place there. It is also possible that frag. 100 refers to this book ; see the note there.*

[a] *Odyssey,* ii. 271.

---

[1] Meineke suggested adding πρὸς φυτουργίαν.
[2] Wyttenbach : ἀλλ' αὐτό.
[3] Something may be omitted. πάνυ κυρίῳ Duebner.
[4] ? συρρεουσῶν ἀρχῶν.

142

Plutarch, *Vita Camilli*, chap. 19.

Οἱ δ'[1] Ἀθηναῖοι καὶ τὴν περὶ Νάξον ἐνίκων ναυ-
μαχίαν, ἧς Χαβρίας ἐστρατήγει, τοῦ Βοηδρομιῶνος
περὶ τὴν πανσέληνον, ἐν δὲ Σαλαμῖνι περὶ τὰς
εἰκάδας, ὡς ἡμῖν ἐν τῷ περὶ ἡμερῶν ἀποδέδεικται.

ΠΕΡΙ ΗΣΥΧΙΑΣ

No work entitled περὶ ἡσυχίας is included in the Lamprias
Catalogue, and some features of this fragment argue against
Plutarchean authorship. It contains three instances of consecutive τε καί ; but it is just possible that they are due to
careless copying by Stobaeus or his source. There are no
examples of Plutarch's favourite ditrochaic clausula ; but
the piece is very short. Two instances of hiatus may be due
to textual corruption.

143

Stobaeus, iv. 16. 18 (iv, p. 398 Hense).

Πλουτάρχου ἐκ τοῦ περὶ ἡσυχίας·

Σοφὸν ἔοικε χρῆμα τὸ τῆς ἡσυχίας πρός τ' ἄλλα
καὶ εἰς ἐπιστήμης[2] καὶ φρονήσεως μελέτην· λέγω δ'
οὐ τὴν καπηλικὴν καὶ ἀγοραίαν ἀλλὰ τὴν μεγάλην,
ἥτις ἐξομοιοῖ θεῷ τὸν αὐτὴν ἀναλαβόντα. αἱ μὲν
γὰρ ἐν ταῖς πόλεσι καὶ τοῖς τῶν ἀνθρώπων ὄχλοις
γινόμεναι μελέται γυμνάζουσι τὴν λεγομένην δρι-
μύτητα, πανουργίαν οὖσαν· ὥστε τοὺς ἐν αὐταῖς
ἄκρους οἷον ὑπὸ μαγείρων τῶν ἐν ταῖς πόλεσι
χρειῶν διαπεποικιλμένους πόσα μὲν οὐχὶ **[3] πόσα

---

[1] δ' added by Anon.　　　[2] F. H. S. : ἐπιστήμην.
[3] πόσα μὲν οὐχὶ added by Wyttenbach.

142

The Athenian victory, under the command of Chabrias, in the naval engagement at Naxos took place in the month of Boëdromiôn at the time of the full moon, that at Salamis about the 20th day of the same month, as I have shown in my work *On Dates*.

ON QUIETUDE

F. Wilhelm, Rh. Mus. *lxxiii (1924), pp. 466 ff., translates into German and accumulates a mass of illustrative material. He notes that the question of retirement from city life was in the air in the latter part of the first century* A.D., *as is shown by the discussions of Seneca,* Epist. *lxviii, Epictetus, iv. 4, Dio Chrysostom, xx, Quintilian, x. 3. 32 ff., Tacitus,* Dialogus, *12 f.*

143

Plutarch, from the work *On Quietude* :

How wise a thing, it would seem, is quietude ! In particular it serves for studying to acquire knowledge and wisdom, by which I do not mean the wisdom of shop and market-place, but that mighty wisdom which makes him that acquires it like to God.[a] Those forms of study that are practised in towns among the crowds of humanity exercise the so-called shrewdness that is really knavery. Hence those who excel in them have been diversified by the needs of city life, like so many fancy products of the culinary art, ⟨and have become ready to do innumerable

---

[a] A phrase originating from Plato, *Theaet.* 176 B.

δ' οὐχὶ καὶ διακονήματα δεινὰ[1] ἐργάζεσθαι; ἡ δ'
ἐρημία, σοφίας οὖσα γυμνάσιον, ἠθοποιὸς ἀγαθὴ
καὶ πλάττει καὶ μετευθύνει[2] τῶν ἀνδρῶν τὰς ψυχάς.
οὐδὲν γὰρ αὐταῖς ἐμπόδιόν ἐστι τῆς αὐξήσεως, οὐδὲ
πρὸς πολλὰ καὶ μικρὰ νόμιμα προσπταίουσαι κάμ-
πτονται εὐθύ,[3] καθάπερ αἱ ταῖς πόλεσιν ἐναπειλημ-
μέναι ψυχαί· ἀλλ' ἐν ἀέρι καθαρῷ καὶ τὰ πολλὰ ἔξω
διαιτώμεναι[4] τῶν ἀνθρώπων ἀνίασιν[5] ὀρθαὶ καὶ
πτεροφυοῦσιν, ἀρδόμεναι τῷ διαυγεστάτῳ τε καὶ
λειοτάτῳ ῥεύματι τῆς ἡσυχίας, ἐν ᾧ τά τε μαθή-
ματα τοῦ νοῦ θεοειδέστερα[6] καὶ καθαρώτερον ὁρᾷ.[7]
διὰ τοῦτό τοι καὶ τῶν θεῶν τὰ ἱερά, ὅσα ἐκ τοῦ
ἀρχαίου πάλαι[8] νενόμισται, τοῖς ἐρημοτάτοις χωρίοις ἐνίδρυσαν[9] οἱ πρῶτοι, μάλιστα δὲ Μουσῶν τε
καὶ Πανὸς καὶ Νυμφῶν καὶ Ἀπόλλωνος καὶ ὅσοι
μουσικῆς ἡγεμόνες θεοί, διακρίναντες, ὡς οἶμαι,
τὰ παιδείας καλὰ[10] τῶν ἐν ταῖς πόλεσι δεινῶν τε
καὶ μιαρῶν τινων.[11]

ΠΕΡΙ ΚΑΛΛΟΥΣ (?)

*The following three fragments are probably excerpted
from the same book, perhaps a dialogue or a " disputatio in
utramque partem," but its title is uncertain ;* ὑπὲρ κάλλους,

[1] ? ταπεινά.
[2] μεγεθύνει Nauck.
[3] εὐθύς Wyttenbach, but hiatus makes probable some more
serious error.
[4] Wyttenbach : διαιτώμενοι.
[5] Meineke : ἀνιᾶσιν.
[6] A : θεωδέστερα SM.
[7] A : ὁρᾶν SM. τὸ δρᾶν Duebner τὸ ὁρᾶν (or ἐνορᾶν) Bernardakis τὸ διορᾶν Hense. Wyttenbach adds ἔστιν.

wrongs⟩ and indeed to perform innumerable dreadful
services. But solitude, being wisdom's training-
ground, is a good character-builder, and moulds and
reforms men's souls. There is nothing to stand in
the way of their development, nor are they straight-
way distorted by collision with many small conven-
tions, as are souls that are confined in towns ; living
in a pure air and for the most part away from the
haunts of men, they grow up erect and sprout their
wings,[a] watered by quietude's streams, so smooth and
pellucid. Here the mind turns to diviner sorts of learning and sees with a clearer vision. This, surely, is the
reason why it was in solitary spots that man founded
all those shrines of the gods that have been long
established from ancient times, above all those of the
Muses,[b] of Pan and the Nymphs, and of Apollo and
all gods who are our guides in music ; to my mind,
they kept the blessings of education away from the
dreadful and abominable influences of the towns.

ON BEAUTY (?)

(*Not in Lamprias Catalogue*)

*attached to the first fragment, may be merely descriptive of
part of its content. Style and rhythm speak against authenticity, even if one admits the probability that several sentences
have suffered mutilation.*

---

[a] A reference to Plato, *Phaedrus*, 251 B.
[b] *Cf. De Curiositate*, 521 D.

---

[8] F. H. S. : πάλαι ἀρχαίου.
[9] ἐνίδρυσαν added by Wyttenbach (after πρῶτοι).
[10] Meineke : τὰς παιδείας κατά. τὰς παιδείας καὶ τὰ Duebner.
[11] τεχνῶν Duebner πόνων Bernardakis σινῶν Hense.

*144

Stobaeus, iv. 21. 12 (iv, p. 485 Hense).

Πλουτάρχου ὑπὲρ κάλλους·

Τί γάρ; οὐ σύνθετον¹ φύσις ἀνθρώπων ἐκ σώματος καὶ ψυχῆς; ἢ θάτερον ἀρκοῦν ἡμῖν; καὶ πῶς
οἷόν τε; τὸ μὲν γὰρ οὐκ ἂν εἴη μὴ χρώμενον ψυχῇ,
ψυχὴ δ᾽ οὐκ ἂν εἴη μὴ ἔχουσα τὸ συνερεῖδον. τί
οὖν; ὥσπερ ἐξ ἴσου κοσμεῖται ἑκάτερα τοῖς συγ-
γενέσιν, ἡ μὲν δικαιοσύνῃ καὶ σωφροσύνῃ καὶ φρονήσει, τὸ δ᾽ ἰσχύι καὶ κάλλει καὶ ὑγιείᾳ. καὶ πῶς
οὐ θαυμαστὸν λέγειν τὰ τῆς ψυχῆς καλά, τὰ τοῦ
σώματος ὑπερορῶντα;

*145

Stobaeus, iv. 21. 13 (iv, p. 485 Hense).

Ἐν ταὐτῷ·

Ἡ γοῦν τοῦ σώματος εὐμορφία ψυχῆς ἐστιν ἔργον σώματι χαριζομένης δόξαν εὐμορφίας. πεσέτω
γοῦν θανάτῳ τὸ σῶμα, καὶ τῆς ψυχῆς μετῳκισμένης,
οὐ στάσις, οὐ χρῶμα, οὐκ ὀφθαλμός, οὐ φωνή, οὐδὲν ἔτι καταλείπεται τῶν ἐρασμίων, προδεδομένον
δ᾽ ὁρᾷς² ὑπὸ τῶν ἀρχαίων οἰκητόρων· ὥστε καὶ τὴν³
ψυχὴν συνυβρίζεις λανθάνων, ἧς ἔστιν ἀνθρώπου
κάλλος.

*146

Stobaeus, iv. 21. 22 (iv, p. 491 Hense).

Πλουτάρχου·

Ἀλλὰ μήν, ὥσπερ ἔφην, οὐδὲν τῶν ἄλλων καλ-

*144

From Plutarch, *In Defence of Beauty* :

What ? Is not man's nature a thing compounded of body and soul ? Or is one enough for us without the other ? How can it be enough ? The former could not exist without the aid of a soul, and soul could not exist if it had nothing to bind it together. Well then, they are both equally, so to speak, adorned by their cognate virtues, the soul by justice, self-control, and wisdom, the body by strength, beauty and health. Surely it would be a strange thing to record the beauties of the soul, but to overlook those of the body.

*145

In the same book :

At any rate the body's comeliness is the work of the soul, which bestows upon the body its appearance of comeliness. Why, the body need only collapse in death, and the soul having migrated from it, neither its stance nor its colour, neither its eye nor its voice, nor anything else remains of all that was lovely : ⟨you see⟩ it forsaken by its ancient inhabitants. So you fail to notice that in insulting the body you insult the soul, to which all the beauty in a human being belongs.

*146

From Plutarch :

But see, as I said, of all beauties that of the body

---

¹ σύνθετος A.
² δ' ὁρᾷς added by F. H. S., *ex. gr.*
³ τὴν added by Duebner.

λῶν[1] κινδύνων γένεσίς ἐστιν, ἀλλὰ μόνου τοῦ σώματος. τὰ μὲν γὰρ τῆς ψυχῆς κάλλη καὶ σωτηρίας
ἐλπίδες εἰσί, φρόνησις, εὐσέβεια, δικαιοπραγία· καὶ
τὸ παιδείας εὐπρόσωπον κάλλος οἴκου καὶ πόλεως
καὶ ἐθνῶν ἀθόρυβος εἰρήνη διατελεῖ γιγνομένη[2]· ἡ
δὲ γυναικῶν εὐμορφία ἀφορμὴ τοῖς πάθεσι καὶ ταῖς
ἐπιθυμίαις.

ΠΕΡΙ ΜΑΝΤΙΚΗΣ

147

Stobaeus, iv. 18 a. 10 (iv, p. 414 Hense).

Πλουτάρχου ἐκ τοῦ περὶ μαντικῆς·

Τῶν τεχνῶν, ὡς ἔοικε, τὰς μὲν ἡ χρεία συνέστη-
σεν ἐξ ἀρχῆς καὶ μέχρι νῦν διαφυλάσσει—

χρειὼ πάντ᾽ ἐδίδαξε, τί δ᾽ οὐ χρειὼ κεν ἀνεύροι
τῶν ἀναγκαίων;—ὑφαντικὴν οἰκοδομικὴν ἰατρικὴν
καὶ ὅσαι περὶ γεωργίαν ἀναστρέφονται· τὰς δ᾽
ἡδονή τις προσηγάγετο καὶ κατέσχε, τὴν τῶν
μυρεψῶν καὶ τῶν[3] ὀψοποιῶν καὶ κομμωτικὴν πᾶσαν καὶ ἀνθοβαφίαν.[4] ἔστι δ᾽ ὧν τὴν πιθανότητα
καὶ τὴν ἀκρίβειαν καὶ τὸ καθάριον ἀγαπῶντες
ἐκμανθάνουσι καὶ περιέπουσιν, ὡς ἀριθμητικὴν καὶ
γεωμετρίαν καὶ κανονικὴν πᾶσαν καὶ ἀστρολογίαν,
ἅς φησιν ὁ Πλάτων καίπερ ἀμελουμένας, "βίᾳ ὑπὸ
χάριτος αὔξεσθαι."

---

[1] καλλῶν added by Bernardakis.
[2] Bernardakis : γενομένη.
[3] τὴν τῶν Bernardakis.　　　　[4] A : ἀνθοβάθειαν.

---

[a] Cf. An Seni, 797 E.

272

alone gives rise to dangers. The beauties of the soul, wisdom, piety, just dealing,[a] give hope of security ; and the beauty of education, fair of face, always leads to undisturbed peace in the household and in societies, civilized or primitive. But the comeliness of women is an incitement to the passions and desires.

ON THE ART OF PROPHECY

(? *Lamprias Catalogue* 71 *or* 131)

147

Plutarch, from the work *On the Art of Prophecy* :

Some of the arts, it seems, were originally developed by necessity, and are preserved by it to this day, like the arts of weaving, of building, of medicine, and every art concerned with agriculture.

Need teaches all ; what could not Need invent [b]

—of what one cannot do without ? Other arts, however, were introduced and maintained by some pleasure, like the art of the scent-makers, the culinary art, all the arts of personal adornment, or that of the dyer. There are still others that men study to acquire and treat with honour because they love the logic, the precision, and the purity of thought that belongs to them : such are arithmetic, geometry, all the theory of music, and astronomy, arts which Plato says " flourish perforce by their own charm," [c] even if neglected.

[b] Archytas, fr. 3 Powell, *Coll. Alex.*, quoted again, frag. 132 ; see note there.
[c] *Republic*, 528 c, quoted again, *Non Posse Suaviter*, 1094 D.

ΠΕΡΙ ΟΡΓΗΣ

The work περὶ ὀργῆς *is not only in the Lamprias Catalogue, but also recorded by Photius. The occurrence three times of* τε καί, *which Plutarch normally avoids, may be due*

148

Stobaeus, iii. 20. 70 (iii, p. 555 Hense).

Πλουτάρχου ἐκ τοῦ περὶ ὀργῆς·

῞Οσα δ' ὀργῇ χρώμενοι πράττουσιν ἄνθρωποι, ταῦτ' ἀνάγκη τυφλὰ εἶναι καὶ ἀνόητα καὶ τοῦ παντὸς ἁμαρτάνειν. οὐ γὰρ οἷόν τ' ὀργῇ χρώμενον λογισμῷ χρῆσθαι, τὸ δ' ἄνευ λογισμοῦ ποιούμενον πᾶν ἄτεχνόν τε καὶ διεστραμμένον. λόγον οὖν ἡγεμόνα χρὴ ποιησάμενον οὕτως ἐπιχειρεῖν τοῖς κατὰ τὸν βίον ἔργοις, τὰς ἑκάστοτε προσπιπτούσας ὀργὰς διωθούμενον[1] καὶ διανεύοντα, ὥσπερ οἱ κυβερνῆται τὰ κύματα προσφερόμενα. ἔστι γοῦν οὐκ ἔλαττον τὸ δέος, ὀργῆς δ'[2] ἀντιπρώρου κυλινδομένης αὐτόν τε καὶ σύμπαντα οἶκον ἔστιν ἄρδην ἀπολέσαι καὶ ἀνατρέψαι[3] μὴ διαπλεύσαντα δεξιῶς. οὐ μὴν ἀλλ' ἐπιμελείας εἰς αὐτὰ δεῖ καὶ μελέτης ᾗ[4] καὶ μάλιστα ἁλίσκονται κατ' ἄκρας. κατορθοῦσι δὲ μάλιστα[5] οἱ παραδεξάμενοι τὸν θυμὸν ὡς σύμμαχον ἀρετῆς, ἀπολαύοντες ὅσον αὐτοῦ χρήσιμόν ἐστιν ἔν τε πολέμῳ καὶ νὴ Δί' ἐν πολιτείαις, τὸ πολὺ δ' αὐτοῦ καὶ τὸ ἐπιπολάζον[6] σπουδάζοντες[7] ἐκκρίνειν καὶ ἐκβάλλειν τῆς ψυχῆς, ὅπερ ὀργή τε καὶ πικρία καὶ

---

[1] Wyttenbach : διορθούμενον.   [2] δ' added by F. H. S.
[3] Wyttenbach : ἀναστρέψαι.   [4] F. H. S. : ἤ.
[5] κατορθοῦσι δὲ μάλιστα added by F. H. S.

ON RAGE

(Lamprias Catalogue 93)

*to modifications by Stobaeus. The text has suffered badly in
transmission, and that printed here includes some uncertain
conjectures to provide a possible sense.*

148

Plutarch, from the work *On Rage* :

All human actions that are done in a rage must be
blind and senseless and entirely miss the mark. It is
not possible to act with calculation when acting in a
rage, and anything done without calculation is un-
skilful and distorted. A man ought, then, to make
reason his guide and so set his hand to life's tasks,
either pushing aside his feelings of wrath whenever
they assail him, or finding a way past, just as pilots
avoid the waves that bear down upon them. Certainly
there is no less cause for fear, but when a wave of
rage comes rolling head on against a man, he may
capsize and utterly destroy both himself and his
whole family if he does not steer his way cleverly
through it. Not that success can be had without
pains and training ; otherwise men meet with utter
disaster. Those men do best who accept anger as
virtue's ally, making use of it in so far as it is helpful
in war *a* and indeed in politics, but endeavouring to
discharge and expel from their souls its abundance
and excess, which we call rage or asperity or quick

---

a Plato, *Republic*, 440 c—441 a. But contrast *De Cohib.
Ira*, 458 e.

---

6 Wyttenbach : ἐπιπόλαιον.
7 σπουδάζοντες added by F. H. S.

ὀξυθυμία¹ λέγεται, νοσήματα² ἥκιστα ταῖς ἀνδρείαις
ψυχαῖς πρέποντα. τίς οὖν ἐν ἡλικίᾳ τούτων γίγνεται μελέτη; ἐμοὶ μὲν δοκεῖ μάλιστ᾽ ἂν ὧδε γίγνεσθαι, πόρρωθεν ἡμῶν προμελετώντων καὶ προ-
απαντλούντων³ τὸ⁴ πλεῖστον, οἷον ἐν οἰκέταις τε καὶ
πρὸς γυναῖκας τὰς γαμετάς. ὁ γὰρ οἴκοι πρᾷος
ἠδκαὶ μοσίᾳ πρᾷος πολὺ μᾶλλον ἔσται, τοιοῦτος
ἔνδοθεν καὶ ὑπὸ τῶν οἴκοι πεποιημένος οἷος αὑτῷ⁵
τῆς αὑτοῦ ψυχῆς εἶναι ἰατρός.⁶

ΠΕΡΙ (or ΚΑΤΑ) ΠΛΟΥΤΟΥ

There is no such title in the Lamprias Catalogue, but
Photius (Sopatros) gives περὶ πλούτου. Hartlich, Leipziger

149

Stobaeus, iv. 31 c. 85 (v, p. 765 Hense).

Πλουτάρχου κατὰ πλούτου·

Φύσει μὲν γὰρ δυσχαλίνωτον ὄρεξις, προσλαβοῦσα
δὲ καὶ πλούτου χορηγίαν ἀχαλίνωτον.

150

Stobaeus, iv. 31 c. 86 (v, p. 765 Hense).

Ἐν ταὐτῷ·

Ἀλλ᾽ ἀπληστία καὶ ἄπιστός ἐστιν ἐν αὐτοῖς

---

¹ καὶ ὀξυθυμία Wyttenbach : δι᾽ ὀξυθυμίαν.
² Hense : νομίσματα. ὀνόματα Wyttenbach.
³ F. H. S. (προαντλούντων Piccolos) : προαπλούντων.
⁴ τὸ added by F. H. S.

temper, disorders that are most unbecoming to manly hearts. Now what training for this can a grown man practise ? It would seem to me to be the most effective method if we were to undertake our preliminary practice well in advance and rid ourselves beforehand of the greatest part of our temper, for example when dealing with our slaves [a] and in our relations with our wives. The man who is good-tempered at home will be much more so in his public life, having been made in his house and by his household such as to be the physician of his own soul.[b]

ON (or AGAINST) WEALTH

(*Not in Lamprias Catalogue*)

Studien, xi, p. 312, suggests that the extracts are from no. 207 of the Lamprias Catalogue, προτρεπτικὸς πρὸς νέον πλούσιον.

149

Plutarch, *Against Wealth* :

Appetite is in itself hard to curb : if it acquires wealth to supply its needs, not hard but impossible.

150

In the same work :

But there is in them an insatiate desire and a mad-

---

[a] *Cf. De Cohib. Ira,* 459 B-E, 462 A.
[b] The Greek is corrupt, and the English translates make-shift corrections.

---

[5] οἷος αὐτῷ Post: αὐτῷ.   [6] ἰατρός F. H. S. *e.g.* : ἀγαθός.

μανία, τοιούτῳ μὲν ἐνθουσιασμῷ χρῆσθαι περὶ τὴν κτῆσιν, ὡς εἰ κτήσαιντο μηκέτι καμουμένους, τοσαύτῃ δ' ἀμελείᾳ¹ περὶ τὰ ληφθέντα, ὡς μὴ γενόμενα. δυσερωτιῶσι δὲ τῶν ἀπόντων, ὑπερορῶντες ὧν ἔχουσιν· οὐδὲν γὰρ οὕτως ἀγαπῶσιν ὡς² ἐλπίζουσιν. οὐκ οἶδα πότερον αὐτοῖς ἄμεινόν ἐστιν, ἔχειν ἢ προσδοκᾶν· ἔχοντες γὰρ οὐ χρῶνται, προσδοκῶντες δὲ κάμνουσι. τί οὖν ἐπαινοῦμεν τοιοῦτον ἀγαθόν, οὗ πέρας ἐστὶν οὐδέν, ἀλλ' ᾧ³ τὸ ληφθὲν ἑτέρων ἀρχή;

151

Stobaeus, iv. 32 a. 16 (v, p. 784 Hense).

Πλουτάρχου κατὰ πλούτου·

Οὐδέποτε λιμὸς ἐγέννησε μοιχείαν, οὐδέποτε ἀπορία χρημάτων ἀσωτίαν. βραχεῖά τίς ἐστι σωφροσύνη τὸ πενητεύειν, ὀλίγη τις εὐνομία τὸ ἀπορεῖσθαι.

*152

Stobaeus, iv. 32 a. 17 (v, p. 784 Hense), follows the preceding fragment without lemma in S, with lemma Ἀρκεσιλάου in MA.

Ἀρκεσίλαος τὴν πενίαν λυπρὰν μὲν ἔλεγεν εἶναι ὥσπερ καὶ τὴν Ἰθάκην, ἀγαθὴν δὲ κουροτρόφον, ἐθίζουσαν συνεῖναι λιτότητι καὶ καρτερίᾳ, καὶ καθόλου γυμνάσιον ἀρετῆς ἔμπρακτον.

¹ Gesner : τοσαύτη δὲ ἀμέλεια.

ness that really passes belief : to be so ecstatic about
making money, as if their toils would be at an end
once they have made it, and to be completely careless
of their acquisitions, as if they had never occurred.
They suffer the pangs of frustrated love for what they
do not possess, yet disregard what is in their hands ;
for nothing gives them satisfaction to match their
hopes. I do not know which is better for them,
possession or expectation. When they possess, they
make no use of their possessions ; when they expect,
they exhaust themselves by their exertions. Why
then do we praise a " good " of this kind ? It is
never completed, but what has been got is a starting-
point for getting more and more.

151

Plutarch, *Against Wealth* :

Hunger never begot adultery, nor lack of money
riotous living. To be poor is a humble form of good
behaviour,[a] to be indigent a limited observation of
the law.

*152

Arcesilaüs said that poverty was, like Ithaca, rough
but a good nurse of men,[b] accustoming them to live
with simplicity and endurance, and generally speaking an effective school of virtue.

[a] A saying ascribed to Socrates, Stobaeus, iv. 32 a. 18.
[b] *Odyssey*, ix. 27 ; *Moralia*, 583 D.

---

[2] ὡς F. H. S. : ὡς δὲ SMA. ὡς ἂ Gaisford, introducing
a hiatus.
[3] Duebner : ὅ.

PLUTARCH'S MORALIA

ΠΕΡΙ ΤΟΥ ΔΙΑΒΑΛΛΕΙΝ (?)

It is uncertain whether there was a book so named ; what appears in Stobaeus to be a title may be no more than an

153

Stobaeus, iii. 20. 59 (iii, p. 551 Hense).

Πλουτάρχου ἐκ τοῦ περὶ διαβολῆς¹·

Οἱ νεώνητοι δοῦλοι πυνθάνονται² οὐκ εἰ δεισιδαίμων ἢ φθονερὸς ὁ δεσπότης, ἀλλ᾽ εἰ ὀργίλος.

154

Stobaeus, iii. 38. 31 (iii, p. 714 Hense).

Πλουτάρχου ἐκ τοῦ περὶ τοῦ³ διαβάλλειν.

Τὸν φθόνον ἔνιοι τῷ καπνῷ εἰκάζουσι· πολὺς γὰρ ἐν τοῖς ἀρχομένοις ὤν, ὅταν ἐκλάμψωσιν ἀφανίζεται. ἥκιστα γοῦν τοῖς πρεσβυτέροις φθονοῦσιν.

155

Stobaeus, iii. 38. 32 (iii, p. 715 Hense).

Πλουτάρχου⁴ ἐκ τοῦ περὶ τοῦ⁵ διαβάλλειν·

Ἱππίας λέγει δύο εἶναι φθόνους· τὸν μὲν δίκαιον, ὅταν τις τοῖς κακοῖς φθονῇ τιμωμένοις· τὸν δ᾽

---

¹ ἐκ τοῦ περὶ διαβολῆς MA, omitted by S Br.
² πυνθάνονται placed after φθονερός by S.
³ περὶ τοῦ added by Hense, who also suggested reading κατὰ τοῦ for ἐκ τοῦ. ἐκ τοῦ διαβάλλειν is omitted by S, and may have been added by MA from the lemma of the next item in the anthology, frag. 155.

280

ON CALUMNY (?)

(Not in Lamprias Catalogue)

indication of the subject-matter of the fragments, none of which seems to preserve Plutarch's own wording.

153

Plutarch, from the work *On Calumny* :

Newly-purchased slaves do not inquire whether their master is superstitious, or jealous, but whether he is quick-tempered.[a]

154

Plutarch, from ⟨the work *On*⟩ *Calumniating* :

Some people [b] compare envy to smoke ; there is much of it at the start, but when once a man's flame is well alight it disappears.[c] Certainly old men are very little envied.

155

Plutarch, from ⟨the work *On*⟩ *Calumniating* :

Hippias [d] says there are two kinds of envy—the legitimate, when one envies or begrudges bad men their honours, and the illegitimate, when one envies

---

[a] Cf. *De Cohibenda Ira*, 462 A, which may be the source of this fragment, as Patzig argues.

[b] Ariston, see *Praecepta Gerendae Reip.* 804 D (*S.V.F.* i. 402).

[c] Cf. *An Seni*, 787 C, perhaps the source of the fragment, as Patzig again argues.

[d] Diels-Kranz, *Frag. d. Vorsokr.* 86 B 16.

---

⁴ MA : τοῦ αὐτοῦ S (no lemma in Br.).
⁵ περὶ τοῦ added by Hense.

ἄδικον, ὅταν τοῖς ἀγαθοῖς. καὶ διπλᾶ τῶν ἄλλων
οἱ φθονεροὶ κακοῦνται· οὐ γὰρ μόνον τοῖς ἰδίοις
κακοῖς ἄχθονται, ὥσπερ ἐκεῖνοι, ἀλλὰ καὶ τοῖς
ἀλλοτρίοις ἀγαθοῖς.

156

Stobaeus, iii. 42. 10 (iii, p. 761 Hense).

Πλουτάρχου ἐκ τοῦ περὶ τοῦ[1] διαβάλλειν·

Ἱππίας φησὶν ὅτι δεινόν ἐστιν ἡ διαβολία, οὕτως
ὀνομάζων, ὅτι οὐδὲ τιμωρία τις κατ' αὐτῶν γέγραπται ἐν τοῖς νόμοις, ὥσπερ τῶν κλεπτῶν. καίτοι
ἄριστον ὂν κτῆμα τὴν φιλίαν κλέπτουσιν, ὥστε ἡ
ὕβρις κακοῦργος οὖσα δικαιοτέρα ἐστὶ τῆς διαβολῆς
διὰ τὸ μὴ ἀφανὴς εἶναι.

ΠΕΡΙ ΤΩΝ ΕΝ ΠΛΑΤΑΙΑΙΣ ΔΑΙΔΑΛΩΝ

*The first of these two fragments treats mythology as a
cover for physical doctrines. In the manner of the Stoics
Hera is identified with the Earth or with air, Zeus with fire,
Apollo with the sun. As was observed by P. Decharme,
Mélanges Weil, pp. 111 ff., this is inconsistent with Plutarch's usual view, namely that a god is a transcendent
being, whom it is wrong to identify with any physical body,
which may nevertheless be his symbol (Pyth. Orac. 400 D)
or vehicle (De Facie, 942 D). Although there are passages
where the distinction is not made (Quaest. Conv. 659 A, De
Facie, 938 F), Decharme was probably right in thinking that
the views of this fragment can hardly have been expressed by
Plutarch in his own person, but must have been put in the
mouth of a character in a dialogue. He found further*

[1] περὶ τοῦ added by Hense.

the good. And envious persons suffer twice as much
as those who are not, since they resent not only their
own troubles, like others, but also other men's
prosperity.

156

Plutarch, from ⟨the work *On*⟩ *Calumniating* :

Hippias [a] says that calumny (which he calls *dia-
bolia*) is a dreadful thing, because there is no penalty
prescribed in the laws for slanderers, as there is for
thieves. Yet they steal the best of possessions,
friendship, so that violence, damaging though it is,
is more honest than calumny, because it is not under-
hand.

ON THE FESTIVAL OF IMAGES
AT PLATAEA

(*Lamprias Catalogue* 201)

*evidence that the work was a dialogue, with its scene near
Mt. Cithaeron, in the word ἐνταῦθα, " here," in chap. 3 init.
and fin. One may also point to the second person plural
μάθοιτ' ἄν in chap. 5 init. Decharme's opinion is shared by
R. Hirzel, Der Dialog, ii. 218, and Wilamowitz (below).*

*According to Pausanias, ix. 3. 35 there were Lesser Daedala
every seventh year and Greater Daedala every sixtieth. At
each Lesser Daedala an oak-tree, miraculously indicated by a
bird in a grove near Alalcomenae, was cut down and shaped
into an image, called a* daidalon. *At the Greater Daedala
fourteen such images that had been so prepared were assigned
to various Boeotian towns, dressed and given a bridal bath
in the Asopus, and placed on carts with a bridesmaid. They
were then taken in procession to the top of Mt. Cithaeron,*

[a] Diels-Kranz, *Frag. d. Vorsokr.* 86 в 17.

where they were burnt with other sacrifices on an altar. This strange rite, of which the story told in chap. 6 is an aetiological myth, is discussed by M. P. Nilsson, Griechische Feste, pp. 50 ff., Farnell, Cults, i, pp. 189 ff., Wilamowitz, Glaube der Hellenen, i, pp. 239 ff., Jacoby, F.Gr.Hist. III b, p. 182.

157

Eusebius, *Praeparatio Evangelii*, iii, Prooem.

Λαβὼν ἀνάγνωθι τοῦ Χαιρωνέως Πλουτάρχου τὰς περὶ τῶν προκειμένων φωνάς, ἐν αἷς σεμνολογῶν παρατρέπει τοὺς μύθους ἐφ᾽ ἃς φησιν εἶναι μυστηριώδεις θεολογίας, ἃς δὴ ἐκκαλύπτων τὸν μὲν Διόνυσον τὴν μέθην εἶναί φησιν . . . τὴν δὲ Ἥραν τὴν γαμήλιον ἀνδρὸς καὶ γυναικὸς συμβίωσιν· εἶθ᾽, ὥσπερ ἐπιλελησμένος τῆς ἀποδόσεως, ἑτέραν ἑξῆς ἐπισυνάψας ἱστορίαν τὴν Ἥραν οὐκέτι ὡς τὸ πρότερον ἀλλὰ τὴν γῆν ὀνομάζει, λήθην δὲ καὶ νύκτα τὴν Λητώ· καὶ πάλιν τὴν αὐτὴν τῇ Λητοῖ φησιν εἶναι τὴν Ἥραν· εἶτ᾽ ἐπὶ τούτοις εἰσάγεται αὐτῷ ὁ Ζεὺς εἰς τὴν αἰθέριον δύναμιν ἀλληγορούμενος. καὶ τί με δεῖ ταῦτα προλαμβάνειν, αὐτοῦ παρὸν ἀκοῦσαι τοῦ ἀνδρὸς ὧδέ πως ἐν οἷς ἐπέγραψεν Περὶ τῶν ἐν Πλαταιαῖς Δαιδάλων τὰ λανθάνοντα τοὺς πολλοὺς τῆς ἀπορρήτου περὶ θεῶν φυσιολογίας ἐκφαίνοντος.

1. Ὅτι μὲν οὖν ἡ παλαιὰ φυσιολογία καὶ παρ᾽ Ἕλλησι καὶ βαρβάροις λόγος ἦν φυσικὸς ἐγκεκαλυμμένος[1] μύθοις, τὰ πολλὰ δι᾽ αἰνιγμάτων καὶ ὑπονοιῶν ἐπίκρυφος,[2] καὶ μυστηριώδης θεολογία, τά

---

[1] ἐγκεκαλυμμένος Vigerius : ἐκκεκαλ- most mss. ἐγγεγραμμένος A. [2] ἀπόκρυφος A.

FRAGMENTS : OTHER NAMED WORKS

The second fragment is not ascribed by Eusebius to any particular work of Plutarch, but in view of its proximity to the first fragment and the nature of its subject-matter, there is high probability in assigning it to the same source.

Both fragments are reproduced, with references to modern literature relevant to them, by A. Tresp, Die Fragmente der griechischen Kultschriftsteller, *pp. 117-123.*

157

Take up Plutarch of Chaeronea and read his statements about our subject, statements in which he majestically converts the myths into what he says are " mystic theologies " ; purporting to reveal these, he says that Dionysus is intoxication . . . and Hera the married life of husband and wife. Then, as if he had forgotten this interpretation, he tacks on directly afterwards a different account : contrary to his previous view he now calls Hera the earth, and Leto forgetfulness and night.[a] Then again he says that Hera and Leto are identical ; next on top of this Zeus is introduced, allegorized into the power of the aether. Why should I anticipate all this, when we can listen to the fellow himself ? In the work he entitled *On the Festival of Images at Plataea* he discloses what most men are unaware of in the secret natural science that attaches to the gods, and does so as follows.

1. Ancient natural science, among both Greeks and foreign nations, took the form of a scientific account hidden in mythology, veiled for the most part in riddles and hints, or of a theology such as is found in

---

[a] This seems to be the origin of Theodoretus, *Cur. Graec. Affect.* iii. 54 (Bernardakis, frag. incert. 134).

τε λαλούμενα τῶν σιγωμένων ἀσαφέστερα[1] τοῖς
πολλοῖς ἔχουσα[2] καὶ τὰ σιγώμενα τῶν λαλουμένων
ὑποπτότερα, κατάδηλόν ἐστιν τοῖς[3] Ὀρφικοῖς ἔπεσι
καὶ τοῖς Αἰγυπτιακοῖς καὶ Φρυγίοις λόγοις· μάλιστα
δ' οἱ περὶ τὰς τελετὰς ὀργιασμοὶ καὶ τὰ δρώμενα
συμβολικῶς ἐν ταῖς ἱερουργίαις τὴν τῶν παλαιῶν
ἐμφαίνει διάνοιαν.

2. Οἷον, ἵνα μὴ μακρὰν τῶν ἐνεστηκότων λόγων
βαδίζωμεν, οὐ νομίζουσιν οὐδ' ἀξιοῦσι κοινωνίαν
εἶναι πρὸς Διόνυσον Ἥρᾳ· φυλάσσονται δὲ συμ-
μιγνύναι τὰ ἱερά, καὶ τὰς Ἀθήνησιν ἱερείας ἀπαν-
τώσας φασὶν ἀλλήλαις μὴ προσαγορεύειν, μηδ'
ὅλως κιττὸν εἰς τὸ τῆς Ἥρας εἰσκομίζεσθαι τέ-
μενος, οὐ διὰ τὰς μυθικὰς καὶ φλυαρώδεις ζηλοτυπίας, ἀλλ' ὅτι γαμήλιος μὲν ἡ θεὸς καὶ νυμφαγωγός,
ἀπρεπὲς δὲ τὸ μεθύειν νυμφίοις καὶ γάμοις ἀναρ-
μοστότατον, ὡς φησιν ὁ Πλάτων· ἀκρατοποσία γὰρ
ταραχὴν[4] ἐμποιεῖ καὶ ψυχαῖς καὶ σώμασιν, ὑφ' ἧς
ἄπλαστα καὶ πεπλανημένα ῥιζοῦται κακῶς τὰ σπει-
ρόμενα καὶ κυϊσκόμενα. πάλιν οἱ θύοντες Ἥρᾳ
τὴν χολὴν οὐ καθαγίζουσιν ἀλλὰ κατορύττουσι
παρὰ τὸν βωμόν, ὡς δέον ἄθυμον καὶ ἄχολον καὶ
καθαρεύουσαν ὀργῆς καὶ πικρίας ἁπάσης τὴν γυναικὸς καὶ ἀνδρὸς εἶναι συμβίωσιν.

3. Τοῦτο δὴ[5] τὸ συμβολικὸν εἶδος ἐν τοῖς λόγοις

---

[1] Reitzenstein : σαφέστερα.
[2] Wyttenbach : ἔχοντα.
[3] τοῖς A : ἐν τοῖς most mss.
[4] All mss. but A add φησί before ταραχὴν.
[5] δὲ A.

---

[a] Cf. De Iside, 362 B ; F. Jacoby, Diagoras ὁ ἄθεος, Abh.
Akad. Wiss. Berlin, 1959, p. 28 and n. 231. Α Φρύγιος λόγος,
first appearing in the third cent. B.C. anonymously, was later

mystery-ceremonies : in it what is spoken is less clear to the masses than what is unsaid, and what is unsaid gives cause for more speculation than what is said. This is evident from the Orphic poems and the accounts given by Phrygians and Egyptians.[a] But nothing does more to reveal what was in the mind of the ancients than the rites of initiation and the ritual acts that are performed in religious services with symbolical intent.

2. To take an instance that will not lead us far from what we have been talking about, it is traditional that there is no association between Hera and Dionysus and it is not thought right that there should be any. Care is taken to keep their rites distinct, and it is said that the priestesses of the two divinities at Athens do not speak to one another if they meet, and that ivy is never introduced into Hera's precincts. The reason is not to be found in the nonsense of mythological stories of jealousy, but in the fact that Hera is the goddess of marriage and leader of the bridal procession, whereas it is unseemly for the bridal pair to be tipsy and, as Plato says, most unsuitable for a wedding.[b] Heavy drinking, he says, causes a disturbance both in mind and in body, as a result of which what is sown and conceived, being unformed and unsettled, has but poor roots. Again at sacrifices to Hera the gall-bladder is not offered to her but buried by the altar, because the life shared by husband and wife should be without anger or gall, and uncontaminated by any ill-temper or bitterness.[c]

3. Now this symbolical aspect occurs more often

ascribed to Democritus, Diels-Kranz, *Fragmente der Vorsokratiker*, 68 B 299.
   [b] *Laws*, 775 B-D.
   [c] *Cf. Praec. Coniug.* 141 E.

καὶ τοῖς μύθοις μᾶλλόν ἐστιν[1]· οἷον ἱστοροῦσι τὴν
Ἥραν ἐν τῇ Εὐβοίᾳ τρεφομένην ἔτι παρθένον ὑπὸ
τοῦ Διὸς κλαπῆναι, καὶ διακομισθεῖσαν ἐνταῦθα
κρύπτεσθαι, Κιθαιρῶνος αὐτοῖς μυχὸν ἐπίσκιόν
τινα[2] καὶ θάλαμον αὐτοφυῆ παρασχόντος· ἐλθούσης
δὲ τῆς Μακρίδος κατὰ ζήτησιν (ἦν δὲ Ἥρας τι-
θήνη) καὶ βουλομένης ἐρευνᾶν, οὐκ ἐᾶν τὸν Κιθαιρῶνα πολυπραγμονεῖν οὐδὲ τῷ χωρίῳ προσάγειν,
ὡς τοῦ Διὸς ἐκεῖ τῇ Λητοῖ συναναπαυομένου καὶ
συνδιατρίβοντος. ἀπελθούσης δὲ τῆς Μακρίδος,
οὕτω τότε μὲν διαλαθεῖν τὴν Ἥραν, ὕστερον δὲ τῇ
Λητοῖ χάριν ἀπομνημονεύουσαν ὁμοβώμιον θέσθαι
καὶ σύνναον· ὥστε καὶ Λητοῖ Μυχίᾳ προθύεσθαι·
τινὲς δὲ Νυχίαν λέγουσι. σημαίνεται δ' ἐν ἑκατέρῳ
τῶν ὀνομάτων τὸ κρύφιον καὶ διαλεληθός. ἔνιοι δὲ
τὴν Ἥραν αὐτὴν ἐκεῖ τῷ Διὶ λάθρα συνοῦσαν καὶ
λανθάνουσαν οὕτω φασὶ Λητὼ[3] Νυχίαν[4] προση-
γορεῦσθαι· φανερῶν δὲ τῶν γάμων γενομένων καὶ
περὶ τὸν Κιθαιρῶνα πρῶτον ἐνταῦθα καὶ τὰς Πλα-
ταιὰς τῆς ὁμιλίας ἀνακαλυφθείσης, Ἥραν Τελείαν
καὶ Γαμήλιον αὐτὴν προσαγορευθῆναι.

4. Οἱ δὲ φυσικῶς μᾶλλον καὶ[5] πρεπόντως ὑπο-
λαμβάνοντες[6] τὸν μῦθον οὕτως εἰς ταὐτὸ τῇ Λητοῖ
συνάγουσι τὴν Ἥραν. γῆ μέν ἐστι ἡ Ἥρα
καθάπερ εἴρηται, νὺξ δ' ἡ Λητὼ " ληθώ " τις οὖσα
τῶν εἰς ὕπνον τρεπομένων. νὺξ δ' οὐδέν ἐστιν ἄλλο

---

[1] ἐστὶν μᾶλλον A.   [2] A : ἐπίσκιόν τινα μυχὸν most mss.
[3] A : Λητώ φασι most mss.
[4] Μυχίαν van Herwerden.
[5] ? καὶ μᾶλλον.   [6] ὑπολαβόντες A.

---

[a] Either a personification of the mountain or a mythical
king of Thebes (Pausanias, ix. 1. 2).

in stories and mythology. For example, they record that when Hera was still a girl, being brought up in Euboea, she was kidnapped by Zeus, transported to these parts and here concealed, Cithaeron [a] providing them with a shaded nook to form a natural marriage-chamber. Macris (she was Hera's nurse [b]) came to look for her ; but when she wanted to make a search of the place Cithaeron prevented her from interfering or approaching the spot by a tale that Zeus was sleeping and dallying with Leto there. Macris went away and thus Hera escaped discovery ; later, to record her gratitude to Leto, she shared her altar and her temple with her. That is why preliminary sacrifice is made to " Leto of the Nook " (mychios), although some say " of the Night " (nychios). Either name, however, signifies the clandestine preservation of secrecy. But there are some who say that Hera herself was given the name of " Leto of the Night " as she there lay with Zeus secretly and undetected ; but when their marriage became public and their association was brought to light—which first happened here on Cithaeron and at Plataea—she was named " Hera of Consummation " and " Hera of Wedlock." [c]

4. But those who prefer to understand the story in a scientific and seemly sense identify Hera and Leto in the following way : Hera is the earth, as has been said, and Leto night, being an oblivion (lêthô [d]) experienced by those who give themselves to sleep, and

---

[b] At *Moralia* 657 E Hera's nurse is called Euboea, for which Macris was another name, Callimachus, *Hymn* iv. 20, etc.

[c] Farnell, *Cults*, i, pp. 195, 244-246.

[d] Plato, *Cratylus*, 406 A suggests a derivation from lêthê, " forgetting."

πλὴν σκιὰ γῆς· ὅταν γὰρ πλησιάσαντα[1] ταῖς δυσμαῖς ἀποκρύψῃ τὸν ἥλιον, ἀναπλατυνομένη μελαίνει τὸν ἀέρα· καὶ τοῦτ᾽ ἔστι τὸ ἐκλειπτικὸν ὀλίσθημα τῶν πανσελήνων, ὅταν τῆς σελήνης περιφερομένης ἡ σκιὰ τῆς γῆς ἐπιψαύσῃ καὶ διαθολώσῃ τὸ φέγγος.

5. Ὅτι δ᾽ οὐκ ἄλλη τίς ἐστι τῆς Ἥρας ἡ Λητώ, μάθοιτ᾽ ἂν ἐνθένδε. τὴν Ἄρτεμιν δήπου[2] θυγατέρα Λητοῦς καλοῦμεν, ἀλλὰ καὶ Εἰλείθυιαν τὴν αὐτὴν ὀνομάζομεν· οὐκοῦν ἥ τε Ἥρα καὶ ἡ Λητὼ δύο εἰσὶ μιᾶς θεοῦ προσηγορίαι. πάλιν ἐκ μὲν Λητοῦς ὁ Ἀπόλλων ἐκ δ᾽ Ἥρας ὁ Ἄρης γέγονε· μία δ᾽ ἐστὶν ἀμφοτέρων δύναμις, καὶ κέκληται Ἄρης μὲν ὡς " ἀρήγων " τοῖς κατὰ βίαν καὶ μάχην συμπτώμασιν, Ἀπόλλων δ᾽ ὡς " ἀπαλλάττων " καὶ " ἀπολύων " τῶν περὶ σῶμα νοσηματικῶν[3] παθῶν τὸν ἄνθρωπον. διὸ καὶ τῶν ἐμπυρωτάτων ἄστρων καὶ πυριφλεγεστάτων ὁ μὲν ἥλιος Ἀπόλλων κέκληται ὁ δὲ πυροειδὴς[4] Ἄρης ἐπωνόμασται. καὶ οὐκ ἀπὸ τρόπου[5] ἐστὶ τὴν αὐτὴν θεὸν Γαμήλιον λέγεσθαι καὶ μητέρα Εἰλειθυίας καὶ Ἡλίου νομίζεσθαι· γάμου μὲν γὰρ τέλος γένεσίς ἐστι, γένεσις δ᾽ ἡ εἰς ἥλιον καὶ φῶς ἐκ σκότους πορεία· καὶ καλῶς ἔφη[6] ὁ ποιητής,

αὐτὰρ ἐπειδὴ τόν γε μογοστόκος Εἰλείθυια
ἐξάγαγε προφόωσδε καὶ ἠελίου ἴδεν αὐγάς.

εὖ ὁ ποιητὴς τῇ μὲν προθέσει τὴν σύνθεσιν συνέθλιψεν,[7] ἐμφαίνων τὸ βεβιασμένον τῆς ὠδῖνος, τέλος

---

[1] F. H. S. : πλησιάσασα.   [2] van Herwerden : ἤδη που.
[3] νοσημάτων καὶ Bernardakis.
[4] πυρροειδὴς A. ? Πυροεὶς Bernardakis.
[5] Gaisford : ἀποτρόπων.
[6] AI omit ἔφη.   ? delete καὶ ... ποιητής.   [7] F. H. S.: ἔθλιψεν.

night is nothing but the earth's shadow. For the earth hides the sun when it has reached the west, and then its shadow spreads upwards to darken the air. And this is the reason for the disappearance of full moons in eclipse ; at that time the shadow of the earth falls upon the moon as it moves in its orbit, and darkens its light.

5. You can gather the identity of Leto and Hera from the fact that we call Artemis daughter of Leto (do we not ?), but also give her the name of Eileithyia. So Hera and Leto are two names for one goddess.[a] Again Apollo was born of Leto and Ares of Hera, but they both have one and the same power : and Ares has his name as giving succour (*arêgôn*) in the violent accidents of battle, and Apollo his as ridding (*apallattôn*) and relieving (*apolyôn*) man of his morbid bodily states. Thus of the fiercest and most flaming heavenly bodies, the sun is called Apollo and the fiery planet has been given the name Ares (Mars). Nor is it inappropriate that the same goddess should have the title Patroness of Marriage and be regarded as mother of Eileithyia and of the Sun, since the purpose of marriage is birth, and birth is the journey out of darkness into the light of the sun. Homer wrote finely :

> When Eileithyia, goddess of birth-pangs,
> Brought him out to the light, and he saw the sun.[b]

It was excellent to force the compound into a single word with the preposition,[c] in order to indicate the forced character of labour, and excellent to make

[a] Eileithyia, the goddess of childbirth, was daughter of Hera : *Iliad*, xi. 271, Hesiod, *Theogony*, 922.

[b] *Iliad*, xvi. 187.

[c] Zenodotus read προφόωσδε as one word, Aristarchus πρὸ φόωσδε as two. Eustathius took it as one word, signifying

291

δὲ τῆς γενέσεως ἐποίησεν ἥλιον ἰδεῖν. οὐκοῦν ἡ
αὐτὴ θεὸς ἐποίησε καὶ γάμον συνελθεῖν, ἵνα γένεσιν
παρασκευάσῃ.

6. Δεῖ δ' ἴσως καὶ τὸν εὐηθέστερον μῦθον εἰπεῖν.
λέγεται γὰρ ὁ Ζεύς, τῆς Ἥρας αὐτῷ διαφερομένης
καὶ μηκέτι φοιτᾶν εἰς ταὐτὸ βουλομένης ἀλλὰ κρυ-
πτούσης ἑαυτήν, ἀμηχανῶν καὶ πλανώμενος Ἀλαλ-
κομενεῖ[1] τῷ αὐτόχθονι συντυχεῖν καὶ διδαχθῆναι
ὑπὸ τούτου, ὡς ἐξαπατητέον τὴν Ἥραν σκηψά-
μενον γαμεῖν ἑτέραν. συνεργοῦντος δὲ τοῦ Ἀλαλ-
κομενέως,[2] κρύφα τεμόντας αὐτοὺς εὐκτέανον καὶ
παγκάλην δρῦν μορφῶσαί τ' αὐτὴν καὶ καταστεῖλαι
νυμφικῶς, Δαιδάλην προσαγορεύσαντας· εἶθ' οὕτως
ἀναμέλπεσθαι μὲν τὸν ὑμέναιον, λουτρὰ δὲ κομίζειν
τὰς Τριτωνίδας Νύμφας, αὐλοὺς δὲ καὶ κώμους τὴν
Βοιωτίαν παρασχεῖν· περαινομένων δὲ τούτων
οὐκέτι τὴν Ἥραν καρτερεῖν, ἀλλὰ καταβᾶσαν ἐκ
τοῦ Κιθαιρῶνος, τῶν Πλαταιατίδων[3] αὐτῇ γυναικῶν
ἑπομένων, ὑπ' ὀργῆς καὶ ζηλοτυπίας θέουσαν ἐλθεῖν
πρὸς τὸν Δία, καὶ τοῦ πλάσματος φανεροῦ γενομένου, διαλλαγεῖσαν μετὰ χαρᾶς καὶ γέλωτος αὐτὴν
νυμφαγωγεῖν· τιμὴν δὲ τῷ ξοάνῳ προσθεῖναι, καὶ
Δαίδαλα τὴν ἑορτὴν προσαγορεῦσαι, κατακαῦσαι δ'
ὅμως αὐτὸ καίπερ ἄψυχον ὂν ὑπὸ ζηλοτυπίας.

7. Ὁ μὲν οὖν μῦθος τοιοῦτος, ὁ δὲ λόγος αὐτοῦ
τοιόσδε. Ἥρας καὶ Διὸς διαφορὰ καὶ στάσις οὐδὲν
ἄλλο πλὴν στοιχείων δυσκρασία καὶ τάραχός ἐστιν,

---

[1] Roscher : ἀλαλκομένει.   [2] Roscher : ἀλαλκομένους.
[3] Mras : πλαταιάδων A : τῶν πλατείδων most mss.

βρέφους πρόοδον εἰς φῶς. For Plutarch's view of the significance of the compound compare Longinus, De Sublimitate,
x. 6 on ὑπὲκ θανάτοιο : τῇ δὲ τοῦ ἔπους συνθλίψει τὸ πάθος ἄκρως
ἀπεπλάσατο.

seeing the sun the consummation of birth. So the same goddess has also created the union of marriage in order to bring birth about.

6. There is a more foolish story, and perhaps it should be told. It is that when Hera fell out with Zeus and would no longer consort with him but hid herself, he wandered around at his wits' end; in this state he fell in with Alalcomeneus the aboriginal,[a] who instructed him that he must trick Hera by a pretence of marrying someone else. Alalcomeneus assisted him in secretly felling a lovely straight-grained oak-tree, which they shaped and dressed like a bride, giving it the name of Daidalê. Then, these preparations made, the wedding-song rang out, and the Nymphs of the river Triton [b] brought the water for the bridal bath, and Boeotia provided pipes and revelry. As all this went forward, Hera could stand it no longer, but came down from Cithaeron, with a retinue of women from Plataea, and ran in anger and jealousy to confront Zeus. The counterfeit being exposed, she was reconciled to him and herself led the bridal procession with joy and laughter; she gave honour to the wooden image, by naming the festival Daidala, but for all that she burnt it up, lifeless though it was, in her jealousy.

7. Such is the story. Its meaning is something like this : the discord and quarrel between Zeus and Hera is nothing but a disturbance of the elements and

---

[a] Alalcomeneus was not only aboriginal, but also the first of all men, according to a poet whose lines are preserved by Hippolytus, *Refutatio*, v, p. 134 ; Page, *Greek Melic Poetry*, adespota 985, Bergk, *Poetae Lyrici Graeci*, iii, adespota 84.

[b] A river running into Lake Copaïs.

ὅταν ἀλλήλοις μηκέτι συμμετρῆται κατὰ κόσμον,
ἀλλὰ καὶ ἀνωμαλίας καὶ τραχύτητος ἐγγενομένης
δυσμαχήσαντα λύσῃ τὴν κοινωνίαν καὶ φθορὰν τῶν
ὅλων ἀπεργάσηται. ἂν μὲν οὖν ὁ Ζεύς, τουτέστιν
ἡ θερμὴ καὶ πυρώδης δύναμις, αἰτίαν παράσχῃ τῆς
διαφορᾶς,[1] αὐχμὸς τὴν γῆν καταλαμβάνει· ἐὰν δὲ
περὶ τὴν Ἥραν, τουτέστι τὴν ὑγρὰν καὶ πνευματι-
κὴν φύσιν, ὕβρις τις ἢ πλεονασμὸς γένηται, ῥεῦμα
ἦλθε πολὺ καὶ συνώμβρισε καὶ κατέκλυσε τὰ πάντα.
τοιούτου δέ τινος γενομένου καὶ περὶ τοὺς τότε
χρόνους, καὶ μάλιστα τῆς Βοιωτίας βυθισθείσης,
ὡς πρῶτον ἀνέδυ τὸ πεδίον καὶ ἡ πλήμμυρα ἐλώ-
φησεν, ὁ μὲν ἐξ εὐδίας κόσμος τοῦ περιέχοντος
ὁμόνοια καὶ διαλλαγὴ τῶν θεῶν ἐλέχθη. πρῶτον
δ᾽ ἀνέσχεν ἐκ τῆς γῆς τῶν φυτῶν[2] ἡ δρῦς, καὶ ταύτην ἠγάπησαν οἱ ἄνθρωποι, τροφὴν[3] βίου καὶ σωτηρίας διαμονὴν παρασχοῦσαν. οὐ γὰρ μόνον τοῖς
εὐσεβέσιν, ὡς Ἡσίοδός φησιν, ἀλλὰ καὶ τοῖς ὑπο-
λειφθεῖσι τῆς φθορᾶς,

ἄκρη μέν τε φέρει βαλάνους, μέσση δὲ μελίσσας.

158

Eusebius, *Praepar. Evang.* iii. 8. 1.

Λέγει δ᾽ οὖν Πλούταρχος ὧδέ πη κατὰ λέξιν·

Ἡ δὲ τῶν ξοάνων ποίησις ἀρχαῖον ἔοικεν εἶναί
τι καὶ παλαιόν, εἴγε ξύλινον μὲν ἦν τὸ πρῶτον εἰς
Δῆλον ὑπὸ Ἐρυσίχθονος Ἀπόλλωνι πεμφθὲν[4] ἐπὶ

[1] F. H. S. : διαφθορᾶς.
[2] F. H. S. : ἐκ τῶν φυτῶν τῆς γῆς.
[3] F. H. S. : τροφῆς.
[4] πεμφθὲν added, *exempli gratia*, by Bolkestein.

their failure to blend, when they no longer preserve their balance in an orderly fashion but, as irregularity and turbulence arise among them, enter on a bitter struggle in which they dissolve their union and work universal destruction. If Zeus,[a] that is to say the hot fiery force, provides the cause of the discord, drought falls on the earth ; if Hera, that is to say the wet and windy matter, gets out of hand and over-abundant, there comes a great flow of water to deluge and inundate everything. Something of the kind happened in those old days : Boeotia in particular was submerged, and when as the flood subsided the plain first reappeared, the good order in the atmosphere that followed the calm weather was spoken of as the concord and reconciliation of the gods ; the first plant to rise from the earth was the oak, and men welcomed it as having provided food to live on and the means by which their preservation would endure.

Its twigs have acorns and its trunk the bee [b]

not for the god-fearing only, as Hesiod tells us, but also for the survivors of the catastrophe.

158

Plutarch, anyway, writes as follows, to quote his own words :

The making of wooden images seems to be an ancient and early practice, if wood was the material of the first statue sent in honour of Apollo by Ery-

[a] These identifications are Stoic, *e.g.*, Cicero, *Nat. Deor.* ii. 66.
[b] Hesiod, *Works and Days*, 233.

τῶν θεωριῶν ἄγαλμα, ξύλινον δὲ τὸ τῆς Πολιάδος
ὑπὸ τῶν αὐτοχθόνων ἱδρυθέν, ὃ μέχρι νῦν Ἀθηναῖοι
διαφυλάττουσιν. Ἥρας δὲ καὶ Σάμιοι ξύλινον εἶχον
ἔδος,[1] ὥς φησι Καλλίμαχος,

> οὔπω Σκέλμιον ἔργον εὔξοον,[2] ἀλλ᾽ ἐπὶ τεθμὸν
> δηναιὸν γλυφάνων ἄξοος[3] ἦσθα σανίς.
> ὧδε γὰρ ἱδρύοντο θεοὺς τότε· καὶ γὰρ Ἀθήνης
> ἐν Λίνδῳ Δαναὸς λιτὸν[4] ἔθηκεν ἔδος.

λέγεται δὲ Πείρας ὁ πρῶτος Ἀργολίδος Ἥρας
ἱερὸν εἰσάμενος τὴν ἑαυτοῦ θυγατέρα Καλλίθυιαν
ἱέρειαν καταστήσας, ἐκ τῶν περὶ Τίρυνθα δένδρων
ὄγχνην τεμὼν εὐκτέανον, Ἥρας ἄγαλμα μορφῶσαι.
πέτραν μὲν γὰρ εἰς θεοῦ κόπτειν εἰκόνα σκληρὰν
καὶ δύσεργον καὶ ἄψυχον οὐκ ἐβούλοντο, χρυσὸν δὲ
καὶ ἄργυρον ἡγοῦντο γῆς ἀκάρπου καὶ διεφθαρ-
μένης χρώματα νοσώδη καὶ κηλῖδας ἐξανθεῖν ὥσπερ
μώλωπας ὑπὸ πυρὸς ῥαπισθείσης· ἐλέφαντι δὲ παίζοντες μὲν ἔσθ᾽ ὅπου προσεχρῶντο ποικίλματι
γλυφῆς.[5]

---

[1] Bentley : εἶδος.
[2] Bentley : εἰσοξόανα or εἰς ξόανον.
[3] δηναιὸν Gaisford γλυφάνων Toup ἄξοος Bentley : δη-
ναιόγλυφον (or δὴ νεό∗γλυφον) ὦναξ θεᾶς.
[4] Isaac Voss : λίθον or λεῖον.
[5] F. H. S. : τρυφῆς. γραφῆς Wyttenbach.

[a] Son of Cecrops ; see Pausanias, i. 18. 5.
[b] Frag. 100 Pfeiffer, from Book iv of Aitia.

sichthon [a] to Delos for the festivals there, and also of the statue of Polias set up by the aboriginals, a statue which the Athenians preserve to this day. The Samians, too, had a wooden icon of Hera, as Callimachus tells [b] :

> Thou wast not yet the polished work of Scelmis, [c]
> But an unchiselled plank, by ancient rule.
> Such gods men set up then : thus Danaüs
> At Lindus placed Athenê's simple icon. [d]

It is said that Peiras, the founder of the temple of Hera at Argos, who appointed his own daughter Callithyia to be her priestess, cut down a straight-grained pear from among the trees near Tiryns and shaped it into an image of Hera. [e] In old times men did not choose to hack a stone into a hard, awkward, lifeless representation of a god ; gold and silver they thought of as pigments due to disease in corrupt, infertile earth or as disfiguring excrescences, swelling up like weals where it had come under the lash of fire; as for ivory, they did on occasion use it light-heartedly to lend variety to their sculpture. [f]

---

[c] Scelmis (?), alias Smilis (Schol. Pausanias, iii. 4. 4), otherwise unknown sculptor who turned a plank, previously the idol, into the first anthropomorphic statue of Hera at Samos, *cf.* Clement, *Protrepticus*, iv. 46. 3, 47. 2 ; E. Buschor, *Ath. Mitt.* lv (1930), p. 4.

[d] Apollodorus, ii. 1. 4. 6. Athena instigated Danaüs' escape with his daughters from Egypt. See C. Blinkenberg, *L'Image d'Athana Lindia*, K. Danske Videnskabsselskab, Hist. fil. Meddelelser, 1917.

[e] *Cf.* Clement, *loc. cit.*, who gives the maker's name as Argus, on the authority of the second book of Demetrius' *Argolica*.

[f] On the importance of early Greek work in ivory, occasionally combined with wood, see R. D. Barnett, *Journ. Hell. Stud.* lxviii (1948), pp. 1 ff.

ΠΕΡΙ ΦΙΛΙΑΣ ΕΠΙΣΤΟΛΗ

Plutarch's name is attached by Stobaeus to two only of these extracts ; the others have merely the title of the book. O. Hense, R.E. ix. 2570, approves Wyttenbach's acceptance of them all, observing that Stobaeus also omits Plutarch's name when quoting from Septem Sapientium Convivium.

159

Stobaeus ii. 31. 82 (ii, p. 215 Wachsmuth).

Ἐκ τῆς περὶ φιλίας ἐπιστολῆς·

Ἡ παιδεία κἂν μηδὲν ἕτερον ἀγαθὸν ἔχῃ,[1] τό γε συμφοιτᾶν δι᾽[2] αὐτὴν νυκτὸς καὶ ἡμέρας ἐκσῴζει[3] κακίας, οἷς ἂν ᾖ τις αἰδώς· καὶ πολλοὶ σφᾶς αὐτοὺς καὶ ἄλλους * *

160

Stobaeus, ii. 46. 15 (ii, p. 262 Wachsmuth).

Ἐκ τῆς περὶ φιλίας ἐπιστολῆς·

Ὡς μέντοι λαμπρόν ἐστιν εὖ ποιεῖν, οὕτως ἀμειπτέον,[4] ἵνα μὴ μόνον ἀχαριστίας ὄφλῃ τις δίκην, ἀλλὰ καὶ βλάβους κοινοῦ τῶν εὖ πεισομένων εἰσαῦθις[5] ἑτέρων ἀνακοπῇ πρὸς εὐεργεσίαν.

---

[1] Meineke : ἔχοι.
[2] δι᾽ added by F. H. S.
[3] Usener : ἔξω. ἔξω τίθησι Duebner.

298

FRAGMENTS : OTHER NAMED WORKS

A LETTER ON FRIENDLINESS

(*Lamprias Catalogue* 132, ? 83)

The extracts have little to do with "friendship" in the narrow sense of the word. Several are concerned with goodwill and concord in social or political fields. This is a possible meaning of the Greek word and it may be that the letter was directed to such aspects of the subject.

159

From the *Letter on Friendliness* :

Even if education provides no other benefit, the very fact of attending school with others for education's sake keeps those pupils who have any sense of shame out of the way of wrong-doing whether by night or by day. Many ⟨have restrained (?)⟩ both themselves and others . . .

160

From the *Letter on Friendliness* :

Yet inasmuch as to confer benefits is a splendid thing, so one ought to make a return, to avoid being condemned not merely for ingratitude but also, by reason of the discouragement given to others' benevolence, for doing a general injury to those who might receive benefits in the future.[a]

[a] Text uncertain.

---

[4] Duebner added τοὺς εὖ ποιοῦντας before ἀμειπτέον ; Usener supposed a lacuna after it.
[5] Wyttenbach : εἰς αὐτούς.

161

Stobaeus, iii. 2. 34 (iii, p. 186 Hense).

Ἐκ τῆς ἐπιστολῆς τῆς περὶ φιλίας·

Κακίας αὐτῶν[1] πλάσσονταί[2] τινες ῥημάτων εὐπρεπείᾳ, τὸ μὲν φιλοσώματον φιλόκαλον, τὸ δ' ἄγροικον[3] ἁπλοῦν, τὸ δὲ φιλάργυρον προμηθὲς ἀποκαλούμενοι.

162

Stobaeus, iii. 2. 35 (iii, p. 186 Hense).

Ἐν ταὐτῷ·

Πολύβουλον εἶναι καὶ πολύτροπον, ἔνθα δεῖ[4] καὶ τέχνης κατ' ἀλλοφύλων πολεμίων, χρήσιμον καὶ ἀναγκαῖον· ἐπίβουλον δ' ἦθος καὶ κακομηχανώτατον διὰ παντὸς ἔχειν καὶ κατὰ πάντων, οὐ τῇ τῶν ἀγχινόων, ὥς τινες οἴονται, τῇ δὲ τοῦ πονηροτάτου μερίδι προστίθημι.

163

Stobaeus, iv. 5. 68 (iv, p. 221 Hense).

Ἐκ τῆς ἐπιστολῆς τῆς περὶ φιλίας[5]·

Μάρτυς δ' ἄριστος ὁ μηθὲν μὲν εὖ παθών, ἀπὸ δὲ τῆς εἰς ἄλλους εὐνοίας κρίνων.

164

Stobaeus, iv. 7. 42 (iv, p. 258 Hense).

Πλουτάρχου ἐκ τῆς ἐπιστολῆς τῆς περὶ φιλίας·

Ἡμερότητι τοίνυν καὶ εὐεργεσίᾳ μᾶλλον ἢ φόβῳ πρὸς εὔνοιαν ὑπακτέον.

FRAGMENTS : OTHER NAMED WORKS

161

From the *Letter on Friendliness* :

Some people disguise their own vices under specious names, calling sensuality ⟨love of beauty, rudeness⟩ simplicity, and avarice foresight.

162

In the same work :

Where trickery is needed against a foreign foe, it is useful and indeed necessary to be full of device and resource. But to have a designing character and to plot mischief at all times and towards all men counts, in my view, not as a sign of quick wits, as some people think, but of complete depravity.

163

From the *Letter on Friendliness* :

The best witness is the man who has received no favour but forms his judgement on the basis of a general goodwill to others.

164

Plutarch, from the *Letter on Friendliness* :

One must induce goodwill, then, by gentleness and helpfulness rather than by fear.

---

[1] Wyttenbach : αὐτῶν.
[2] περιπλάσσονται Jacobs.
[3] φιλόκαλον τὸ δ' ἄγροικον added by Hense.
[4] ? ἔνθ' ἀπάτης δεῖ.   [5] No lemma in S.

165

Stobaeus, iv. 7. 43 (iv, p. 258 Hense).

Ἐν ταὐτῷ·

Ἠπίους οὖν εἶναι δεῖ μετὰ τοῦ ἔμφρονος[1] εἰς τὸ κοινῇ λυσιτελές.

166

Stobaeus, iv. 12. 11 (iv, p. 344 Hense).

Ἐκ τῆς ἐπιστολῆς τῆς περὶ φιλίας·

Ἔτι δὲ κολάσεως ἀπαραιτήτου[2] φόβος αἴτιός ἐστιν ἀπονοίας· ὁ γὰρ ὄλεθρον αὐτοῦ προλαβὼν ὁμόσε χωρεῖ κινδύνοις.

167

Stobaeus, iv. 28. 8 (v, p. 678 Hense).

Ἐκ τῆς ἐπιστολῆς τῆς περὶ φιλίας[3]·

Γάμος γὰρ ἀπὸ μὲν φιλίας διττῆς κράσεως[4] βελτίων, ἑτέρως δὲ σφαλερός.

168

Stobaeus, iv. 31. 126 (v, p. 778 Hense).

Ἐκ τῆς ἐπιστολῆς τῆς περὶ φιλίας·

Πλούτῳ μέντοι χρηστέον ὡς ὕλῃ τινός,[5] οὐκ[6] ἐπὶ παντὸς ὁμοίως.

302

FRAGMENTS : OTHER NAMED WORKS

165

In the same work :

One should act kindly, but also intelligently, to secure what is to the common interest.

166

From the *Letter on Friendliness* :

Further, a fear of unmerciful punishment is responsible for desperation, since a man who foresees his own destruction will take dangerous courses.

167

From the *Letter on Friendliness* :

A marriage is better if it arises from the blending of affection on either side ; otherwise it is liable to go wrong.

168

From the *Letter on Friendliness* :

Wealth should, however, be used as the raw material for something, not indiscriminately.

---

¹ ἔμφρονας Elter.
² F. H. S. : ἀπαραίτητος.
³ S has the lemma belonging to the next passage, *viz.*, Πλουτάρχου ἐκ τῶν γαμικῶν παραγγελμάτων.
⁴ ὅπου . . . κρᾶσις Piccolos.
⁵ ? τινὸς ἀγαθοῦ Duebner (βελτίονος Hense).
⁶ ? ἀλλ' οὐκ Hense.

169

Stobaeus, iv. 31. 127 (v, p. 779 Hense).

Ἐν ταὐτῷ·

Ἀρετὴν οὖν τοῖς πᾶσι μᾶλλον εὐκτέον ἢ πλοῦτον[1]
ἀνοήτοις σφαλερόν· ὑπὸ γὰρ χρημάτων αὔξεται
κακία. καὶ ὅσῳ τις ἂν ἄφρων ᾖ, τοσούτῳ πλέον
ἐξυβρίζει, τὸ λυσσῶδες αὐτοῦ[2] τῶν ἡδονῶν ἐκπλη-
ροῦν ἔχων.

170

Stobaeus, iv. 33. 20 (v, p. 805 Hense).

Ἐκ τῆς ἐπιστολῆς τῆς περὶ φιλίας·

Ἐν πενίᾳ μέν τις διετέλεσεν εὐδαίμων, ὡς[3] ἥκιστα δὲ πλουτῶν[4] κἂν[5] ἀρχαῖς.

*171

Τοσοῦτον ὑπεραίρει πενίας ἀγαθόν, ὥστ᾽ αἰσχροῦ
πλούτου νόμιμος ἀνὴρ ἀλλάξαιτ᾽ ἂν πενίαν· εἴ γε
μὴ τῶν ποτ᾽ Ἀθηναίων ὁ πλουσιώτατος ἀμείνων
ἦν Ἀριστείδου καὶ Σωκράτους[6] ἐν πενίᾳ τῆς ἀρετῆς[7]·
ὁ δὲ πλοῦτος ἐκείνου[8] καὶ αὐτὸς ἐξίτηλός τε καὶ
ἀνώνυμος. φαύλῳ γὰρ ἅμα τῷ θανάτῳ πάντα
συνοίχεται, τὸ δὲ καλὸν αἰώνιον.

---

[1] πλοῦτον τὸν Schwartz.   [2] Meineke : αὐτοῦ.
[3] Gesner : ὅς.   [4] δ᾽ ἐν πλούτῳ Boissonade.
[5] Schwartz : καί.
[6] Θεμιστοκλῆς ὁ Νεοκλέους deleted by Valckenaer after Σωκράτους.   [7] ? after ἀρετῆς add, e.g., ἀντεχομένων.
[8] αὐτοῦ deleted by Duebner after ἐκείνου. ? ὁ δὲ πλοῦτος
αὐτοῦ καὶ αὐτὸς ἐκεῖνος.

---

[a] In the mss. of Stobaeus this is continuous with the pre-

169

In the same work :

So all men should pray for virtue rather than for riches, which are dangerous to the foolish, since faults are made worse by money. And the more unintelligent a man is, the more extravagant are his excesses ; there is a madness in his pleasures, and he has the means to gratify it.

170

From the *Letter on Friendliness* :

It has been known for a man to continue happy in poverty, but to be far from happy when rich and in positions of authority.

*171 *a*

So much does it (?) lift a good man above poverty that a law-abiding man would prefer poverty to shameful wealth. Unless indeed the richest Athenian of all time *b* was a better man than Aristides and Socrates for all that he was poor in virtue (?). But that man's wealth is itself, like him, extinct and nameless, for an inferior man's possessions all depart with him at his death, but what is truly fine is everlasting.

ceding fragment. Meineke saw that there is no connexion between them. Since a lemma must have been omitted, this fragment may not be drawn from Plutarch (so Duebner) ; certainly its present form of disjointed platitudes is not characteristic of him, nor is the consecutive τε καί of the penultimate sentence.

b Valckenaer supposed Callias to be meant (Teles, p. 48. 3 Hense), although the author implies that the man's name was forgotten.

ΠΕΡΙ ΦΥΣΕΩΣ ΚΑΙ ΠΟΝΩΝ

If this is a genuine title, it is unique in Photius' list (p. 2), in that there is appended to it a brief account of its

172

Photius, *Bibliotheca*, 161 (103 a Migne).

. . . Περί τε φύσεως καὶ πόνων, ὅπως τε πολλοὶ πολλάκις πόνῳ τὴν φύσιν οὐκ εὖ φερομένην ὤρθωσαν, ἕτεροι δὲ καλῶς ἔχουσαν ἐξ ἀμελείας διέφθειραν, ὅπως τε ἔνιοι ἐν μὲν νέοις βραδεῖς ἐνεωρῶντο πᾶσι καὶ ἀσύνετοι, ἀκμασάντων δὲ εἰς τὸ ταχὺ καὶ συνετὸν αὐτοῖς ἡ φύσις ἐξέλαμψεν.

ΠΕΡΙ ΨΥΧΗΣ

Three certain fragments of this book survive, and two others are assigned to it with some probability. These two are preserved by Stobaeus, in whose mss. *they are ascribed to a work* περὶ ψυχῆς *by Themistius. Wyttenbach in his edition of* De Sera Numinis Vindicta *(1772), p. 129, claimed them for Plutarch on the convincing grounds that their style is characteristically Plutarchean and that they are extracts from a dialogue featuring his brother Timon* [a] *and a relation by marriage, Patrocleas (see* L.C.L. vii, p. 575). *If anyone were disposed to think that Themistius might have imitated Plutarch's style and made use of his relatives in a dialogue of his own, such a fancy could not survive a discovery made by M. R. James* (C.R. xiv [1900], p. 23). *He showed that phrases from one of the fragments are quoted, without naming the author, by Clement of Alexandria (Ecl. Proph.*

---

[a] He may have had the leading part, as Lamprias does in *De Facie* (so R. Hirzel, *Der Dialog*, ii, p. 216).

ON NATURAL ENDOWMENT AND HARD WORK

(Not in Lamprias Catalogue)

content ; *if it is nothing but the description of some extract, it is unique in not being a true title.*

172

On Natural Endowment and Hard Work, how many men have often by hard work corrected an inadequate natural endowment, while others have spoiled a good one by neglect ; also how some men have in their youth given everyone the impression of being slow and unintelligent, but when they reached their prime, a sudden development of personality made them quick and intelligent.

ON THE SOUL

(Lamprias Catalogue 209)

34, 35), who elsewhere made free unacknowledged use of Plutarch, and who lived long before Themistius.

Opinions differ about four other short fragments (203-206) elsewhere assigned by Stobaeus to Themistius, περὶ ψυχῆς. If Stobaeus, or a predecessor, excerpted a work entitled περὶ ψυχῆς, which was really by Plutarch but which he believed to be by Themistius, these fragments, too, will belong to Plutarch.[b] But there may be some other reason for the assignment to Themistius of the two certainly Plutarchean fragments ; for example, a genuine extract from Themistius' περὶ ψυχῆς (if such a work existed) may have fallen out to-

---

[b] F. Bücheler, *Rh. Mus.* xxvii (1872), p. 524, translates a Syriac version of a Greek ms. that contained works by both authors.

*gether with the correct lemma for the first extract from
Plutarch : in that case it would need some other argument
to prove that the four short fragments were not taken from
Themistius.*[a]* In this uncertainty I have not included them
here. It may be doubted whether it was right to include even
the two fragments from Stobaeus that are indubitably by*

173

Origenes, *Contra Celsum*, v. 57.

Παράδοξα δὲ πράγματα τοῖς ἀνθρώποις ἐπιφαί-
νεσθαί ποτε καὶ τῶν Ἑλλήνων ἱστόρησαν οὐ μόνον
οἱ ὑπονοηθέντες ἂν ὡς μυθοποιοῦντες ἀλλὰ καὶ οἱ[1]
πολὺ ἐπιδειξάμενοι γνησίως φιλοσοφεῖν καὶ φιλ-
αληθῶς ἐκτίθεσθαι τὰ εἰς αὐτοὺς φθάσαντα. τοιαῦτα
δ' ἀνέγνωμεν παρὰ . . . τῷ Χαιρωνεῖ Πλουτάρχῳ
ἐν τοῖς περὶ ψυχῆς.

174

Aulus Gellius, i. 3. 31.

Super hoc eodem Chilone Plutarchus philosophus
in libro περὶ ψυχῆς primo verbis his[2] ita scripsit :
Χείλων ὁ παλαιός, ἀκούσας τινὸς λέγοντος μηδένα
ἔχειν ἐχθρόν, ἠρώτησεν εἰ μηδένα φίλον ἔχει, νομί-
ζων ἐξ ἀνάγκης ἐπακολουθεῖν καὶ συνεμπλέκεσθαι[3]
φιλίαις ἀπεχθείας.[4]

175

Aulus Gellius, xv. 10.

Plutarchus in librorum quos περὶ ψυχῆς inscripsit

¹ οἱ Guiet : οἷον.   ² *his* A : omitted by RPV.

FRAGMENTS : OTHER NAMED WORKS

Plutarch, since it is only a hypothesis that they come from his work entitled περὶ ψυχῆς ; *but it seemed convenient to retain their traditional place, which may after all be correct.*

There is a translation of fragments 177, 178 by A. O. Prickard, Plutarch, Select Essays, vol. ii (1918), pp. 214 ff.

173

That extraordinary events are sometimes manifested to men has been recorded not only by those Greek authors who might be suspected of inventing stories but also by those who have made a great display of a genuine pursuit of philosophy and of a regard for the truth in setting down what evidence reached them. Such accounts I have read in . . . Plutarch of Chaeronea in his work *On the Soul.*[b]

174

In the first volume of his book *On the Soul* the philosopher Plutarch wrote in these words about this same Chilon : Chilon of old, hearing someone say that he had no enemies, asked whether he had no friends, holding that enmities necessarily follow upon friendships and are interwoven with them.[c]

175

Plutarch, in the first of the books he entitled *On*

[a] O. Hense, *Rh. Mus.* lxxiii (1920), p. 301.
[b] Origen is here opposing pagan scepticism about the Resurrection.
[c] The same anecdote is told in *De Capienda ex Inimicis Utilitate*, 86 c and *De Amicorum Multitudine*, 96 A.

---

[3] Duebner : συνενπλεκεσθαι. συμπλέκ- 86 c, 96 A.
[4] Hosius : σφιλιασαπεχθειαισ.

primo cum de morbis dissereret in animos hominum
incidentibus, virgines[1] dixit Milesii nominis, fere quot
tum in ea civitate erant, repente sine ulla evidenti
causa voluntatem cepisse obeundae mortis ac deinde
plurimas vitam suspendio amississe. id cum accideret
in dies crebrius neque animis earum mori persever-
antium medicina adhiberi quiret, decrevisse Milesios
ut virgines, quae corporibus suspensis demortuae
forent, ut hae omnes nudae cum eodem laqueo quo[2]
essent praevinctae efferrentur. post id decretum
virgines voluntariam mortem non petisse pudore solo
deterritas tam inhonesti funeris.

176

Eusebius, *Praepar. Evang.* xi. 36. 1. [Theodoretus, *Cur.
Gr. Aff.* xi. 46, gives an abbreviated version.]

Συγγενῆ δὲ τούτοις καὶ ὁ Πλούταρχος ὧδέ πη ἐν
τῷ πρώτῳ περὶ ψυχῆς ἱστορεῖ·

'Αντύλλῳ δὲ τούτῳ καὶ αὐτοὶ παρῆμεν ἅμα[3] Σω-
σιτέλει καὶ 'Ηρακλέωνι διηγουμένῳ.[4] νοσῶν γὰρ
ἔναγχος ἀβιώτως ἔχειν ἐδόκει τοῖς ἰατροῖς· ἀνενεχ-
θεὶς δὲ μικρὸν ἔκ τινος οὐ βεβαίου[5] καταφορᾶς, ἄλλο
μὲν οὐδὲν οὔτ' ἔπραξεν οὔτ' εἶπε παρακινητικόν,

---

[1] *uirgines* γ : *uirginem* δ : *uirginum* Hertz.
[2] *quo* T (*a florilegium*) : *qui* γδ (" an recte " Hosius).
[3] Theodoretus : ἀλλὰ Eusebius.
[4] Theodoretus : διηγησώμεθα or διηγήσομαι Eusebius.
[5] Eusebius (or βεβαίας) : βιαίου Theodoretus.

---

[a] This story is also told in *Mulierum Virtutes*, 249 B-C.
The point may be that concern about the fate of the body

the Soul, when discussing the diseases that attack men's minds, tells this story.[a]   The unmarried daughters of the citizens inhabiting Miletus at that time almost without exception took a sudden whim to commit suicide, without there being any obvious reason for it, and subsequently many ended their lives by hanging themselves.   Such incidents became daily more frequent, and when no cure was to be had for this demented persistence in dying, the Milesians introduced a regulation that all girls who died by hanging themselves should be carried naked to burial, retaining the identical noose that had been round their neck.   After this regulation had been made the girls no longer committed suicide, deterred by nothing but the shame of such a disgraceful funeral.

176

Plutarch, too, records happenings akin to these (*sc.* Plato's myth of Er) much as follows in the first book *On the Soul* :

We were ourselves present on the occasion when Antyllus here recounted to Sositeles and Heracleon [b] how he had shortly before been ill and the doctors had thought he would not live.   On partially coming out of a kind of unsettled trance he showed no sign by act or word that his mind was affected except that

after death is logical only if a soul will survive that could be distressed at any indignities the body suffers.

[b] Heracleon from Megara recurs in *De Sollertia Animalium*, 965 c, and as a character in the dialogue *De Defectu Oraculorum*, where he is not readily satisfied, 412 E, 418 D, 421 E. The other two are unknown, unless Sositeles is a mistake for the poet Sosicles from Coroneia, *Quaest. Conv.* 618 F, 638 B, 677 D, and Lamprias Catalogue, no. 57.

ἔλεγε δὲ τεθνάναι καὶ πάλιν ἀφεῖσθαι καὶ μὴ τεθνή-
ξεσθαι τὸ παράπαν ὑπὸ τῆς ἀρρωστίας ἐκείνης,
ἀλλὰ καὶ κακῶς ἀκηκοέναι τοὺς ἀγαγόντας αὐτὸν
ὑπὸ τοῦ κυρίου· πεμφθέντας γὰρ ἐπὶ Νικανδᾶν,
αὐτὸν ἥκειν ἀντ᾽ ἐκείνου κομίζοντας. ὁ δὲ Νικαν-
δᾶς ἦν σκυτοτόμος, ἄλλως δὲ τῶν ἐν παλαίστραις
γεγονότων καὶ¹ πολλοῖς συνήθης καὶ γνώριμος.
ὅθεν οἱ νεανίσκοι προσιόντες ἔσκωπτον αὐτὸν ὡς
ἀποδεδρακότα καὶ διεφθαρκότα τοὺς ἐκεῖθεν ὑπη-
ρέτας· αὐτὸς μέντοι δῆλος ἦν εὐθὺς ὑποθραττόμενος
καὶ δυσχεραίνων· τέλος δὲ πυρετοῦ προσπεσόντος,
ἐξαίφνης ἀπέθανε τριταῖος. οὗτος δ᾽ ἀνεβίω καὶ
περίεστιν εὖγε ποιῶν, ἡμῖν ξένων ἐπιεικέστατος.

177

Stobaeus, iv. 52. 48 (v, p. 1087 Hense).

Θεμιστίου ἐκ τοῦ² περὶ ψυχῆς·

Ταῦτα τοῦ Τίμωνος εἰπόντος, ὑπολαβὼν ὁ Πατροκλέας, " ὁ μὲν λόγος," εἶπεν, " οὐχ ἧττον ἰσχυρὸς
ἢ παλαιός, ἔχει δ᾽ ὅμως ἀπορίας. εἰ γὰρ ἡ δόξα
τῆς ἀφθαρσίας παμπάλαιός ἐστι, πῶς αὖ πάλιν τὸ

---

¹ Wilamowitz omits καὶ.
² ἐκ τοῦ omitted by S.

ᵃ Lit., " was one of those who had been in the wrestling-
schools " ; but these were places of learning as well as exercise, cf. 749 c, φιλοσοφοῦντες ἐν ταῖς παλαίστραις. A plausible
emendation would give the meaning " had many friends
among the educated."

ᵇ Wilamowitz, Hermes, lxi (1926), p. 291, thinks that
Antyllus really dreamed this dream. It would be safer to say
that probably he, and certainly Plutarch, recounted the story

he said that he had died and had been released again,
and that he was not going to die of his present illness
at all ; on the contrary, those who had fetched him
had been reprimanded by their master for returning
with him instead of the Nicandas for whom they had
been sent. This Nicandas was a shoemaker, but for
all that he had had some education [a] and had many
friends and acquaintances. So the young lads would
go up and make fun of him for having cut and run or
bribed the officers from the other world. Nicandas,
however, thought it no joke ; from the first he was
uneasy and clearly did not like the affair. The end
of it was that a fever attacked him, and two days
later he died suddenly.[b] But our friend here was
restored to life and is still with us, I am glad to say,
as we have no kinder host.

177

Themistius, from his work *On the Soul* :

These remarks of Timon were taken up by Patrocleas. " Your argument," he said, " is as powerful
as it is ancient, yet it involves some difficulties. For
if the belief in immortality is of remote antiquity,

in good faith. H. J. Rose, *Proc. Camb. Phil. Soc.* 1926, p.
13, points out that St. Augustine must have credited the vision
he reports in *De Cura Pro Mortuis*, chap. 15 ; the same must
be said of Bede and the vision he reports in *Hist. Eccl.* iii. 19.
Such stories, current in real life (Aristotle, *De Somno*, 456 b
12), provide the basis for literary developments like the
myth of Er or Plutarch's own inventions in *De Genio Socratis*
and *De Sera Numinis Vindicta*. For further examples see
Proclus, *In Rempublicam*, ii. 113-116 Kroll, and for a
modern case *Proc. Soc. Psych. Research*, viii (1892), p. 180
(a reference I owe to Professor C. D. Broad).

τοῦ θανάτου δέος πάντων πρεσβύτατον εἰκὸς[1] εἶναι
τῶν φόβων εἰ μὴ νὴ Δία καὶ πάντας ἡμῖν τοῦτο
τοὺς ἄλλους ἐγγεγέννηκεν; οὐ γὰρ νεαρὸν οὐδὲ
πρόσφατόν ἐστι[2] τὸ κλαίεσθαι τὸν τεθνηκότα, καὶ
ταῦτα δὴ τὰ θρηνώδη καὶ δύσφημα τῶν ὀνομάτων
ἐπιλέγεσθαι, τὸν ἄθλιον καὶ τὸν οἰκτρόν.''

'' 'Αλλ' οὕτω μέν,'' ἔφη ὁ Τίμων, '' λογιζόμενοι[3]
καὶ τὰ ἄφθαρτα δοξάζουσι[4] συνδιαλύεσθαι[5] τοῖς[6]
φθειρομένοις. ὅτι μὲν οὖν τὸ μετηλλαχέναι καὶ
μεθίστασθαι καὶ οἴχεσθαι τὸν τεθνηκότα δυσχεροῦς
οὐδενὸς ἁπλῶς, ἀμείψεως δέ τινος ἢ μεταβολῆς
ὑπόνοιαν δίδωσιν, οὐκ ἄδηλόν ἐστι· ὅποι[7] δ' αὕτη
γίγνεται τοῖς μεταλλάττουσιν ἡ μεταβολή, καὶ
πότερον εἰς χεῖρον ἢ βέλτιον, ἐκ τῶν ἄλλων ὀνομάτων σκοπῶμεν. αὐτὸ τοίνυν τὸ τοῦ θανάτου
πρῶτον οὐχ ὑπὸ γῆν ἔοικεν οὐδὲ κάτω δεικνύναι[8]
χωροῦν τὸ μετηλλαχὸς ἀλλ' ἄνω φερόμενον καὶ
θέον· διὸ[9] δὴ καὶ λόγον ἔχει καθάπερ ἐκ καμπῆς[10]
τινος ἀνείσης οἷον ἐξάττειν[11] καὶ ἀναθεῖν[12] τὴν ψυχὴν
ἀποπνέοντος τοῦ σώματος ἀναπνέουσαν αὐτὴν καὶ
ἀναψύχουσαν. ὅρα δὲ τὸ ἀντικείμενον θανάτῳ, τὴν
γένεσιν, ὡς τοὐναντίον δηλοῖ ῥοπήν τινα κάτω καὶ
νεῦσιν ἐπὶ γῆν ἐκείνου τοῦ περὶ τὴν τελευτὴν πάλιν
ἀναθέοντος· ᾗ[13] καὶ γενέθλιον τὴν πρώτην[14] ἡμέραν
καλοῦσιν, ὡς ἄθλων καὶ πόνων μεγάλων ἀρχὴν

---

[1] εἰκὸς added by Hense (before πάντων).
[2] Tr. : ἔσται.   [3] Tr. : λογιζομένοις.
[4] A : δόξουσι.   [5] Bernardakis : διανοεῖσθαι.
[6] τοῖς added by Wyttenbach, who proposed δόξουσι τὰ αὐτὰ
διανοεῖσθαι τοῖς.
[7] Meineke : ὅπου A ποῦ S.
[8] Valckenaer : μιγνύναι.
[9] Bernardakis : ὅ.   [10] Wyttenbach : εἰ κάμπης.
[11] Koenius : ἐξάπτειν.   [12] Valckenaer : ἀναθεῖναι.

314

how (we may object) can the dread of death be the oldest of all fears, if indeed it has not engendered in us all our other fears ?[a] Certainly it is no novel, modern custom to wail over a dead man, or that those sinister words of lamentation, ' poor fellow,' ' wretched fellow,' should be used of him."

" To argue like that," replied Timon, " is to take the view that the imperishable shares in the dissolution of that which perishes. Now it is clear enough that to say that the dead man has ' passed away,' ' departed,' or ' left us ' carries no suggestion of anything that is in itself unpleasant,[b] only one of some change or transition. But where does this transition take those who pass away, and is the change for the better or for the worse ? Let us consider the matter from the evidence of the rest of our vocabulary. First of all the very word ' death ' (*thanatos*) seems to indicate that the departed do not go down below the earth but rises and races upwards (*theon anô*) ; hence it is reasonable to believe that the soul, when expired by the body, shoots forth and races upwards, as if at the release of a spring,[c] and itself draws breath and is revivified. And observe that on the contrary the opposite of death, namely birth, expresses by its name (*genesis*) a downward trend and earthward inclination (*epi gên neusis*)[d] of that which at life's close races upward once again. Thus, too, men call their first their natal day (*genethlion*), a word suggesting the beginning of great trials and tribulations

---

[a] The Epicurean view, Lucretius, iii. 38 ff.
[b] *Cf. Non Posse Suaviter*, 1104 c.
[c] *Cf. Moralia*, 611 f and note.
[d] *Cf. Moralia*, 566 a.

---

[13] Wyttenbach : ἤ.   [14] πρώτην added by F. H. S.

γενομένην. μᾶλλον δ' ἴσως ἀφ' ἑτέρας ταὐτὸ συζυ-
γίας κατοψόμεθα καὶ σαφέστερον. ἀπολύεσθαι γὰρ
τὸν ἀποθνήσκοντα καὶ τὴν τελευτὴν ἀπόλυσιν καλοῦσιν, ἂν δὲ ἔρῃ, καὶ τοῦ¹ σώματος. τοῦτο γὰρ
' δέμας ' ὀνομάζουσιν, ὡς ' δεδεμένης ' ὑπ' αὐτοῦ
τῆς ψυχῆς ἐνταῦθα παρὰ φύσιν· οὐδὲν γὰρ ἐν ᾧ
πέφυκεν εἶναι κατέχεται βίᾳ, καὶ τὸ² δεδέσθαι τήν
τε ' βίαν ' ταύτην παραγαγόντες ὠνόμασαν ' βίον,'
ὥσπερ οἶμαι τὴν ' ἑσπέραν ' Ὅμηρος ' ἕσπερον.'
ὅθεν ἀντίφωνον τοῦ βίου ὄνομα γέγονε τὸ ἀναπαύε-
σθαι τὸν θνήσκοντα, μεγάλης καὶ παρὰ φύσιν ἀναγ-
κης ἀπαλλαττόμενον.''

178

Stobaeus, iv. 52. 49 (v, p. 1089 Hense).

Ἐν ταὐτῷ·

'' Οὕτω κατὰ τὴν εἰς τὸ ὅλον μεταβολὴν καὶ
μετακόσμησιν³ ὀλωλέναι τὴν ψυχὴν λέγομεν ἐκεῖ
γενομένην⁴· ἐνταῦθα δ' ἀγνοεῖ,⁵ πλὴν ὅταν ἐν τῷ
τελευτᾶν ἤδη γένηται· τότε⁶ δὲ πάσχει πάθος οἷον
οἱ τελεταῖς μεγάλαις κατοργιαζόμενοι. διὸ καὶ τὸ
ῥῆμα τῷ ῥήματι καὶ τὸ ἔργον τῷ ἔργῳ τοῦ τελευτᾶν
καὶ τελεῖσθαι προσέοικε. πλάναι τὰ πρῶτα καὶ

---

¹ ἔρῃ καὶ Prickard : ἔρημαι. τοῦ was added by Duebner,
to fill a lacuna in S. These corrections are very uncertain.
² Gesner : τῷ.
³ Wyttenbach : κατακόσμησιν S κατασκόμησιν A.
⁴ S : γεγονέναι A. γεγονυῖαν Cobet.
⁵ Gesner : ἀγνοεῖν.
⁶ Wyttenbach : τό.

ᵃ The view that the body is the prison of the soul is Orphic
and Pythagorean. The etymology which connects δέμας with

(*genesis athlôn*). And maybe we shall see the same
thing better and even more clearly from another set
of words : men say that the dying man ' is released '
and call his end ' a release,' and, if you ask them,
they in fact mean thereby a release from the body,
which they name the ' frame ' (*demas*), because the
soul is unnaturally imprisoned (*dedemenês*) therein [a] :
for nothing is forcibly detained in a place where it is
natural for it to be. To this forcible (*bian*) imprison-
ment they have by a change of termination given the
name of life (*bion*) ; a parallel, I believe, is Homer's
use of the word *hesperos* for *hespera* (evening).[b] And
so in contrast to the name ' life ' stands the phrase
' going to his rest,' used of the dying man, as he
escapes from the grievous and unnatural constraint of
living.''

178

In the same work :

'' Thus we say that the soul that has passed thither
is dead (*olôlenai*), having regard to its complete (*eis to
holon*) change and conversion. In this world it is
without knowledge, except when it is already at the point
of death ; but when that time comes, it has an
experience like that of men who are undergoing
initiation into great mysteries [c] ; and so the verbs
teleutân (die) and *teleisthai* (be initiated), and the
actions they denote, have a similarity. In the

δέω (bind, imprison), δεσμός (fetter), etc. is found, Eustathius, 1476. 52.
  [b] *e.g. Odyssey*, i. 423, ἐπὶ ἕσπερος ἦλθε. Homer does not
use ἑσπέρα at all.
  [c] G. E. Mylonas, *Eleusis and the Eleusinian Mysteries*,
pp. 264 ff., argues that the following passage throws no light
on what happened at Eleusis.

περιδρομαὶ κοπώδεις καὶ διὰ σκότους τινὲς[1] ὕποπτοι
πορεῖαι καὶ ἀτέλεστοι, εἶτα πρὸ τοῦ τέλους αὐτοῦ
τὰ δεινὰ πάντα, φρίκη καὶ τρόμος καὶ ἰδρὼς καὶ
θάμβος· ἐκ δὲ τούτου φῶς τι θαυμάσιον ἀπήντησεν
καὶ[2] τόποι καθαροὶ καὶ λειμῶνες ἐδέξαντο, φωνὰς
καὶ χορείας καὶ σεμνότητας ἀκουσμάτων ἱερῶν καὶ
φασμάτων ἁγίων ἔχοντες[3]· ἐν αἷς ὁ παντελὴς ἤδη
καὶ μεμυημένος ἐλεύθερος γεγονὼς καὶ ἄφετος
περιιὼν ἐστεφανωμένος ὀργιάζει καὶ σύνεστιν ὁσίοις
καὶ καθαροῖς ἀνδράσι, τὸν ἀμύητον ἐνταῦθα τῶν
ζώντων καὶ[4] ἀκάθαρτον ἐφορῶν ὄχλον ἐν βορβόρῳ
πολλῷ[5] καὶ ὁμίχλῃ πατούμενον ὑφ' ἑαυτοῦ καὶ
συνελαυνόμενον, φόβῳ δὲ θανάτου τοῖς κακοῖς ἀπι-
στίᾳ τῶν ἐκεῖ ἀγαθῶν ἐμμένοντα. ἐπεὶ τό γε παρὰ
φύσιν τὴν πρὸς τὸ σῶμα τῇ ψυχῇ συμπλοκὴν εἶναι
καὶ σύνερξιν ἐκεῖθεν ἂν συνίδοις.''

" Πόθεν; " ἔφη ὁ Πατροκλέας.

" Ὅτι τῶν περὶ ἡμᾶς παθῶν ὁ ὕπνος ἥδιστόν
ἐστι. πρῶτα μὲν γὰρ αἴσθησιν ἀλγηδόνος πάσης[6]
σβέννυσι διὰ τὴν ἡδονὴν πολλῷ τῷ οἰκείῳ κεραννυ-
μένης[7]· ἔπειτα τῶν ἄλλων ἐπιθυμιῶν κρατεῖ, κἂν
ὦσι σφοδρόταται. καὶ γὰρ πρὸς ἡδονὴν οἱ φιλοσώ-
ματοι[8] δυσανασχετοῦσιν, ἐπιόντος αὐτοῖς τοῦ καθεύδειν, καὶ περιβολὰς ἐρωμένων προΐενται κατα-
δαρθάνοντες. καὶ τί δεῖ ταῦτα λέγειν, ὅπου[9] καὶ
τὴν ἀπὸ τοῦ μανθάνειν καὶ διαλέγεσθαι καὶ φιλοσοφεῖν ἡδονὴν καταλαμβάνων ὁ ὕπνος ἀποκλείει,

---

[1] Wyttenbach : τινός.　　　　[2] Duebner : ἦ.
[3] φωνὰς καί τινας ὄψεις ἁγίων φασμάτων ⟨ἔχοντες⟩ Clement.
[4] καί added by F. H. S.
[5] Tr. : πολλά.
[6] Dobree : πᾶσι.
[7] κεραννυμένην Wyttenbach.

beginning there is straying and wandering, the weariness of running this way and that, and nervous journeys through darkness that reach no goal, and then immediately before the consummation every possible terror, shivering and trembling and sweating and amazement. But after this a marvellous light meets the wanderer, and open country and meadow lands welcome him ; and in that place there are voices and dancing and the solemn majesty of sacred music and holy visions. And amidst these, he walks at large in new freedom, now perfect and fully initiated, celebrating the sacred rites, a garland upon his head, and converses with pure and holy men ; he surveys the uninitiated, unpurified mob here on earth, the mob of living men who, herded together in mirk and deep mire, trample one another down and in their fear of death cling to their ills, since they disbelieve in the blessings of the other world. For the soul's entanglement with the body and confinement in it are against nature, as you may discern from this."

"And what may that be ? " asked Patrocleas.

" The fact that sleep is the most pleasant of our experiences. In the first place, by reason of the pleasure it brings, it extinguishes the consciousness of any pain, as that pain is diluted by a large element of what our constitution welcomes. Then it prevails over all other appetites, however violent they may be. Why, the sensual are impatient of pleasure when sleep approaches, and as they surrender to it cast off the embraces of those they love. But why should I mention this, seeing that when sleep lays hold on us it excludes even the pleasure of learning and discus-

---

[8] Valckenaer : φιλομουσότατοι.   [9] Gesner : ὅτι οὐ.

τῆς ψυχῆς ὥσπερ ἀπὸ ῥεύματος λείου καὶ βαθέος
ὑποφερομένης; ἡδονὴ δὲ δὴ¹ πᾶσα μὲν ἴσως οὐσίαν
ἔχει καὶ φύσιν ἀλγηδόνος² ἀπαλλαγήν, αὕτη δὲ καὶ
παντάπασιν· οὐδενὸς γὰρ ἔξωθεν οἷον ἐπιτερποῦς
καὶ κινητικοῦ προσιόντος, ἡδόμεθα καταδαρθάνον
τες. ἀλλ' ἐπίπονόν τινα καὶ κοπώδη καὶ σκληρὰν
ἔοικεν ἐξαιρῶν³ ὕπνος διάθεσιν ἥδιστον εἶναι· αὕτη
δ' ἐστὶν οὐχ ἑτέρα τῆς πρὸς τὸ σῶμα τὴν ψυχὴν
συνδεούσης. χωρίζεται γὰρ⁴ ἐν τῷ καθεύδειν ἀνα
τρέχουσα καὶ συλλεγομένη πρὸς ἑαυτὴν ἐκ τοῦ
διατετάσθαι πρὸς τὸ σῶμα καὶ διεσπάρθαι ταῖς
αἰσθήσεσι. καίτοι λέγουσί τινες ὡς καταμίγνυσι
μᾶλλον ὁ ὕπνος πρὸς τὸ σῶμα τὴν ψυχήν, οὐκ
ὀρθῶς λέγοντες· ἀντιμαρτυρεῖ γὰρ τῇ ἀναισθησίᾳ
καὶ ψυχρότητι καὶ βάρει καὶ ὠχρότητι τὸ σῶμα
κατηγοροῦν τῆς ψυχῆς ἔκλειψιν μὲν ὅταν τελευτήσῃ
μετάστασιν δ' ὅταν καθεύδῃ. καὶ τοῦτ' ἐστὶ τὸ
τὴν ἡδονὴν ποιοῦν, ἀπόλυσις καὶ ἀνάπαυλα⁵ τῆς
ψυχῆς, ὥσπερ ἄχθος κατατιθεμένης καὶ πάλιν
ἀναλαμβανούσης καὶ ὑποδυομένης.⁶ φεύγειν γὰρ
ἔοικε κομιδῇ τὸ σῶμα θνήσκουσα δραπετεύειν δὲ
καταδαρθάνουσα. διὸ θνήσκουσι μὲν ἔνιοι μετὰ
πόνων καθεύδουσι δὲ μεθ' ἡδονῆς ἅπαντες· ὅπου
μὲν γὰρ ἀπορρήγνυται παντάπασιν ὁ δεσμός, ὅπου
δ' ἐνδίδωσι καὶ χαλᾶται καὶ γίγνεται μαλακώτερος,
οἷον ἀμμάτων ἀφιεμένων τῶν⁷ αἰσθήσεων παραλυο-

----

¹ δὲ δὴ Wyttenbach : δ' ἤδε.
² τὴν τῆς ἀλγηδόνος Clement.
³ Wyttenbach : ἐξαίρων.
⁴ ἡ ψυχὴ added by A.
⁵ Wyttenbach : ἀπόλαυσιν καὶ ἀνάπαυλαν.

sion and philosophy, as its smooth deep current bears the soul away ? Again it may be true that every pleasure is in nature and essence relief from pain [a]; it is certainly true of the pleasure of sleep. We find pleasure in falling asleep, although there is no access of any external pleasurable stimulus ; no, sleep is, it would seem, the height of pleasure because it removes an oppressive, wearisome, fatiguing condition, and that condition is no other than the one that binds the soul to the body. For in sleep the soul is dissociated, as it retires and concentrates upon itself, having previously been extended to fit the body and dispersed through the organs of sense.[b] There are, to be sure, those who claim that sleep causes the soul to be more fully commingled with the body, but they are mistaken. The body gives evidence to the contrary, witnessing by its lack of sensation, its coldness, its heaviness, and its pallor, that the soul leaves it temporarily in sleep just as it abandons it in death. This is what causes the pleasure of sleep— the soul's release and respite, when it lays down its burden, as it were, later to take it up and shoulder it again. For it would appear that, whereas in dying the soul escapes from the body altogether, in falling asleep it only plays truant. That is why death is sometimes accompanied by pains, but sleep invariably by pleasure. In the one case the bond is completely snapped ; in the other it gives and is slackened off and becomes easier, when the knots are, so to speak,

---

[a] Timon accepts, at least for the sake of his argument, the Epicurean view of pleasure.

[b] *Cf.* Aristotle, frag. 10 b Ross, Walzer, 60 Rose.

---

[6] Wyttenbach : ἀποδυομένης.

[7] Wyttenbach : ὀμμάτων ἀφαιμάτων.

μένων καὶ προϊεμένων τὴν περὶ τὸ σῶμα τῆς ψυχῆς
ἔντασιν.''[1]

'' Εἶτα πῶς,'' εἶπεν ὁ Πατροκλέας,[2] '' οὐ δυσφο-
ροῦμεν οὐδ' ἀλγοῦμεν ἐγρηγορότες; ''

'' Πῶς δέ,'' ἔφη ὁ Τίμων,'' κειρομένων μὲν αἰσθάνεται κουφότητος ἡ κεφαλὴ καὶ ῥαστώνης, κομών-
των δὲ βαρύτητος αἴσθησιν οὐ πάνυ παρεῖχεν; καὶ
λυθέντες μὲν ἐκ δεσμῶν ἥδονται, δεδεμένοι δ' οὐκ
ἀλγοῦσι; καὶ φῶς ἐπεισενεχθὲν ἐξαίφνης συμποσίῳ
τινὶ συνηρεφεῖ[3] θόρυβον καὶ κρότον ὑφ' ἡδονῆς
ἐποίησε, πρότερον δὲ τὸ ἀλαμπὲς ἐδόκει μὴ ἐνοχλεῖν
μηδὲ λυπεῖν τὴν ὄψιν· ἐν γὰρ αἴτιον, ὦ φίλε,[4] τούτων ἁπάντων, ὅτι τῷ[5] παρὰ φύσιν τὸ κατὰ μικρὸν
συνήθη[6] καὶ σύντροφον ἐποίει τὴν αἴσθησιν, ὥστε
μὴ πάνυ δυσχεραίνειν πάσχουσαν, ἀπαλλαγείσης δὲ
καὶ μεταβαλούσης εἰς τὴν φύσιν, φαίνεται παρευ-
θὺς[7] τῷ οἰκείῳ τἀλλότριον καὶ τῷ ἡδομένῳ τὸ
λυποῦν ὅτι παρῆν[8] βαρῦνον. οὕτω δὴ καὶ τὴν
ψυχὴν τῇ πρὸς τὰ θνητὰ πάθη καὶ μέρη καὶ ὄργανα[9]
κοινωνίᾳ τὸ παρὰ φύσιν καὶ ἀλλότριον οὐ πάνυ
δοκεῖ πιέζειν ὑπὸ μακρᾶς[10] συνηθείας· αἰσθάνεται δὲ
ῥαστώνης καὶ κουφότητος[11] μεθ' ἡδονῆς ἀφιεμένη[12]
τῶν διὰ τοῦ σώματος ἐνεργειῶν· ἐκείναις γὰρ
ἐνοχλεῖται καὶ περὶ ἐκείνας ἐκπονεῖται καὶ ἀπ'
ἐκείνων[13] σχολῆς δεῖται καὶ ἀναπαύσεως· ἃ δ' αὐτὴ
καθ' αὑτὴν ἐνεργεῖ κατὰ φύσιν, τὸ σκοπεῖν ἀεί τι

---

[1] Wyttenbach : ἐν πᾶσιν.
[2] Duebner : πατροκλεύς.
[3] τινὶ συνηρεφεῖ added by F. H. S. from Clement; see p. 306.
[4] Wyttenbach : ὤφειλε.
[5] Wyttenbach : τό.   [6] Hartman : σύνηθες.
[7] Duebner (or εὐθὺς) : γὰρ εὐθύς.
[8] καὶ omitted by F. H. S. after παρῆν.

undone and the senses unfasten and throw off the
strings that strain the soul to the body."

" Then how is it," said Patrocleas, " that we feel
no discomfort or pain when awake ? "

"And how is it," retorted Timon, " that the head
has a sense of lightness and relief when the hair is cut,
but affords no sensation whatever of heaviness while it
is long ? And why do men released from fetters feel
pleasure,[a] but no pain when wearing them ? Why do
lights suddenly brought into a shadowy banqueting
hall give pleasure and cause a stir of applause, whereas the dimness did not previously seem to trouble
or pain the eyes ? There is a single reason, my dear
friend, for all these facts : gradual change accustomed
and habituated the seat of sensation to an unnatural
condition, so that it did not feel any actual discomfort
at what it was enduring, but on its being freed and
reverting to nature it immediately recognizes the previous burdensome presence of what was alien alongside what was natural, and of painful feeling alongside
pleasurable. Similarly, you see, with the soul : in
its association with mortal limbs, organs, and affections, that which is unnatural and alien to it seems,
because of long familiarity, not to be at all oppressive ;
yet it has a feeling of relief and lightness, accompanied
by pleasure, on release from its bodily activities. It
is by them that it is harassed, on them that it wears
itself out, from them that it needs rest and relaxation.
But where its own natural activities are concerned—

---

[a] *Cf.* Plato, *Phaedo*, 60 b-c.

---

⁹ καὶ ὄργανα omitted by S.
¹⁰ Gesner : μικρᾶς.
¹¹ Gesner : ῥαστώνη καὶ κουφότητι.
¹² Gesner : ἐφιεμένη.   ¹³ Tr. : ἐκείνης.

καὶ λογίζεσθαι καὶ μνημονεύειν καὶ θεωρεῖν, πρὸς
ταῦτα ἄτρυτός ἐστι καὶ ἀκόρεστος. καὶ γὰρ ὁ
κόρος κόπος ἐν ἡδοναῖς ἔοικεν εἶναι τῷ μετὰ[1]
σώματός τι τὴν ψυχὴν πάσχειν, ἐπεὶ πρός γε τὰς
αὐτῆς[2] ἡδονὰς οὐκ ἀπαγορεύει.[3] συμπεπλεγμένη
δέ, ὥσπερ εἴρηται,[4] τῷ σώματι ταὐτὰ τῷ Ὀδυσσεῖ
πέπονθεν· ὡς γὰρ ἐκεῖνος τῷ ἐρινεῷ προσφὺς εἴχετο
καὶ περιέπτυσσεν οὐ ποθῶν οὐδ' ἀγαπῶν ἐκεῖνον,
ἀλλὰ δεδιὼς ὑποκειμένην τὴν Χάρυβδιν, οὕτως
ἔοικεν ἡ ψυχὴ τοῦ σώματος[5] ἔχεσθαι καὶ περιπε-
πλέχθαι δι' εὔνοιαν οὐδεμίαν αὐτοῦ καὶ χάριν, ἀλλ'
ὀρρωδοῦσα τοῦ θανάτου τὴν ἀδηλότητα.[6]

κρύψαντες γὰρ ἔχουσι θεοὶ βίον ἀνθρώποισι

κατὰ τὸν σοφὸν Ἡσίοδον, οὐ σαρκίνοις τισὶ δεσμοῖς
πρὸς τὸ σῶμα τὴν ψυχὴν κατατείναντες, ἀλλ' ἕνα
δεσμὸν αὐτῇ καὶ μίαν φυλακὴν μηχανησάμενοι καὶ
περιβαλόντες, τὴν ἀδηλότητα καὶ ἀπιστίαν τῶν μετὰ
τὴν τελευτήν· ἐπεὶ τήν γε πεισθεῖσαν, ὅσα ἀνθρώπους περιμένει τελευτήσαντας καθ' Ἡράκλειτον,
οὐδὲν ἂν κατάσχοι."

ΣΤΡΩΜΑΤΕΙΣ

*It does Eusebius no credit that he was taken in by the
ascription to Plutarch of a puerile compilation from which
he quoted in order to discredit Greek philosophy. Its char-*

---

[1] ? μετὰ τοῦ.
[2] Wyttenbach : τε τὰς αὐτάς.
[3] Wyttenbach : οὐ κατηγοροῦσι.
[4] εἱρκτῇ Wyttenbach.
[5] τοῦ σώματος added by Hense.
[6] Tr. : εἰδωλότητα.

always to be inquiring, reasoning, remembering, or contemplating—there it is indefatigable and insatiable. Satiety (*koros*) seems indeed to be nothing but a wearying (*kopos*) in pleasures, because the soul suffers when associated with the body. Where its own pleasures are concerned, the soul does not flag. But being entangled, as has been said, with the body, it is in the same case as Odysseus. Just as he clung tightly to the fig-tree,[a] clasping it, not out of any love or affection for it, but in fear of Charybdis that lay below him, so it would seem that the soul clings to the body and embraces it, not through any kindly feeling or goodwill towards it, but in horror of death's uncertainty. ' For the gods keep life concealed from human ken,' as that wise man Hesiod says.[b] They have not strained the soul tight to the body by any bonds of flesh : the one bond they have contrived for it, the one prison in which they have confined it, is our uncertainty about what follows death, and our unwillingness to believe. For if a soul were confident of all that, in Heraclitus's words, ' awaits men who have met their end,' [c] there is nothing that could hold it.'' [d]

A PATCHWORK

acter is not over-harshly described by Diels, Doxographi Graeci, *156 f. The greater part of it he shows to be originally derived from Theophrastus's* Φυσικαὶ Δόξαι, *and it preserves*

---

[a] *Odyssey*, xii. 432. The same comparison is found at *De Tranquillitate Animi*, 476 B.

[b] *Works and Days*, 42.

[c] Diels-Kranz, *Frag. d. Vorsokr.* 22 B 27.

[d] This may have been suggested by Plato, *Cratylus*, 403.

in its garbled way some elements from that work not otherwise known, particularly concerning Anaximander (cf. ibid., 132-144).   Into this original stratum it inserts, after the paragraph on Democritus, brief accounts of Epicurus and Aristippus.   No. 62 in the Lamprias Catalogue is Στρωματεῖς ἱστορικοὶ ⟨καὶ⟩ ποιητικοί.   This may be identical with the book used by Eusebius, since that catalogue contains other spurious works.   On the other hand, if there was a genuine work of this name, it may have suggested the ascription to Plutarch of this forgery.

The title Στρωματεῖς for a Miscellany was known to Aulus Gellius (praef. 7), possibly from a work of that name composed in the time of Trajan by Caesellius Vindex.   The word is otherwise known in the sense of " bed-coverings," and its use for a Miscellany is explained by supposing such coverings to have been of patchwork or otherwise variegated.

K. Mras, Wiener Studien, lxviii (1955), pp. 88 ff., who maintains that the miscellany comprised notes made by Plu-

*179

Eusebius, *Praeparatio Evangelii*, i. 7. 16.

Τούτῳ δ' ἂν εὕροις συμφώνους καὶ τοὺς πλείστους τῶν παρ' Ἕλλησι φιλοσόφων, ὧν ἐγώ σοι τὰς περὶ ἀρχῶν δόξας καὶ τὰς πρὸς ἀλλήλους διαστάσεις καὶ διαφωνίας, ἐκ στοχασμῶν ἀλλ' οὐκ ἀπὸ καταλήψεως ὁρμηθείσας, ἀπὸ τῶν Πλουτάρχου Στρωματέων ἐπὶ τοῦ παρόντος ἐκθήσομαι. σὺ δὲ μὴ παρέργως, σχολῇ δὲ καὶ μετὰ λογισμοῦ θέα τῶν δηλουμένων τὴν πρὸς ἀλλήλους διάστασιν.

1. Θάλητα πρῶτον πάντων φασὶν ἀρχὴν τῶν ὅλων ὑποστήσασθαι τὸ ὕδωρ· ἐξ αὐτοῦ γὰρ εἶναι τὰ πάντα καὶ εἰς αὐτὸ χωρεῖν· (2) μεθ' ὃν Ἀναξί-

---

[a] Of Chios (the Stoic) according to the mss., of Ceos (the

326

tarch for his own use, argues that Eusebius also took from the same source without acknowledgement, contrary to his usual practice, a passage on Ariston,[a] P.E. xv. 62. 7-13. He bases his argument on the structure of Eusebius' work and on a quotation from Homer common to both places. He does not seem to me to establish more than a bare possibility, and as the passage does not resemble the acknowledged extracts in style, I do not think it justifiable to print it here.

It need hardly be said that these extracts must be approached with extreme caution. To consider what truth can be found in them would go beyond what is reasonable in this edition. The non-specialist reader may be referred for a general orientation to G. S. Kirk and J. E. Raven, The Presocratic Philosophers (Cambridge, 1957), or to W. K. C. Guthrie, History of Greek Philosophy (Cambridge, 1962). I have been chary of admitting into the text conjectural emendations, which may restore historical truth rather than the wording of the compiler.

*179

You would find most of the Greek philosophers agreeing with this (*i.e.*, that the world is a product of chance). I will now set out, from the *Patchwork* of Plutarch, their opinions about the origins of things and their differences and disputes, which arose from guesswork and not from a grasp of truth. You must not take it lightly, but devote time and thought to observing the disagreement among them in the views here expounded.

1. They say that Thales was the first man to suppose that the origin of all things is water, arguing that everything came from it and passed into it ; (2) [b] and that after him Anaximander, who had been

Peripatetic) according to Mras ; perhaps a conflation of the two, who were confused by the 2nd century A.D. at latest.

[b] Diels-Kranz, *Frag. d. Vorsokr.* 12 A 10.

μανδρον, Θάλητος ἑταῖρον γενόμενον, τὸ ἄπειρον
φάναι τὴν πᾶσαν αἰτίαν ἔχειν τῆς τοῦ παντὸς γενέ-
σεώς τε καὶ φθορᾶς· ἐξ οὗ δή φησι τούς τε οὐρανοὺς
ἀποκεκρίσθαι, καὶ καθόλου τοὺς ἅπαντας ἀπείρους
ὄντας κόσμους. ἀπεφήνατο δὲ τὴν φθορὰν γίγνεσθαι καὶ πολὺ πρότερον τὴν γένεσιν ἐξ ἀπείρου
αἰῶνος ἀνακυκλουμένων πάντων[1] αὐτῶν.

Ὑπάρχειν δέ φησι τῷ μὲν σχήματι τὴν γῆν
κυλινδροειδῆ, ἔχειν δὲ τοσοῦτον βάθος ὅσον ἂν εἴη
τρίτον πρὸς τὸ πλάτος. φησὶ δὲ τὸ[2] ἐκ τοῦ ἀϊδίου
γόνιμον θερμοῦ τε καὶ ψυχροῦ[3] κατὰ τὴν γένεσιν
τοῦδε τοῦ κόσμου ἀποκριθῆναι, καί τινα ἐκ τούτου
φλογὸς σφαῖραν περιφυῆναι τῷ περὶ τὴν γῆν ἀέρι
ὡς τῷ δένδρῳ φλοιόν, ἧς[4] ἀπορραγείσης καὶ εἴς
τινας ἀποκλεισθείσης κύκλους ὑποστῆναι τὸν ἥλιον
καὶ τὴν σελήνην καὶ τοὺς ἀστέρας. ἔτι φησὶν ὅτι
κατ᾽ ἀρχὰς ἐξ ἀλλοειδῶν ζώων ὁ ἄνθρωπος ἐγεν-
νήθη, ἐκ τοῦ τὰ μὲν ἄλλα δι᾽ ἑαυτῶν ταχὺ νέμεσθαι,
μόνον δὲ τὸν ἄνθρωπον πολυχρονίου δεῖσθαι τιθη-
νήσεως· διὸ καὶ κατ᾽ ἀρχὰς οὐκ ἄν ποτε τοιοῦτον
ὄντα διασωθῆναι. ταῦτα μὲν οὖν ὁ Ἀναξίμανδρος.

3. Ἀναξιμένην δέ φασι τὴν τῶν ὅλων ἀρχὴν
τὸν ἀέρα εἰπεῖν, καὶ τοῦτον εἶναι τῷ μὲν μεγέθει[5]

---

[1] ? πάντων τῶν, cf. Marcus Aurelius, ii. 14. 5, πάντα ἐξ ἀϊδίου
ὁμοειδῆ ἀνακυκλούμενα. Heidel would omit πάντων.

[2] δέ τι Diels.   [3] γονίμου θερμόν τε καὶ ψυχρὸν Mullach.

[4] ἧστινος other mss.   [5] μεγέθει Zeller : γένει.

---

[a] The words οὐρανός, "heaven," and κόσμος, "world," are
ambiguous. Probably the writer understood by κόσμος any
system like that in which he supposed himself to live, con-
sisting of earth, air, and celestial bodies enclosed by an
outer shell, the οὐρανός, or "heaven." The problems of the
"innumerable worlds" are lucidly discussed by W. K. C.
Guthrie, *History of Greek Philosophy*, i, pp. 106-115.

his associate, said that " the Infinite " was solely responsible for the coming-to-be and the passing-away of the universe. Anaximander states that the various heavens have been secreted out of this Infinite, as more generally have been all the worlds, which are infinite in number.[a] He declared that passing-away and (much earlier) coming-to-be take place as they[b] all repeat a cycle from infinite time.

He says that the earth is cylindrical in shape, and has a depth such as to be a third of its breadth. He says that what is generative of hot and cold from the eternal was separated off[c] at the coming-to-be of this world, and that from this a sort of ball of flame grew round the air surrounding the earth, like the bark round a tree. When this had been torn off and shut up in certain rings, the sun, moon, and stars[d] came into existence. Further he says that originally man was born from animals of a different species, his reason being that whereas other animals quickly get their own food, man alone needs a long period of suckling. So that, if he was also originally so constituted, he would not have survived. So much for Anaximander.[e]

3.[f] They say that Anaximenes said that the origin of all things is the air, and that it is infinite in extent,

---

[b] As the text stands, " they " seems to mean the worlds ; but a very easy change would give the meaning " as all things recur identically in a cycle."

[c] A small and probable change gives " something generative of hot and cold was separated off from the eternal."

[d] Including the planets.

[e] On whom see C. H. Kahn, *Anaximander and the Origins of Greek Cosmology* (1960), C. J. Classen, *Hermes*, xc (1962), p. 159, M. C. Stokes, *Phronesis*, viii (1963), p. 5 : references to earlier literature will be found there.

[f] Diels-Kranz, *Frag. d. Vorsokr.* 13 A 6.

ἄπειρον, ταῖς δὲ περὶ αὐτὸν ποιότησιν ὡρισμένον·
γεννᾶσθαί τε πάντα κατά τινα πύκνωσιν τούτου
καὶ πάλιν ἀραίωσιν. τήν γε μὴν κίνησιν ἐξ αἰῶνος
ὑπάρχειν· πιλουμένου δὲ τοῦ ἀέρος, πρώτην γεγε-
νῆσθαι λέγει τὴν γῆν, πλατεῖαν μάλα· διὸ καὶ κατὰ
λόγον αὐτὴν ἐποχεῖσθαι τῷ ἀέρι. καὶ τὸν ἥλιον κα
τὴν σελήνην καὶ τὰ λοιπὰ ἄστρα τὴν ἀρχὴν τῆς
γενέσεως ἐκ γῆς ἔχειν· ἀποφαίνεται γοῦν τὸν ἥλιον
γῆν, διὰ δὲ τὴν ὀξεῖαν κίνησιν καὶ μάλ' ἱκανῶς[1]
θερμότητα[2] λαβεῖν.[3]

4. Ξενοφάνης δ' ὁ Κολοφώνιος, ἰδίαν τινὰ ὁδὸν
πεπορευμένος καὶ παρηλλαχυῖαν πάντας τοὺς προ-
ειρημένους, οὔτε γένεσιν οὔτε φθορὰν ἀπολείπει,
ἀλλ' εἶναι λέγει τὸ πᾶν ἀεὶ ὅμοιον· εἰ γὰρ γίγνοιτο
τοῦτο, φησίν, ἀναγκαῖον πρὸ τούτου μὴ εἶναι· τὸ
μὴ ὂν δ' οὐκ ἂν γένοιτο οὐδ' ἂν τὸ μὴ ὂν ποιήσαι
τι οὔτε ὑπὸ τοῦ μὴ ὄντος γένοιτ' ἄν τι. ἀποφαίνεται δὲ καὶ τὰς αἰσθήσεις ψευδεῖς, καὶ καθόλου
σὺν αὐταῖς καὶ αὐτὸν τὸν λόγον διαβάλλει. ἀποφαίνεται δὲ καὶ τῷ χρόνῳ καταφερομένην συνεχῶς
καὶ κατ' ὀλίγον τὴν γῆν εἰς τὴν θάλασσαν χωρεῖν.
φησὶ δὲ καὶ τὸν ἥλιον ἐκ μικρῶν καὶ πλειόνων πυ-
ριδίων[4] ἀθροίζεσθαι. ἀποφαίνεται δὲ καὶ περὶ θεῶν
ὡς οὐδεμιᾶς ἡγεμονίας ἐν αὐτοῖς οὔσης· οὐ γὰρ
ὅσιον δεσπόζεσθαί τινα τῶν θεῶν, ἐπιδεῖσθαί τε
μηδενὸς αὐτῶν μηδένα μηδ' ὅλως· ἀκούειν δὲ καὶ

---

[1] εἰκότως Toup.
[2] θερμότητα or θερμότητος one late MS.: θερμοτάτην the rest.
θερμὴν ταύτην Diels.

but definite in its qualities ; and that all things are generated by a kind of condensation, and contrary rarefaction, of this air. Change, however, existed from all time. And he says that when the air was compressed the earth came into being first ; it is very broad and accordingly rides upon the air ; and the sun and moon and other stars have the origin of their coming-to-be from earth. At any rate, he declares that the sun is earth, but that through its rapid motion it acquired heat quite adequately.[a]

4.[b] Xenophanes of Colophon, having taken his own way, which was distinct from that of all the philosophers previously mentioned, does not admit either coming-to-be or passing-away, but says that the sum of things is always the same. For if it should come-to-be, he says, necessarily it would not exist previously. But what does not exist would not come to be nor could it make anything, and nothing could come into existence as a result of it. He declares, too, that the senses are deceptive, and entirely impugns reason itself along with them. And he declares, too, that in the course of time the earth is continually and gradually carried down to join the sea. He says also that the sun is formed by the collection of a large number of small fires. And his account of the gods is that there is no supremacy among them, since religion forbids that any god should have a master, and none of them lacks anything in any way whatever. They hear and see as a

---

[a] Anaximenes believed the heavenly bodies to be fiery. This sentence may be due to confusion with Anaxagoras, whom it fits.   [b] Diels-Kranz, *Frag. d. Vorsokr.* 21 A 32.

---

³ κίνησιν before λαβεῖν omitted by Zeller : καῦσιν Diels.
⁴ Toup : πυρίων.

ὁρᾶν καθόλου καὶ μὴ κατὰ μέρος. ἀποφαίνεται δὲ
καὶ τὴν γῆν ἄπειρον εἶναι καὶ κατὰ[1] πᾶν μέρος[2] μὴ
περιέχεσθαι ὑπ' ἀέρος· γίγνεσθαι δ' ἅπαντα ἐκ γῆς.
τὸν δ' ἥλιόν φησι καὶ τὰ ἄστρα ἐκ τῶν νεφῶν
γίγνεσθαι.

5. Παρμενίδης δ' ὁ Ἐλεάτης, ἑταῖρος Ξενοφά-
νους, ἅμα μὲν καὶ τῶν τούτου δοξῶν ἀντεποιήσατο,
ἅμα δὲ καὶ τὴν ἐναντίαν ἐνεχείρησε στάσιν. ἀίδιον
μὲν γὰρ τὸ πᾶν καὶ ἀκίνητον ἀποφαίνεται κατὰ[3]
τὴν τῶν πραγμάτων ἀλήθειαν· εἶναι γὰρ αὐτὸ

μοῦνον[4] μουνογενές τε καὶ ἀτρεμὲς ἠδ' ἀγένητον·

γένεσιν δὲ τῶν καθ' ὑπόληψιν ψευδῆ δοκούντων
εἶναι· καὶ τὰς αἰσθήσεις ἐκβάλλει ἐκ τῆς ἀληθείας·
φησὶ δ' ὅτι, εἴ τι παρὰ τὸ ὂν ὑπάρχει, τοῦτο οὐκ
ἔστιν ὄν, τὸ δὲ μὴ ὂν ἐν τοῖς ὅλοις οὐκ ἔστιν. οὕτως
οὖν τὸ ὂν ἀγένητον ἀπολείπει, λέγει δὲ τὴν γῆν
τοῦ πυκνοῦ καταρρυέντος ἀέρος[5] γεγονέναι.

6. Ζήνων δ' ὁ Ἐλεάτης ἴδιον μὲν οὐδὲν ἐξέθετο,
διηπόρησε δὲ περὶ τούτων ἐπὶ πλεῖον.

7. Δημόκριτος δ' ὁ Ἀβδηρίτης ὑπεστήσατο τὸ
πᾶν ἄπειρον διὰ τὸ μηδαμῶς ὑπό τινος αὐτὸ δεδη-
μιουργῆσθαι, ἔτι δὲ καὶ ἀμετάβλητον αὐτὸ λέγει·
καὶ καθόλου, οἷον τὸ πᾶν ἐστι, ῥητῶς ἐκτίθεται,
μηδεμίαν ἀρχὴν ἔχειν τὰς αἰτίας τῶν νῦν γιγνο-
μένων, ἄνωθεν δ' ὅλως ἐξ ἀπείρου χρόνου προκατ-
έχεσθαι τῇ ἀνάγκῃ πάνθ' ἁπλῶς τὰ γεγονότα καὶ

[1] κατά] τὸ κάτω Diels.
[2] Brandis places κατὰ πᾶν μέρος after μὴ; perhaps it belongs after ἀέρος.
[3] καὶ before κατὰ deleted by Duebner.
[4] οὖλον Parmenides.
[5] ἀέρος deleted by Patin.

whole and not with part of themselves. He declares, too, that the earth is without limits and is not surrounded by air on all sides, and that all things come from earth. But he says that the sun and the stars come from the clouds.

5.[a] Parmenides of Elea, Xenophanes' associate, appropriated his doctrines but simultaneously maintained the opposite position. On the one hand he declares the sum of things to be eternal and unchanging, if we keep to the truth of the facts ; for it is

Alone, unique, unshaken, and unborn.[b]

He says that coming-to-be belongs to the things that appear to exist through false supposition, and he expels the senses from reality. He says that if there is anything besides what exists, it is not existent. But the non-existent has no place in the whole of things. So he concludes that what exists did not come to be. But he says that the earth came into being when the dense air was precipitated.

6. Zeno of Elea put forward no views of his own, but argued further on these matters.

7.[c] Democritus of Abdera supposed that the sum of things is infinite because it certainly has not been fashioned by anyone. Further he says that it is immutable. And in general he explicitly explains the nature of the sum of things. He says that the causes of present events have no beginning and that absolutely everything that was, is, and shall be is completely determined previously by necessity

[a] Diels-Kranz, *Frag. d. Vorsokr.* 28 A 22.
[b] A misquotation, also met in the parallel version of Aëtius, of Parmenides B 8. 3-4 (Diels-Kranz).
[c] Diels-Kranz, *Frag. d. Vorsokr.* 68 A 39.

PLUTARCH'S MORALIA

ἐόντα καὶ ἐσόμενα. ἡλίου δὲ καὶ σελήνης γένεσίν
φησι κατ' ἰδίαν· φέρεσθαι ταῦτα μηδέπω τὸ παράπαν ἔχοντα θερμὴν φύσιν μηδὲ μὴν καθόλου λαμ-
πρότητα,[1] τοὐναντίον δ' ἐξωμοιωμένην τῇ περὶ τὴν
γῆν φύσει· γεγονέναι γὰρ ἑκάτερον τούτων πρότερον
ἔτι κατ' ἰδίαν ὑποβολήν τινα κόσμου, ὕστερον δέ,
μεγεθοποιουμένου τοῦ περὶ τὸν ἥλιον κύκλου, ἐν-
αποληφθῆναι[2] ἐν αὐτῷ τὸ πῦρ.

8. Ἐπίκουρος Νεοκλέους Ἀθηναῖος τὸν περὶ
θεῶν τῦφον πειρᾶται καταστέλλειν· ἀλλὰ καὶ οὐδέν,
φησί, γίγνεται ἐκ τοῦ μὴ ὄντος· ὅτι τὸ πᾶν ἀεὶ
τοιοῦτον ἦν καὶ ἔσται τοιοῦτον· ὅτι οὐδὲν ξένον ἐν
τῷ παντὶ ἀποτελεῖται παρὰ τὸν ἤδη γεγενημένον
χρόνον ἄπειρον· ὅτι πᾶν ἐστι σῶμα, καὶ οὐ μόνον
ἀμετάβλητον ἀλλὰ καὶ ἄπειρον· ὅτι τέλος τῶν ἀγαθῶν ἡ[3] ἡδονή.

9. Ἀρίστιππος ὁ Κυρηναῖος τέλος ἀγαθῶν τὴν
ἡδονὴν κακῶν δὲ τὴν ἀλγηδόνα· τὴν δ' ἄλλην φυ-
σιολογίαν περιγράφει, μόνον ὠφέλιμον εἶναι λέγων
τὸ ζητεῖν

ὅττι τοι ἐν μεγάροισι κακόν τ' ἀγαθόν τε τέτυκται.

10. Ἐμπεδοκλῆς ὁ Ἀκραγαντῖνος στοιχεῖα τέσσαρα, πῦρ, ὕδωρ, αἰθέρα, γαῖαν· αἰτίαν[4] δὲ τούτων
φιλίαν καὶ νεῖκος· ἐκ πρώτης φησὶ τῆς τῶν στοι-

---

[1] Diels : λαμπροτάτην (retained by Kranz, Mras).
[2] ἐναπολειφθῆναι mss., but corrected in some.
[3] ἡ added by Diels.   [4] ? αἴτια Kranz.

---

[a] Epicurus rejects the view that the heavenly bodies were
formed separately from the world, Diogenes Laertius, x. 90.
[b] This suggests that the sun and moon were first formed

from infinite time past. He affirms an independent birth of the sun and the moon.[a] They were borne along without yet possessing any heat whatsoever or indeed any brightness at all, but having on the contrary a nature resembling that of the earth. For they had come into existence still earlier, each of them at an independent laying of the foundation for a world [b]; later when the sun's orb increased, its fire was enclosed in it.

8. Epicurus, son of Neocles, an Athenian, tries to suppress the nonsense talked about gods. Moreover nothing, he says, comes to be from what does not exist. He says that the sum of things always was and will be as it is ; that nothing strange is produced in the sum of things that has not occurred in the infinite time that has already been ; that everything is corporeal, and is not merely immutable, but also infinite ; that the supreme good is pleasure.

9.[c] Aristippus of Cyrenê says that the supreme good is pleasure, the supreme evil pain. He rejects all natural science, saying that there is no use in inquiring about anything but what

Is fashioned good or bad within your halls.[d]

10.[e] Empedocles of Acragas gives four elements, fire, water, air, and earth. Responsible for them are Love and Strife. He says that the air, separated off

in abortive worlds and later taken up into ours. But if κόσμου has been misplaced, the original sense may have been that their " foundations " were laid before the beginning of our world, and that they were later built up in it to their present size.

[c] Fragments 159 A, 144 Mannebach, 1 B 19 Giannantoni.

[d] *Odyssey*, iv. 392. Cited by Plutarch, *Mor.* 122 D, 1063 D, and in Eusebius, *Praepar. Evang.* xv. 62. 11.

[e] Diels-Kranz, *Frag. d. Vorsokr.* 31 A 30.

χείων κράσεως ἀποκριθέντα τὸν ἀέρα περιχυθῆναι
κύκλῳ· μετὰ δὲ τὸν ἀέρα τὸ πῦρ ἐκδραμὸν καὶ οὐκ
ἔχον ἑτέραν χώραν ἄνω ἐκτρέχειν ὑπὸ[1] τοῦ περὶ τὸν
ἀέρα πάγου. εἶναι δὲ κύκλῳ περὶ τὴν γῆν φερό-
μενα δύο ἡμισφαίρια, τὸ μὲν καθόλου πυρὸς τὸ δὲ
μικτὸν ἐξ ἀέρος καὶ ὀλίγου πυρός, ὅπερ οἴεται τὴν
νύκτα εἶναι. τὴν δ' ἀρχὴν τῆς κινήσεως συμβῆναι
ἀπὸ τοῦ τετυχηκέναι κατὰ[2] τὸν ἀθροισμὸν ἐπιβρί-
σαντος τοῦ πυρός.[3] ὁ δ' ἥλιος τὴν φύσιν οὐκ ἔστι
πῦρ ἀλλὰ τοῦ πυρὸς ἀντανάκλασις ὁμοία τῇ ἀφ'
ὕδατος γιγνομένῃ. σελήνην δέ φησι συστῆναι καθ'
ἑαυτὴν ἐκ τοῦ ἀπολειφθέντος[4] ἀέρος ὑπὸ τοῦ πυρός·
τοῦτον γὰρ παγῆναι καθάπερ καὶ τὴν χάλαζαν· τὸ
δὲ φῶς αὐτὴν ἔχειν[5] ἀπὸ τοῦ ἡλίου. τὸ δ' ἡγεμο-
νικὸν οὔτ' ἐν κεφαλῇ οὔτ' ἐν θώρακι ἀλλ' ἐν
αἵματι· ὅθεν καθ' ὅ τι ἂν μέρος τοῦ σώματος πλεῖον
ᾖ παρεσπαρμένον, οἴεται[6] κατ' ἐκεῖνο προτερεῖν
τοὺς ἀνθρώπους.

11. Μητρόδωρος ὁ Χῖος ἀίδιον εἶναί φησι τὸ πᾶν,
ὅτι, εἰ ἦν γενητόν, ἐκ τοῦ μὴ ὄντος ἂν ἦν· ἄπειρον
δέ, ὅτι ἀίδιον· οὐ γὰρ ἔχειν ἀρχὴν ὅθεν ἤρξατο
οὐδὲ πέρας οὐδὲ τελευτήν. ἀλλ' οὐδὲ κινήσεως
μετέχειν τὸ πᾶν· κινεῖσθαι γὰρ ἀδύνατον μὴ μεθι-
στάμενον· μεθίστασθαι δ' ἀναγκαῖον ἤτοι εἰς πλῆρες
ἢ εἰς κενόν. πυκνούμενον δὲ τὸν ἀέρα ποιεῖν νε-

---

[1] Kranz suggests adding κατεχόμενον before ὑπό.
[2] κατά] κατά τι Diels.
[3] ἐπιβρῖσαν τὸ πῦρ Bernardakis.
[4] ἀπολειφθέντος one important ms. (A): ἀποληφθέντος the
rest. [5] ἔχειν AH : σχεῖν the rest.
[6] τὸ ἡγεμονικόν omitted by Bernardakis before οἴεται, which
Diels deletes as well.

---

[a] Since mist was regarded as a form of air, air was thought

from the original mixture of the elements, flowed around to encircle them ; and after the air the fire ran out, and finding no other place, ran out upwards, to a position below the crystallized mass of the air.[a] And there are two hemispheres, revolving round the earth, one entirely of fire, the other a mixture of air and a little fire : the latter he thinks to be night. The origin of their motion came about by a chance effect, when the fire weighed down heavily as a result of its concentration. The sun is not in reality fire, but a reflection of fire like that which comes about from water. The moon, he says, had its independent origin, by the action of fire, from the air that was left behind. For it was solidified, just as hail is. But the moon gets her light from the sun. The centre of command in the soul is not in the head nor the chest, but in the blood. Hence, in whatever part of the body it is diffused in greatest quantity, it is in that, he thinks, that men excel.

11.[b] Metrodorus of Chios says that the sum of things is eternal, because if it had a birth, it would come from the non-existent, and that it is infinite because it is eternal, since it has no beginning from which it started, nor any limit or end. Nor does the sum of things have any movement ; it is impossible to move without change of place, and change of place must be either into what is occupied or into what is empty.[c] When the air is condensed it forms clouds,

to be capable of freezing, as mist does ; hail was evidence that air could become solid.

[b] Diels-Kranz, *Frag. d. Vorsokr.* 70 A 4. He was a pupil of Democritus.

[c] Zeller, *Philosophie der Griechen*, i, p. 1186, marked a lacuna here ; at some stage there must have been a longer text, but not in Eusebius (so Mras) and perhaps not in Ps.-Plutarch.

φέλας, εἶτα ὕδωρ, ὃ καὶ κατιὸν ἐπὶ τὸν ἥλιον
σβεννύναι αὐτὸν καὶ πάλιν ἀραιούμενον ἐξάπτεσθαι·
χρόνῳ δὲ πήγνυσθαι τῷ ξηρῷ τὸν ἥλιον καὶ ποιεῖν ἐκ
τοῦ λαμπροῦ ὕδατος ἀστέρας, νύκτα τε καὶ ἡμέραν
ἐκ τῆς σβέσεως καὶ ἐξάψεως καὶ καθόλου τὰς ἐκ-
λείψεις ἀποτελεῖν.

12. Διογένης ὁ Ἀπολλωνιάτης ἀέρα[1] ὑφίσταται
στοιχεῖον· κινεῖσθαι δὲ τὰ πάντα ἀπείρους τ' εἶναι
τοὺς κόσμους. κοσμοποιεῖ δ' οὕτως· ὅτι τοῦ παντὸς κινουμένου καὶ ᾗ μὲν ἀραιοῦ ᾗ δὲ πυκνοῦ
γιγνομένου, ὅπου συνεκύρησε τὸ πυκνόν, συστρο-
φὴν[2] ποιῆσαι, καὶ οὕτω τὰ λοιπὰ[3] κατὰ τὸν αὐτὸν
λόγον· τὰ κουφότατα τὴν ἄνω τάξιν λαβόντα τὸν
ἥλιον ἀποτελέσαι.

---

[1] ἀέρα one ms. : αἰθέρα.

then rain, which descends on the sun and puts it out. When the air is rarefied again, it catches fire. In time the sun is solidified by the dry stuff (?) and makes stars out of the bright water, and causes night and day and, in general, eclipses by being put out and taking fire.

12.[a] Diogenes of Apollonia supposes air to be the elemental substance. Everything is in motion, and the worlds are innumerable. His cosmology is as follows. He says that the whole was in motion and became rare in some places and dense in others, and where the dense came together it formed an aggregate, and thus the rest happened in the same way, while the lightest elements, taking a position up above, formed the sun.

[a] Diels-Kranz, *Frag. d. Vorsokr.* 64 A 6.

---

[2] συστροφὴν] ? συστραφὲν γῆν Diels : τὴν γῆν συστροφῇ Kranz.   [3] λοιπά· καὶ Duebner.

OTHER FRAGMENTS

180

Aelian, frag. 108 (Suidas, *s.vv.* ἐγγώνιος, Ἰόρτιος, Μαικήνας).

Ἐν τῷ συνδείπνῳ¹ τῷ τοῦ Μαικήνα τράπεζα ἐγγώνιος ἦν ὑπὸ τῇ κλισίᾳ τὸ μέγεθος μεγίστη καὶ κάλλος ἄμαχος. καὶ οἷα εἰκὸς ἐπήνουν ἄλλοι ἄλλως αὐτήν· ὁ δὲ Ἰόρτιος,² οὐκ ἔχων ὅ τι παρ' ἑαυτοῦ τερατεύσασθαι,³ σιγῆς γενομένης, "ἐκεῖνο δὲ οὐκ ἐννοεῖτε,⁴ ὦ φίλοι συμπόται, ὡς στρογγύλη ἐστὶ καὶ ἄγαν περιφερής." ἐπὶ τοίνυν τῇ ἀκράτῳ κολακείᾳ, ὡς τὸ εἰκός, γέλως κατερράγη. Πλούταρχος.

181

Aulus Gellius, iii. 5.

Plutarchus refert Arcesilaum philosophum vehementi verbo usum esse de quodam nimis delicato divite, qui incorruptus tamen et a stupro integer dicebatur. nam cum vocem eius infractam capillumque arte compositum et oculos ludibundos atque illecebrae voluptatisque plenos videret, " nihil interest," inquit, " quibus membris cinaedi sitis, posterioribus an prioribus."

---

¹ ? συνδειπνίῳ.   ² ? Ἑόρτιος Dessau.
³ τερατεύσαιτο ed. pr. Suidae.   ⁴ Bernardakis added εἶπεν.

ᵃ R. Hirzel, *Der Dialog*, ii, p. 6, n. 1, suggests that the anecdote is derived from Maecenas' *Symposium*.
ᵇ A unique, but not impossible name, *R.E.* ix. 2. 1929.
ᶜ Plutarch is occasionally used by Aelian, who is, however,

180

At Maecenas' banquet [a] there was a rectangular
table alongside his couch, of the largest size and
superb beauty ; as might be expected, the guests
found various ways to praise it. Iortius [b] could not
invent any original extravagance, so in an interval of
silence he remarked, " But, my dear fellow-guests,
there is something you have not noticed : it is round
and exceedingly circular." Naturally there was a
burst of laughter at this undiluted piece of flattery.
Plutarch. [c]

181

Plutarch records that the philosopher Arcesilaüs
used a forcible expression about an over-effeminate
rich man, who was said, however, to be no pervert,
and to allow no acts of indecency towards himself. Observing the man's mincing voice, carefully arranged
hair, and mischievous eyes, full of alluring volup-
tuousness, " It makes no difference," he remarked,
" which parts of your body you use for your lewd
practices, the hind or the front." [d]

not given to naming a source in this way. One can neither
accept nor reject the fragment with confidence.
  [d] Cf. De Tuenda Sanitate, 126 A, Quaest. Conviv. 705 E.
Perhaps Gellius, whose absolute veracity cannot be maintained, took Arcesilaüs' mot from Quaest. Conviv. with which
he was conversant, and invented for it this setting, which does
not agree with that in De Tuenda Sanitate.

182

Damascius, *Vita Isidori*, 64 Westermann (= Photius, *Bibl.*
242 ; Migne, ciii. 1265).

Τούτου (*sc.* Σεβήρου) ὁ ἵππος . . . ψηχόμενος
σπινθῆρας ἀπὸ τοῦ σώματος πολλούς τε καὶ μεγά-
λους ἠφίει . . . ἀλλὰ καὶ Τιβερίῳ ὄνος, ὡς Πλούταρχος ὁ Χαιρωνεύς φησιν, ἔτι μειρακίῳ ὄντι καὶ
ἐν Ῥόδῳ ἐπὶ λόγοις ῥητορικοῖς διατρίβοντι τὴν
βασιλείαν διὰ τοῦ αὐτοῦ παθήματος προεμήνυσεν.

183

Etymologicum Magnum, 184. 30.

Πλούταρχος δὲ ἀπὸ τοῦ ὀπίσω τὸ ἄψ λέγει εἶναι,
τοῦ ο εἰς α τραπέντος καὶ τοῦ π εἰς ψ.

184

Eunapius, *Vitae Sophistarum*, ii. 7.

Αὐτίκα οὖν ὁ θεσπέσιος Πλούταρχος τόν τε
ἑαυτοῦ βίον ἀναγράφει τοῖς βιβλίοις ἐνδιεσπαρ-
μένως καὶ τὸν τοῦ διδασκάλου, καὶ ὅτι γε Ἀμ-
μώνιος Ἀθήνησιν ἐτελεύτα, οὐ βίον προσειπών
. . . ἀλλὰ τὸ ἴδιον καὶ τὸ[1] τοῦ διδασκάλου καθ'
ἕκαστον τῶν βιβλίων ἐγκατέσπειρεν ὥστε εἴ τις
ὀξυδορκοίη περὶ ταῦτα[2] ἀνιχνεύων κατὰ τὸ προσ-
πῖπτον καὶ φαινόμενον, καὶ σωφρόνως τὰ κατὰ
μέρος ἀναλέγοιτο, δύνασθαι τὰ πλεῖστα τῶν βε-
βιωμένων αὐτοῖς εἰδέναι.

344

OTHER FRAGMENTS

182

Severus' horse emitted many large sparks while being groomed. . . . But Tiberius, too, when still a young man living in Rhodes to study oratory, received a prediction of his future throne, as Plutarch of Chaeronea relates, from a donkey which exhibited the same phenomenon.[a]

183

Plutarch says that *aps* is derived from *opisô, o* having been converted into *a* and *p* into *ps*.[b]

184

For example that marvellous man Plutarch records his own life in scattered notices throughout his books, and also that of his teacher : and so doing, he writes that Ammonius " ended " at Athens, without adding the words " his life." . . . But he had the habit of inserting here and there in all his books what concerned himself and his master, so that if one has a keen eye for these things, following up obvious clues that present themselves, and carefully collects the details, one can learn most of the incidents of their lives.

---

[a] Possibly, but not necessarily, in the lost *Life of Tiberius*.
[b] Both words mean back.

---

[1] τὸ added by Cobet.
[2] καὶ after ταῦτα deleted by Vollebregt.

185

Geoponica, xiii. 9.

Πλούταρχος λεπτοκάρυον προσάπτει τοῖς κλινό-
ποσιν εἰς τὸ μὴ προσιέναι τὸν σκορπίον αὐτοῖς·
φησὶ γὰρ τῷ λεπτοκαρύῳ μὴ προσιέναι τὸν
σκορπίον.

186

Isidorus of Pelusium, *Letters*, ii. 42.

Πλουτάρχῳ δὲ δοκεῖ τὸ σαφὲς καὶ λιτὸν[1] γνήσιον
εἶναι ᾿Αττικισμόν· οὕτω γάρ, φησίν, ἐλάλησαν οἱ
ῥήτορες. Γοργίας δ᾿ ὁ Λεοντῖνος πρῶτος τὴν νόσον
ταύτην εἰς τοὺς πολιτικοὺς λόγους εἰσήγαγε τὸ
ὑψηλὸν καὶ τροπικὸν[2] ἀσπασάμενος καὶ τῇ σαφηνείᾳ
λυμηνάμενος. ἥψατό τε, φησίν, ἡ νόσος αὕτη καὶ
τοῦ θαυμαστοῦ Πλάτωνος.

*187

John of Antioch, *Archaeologia* (*Anecdota Graeca*, ii, p. 388
Cramer).

᾿Ιορδάνης λέγεται ὁ ποταμὸς διότι δύο ἅμα μίγ-
νυνται ποταμοί, ᾿Ιόρ τε καὶ Δάνης, καὶ ἀποτελοῦσιν
αὐτόν, ὥς φησι Πλούταρχος.

188

Lydus, *De Mensibus*, iv. 148.

Εἰλείθυια ⟨δ᾿ ἐστὶν ἡ τ⟩ῶν τικτουσῶν ἔφ⟨ορος,

---

[1] Ruhnken: λεῖον.   [2] Bernardakis: τυπικόν.

OTHER FRAGMENTS

185

Plutarch attaches a filbert to the feet of a bedstead to keep scorpions away. For he says that the scorpion will not go near a filbert.

186

Plutarch thinks that a clear, simple style constitutes genuine Atticism. That, he explains, is how their public speakers talked. Gorgias from Leontini was the first to introduce this malady into political oratory, by showing a liking for elevated language and figures of speech and by doing violence to clarity. This disease, as Plutarch says, attacked even that wonderful man Plato.[a]

*187

The river Jordan is so called because two rivers mingle to form it, the Jor and the Danes, as Plutarch says.[b]

188

Eileithyia is the guardian of women in childbirth

[a] See E. Norden, *Kunstprosa*, i, p. 380. R. Hirzel, *Plutarch*, p. 80[7], does not believe that Plutarch of Chaeronea is meant; R. Volkmann, *Leben, Schriften und Philosophie des Plutarch von Chaeronea*, ii, VIII, thinks that the neo-Platonist is intended, but this is chronologically impossible if frag. 192 is to be associated, as seems likely, with this report. Plato's alleged Gorgianism is criticized by Dionysius of Halicarnassus, *Dem.* chap. 5, *Ad Pomp.* 2. 6.

[b] It is most unlikely that Plutarch said anything of the sort. This does not even come from the spurious *De Fluviis*.

ὅ)πω⟨ς τὸ ἕν⟩, ὥς φησι Πλούτ⟨αρχος, ὁμ⟩οίως
ἑαυτῇ[1] δ⟨ύο ποιή⟩σειε.[2]

189

John Malalas, *Anecdota Graeca*, ii, p. 232 Cramer.
[*Chronicon Anon.* (*Anecdota graeca*, ii, p. 380 Cramer) and
Tzetzes, *Chiliades*, iv. 385, probably derive from Malalas.]

Ὁ δὲ Πλούταρχός φησιν ὅτι σφαῖρα πυρὸς κατ-
ενέχθη εἰς τὴν Κελτικὴν χώραν ὑπὸ τοῦ θεοῦ καὶ[3]
κατέκαυσε τοὺς Γίγαντας, καὶ εἰς τὸν Ἠριδανὸν[4]
ποταμὸν ἐνεχθεῖσα ἡ σφαῖρα ἐσβέσθη.

190

John Malalas, *Chronicon*, col. 130 Migne, vol. xcvii (= Ox.).
An extract is to be found in Cramer's *Anecdota graeca*, ii
(= An.).   Malalas is adapted by Cedrenus, i. 82 (Migne, col.
112) and mutilated in the *Passio S. Catharinae* and *Passio S.
Luciae* (S. Costanza, *Byz. Zeitschrift*, lii [1959], p. 247).

῏Ησαν γὰρ καὶ αὐτοὶ ἀγαλμάτων ποιηταὶ καὶ
μυστηρίων ἐξηγηταὶ καὶ τελεσταί (*sc.* Aegyptii,
Babylonii, Phryges, etc.), ἀφ᾽ ὧν μάλιστα εἰς
Ἕλληνας ἤχθη ἡ αὐτὴ θρησκεία . . . Ἴωνες δὲ
οἱ ἐκ τῆς Ἰὼ τούτων ἀρχηγοὶ ἐγένοντο . . .
οὕστινας μεμφόμενος ὁ Χερονήσιος[5] Πλούταρχος
τῇ παλαιᾷ φιλοσοφίᾳ[6] παρ᾽ Ἕλλησι καὶ βαρβάροις
ἐπαινουμένῃ[7] ἐξέθετο ὡς πλάνην ἀγαλμάτων τινὲς
εἰσάγουσιν. αὐτὸς[8] δέ φησι τοὺς κατ᾽ οὐρανὸν
φωστῆρας θεοποιεῖν ἔδοξεν, τὸν ἥλιον καὶ τὴν
σελήνην παρεισάγων ὡς ἡ τῶν Αἰγυπτίων θεολογία
ἔχει αὐτοὺς[9] τὸν σύμπαντα κόσμον διοικεῖν τρέφον-
348

OTHER FRAGMENTS

so that she might make what is one two, as Plutarch says, similarly to herself.[1]

189

Plutarch says that a ball of fire came down by an act of God into the land of the Celts and consumed the Giants, and plunging into the river Po was there quenched.

190

They also (*sc.* the Egyptians, Babylonians, Phrygians, etc.) were makers of images and guides to mysteries and initiators into sacred rites, and indeed it was from them that this worship was brought to the Greeks. . . . the Ionians, the descendants of Io, were the leaders in this . . . Plutarch of the Chersonese, censuring them by the old philosophy that was approved[2] among Greeks and foreign nations, declared that certain persons introduced " an imposture of images." He himself, thinking it right (he says) to make gods of the luminaries of heaven, brought forward the sun and moon, as the theology of the Egyptians understands them ; he says that they[3] direct the whole world, nourishing and increasing all

---

[1] ἑαυτὴν MSS.
[2] Supplements due to Hase.
[3] καὶ added by F. H. S.
[4] Cramer (and Tzetzes) : Κρηδανὸν.
[5] This common error is probably that of Malalas.
[6] An. : ἡ παλαιὰ φιλοσοφία Ox.
[7] ἐπαινουμένη om. Ox.
[8] ? αὐτοῖς.
[9] περιέχει. αὐτοὺς γὰρ λέγει Cedrenus.

τας καὶ αὐξάνοντας τὰ πάντα τῇ τριμερεῖ[1] κινήσει
τῶν πέντε πλανητῶν καὶ τῆς λοιπῆς ἀστροθεσίας
κατὰ γένεσιν καὶ †ἀέρα.[2]

191

Philoponus, *in Aristotelis Meteorologica*, i, p. 82 (*Comm.
Arist. Graec.* xiv, p. 26).

[Διὰ τί μὴ συνίσταται νέφη ἐν τῷ πολὺ τῆς γῆς
ὑπερανεστηκότι τόπῳ; ὅτι γὰρ οὐ συνίσταται, ἐκ
τῆς μακρᾶς ἱστορίας ἐστὶ δῆλον· τὰ γὰρ ὑψηλότατα
τῶν ὀρῶν ὑπερνεφῆ τ' ἐστὶ καὶ ὑπερήνεμα.] *τέφραν γὰρ ἔν τισι τούτων ἀποθέμενοί τινες ἢ καὶ ἐκ
θυσιῶν τῶν ἐν ἐκείνοις γινομένων ἀπολελοιπότες
μετὰ πλείστους ἐνιαυτοὺς περιεργασάμενοι, κειμένην εὗρον αὐτὴν οὕτως ὡς ἔθεσαν. καὶ ἐν Κυλ-
λήνῃ δέ φασιν ('Αρκαδίας δ' ὄρος ἐστὶ τοῦτο λίαν
ὑψηλόν) θύσαντές τινες ἐν τῷ ἐπιόντι θέρει πάλιν
θῦσαι ἀνελθόντες ἔτι τὴν τέφραν τῶν ἱερείων οὕτω
κειμένην εὗρον μήτε ὑπ' ὄμβρων κατακλυσθεῖσαν
μήτε ὑπὸ πνευμάτων διεσκεδασμένην.* ἱστορεῖ δὲ
Πλούταρχος καὶ γράμματα μεῖναι εἰς ἑτέραν τῶν
ἱερέων ἀνάβασιν ἐκ τῆς προτέρας ἐν τῷ 'Ολύμπῳ τῷ
Μακεδονικῷ.

[1] Cedrenus : τρίτῃ μερικῇ An. : τρίτῃ Ox.
[2] ἀστέρας Cedrenus.

[a] The history of this idea is traced by W. Capelle, Pauly-
Wissowa, *R.E.*, suppl. vi, cols. 351-354. Contrast Lucretius,
vi. 459 ff.

[b] Arrian, fr. 4 Roos (= Stob. i. 246. 19 Wachsmuth) records that the ash of sacrifice remained undisturbed on Mt.
Oeta.

things by the threefold motion of the five planets and the rest of the constellations, as things come into being and . . .

This unreliable fragment should perhaps be associated with frag. 213. It was a common confusion among late Greeks to ascribe Plutarch to the Chersonese instead of to Chaeronea. The phrase "imposture of images" comes from Sophocles, frag. 1025 Nauck, 1126 Pearson, quoted in full by Cedrenus, but it may of course have been quoted by Plutarch.

191

[Why do clouds not form in the region high above the earth ? That they do not, is clear from long observation. The highest mountains are above the clouds and above the winds.^a] *Evidence of this is provided by the fact that persons who have deposited ash on certain summits, or left it there after sacrifices performed upon them, have discovered it lying as they had left it when they investigated many years later.^b They say, too, that on Cyllenê (a very high mountain in Arcadia) certain persons, who had sacrificed and ascended to sacrifice again the next summer, found the ash from their sacrifice still lying there just as it had been, neither washed away by rains nor scattered by winds.* Plutarch ^c records that writings also remained on Olympus in Macedonia from one ascent of the priests to the next.

^c Elsewhere Philoponus usually intends the neo-Platonist by Πλούταρχος ; e.g., frequently in his commentary on *De Anima*. But at *De Aet. Mundi*, vi. 27, the name denotes our Plutarch, who mentions the windlessness of high mountains at *Moralia*, 938 A-B, 951 B.

Philostratus, *Epistula* 73.

Πεῖθε δὴ καὶ σύ, ὦ βασίλεια, τὸν θαρσαλεώτερον
τοῦ Ἑλληνικοῦ Πλούταρχον μὴ ἄχθεσθαι τοῖς σο-
φισταῖς μηδ' ἐς διαβολὰς καθίστασθαι τοῦ Γοργίου.

193

Porphyry, *De Abstinentia*, iii. 18.

Ἀρχὴν δέ, ὡς καὶ Πλούταρχός φησιν, οὐκ ἐπεὶ
δεῖταί τινων ἡμῶν ἡ φύσις καὶ χρώμεθα τούτοις,
ἤδη ἐπὶ πᾶν προακτέον καὶ πρὸς πάντα τὴν ἀδικίαν.
δίδωσι μὲν γὰρ καὶ παρέχει τοῖς ἀναγκαίοις τὴν
ἄχρι τινὸς βλάβην (εἴ γε βλάβη τὸ λαμβάνειν τι
παρὰ τῶν φυτῶν, καίτοι ζώντων μενόντων)· τὸ δ'
ἐκ περιουσίας καὶ πρὸς ἡδονὴν ἀπολλύειν[1] ἕτερα
καὶ φθείρειν τῆς παντελοῦς ἦν ἀγριότητος καὶ
ἀδικίας· καὶ ἡ τούτων ἀποχὴ οὔτε πρὸς τὸ ζῆν
οὔτε πρὸς τὸ εὖ ζῆν ἡμᾶς ἠλάττου. εἰ μὲν γὰρ ὡς
ἀέρος καὶ ὕδατος φυτῶν τε καὶ καρπῶν, ὧν ἄνευ
ζῆν ἀδύνατόν ἐστιν, οὕτω φόνου ζώων καὶ βρώσεως
σαρκῶν ἐτυγχάνομεν δεόμενοι πρὸς τὸν βίον, ἀναγκαίαν ἡ φύσις συμπλοκὴν εἶχεν ἂν πρὸς ταύτην τὴν
ἀδικίαν· εἰ δὲ πολλοὶ μὲν ἱερεῖς θεῶν πολλοὶ δὲ

---

[1] Reiske : ἀπολαύειν.

---

[a] Julia Domna; that Plutarch was long dead would not deter Philostratus, as Norden noted, from this request. There
is no need to invent some unknown Plutarch to account for
this fragment and frag. 186.

[b] There is nothing to show what work of Plutarch was
used by Porphyry : Bernays' guess (*Theophrast über die*

192

So add your voice, my Empress,[a] to urge Plutarch, that most audacious representative of Greece, not to be vexed with the sophists or start slandering Gorgias.

193

There is absolutely no reason, as indeed Plutarch says,[b] why just because our nature requires certain things and we lay hands on these things, our wrong-doing should be carried to all lengths and extended to all creatures.[c] Nature allows as a concession to the necessities of life the doing of a limited amount of damage—if to take some part of a plant or tree is to damage it, in spite of the fact that it remains alive—but, having other resources, to kill and destroy other beings for pleasure was an act of unmitigated savagery and wrong-doing. To abstain from animal foods used to make us no less able either to maintain life or to lead a good life. If it were really the case that we needed to slaughter animals and eat their flesh in order to live, in the way that we need air and water, plants and fruits, without which life is impossible, our nature would necessarily involve us in this wrong-doing. The fact is, however, that many

Frommigkeit, p. 149) that it was a lost part of the second speech *De Esu Carnium* has nothing to recommend it.

[c] The latter part of the fragment contains an open attack on the Stoics, who may be in mind from the beginning. They maintained that men could not wrong animals, which existed to be used by mankind ; the fact that animals were irrational meant that men had no fellow-feeling or obligations towards them.

βασιλεῖς βαρβάρων ἁγνεύοντες ἄπειρα δὲ γένη ζῴων
τὸ παράπαν οὐ θιγγάνοντα τῆς τοιαύτης τροφῆς
ζῶσι καὶ τυγχάνουσι τοῦ κατὰ φύσιν τέλους, πῶς
οὐκ ἔστιν ἄτοπος ὁ κελεύων, εἴ τισιν ἀναγκαζόμεθα[1]
πολεμεῖν, μηδ᾽ οἷς ἔξεστιν εἰρηνικῶς ὁμιλεῖν, ἀλλ᾽
ἢ πρὸς μηδὲν τῇ δικαιοσύνῃ χρωμένους ζῆν ἢ πρὸς
πάντα χρωμένους μὴ ζῆν; ὥσπερ οὖν ἐπ᾽ ἀνθρώπων ὁ μὲν αὑτοῦ[2] σωτηρίας ἕνεκα καὶ παίδων καὶ[3]
πατρίδος ἢ χρήματά τινων παραιρούμενος ἢ χώραν
ἐπιτρίβων καὶ πόλιν ἔχει[4] πρόσχημα τῆς ἀδικίας
τὴν ἀνάγκην, ὅστις δὲ ταῦτα δρᾷ διὰ πλοῦτον ἢ
κόρον ἢ ἡδονὰς τρυφῶσας καὶ ἀποπληρώσεις οὐκ
ἀναγκαίων ποριζόμενος ἐπιθυμιῶν, ἄμικτος εἶναι
δοκεῖ καὶ ἀκρατὴς καὶ πονηρός· οὕτω τὰς μὲν εἰς
φυτὰ βλάβας καὶ πυρὸς καὶ ναμάτων ἀναλώσεις
κουράς τε προβάτων καὶ γάλα βοῶν τ᾽ ἐξημέρωσιν
καὶ κατάζευξιν ἐπὶ σωτηρίᾳ καὶ διαμονῇ τοῖς χρω-
μένοις ὁ θεὸς δίδωσι συγγνώμων[5]· ζῷα δ᾽ ὑπάγειν
σφαγαῖς καὶ μαγειρεύειν ἀναπιμπλαμένους φόνου,
μὴ τροφῆς ἢ πληρώσεως χάριν ἀλλ᾽ ἡδονῆς, καὶ
λαιμαργίας ποιουμένους τέλος, ὑπερφυῶς[6] ὡς ἄνο-
μον καὶ δεινόν. ἀρκεῖ γὰρ ὅτι μηδὲν πονεῖν δεομένοις χρώμεθα προκάμνουσι καὶ μοχθοῦσιν,[7]

ἵππων ὄνων τ᾽ ὀχεῖα[7] καὶ ταύρων γονάς,

---

[1] Nauck : ἀναγκαζοίμεθα.
[2] Hercher : αὑτοῦ. τῆς αὑτοῦ Fogerolles.
[3] Hercher : ἤ. [4] Valentine : ἔχειν.
[5] Duebner : συγγνώμην. ? συγγνώμην ἔχοντα.
[6] Abresch : ὑπερφυὲς.
[7] Reiske : μόχθους and ὀχείαν.

priests of the gods and many kings of foreign nations practise a ritual abstinence from flesh, and countless species of animals do not touch such food at all ; yet they keep alive and attain full realization of their nature. How, then, can it be anything but absurd to tell us that if we are forced to wage war on some creatures, we should not live at peace even with those with whom peace is possible, but that we must choose either to treat none justly and to live or to treat all justly and not to live ? [a] The man who, in dealing with human beings, takes other people's possessions or destroys their territory or their town for the sake of his own safety or that of his children or his country has necessity as a pretext for his wrong-doing, but anyone who perpetrates such acts in the pursuit of wealth, or in the arrogance of success, or to provide himself with luxurious pleasures and the satisfaction of unnecessary desires, is generally regarded as savage, self-indulgent, and wicked. Similarly God indulgently grants us the damage we do to plants, the fire and running water we use up, the shearing of sheep and the milk they yield, the domestication and yoking of cattle, as being for the preservation and continuance of those who exploit them. But to bring animals to the slaughter, and to defile ourselves with murder by butchering them, not for the sake of food or the satisfaction of hunger, but in pursuit of pleasure and making gluttony our aim in life, that is a monstrously unnatural and dreadful act. It is enough that we take beasts that have no need to work and employ them to toil and labour for us, subjugating and bringing to the yoke

> Jack-ass and stallion and the seed of bulls,

[a] *Cf. De Sollertia Animalium* 964, A.

ὡς Αἰσχύλος φησίν,

ἀντίδουλα[1] καὶ πόνων ἐκδέκτορα

χειρωσάμενοι καὶ καταζεύξαντες.

Ὁ δ' ἀξιῶν ἡμᾶς ὄψῳ μὴ χρῆσθαι βοΐ μηδὲ πνεῦμα καὶ ζωὴν διολλύντας καὶ διαφθείροντας ἡδύσματα πλησμονῆς καὶ καλλωπίσματα προτίθεσθαι[2] τραπέζης τίνος ἀναγκαίου πρὸς σωτηρίαν ἢ καλοῦ πρὸς ἀρετὴν ἀφαιρεῖται τὸν βίον;

Οὐ μὴν ἀλλὰ καὶ τοῖς ζῴοις τὰ φυτὰ παραβάλλειν κομιδῇ βίαιον· τὰ μὲν γὰρ αἰσθάνεσθαι πέφυκε καὶ ἀλγεῖν καὶ φοβεῖσθαι καὶ βλάπτεσθαι, διὸ καὶ ἀδικεῖσθαι· τοῖς δ' οὐδέν ἐστιν αἰσθητόν, οὕτως δ' οὐδὲ ἀλλότριον οὐδὲ κακὸν οὐδὲ βλάβη τις οὐδ' ἀδικία· καὶ γὰρ οἰκειώσεως πάσης καὶ ἀλλοτριώσεως ἀρχὴ τὸ αἰσθάνεσθαι, τὴν δ' οἰκείωσιν ἀρχὴν τίθενται δικαιοσύνης οἱ ἀπὸ Ζήνωνος. πῶς δ' οὐκ ἄλογον πολλοὺς τῶν ἀνθρώπων ἐπ' αἰσθήσει μόνον ζῶντας ὁρῶντας νοῦν δὲ καὶ λόγον οὐκ ἔχοντας, πολλοὺς δὲ πάλιν ὠμότητι καὶ θυμῷ καὶ πλεονεξίᾳ τὰ φοβερώτατα τῶν θηρίων ὑπερβεβληκότας, παιδοφόνους καὶ πατροκτόνους τυράννους καὶ βασιλέων[3] ὑπουργούς, πρὸς μὲν τούτους οἴεσθαι δίκαιόν τι[4] εἶναι ἡμῖν, πρὸς δὲ τὸν ἀροτῆρα βοῦν καὶ τὸν σύντροφον κύνα καὶ τὰ γάλακτι μὲν τρέφοντα κουρᾷ δὲ κοσμοῦντα θρέμματα μηδὲν εἶναι, πῶς οὐ παραλογώτατόν ἐστι;

Ἀλλ' ἐκεῖνο νὴ Δία τοῦ Χρυσίππου πιθανόν,[5] ὡς

---

[1] 964 F : ἂν δοῦλα. [2] Abresch : προστίθεσθαι or τίθεσθαι.
[3] βασάνων Wyttenbach. [4] δίκαιόν τι added by Reiske.
[5] ἢ after πιθανόν deleted by Bernardakis. ἢν Duebner.

---

[a] Frag. 194 Nauck, 336 Mette, from *Prometheus Lyo-*

356

as Aeschylus puts it,

> To serve for slaves and substitutes in toil.[a]

If a man requires that we should not use the ox as meat, nor destroy and make away with breath and life in order to serve up sauces for our satiety and make a show on our tables, does he rob our life of anything necessary to its preservation or of anything fine, that can contribute to its goodness ?

However, to put plants and animals on a par is a fairly violent proceeding. Animals are so constituted as to have sense-perception, to feel pain and fear, to be injured, and therefore to be wronged ; but nothing is perceptible to plants, and so nothing is to them alien or bad, nor anything an injury or wrong. Sense-perception is, in fact, the origin of all feeling of affinity or aversion,[b] and Zeno's followers suppose that the feeling of affinity is the origin of justice.[c] But when we see many men whose lives are guided by sense-perception alone, without use of mind or reason, and many again outdoing the most fearsome of beasts in cruelty, anger, and greed—despotic rulers who murder their children and kill their fathers, or creatures that kings use to serve their purposes—can it be anything but utterly unreasonable to imagine that with them we have something in common, but nothing with the ox at the plough, or the dog that shares our home, or the sheep that feed us with their milk and clothe us with their fleeces ? [d]

But really I must say that is a plausible view of

menos. Cited also, *De Fortuna*, 98 c, *De Sollertia Animalium*, 964 f.   [b] *Cf. De Esu Carnium*, 997 e.
[c] *Stoic. Vet. Frag.* i. 197.
[d] *Cf. Stoic. Vet. Frag.* iii. 346. Although this paragraph may contain elements drawn from Plutarch, it seems to be of Porphyry's composition.

ἡμᾶς αὐτῶν[1] καὶ ἀλλήλων οἱ θεοὶ χάριν ἐποιήσαντο,
ἡμῶν δὲ τὰ ζῷα, συμπολεμεῖν μὲν ἵππους καὶ συν-
θηρεύειν κύνας, ἀνδρείας δὲ γυμνάσια παρδάλεις
καὶ ἄρκτους καὶ λέοντας· ἡ δ' ὗς (ἐνταῦθα γάρ ἐστι
τῶν χαρίτων τὸ ἥδιστον) οὐ δι' ἄλλο τι πλὴν θύε-
σθαι ἐγεγόνει,[2] καὶ τῇ σαρκὶ τὴν ψυχὴν ὁ θεὸς οἷον
ἅλας ἐνέμιξεν, εὐοψίαν ἡμῖν μηχανώμενος· ὅπως δὲ
ζωμοῦ καὶ παραδειπνίων ἀφθονίαν ἔχωμεν, ὄστρεά
τε παντοδαπὰ καὶ ἀκαλήφας καὶ γένη πτηνῶν
ποικίλα παρεσκεύασεν, οὐκ ἀλλαχόθεν, ἀλλ'[3] αὐτοῦ[4]
μέγα μέρος ἐνταῦθα τρέψας εἰς γλυκυχυμίας[5] τὰς
τιτθὰς ὑπερβαλλόμενος καὶ καταπυκνώσας ταῖς
ἡδοναῖς καὶ ἀπολαύσεσι τὸν περίγειον τόπον. ὅτῳ
δὴ ταῦτα δοκεῖ τι τοῦ πιθανοῦ καὶ θεῷ πρέποντος
μετέχειν, σκοπείτω τί πρὸς ἐκεῖνον ἐρεῖ τὸν λόγον,
ὃν Καρνεάδης ἔλεγεν, ὡς[6] ἕκαστον τῶν φύσει γεγονότων, ὅταν τοῦ πρὸς ὃ πέφυκε καὶ γέγονε τυγχάνῃ τέλους, ὠφελεῖται· κοινότερον δὲ τὸ[7] τῆς
ὠφελείας, ἣν εὐχρηστίαν οὗτοί λέγουσιν, ἀκουστέον·
ἡ δ' ὗς φύσει γέγονε πρὸς τὸ σφαγῆναι καὶ κατα-
βρωθῆναι· καὶ τοῦτο πάσχουσα τυγχάνει τοῦ πρὸς
ὃ πέφυκε καὶ ὠφελεῖται.

---

[1] Hercher : αὐτῶν.
[2] ? γέγονε.
[3] F. H. S. : ἀλλ' ὡς.
[4] Wyttenbach : αὐτοῦ.
[5] F. H. S. : γλυκυθυμίας.
[6] ὡς added by F. H. S.
[7] τὸ added by Abresch.

---

[a] Cf. Cicero, Nat. Deorum, ii. 37 (S.V.F. ii. 1153).
[b] A saying ascribed by Clement, Strom. vii. 6. 33 (S.V.F.
i. 516) to Cleanthes; Quaest. Conv. 685 c, and Cicero, Nat.
Deorum, ii. 160 (S.V.F. ii. 1154), Fin. v. 38 (S.V.F. ii. 723),
make the point clearer : the pig's " soul " (the word does

Chrysippus according to which the gods created us to serve their purposes and those of our fellow-men, animals, on the other hand, to serve ours,[a] horses to accompany us to the wars, dogs to the hunt, panthers, bears, and lions as a school for training in bravery. As for the pig—and here is the most delightful of all his charming ideas—it was brought into existence for no other purpose but to be sacrificed, and God impregnated its flesh with life as it were with salt,[b] thereby contriving for us an abundant supply of meat. And in order that we should have plenty of soup and of side-dishes he provided all kinds of shell-fish, and sea-nettles, and the various species of birds, and this not from any extraneous source—no, he has converted a large part of his own self here on earth into sweet flavours and juices, in this outdoing any wet-nurse, and has contrived " a concentration of pleasures "[c] and sensual enjoyments in the terrestrial regions. Now if anyone thinks this is at all plausible or a fitting activity for God, he should consider what reply to make to the argument used by Carneades. When any creature attains the natural end for which it was created, it thereby derives an advantage. ("Advantage" must be understood in the wider sense of the word, what these Stoics call " utility.")[d] The pig has been created to be killed and eaten. When this happens to it, therefore, it attains its natural end and thereby derives an advantage !

not imply any rational or spiritual functions) was given it in order that its flesh should not go putrid.

[c] An Epicurean term (Κυρία Δόξα 12) maliciously attached to the Stoic pantheistic God.

[d] The Stoics confined ὠφέλεια, " advantage," and related words to what aided morality ; εὐχρηστία, " utility," was allowed to what was serviceable to meet natural needs.

Καὶ μὴν εἰ πρὸς ἀνθρώπων χρῆσιν ὁ θεὸς μεμηχάνηται τὰ ζῷα, τί χρησόμεθα μυίαις, ἐμπίσι,
νυκτερίσιν, κανθάροις, σκορπίοις, ἐχίδναις, ὧν τὰ
μὲν ὁρᾶν εἰδεχθῆ καὶ θιγγάνειν μιαρὰ καὶ κατ'
ὀδμὰς δυσανάσχετα καὶ φθέγγεται δεινὸν καὶ ἀτερ-
πές, τὰ δ' ἄντικρυς ὀλέθρια τοῖς τυγχάνουσιν;[1]
φαλαίνας τε[2] καὶ πρίστεις καὶ τὰ ἄλλα κήτη, " ἃ
μυρία βόσκειν" Ὅμηρός φησιν " ἀγάστονον Ἀμφι-
τρίτην," τί οὐκ ἐδίδαξεν ἡμᾶς ὁ δημιουργός, ὅπῃ
χρήσιμα τῇ φύσει γέγονε; εἰ δ' οὐ πάντα φασὶν
ἡμῖν καὶ πρὸς ἡμᾶς γεγονέναι, πρὸς τῷ σύγχυσιν
ἔχειν πολλὴν καὶ ἀσάφειαν τὸν διορισμὸν οὐδὲ
ἐκφεύγομεν τὸ ἀδικεῖν, ἐπιτιθέμενοι καὶ χρώμενοι
βλαβερῶς τοῖς οὐ δι' ἡμᾶς ἀλλ' ὥσπερ ἡμεῖς κατὰ
φύσιν γεγενημένοις. ἐῶ λέγειν ὅτι τῇ χρείᾳ τὸ
πρὸς ἡμᾶς ὁρίζοντες οὐκ ἂν φθάνοιμεν ἑαυτοὺς
ἕνεκα τῶν ὀλεθριωτάτων ζῴων, οἷα κροκόδειλοι
καὶ φάλαιναι καὶ δράκοντες, γεγονέναι συγχωροῦν-
τες. ἡμῖν μὲν γὰρ οὐδὲν ἀπ' ἐκείνων ὑπάρχει τὸ
παράπαν ὠφελεῖσθαι· τὰ δὲ ἁρπάζοντα καὶ δια-
φθείροντα τοὺς παραπίπτοντας ἀνθρώπους βορᾷ
χρῆται, μηδὲν ἡμῶν κατὰ τοῦτο δρῶντα χαλεπώ-
τερον, πλὴν ὅτι τὰ μὲν ἔνδεια καὶ λιμὸς ἐπὶ ταύτην
ἄγει τὴν ἀδικίαν, ἡμεῖς δ' ὕβρει καὶ τρυφῆς ἕνεκα,
καὶ[3] παίζοντες πολλάκις ἐν θεάτροις καὶ κυνηγε-
σίοις, τὰ πλεῖστα τῶν ζῴων φονεύομεν.

[1] ἐντυγχάνουσιν Reiske.
[2] δὲ Bernardakis. ? δέ γε.
[3] καὶ added by F. H. S.

---

[a] *Odyssey*, xii. 97.
[b] *Cf.* Celsus as quoted by Origen, *Contra Celsum*, v. 78.

Moreover, if God has contrived animals for the use of mankind, what use are we to make of flies, mosquitoes, bats, dung-beetles, scorpions, and vipers, some of which are repulsive to look at, or disgusting to touch, or have an intolerable smell, or make alarming or unpleasant sounds, while others are downright deadly to those that come upon them ? As for whales and sawfish and all the other monsters which, according to Homer,

> In thousands groaning Amphitritê feeds,[a]

why has not the Artisan of the world explained the use for which Nature created them ? If on the other hand the Stoics admit exceptions to the rule that all creatures were created for us and for our benefit, not only is the dividing-line an extremely obscure and confused one, but since it follows that we attack and harmfully use animals that have not been created on our account but are products of nature on a par with ourselves, we do not even escape from the charge of doing wrong. I will refrain from observing that if we constitute usefulness the mark of what is created for our benefit, we might as well at once concede that we ourselves have been created for the sake of the most deadly animals, like crocodiles, whales, and snakes.[b] For whereas we derive absolutely no advantage from them, they carry off and kill the human beings that fall in their way, to feed upon them ; in this they act no more cruelly than we do ; except that need and hunger lead them to do us such wrong, whereas most of the animals that we kill, we murder wantonly and for the sake of our luxuries, often indeed for sport in theatres and in the chase.[c]

[c] *Cf. De Sollertia Animalium*, 965 A.

(a) Porphyry, Περὶ ἀγαλμάτων, frag. 8 Bidez (Eusebius, *Praepar. Evang.* ii. 23).

Τοῦ δ' αὖ πυρὸς τὴν δύναμιν προσειπόντες
Ἥφαιστον ἀνθρωποειδὲς μὲν αὐτοῦ τὸ ἄγαλμα
πεποιήκασιν, πῖλον δὲ περιέθεσαν κυάνεον τῆς
οὐρανίου σύμβολον περιφορᾶς ἔνθα τοῦ πυρὸς τὸ
ἀρχοειδές τε καὶ ἀκραιφνέστατον· τὸ δ' εἰς γῆν
κατενεχθὲν ἐξ οὐρανοῦ πῦρ ἀτονώτερον, δεόμενόν
τε στηρίγματος καὶ βάσεως τῆς ἐφ' ὕλης· διὸ
χωλεύει[1] ὕλης δεόμενον εἰς ὑπέρεισμα. καὶ ἡλίου
δὲ τὴν τοιάνδε δύναμιν ὑπολαβόντες Ἀπόλλωνα
προσεῖπον ἀπὸ τῆς τῶν ἀκτίνων αὐτοῦ πάλσεως·
ἐννέα δ' ἐπᾴδουσιν[2] αὐτῷ Μοῦσαι, ἥ θ' ὑποσελήνιος
σφαῖρα καὶ ἑπτὰ πλανητῶν καὶ μία ἡ τῆς ἀπλανοῦς.
περιέθεσαν δ' αὐτῷ τὴν δάφνην, τοῦτο μὲν ὅτι
πυρὸς πλῆρες τὸ φυτὸν καὶ διὰ τοῦτο ἀπεχθὲς δαί-
μοσιν, τοῦτο δ' ὅτι λάλον καιόμενον εἰς παράστασιν
τοῦ προφητεύειν τὸν θεόν.

(b) Lydus, *de Mensibus*, iv. 86.

Ὁ δὲ Χαιρωνεύς φησιν ὅτι τοῦ πυρός . . . ἀ-
κραιφνέστατον.

(c) Lydus, *ibid.* iv. 4. *Geoponica*, xi. 2. 4.

Τὴν δάφνην δὲ οἱ παλαιοὶ τῷ Ἀπόλλωνι καθιε-
ροῦσιν ὅτι πυρὸς πλῆρες τὸ φυτόν, ὥς φησιν ὁ
Πλούταρχος,[3] καὶ ὁ Ἀπόλλων πῦρ· ἥλιος γάρ ἐστιν.
ὅθεν καὶ ἀπεχθάνεται δαίμοσι τοῦτο τὸ φυτόν, καὶ
ἔνθεν ἂν εἴη δάφνη ἐκποδὼν δαίμονες, καὶ ἐν ταῖς

---

[1] ? χωλεύειν.
[2] F. H. S. : ἐπᾴδουσαι.

OTHER FRAGMENTS

194

(*a*) Then again, giving to the power of fire the appellation of Hephaestus, they made his image in human shape and placed on his head a dark blue cap as a symbol of the revolving vault of heaven, where the archetypal and purest form of fire is to be found. The fire that is carried down to earth from the heavens is less tense and vigorous, and needs its material support and foundation. That is why it is " lame," as needing matter to support it.[a] Moreover, taking the power of the sun to be of this sort they called it Apollo from the vibration of its rays (*a*[*ctinôn*] *palsis*).[b] And nine Muses sing to accompany him, the sublunary sphere and seven spheres of planets and the one sphere of the fixed stars. They made the bay-tree his attribute, for one thing because this plant is full of fire and therefore repugnant to demons, for another because when it is burnt it chatters, and so represents the prophetic activity of the god.

(*b*) The sage of Chaeronea says that the power of fire . . . purest form of fire is to be found.

(*c*) The ancients consecrate the bay-tree to Apollo because the plant is full of fire, as Plutarch says, and Apollo is fire. For he is the sun. Hence this plant is hated by demons, and they depart from any place where bay may be, and men think that when they

[a] *De Facie*, 922 B, Cornutus, chap. 19, and Heraclitus, *Alleg. Homer.* chap. 26, who applies the word " lame " to fire itself, as is done here, instead of using it of the personification of Hephaestus.

[b] *Cf.* the derivation from ἀκτίνων βολάς, *Vit. et Poes. Hom.*, chap. 202.

---

[3] ὡς φησιν ὁ Πλούταρχος one MS. (S) only.

μαντείαις καίοντες ταύτην οἱ ἄνθρωποι παράστασιν
προφητείας δοκοῦσιν εὑρηκέναι.

195

Proclus, *in Timaeum*, i, p. 415 Diehl.

Καὶ δεῖ μεμνῆσθαι καὶ ὧν ὁ Χαιρωνεὺς εἶπε περὶ
τοῦ τῆς προνοίας ὀνόματος, ὡς Πλάτωνος οὕτως
τὴν θείαν αἰτίαν καλέσαντος.

196

Proclus, *in Euclidem*, ii, p. 35.

Ποσότητα δὲ λέγουσιν αὐτὴν (*sc.*, τὴν γωνίαν)
ὅσοι φασὶ τὸ πρῶτον διάστημα ὑπὸ τὸ σημεῖον
εἶναι τὴν γωνίαν· ὧν καὶ Πλούταρχός ἐστιν, εἰς
τὴν αὐτὴν δόξαν συνωθῶν καὶ τὸν Ἀπολλώνιον.
" δεῖ γὰρ εἶναί τι," φησί, " διάστημα πρῶτον ὑπὸ
τὴν κλάσιν τῶν περιεχουσῶν γραμμῶν ἢ ἐπι-
φανειῶν."

*197

Prolegomenon in Hermogenis περὶ στάσεων Appendices
(p. 217 Rabe).

Ἐκ τῶν Πλουτάρχου εἰς τὸν Πλάτωνος Γοργίαν·

Ὅρος ῥητορικῆς κατὰ Γοργιάν· ῥητορικὴ ἐστι
τέχνη περὶ λόγους τὸ κῦρος ἔχουσα, πειθοῦς δημι-

---

[a] ? *Timaeus*, 30 b, 44 c.
[b] P. ver Eecke, *Proclus de Lycie*, 1948, p. 114, thinks the
neo-Platonist is meant.

burn it as they seek oracular responses, they have found a representation of prophecy.

Fragment discovered by E. Bickel, *Diatribe in Senecae philosophi fragmenta*, i. 103. But J. Bidez, *Vie de Porphyre*, p. 147, supports the view of F. Börtzler, *Porphyrios' Schrift von den Gottesbildern*, p. 61, that the reference to Plutarch in Lydus is an error.

195

One must also remember what the philosopher of Chaeronea said about the name Providence, as being that by which Plato called the Divine Cause.[a]

196

The angle is treated as a quantity by all those who say that an angle is " the first distance under the point." Plutarch [b] belongs to their number, and attempts to foist the same view on Apollonius.[c] There must, he says, be some first distance under the deflection of the enclosing lines or surfaces.[d]

*197

From Plutarch's *Commentary on Plato's Gorgias* [e] :

Definition of rhetoric according to Gorgias. Rhetoric is an art authoritative in the field of discourse, a

---

[c] Apollonius of Pergê, c. 265–170 B.C., famous for his work on conic sections.

[d] What follows is Proclus' refutation of Plutarch (M. Steck, *Proklus, Kommentar zum ersten Buch von Euklids Elementa*). For an account of the controversy see T. L. Heath, *The Thirteen Books of Euclid's Elements*, i, pp. 176-177.

[e] There is nothing to show which Plutarch is intended ;

365

ουργὸς ἐν πολιτικοῖς λόγοις περὶ παντὸς τοῦ προ-
τεθέντος πιστευτικῆς καὶ οὐ διδασκαλικῆς· εἶναι δὲ
αὐτῆς τὴν πραγματείαν ἰδίαν μάλιστα περὶ δίκαια
καὶ ἄδικα ἀγαθά τε καὶ κακὰ καλά τε καὶ αἰ-
σχρά.

*198

Scholia in Platonis *Gorgiam*, 462 ε (307. 12 Hermann).

Ἰστέον ὅτι διαφέρει ἐπιτήδευμα καὶ ἐπιτήδευσις·
αὕτη μὲν γὰρ ἐνέργειαν δηλοῖ, ἐκεῖνο δὲ οἷον οὐσίαν,
ὧς φησι Πλούταρχος.

*199

Ibid. 495 D (318. 26 Hermann).

῏Ω σοφώτατε σύ· κατ᾽ εἰρωνείαν ὑπὸ Καλλικλέους
εἴρηται, ὧς φησι Πλούταρχος.

200

*This fragment and the following are ascribed in Stobaeus
to Porphyry, that is to say, the preceding fragment is introduced by the word* Πορφυρίου *and they by the words* τοῦ αὐτοῦ.
*They were claimed for Plutarch by Bernardakis, probably
rightly. The style, vocabulary and rhythm all suggest that
he is the author : they are definitely not those of Porphyry.
The quotations contained in them are all such as he might
have made. With Empedocles he was familiar and actually*

but observe frags. 186, 192. R. Beutler, *R.E.* xxi. 969,
inclines to ascribe this fragment and the two following ones
to the neo-Platonist. It summarizes Plato, *Gorgias*, 450 B—
456 c.

worker of persuasion in political speeches on any subject proposed, a persuasion that creates belief without giving instruction. He says that its proper business has particular reference to what is just and unjust, good and bad, honourable and disgraceful.

*198 *a*

One must know that *epitêdeuma* (a pursuit) differs from *epitêdeusis* (the practice of a pursuit). As Plutarch says, the latter indicates an activity, the former a quasi-substance.

*199

" How wise you are ! " Said ironically by Callicles, as Plutarch says.

200

quotes the same line elsewhere ; Odyssey, iv. 563 is given the same interpretation in De Facie, 942 F, 944 c ; and he seems to have had an interest in Timotheüs, whom he quotes in twelve other places. On the other hand Porphyry gave, at one time at least, a different interpretation of Odyssey, x. 190-191 (see Wachsmuth's note).

If Stobaeus (or his MSS.) are mistaken in their ascription, the mistake may have come about in various ways. The most likely are (1) that before these two fragments there once stood an extract, now fallen out, that was ascribed to Plutarch, (2) that the fragments were indeed taken from a work by

a This fragment and the next are ascribed by C. F. Hermann to the neo-Platonist. The only other time a Plutarch is mentioned in the old scholia to Plato (*Alcibiades*, 122 B), the reference is to ours.

Porphyry, but that he had included in it passages from Plutarch ; he might have done so without acknowledgement,

Stobaeus, i. 44. 60 (i, p. 445 Wachsmuth).

Τοῦ αὐτοῦ (*sc.* Πορφυρίου)·

Τὰ δὲ παρ' Ὁμήρῳ[1] περὶ τῆς Κίρκης λεγόμενα θαυμαστὴν ἔχει τὴν[2] περὶ ψυχὴν θεωρίαν. λέγεται γὰρ οὕτως,

οἱ δὲ συῶν μὲν ἔχον κεφαλὰς φωνήν τε τρίχας τε καὶ δέμας· αὐτὰρ νοῦς ἦν ἔμπεδος ὡς τὸ πάρος περ.

ἔστι τοίνυν ὁ μῦθος αἴνιγμα τῶν περὶ ψυχῆς ὑπό τε Πυθαγόρου λεγομένων καὶ Πλάτωνος, ὡς ἄφθαρτος οὖσα τὴν φύσιν καὶ ἀίδιος, οὔ τι μὴν ἀπαθὴς οὐδ' ἀμετάβλητος, ἐν ταῖς λεγομέναις φθοραῖς καὶ τελευταῖς μεταβολὴν ἴσχει καὶ μετακόσμησιν εἰς ἕτερα σωμάτων εἴδη, καθ' ἡδονὴν διώκουσα τὸ πρόσφορον καὶ οἰκεῖον ὁμοιότητι καὶ συνηθείᾳ βίου διαίτης· ἔνθα δὴ τὸ μέγα[3] παιδείας ἑκάστῳ καὶ φιλοσοφίας ὄφελος, ἂν μνημονεύουσα τῶν καλῶν ἡ ψυχὴ καὶ δυσχεραίνουσα τὰς αἰσχρὰς καὶ παρανόμους ἡδονὰς δύνηται κρατεῖν καὶ προσέχειν αὑτῇ[4] καὶ φυλάττειν μὴ λάθῃ θηρίον γενομένη καὶ στέρξασα σώματος οὐκ εὐφυοῦς[5] οὐδὲ καθαροῦ πρὸς ἀρετὴν φύσιν ἄμουσον καὶ ἄλογον καὶ τὸ ἐπιθυμοῦν καὶ[6] θυμούμενον μᾶλλον ἢ τὸ φρόνιμον αὐξάνοντος[7] καὶ τρέφοντος.

----

[1] Ὁμήρῳ P : Ὁμήρου F.
[2] τὴν] τῶν Heeren.
[3] Bernardakis : μετά. *Cf.* Plato, *Phaedo*, 107 D.
[4] Heeren : αὐτῆς.

OTHER FRAGMENTS

just as he copied, with minor changes, extensive passages from De Sollertia Animalium *in the third book of his* De Abstinentia.

From the same author :

Homer's account of Circê contains an admirable interpretation of the soul's condition. The words are as follows :

> They had the heads of swine, the voice, the hair,
> The shape ; yet still unchanged their former mind.[a]

The story is a riddling version of what Plato and Pythagoras said about the soul, how although imperishable of nature and eternal, it is in no way impassible or immutable, but at the times of its so-called death and destruction it experiences an alteration and recasting which bring a change of outward bodily shape ; it then follows its own tastes by looking for a shape that suits it and is appropriate by reason of a familiar similarity in its way of life.[b] And there, they say, is the great benefit that each individual derives from education and philosophy, should his soul remember all that is fine and beautiful and feel distaste for ugly, illicit pleasures ; then it will be able to retain control and look to itself and guard against the danger that, before it knows what has happened, it may become a beast, having taken a liking to a body that is naturally gross and irrational, one unclean and without innate disposition to goodness, one that strengthens and feeds in it the source of appetite and anger rather than that of intelligence.

---

[a] *Odyssey*, x. 239-240.   [b] Plato, *Phaedo*, 81 E.

---

[5] Heeren : ἀφνούς.   [6] Wachsmuth : ἤ.
[7] F. H. S. : αὔξαντος, altered in P to αὔξοντος.

Αὐτῆς γὰρ τῆς μετακοσμήσεως εἱμαρμένη καὶ
φύσις ὑπὸ Ἐμπεδοκλέους δαίμων ἀνηγόρευται

σαρκῶν ἀλλογνῶτι περιστέλλουσα χιτῶνι

καὶ μεταμπίσχουσα τὰς ψυχάς, Ὅμηρος δὲ τὴν
ἐν κύκλῳ περίοδον καὶ περιφορὰν παλιγγενεσίας
Κίρκην προσηγόρευκεν, Ἡλίου παῖδα τοῦ πᾶσαν
φθορὰν γενέσει καὶ γένεσιν αὖ πάλιν φθορᾷ συνάπ-
τοντος ἀεὶ καὶ συνείροντος. Αἰαίη δὲ νῆσος ἡ δεχομένη τὸν ἀποθνῄσκοντα μοῖρα καὶ χώρα τοῦ
περιέχοντος, εἰς ἣν ἐμπεσοῦσαι πρῶτον αἱ ψυχαὶ
πλανῶνται καὶ ξενοπαθοῦσι καὶ ὀλοφύρονται καὶ
οὐκ ἴσασιν ὅπῃ ζόφος

οὐδ' ὅπῃ ἠέλιος φαεσίμβροτος εἶσ' ὑπὸ γαῖαν,

ποθοῦσαι δὲ καθ' ἡδονὰς τὴν συνήθη καὶ σύντροφον
ἐν σαρκὶ καὶ μετὰ σαρκὸς δίαιταν ἐμπίπτουσιν[1]
αὖθις εἰς τὸν κυκεῶνα, τῆς γενέσεως μιγνύσης εἰς
ταὐτὸ καὶ κυκώσης ὡς[2] ἀληθῶς ἀΐδια καὶ θνητὰ καὶ
φρόνιμα καὶ παθητὰ καὶ ὀλύμπια καὶ γηγενῆ,
θελγόμεναι καὶ μαλασσόμεναι[3] ταῖς ἀγούσαις αὖθις
ἐπὶ τὴν γένεσιν ἡδοναῖς, ἐν ᾧ δὴ μάλιστα πολλῆς
μὲν εὐτυχίας αἱ ψυχαὶ δέονται πολλῆς δὲ σωφροσύνης, ὅπως μὴ τοῖς κακίστοις ἐπισπόμεναι[4] καὶ
συνενδοῦσαι μέρεσιν ἢ πάθεσιν αὐτῶν κακοδαίμονα
καὶ θηριώδη βίον ἀμείψωσιν. ἡ γὰρ λεγομένη καὶ

---

[1] Canter : ἐμπίπτουσα.   [2] Canter : ἕως.
[3] Meineke : θελγόμενα καὶ μαλασσόμενα.
[4] Canter : ἐπισπώμεναι.

---

[a] Frag. B 126, quoted also, De Esu Carnium, 998 c.
[b] κίρκος (or more commonly κρίκος) means " ring."
Parallels for the symbolical interpretations that follow may
be found in an article by E. Kaiser, Mus. Helv. xxi (1964),
p. 205.

Now Fate and Nature, the causes of the actual re-fashioning, are designated by Empedocles the Power "that wraps in unfamiliar shirt of flesh," [a] that is, gives the souls their new dress, but Homer has called the cyclical revolution and recurrence of rebirth by the name of Circê,[b] child of the Sun, since the Sun forever joins every death to birth and birth again to death in unending succession.[c] The island of Aeaea[d] is that appointed region of space which receives every man when he dies, where the souls wander on their first arrival, feeling themselves strangers and lamenting their fate and not knowing in what direction lies the West

> Nor where the Sun that gives its light to men
> Descends beneath the Earth.[e]

Longing, according to their tastes, for their accustomed and familiar way of life in the flesh and with the flesh, they fall once again into that brew (*kukeôn*),[f] where birth commingles and literally stirs together (*kukôsês*) what is eternal and what is mortal, thought and emotion, the heavenly and the earth-born ; they are bewitched and enfeebled by the pleasures that draw them back to birth. Then indeed souls stand in need of great good fortune and great self-control if they are not to follow, and give way to, their worst parts or passions, and so pass into a miserable and bestial way of life. Here, it seems,

[c] That the sun is the cause of sublunary change, including birth and death, is a commonplace : Plato, *Rep.* 509 B, Aristotle, *Met.* Λ 1071 a 15, *Gen. et Corr.* B 338 b 3.

[d] Associated with αἰαῖ, a cry of lamentation, *cf. De Vita et Poesi Homeri*, 126.

[e] *Odyssey*, x. 190-191.

[f] A reference to the posset with which Circê turned her victims into animals, *Odyssey*, x. 234 ff.

νομιζομένη τῶν ἐν Ἅιδου τρίοδος ἐνταῦθά που
τέτακται περὶ τὰ τῆς ψυχῆς σχιζομένη[1] μέρη, τὸ
λογιστικὸν καὶ θυμοειδὲς καὶ ἐπιθυμητικόν, ὧν
ἕκαστον ἀρχὴν ἐξ αὑτοῦ καὶ ῥοπὴν ἐπὶ τὸν οἰκεῖον
βίον ἐνδίδωσι. καὶ οὐκέτι ταῦτα μῦθος οὐδὲ ποίησις ἀλλ' ἀλήθεια καὶ φυσικὸς λόγος. ὧν μὲν γὰρ
ἐν τῇ μεταβολῇ καὶ γενέσει τὸ ἐπιθυμητικὸν ἐξαν-
θοῦν ἐπικρατεῖ καὶ δυναστεύει, τούτοις εἰς ὀνώδη
καὶ ὑώδη[2] σώματα καὶ βίους θολεροὺς καὶ ἀκαθάρ-
τους ὑπὸ φιληδονίας καὶ γαστριμαργίας φησὶ γίνεσθαι[3] τὴν μεταβολήν. ὅταν δὲ φιλονεικίαις σκλη-
ραῖς καὶ φονικαῖς[4] ὠμότησιν ἔκ τινος διαφορᾶς ἢ
δυσμενείας ἐξηγριωμένον ἔχουσα παντάπασιν ἡ
ψυχὴ τὸ θυμοειδὲς εἰς δευτέραν γένεσιν ἀφίκηται,
πλήρης οὖσα προσφάτου πικρίας καὶ βαρυφροσύνης[5]
ἔρριψεν ἑαυτὴν εἰς λύκου φύσιν ἢ λέοντος, ὥσπερ
ὄργανον ἀμυντικὸν τὸ σῶμα τῷ κρατοῦντι προσιεμένη[6] πάθει καὶ περιαρμόσασα. διὸ δεῖ[7] μάλιστα
περὶ τὸν θάνατον ὥσπερ ἐν τελετῇ καθαρεύοντα
παντὸς ἀπέχειν πάθους φαύλου[8] τὴν ψυχὴν καὶ
πᾶσαν ἐπιθυμίαν χαλεπὴν κοιμήσαντα καὶ φθόνους
καὶ δυσμενείας καὶ ὀργὰς ἀπωτάτω τιθέμενον τοῦ
φρονοῦντος ἐκβαίνειν τοῦ σώματος. οὗτος ὁ χρυ-

---

[1] Heeren : σχιζόμενα.
[2] ὀνώδη Canter, ὑώδη added by Wachsmuth : εἰς νωθῆ καὶ
F ἰσονωθῆ καὶ P. εἰς νωθῆ Heeren.
[3] Bernardakis : γενέσθαι.   [4] Meineke : φοινικαῖς.
[5] Heeren : βαρυφρόνης.   [6] F. H. S. : προϊεμένη.
[7] Canter : δή.   [8] P² : φαύλην FP¹.

---

[a] Plato, *Phaedo*, 108 A, *Gorgias*, 524 A.
[b] Plato, *Phaedo*, 81 E. Although Homer's Circê perhaps

is the right interpretation of that belief in the under-world crossroads [a] of which men tell : the parting of the ways refers to the parts of the soul, the reasoning, the spirited, and the appetitive, each of which gives an impulse and inclination towards the manner of life appropriate to itself. And with this we pass from mythology and poetic invention to truth and the laws of nature. The men whose appetitive element erupts to prevail and dominate at this time of change and birth suffer a transmutation by reason of their sensuality and gluttony, so Homer means, into the bodies of donkeys [b] and swine, to lead their lives in mud and uncleanliness. In another soul the spirited element has grown utterly savage through stubborn rivalries and murderous cruelties, that sprang from some quarrel or enmity ; when such a one comes to his second birth, full of fresh bitterness and indigna-tion, he throws himself into the shape of a wolf [c] or lion, welcoming this body and fastening it to himself as an organ of retaliation that will serve his dominant passion.[d] So one should never keep oneself so pure as at the time of one's death, as if taking part in a rite of initiation ; one should restrain the soul from all evil passions, put all troublesome appetites to sleep, keep feelings of envy, ill-will, and anger as far from the seat of reason as possible, and thus withdraw from the body. " Hermes with his golden

turned men into swine only, she is often represented as giving them other animal forms : donkeys, *e.g. Coniug. Praec.* 139 A ; wolves, *e.g.* Virgil, *Aen.* vii. 18.

[c] Plato, *Phaedo*, 82 A. The wolves and lions of *Odyssey*, x. 213, may have been genuine wild animals, not bewitched human beings ; Eustathius, 1656. 38, regards their status as not determinable.

[d] There are points of contact between these two sentences and *De Sera Numinis Vindicta*, 565 D.

σόρραπις Ἑρμῆς ἀληθῶς ὁ λόγος ἐντυγχάνων καὶ
δεικνύων ἐναργῶς τὸ καλὸν ἢ παντάπασιν εἴργει
καὶ ἀπέχει[1] τοῦ κυκεῶνος, ἢ πιοῦσαν[2] ἐν ἀνθρωπίνῳ
βίῳ καὶ ἤθει διαφυλάσσει πλεῖστον χρόνον, ὡς
ἀνυστόν ἐστι.

201

Stobaeus, i. 49. 61 (i, p. 448 Wachsmuth).

Τοῦ αὐτοῦ·

Πάλιν αἰνιττόμενος ὅτι ταῖς τῶν εὐσεβῶς βεβιω-
κότων ψυχαῖς μετὰ τὴν τελευτὴν οἰκεῖός ἐστι τόπος
ὁ περὶ τὴν σελήνην, ὑπεδήλωσεν εἰπών,

   ἀλλά σ᾽ ἐς ἠλύσιον πεδίον καὶ πείρατα γαίης
   ἀθάνατοι[3] πέμψουσιν, ὅθι ξανθὸς Ῥαδάμανθυς,

ἠλύσιον μὲν πεδίον εἰκότως προσειπὼν τὴν τῆς σελήνης ἐπιφάνειαν ὑφ᾽ ἡλίου καταλαμπομένην, '' ὅτ᾽
ἀέξεται[4] ἀλίου[5] αὐγαῖς,'' ὥς φησι Τιμόθεος, πέρατα
δὲ γῆς τὰ ἄκρα νυκτός. ἣν σκιὰν τῆς γῆς εἶναι
λέγουσιν οἱ μαθηματικοὶ πολλάκις ἐπιψαύουσαν τῆς
σελήνης, ὡς τοῦτο τῆς γῆς πέρας ἐχούσης, οὗ τῇ
σκιᾷ μακρότερον οὐκ ἐξικνεῖται.

*202

Stobaeus, iii. i. 199 (iii, p. 150 Hense).

Πυθαγορικά·

Καὶ μὴν οὐδέν ἐστιν οὕτω τῆς Πυθαγορικῆς

[1] ἀπέχει F : ἀνέχει P.   [2] Canter : ποιοῦσαν.
[3] P[2], Homer : ἀθάνατον.   [4] Meineke : αὔξεται.
         [5] Meineke : ἠλίου F : ἡελίου P.

---

[a] *Odyssey*, x. 277.
[b] Heraclitus, *Hom. Alleg.*, chap. 72, Eustathius, 1658. 26.

wand " [a] is this faculty of reason,[b] which in very truth converses with the soul and shows it clearly what is its good, and either bars and restrains it entirely from drinking of the posset,[c] or preserves it, if it does drink, in a human life and character for so long as is feasible.

201

From the same author :

Again wishing to hint that after death the souls of those who have lived righteous lives have for their own the regions around the moon, he suggested this by saying :

> Thee to the Elysian plain and earth's extremes
> The Gods shall send, where Rhadamanthys dwells,
> The golden-haired.[d]

He aptly gave the name of " Elysian plain " to the surface of the moon that is illuminated by the sun,[e] when, in the words of Timotheüs,[f] " the sun's rays bless it " ; and by " Earth's extremities " he means the limit of night. Astronomers say that night is the Earth's shadow, which often touches the moon ; and so he means that the earth has as its extremity the point beyond which its shadow does not reach.[g]

*202

Pythagorean Views :

Moreover nothing is so characteristic of the Pytha-

---

[c] *Cf.* Plato, *Phaedo*, 82 B, 114 C ; the best of philosophers escape reincarnation.

[d] *Odyssey*, iv. 563, quoted also, *De Facie*, 942 F, 944 C.

[e] The etymology is *Elysium* from *Helios*.

[f] Frag. 13 Diehl. [g] *Cf. De Facie*, 942 F.

φιλοσοφίας ἴδιον, ὡς τὸ συμβολικόν, οἶον ἐν τελετῇ μεμιγμένον φωνῇ καὶ σιωπῇ διδασκαλίας γένος· ὥστε μὴ λέγειν

ἀείσω ξυνετοῖσι, θύρας δ' ἐπίθεσθε βέβηλοι,

ἀλλ' αὐτόθεν ἔχειν φῶς καὶ χαρακτῆρα τοῖς συνήθεσι τὸ φραζόμενον, τυφλὸν δὲ καὶ ἄσημον εἶναι τοῖς ἀπείροις. ὡς γὰρ ὁ ἄναξ ὁ ἐν Δελφοῖς οὔτε λέγει οὔτε κρύπτει ἀλλὰ σημαίνει κατὰ τὸν Ἡράκλειτον, οὕτω τῶν Πυθαγορικῶν συμβόλων καὶ τὸ φράζεσθαι δοκοῦν κρυπτόμενόν ἐστι καὶ τὸ κρύπτεσθαι νοούμενον.

*203

Stobaeus, iii. 13. 68 (iii, p. 468 Hense).

Θεμιστίου[1] περὶ ψυχῆς·

Εἰ μὲν οὖν ὀρθῶς ἐπὶ Πλάτωνος εἶπε Διογένης, '' τί δαὶ ὄφελος ἡμῖν ἀνδρὸς ὃς πολὺν ἤδη χρόνον φιλοσοφῶν οὐδένα λελύπηκεν; '' ἕτεροι κρινοῦσιν.[2] ἴσως γὰρ ὡς τὸ μέλι[3] δεῖ καὶ τὸν λόγον τοῦ φιλοσόφου τὸ γλυκὺ δηκτικὸν ἔχειν τῶν ἡλκωμένων.

[1] Θεμιστίου omitted by L.
[2] Second hand in Par. 1985 : κρίνουσιν.
[3] Wyttenbach : μὲν.

---

[a] Kern, *Orphicorum Fragmenta*, 334. The first two words are quoted by Plutarch, *Quaest. Conv.* 636 D.

gorean philosophy as its use of symbols, a kind of instruction compounded of speech and of silence, as in a mystic ritual : as a result they do not say :

> To those with understanding I shall sing ;
> But close your doors, all ye who are profane,[a]

but what they signify is immediately lucid and clear of feature for those to whom it is familiar, but dark and meaningless to the ignorant. Just as the Lord who is at Delphi " neither affirms nor conceals but indicates," to quote Heraclitus,[b] so with the Pythagorean symbols what seems to be made known is really being concealed, and what seems to be concealed is discerned by the mind.

Ascribed to Plutarch by Wyttenbach on grounds of matter and style. This, although more likely than Meineke's ascription to Aristoxenus' Πυθαγορικαὶ Ἀποφάσεις, the other fragments of which are quite different in style, is yet far from certain.

*203 [c]

Themistius, *On the Soul* :

I leave it to others to decide whether Diogenes was right in his comment on Plato : " What use to us," he asked, " is a man who has practised philosophy so long without causing anyone pain ? "[d] It may well be that the talk of a philosopher should have a sweetness that stings ulcers in the mind, as honey stings bodily sores.[e]

[b] Diels-Kranz, *Fragmente der Vorsokratiker*, 22 B 93 ; also quoted, *De Pyth. Orac.* 404 D.
[c] On the reasons for and against attributing frags. 203-206 to Plutarch see p. 307.   [d] Cf. *Moralia*, 452 D.
[e] Cf. *Moralia*, 59 D, *Life of Phocion*, chap. 2.

*204

Stobaeus, iv. 22. 89 (iv, p. 530 Hense).

Θεμιστίου ἐκ τοῦ περὶ ψυχῆς·

'Αλλ' οὖν¹ μάλιστα διψῶν ἀπέθανε τῆς γυναικός,
ἐρῶν ἐρώσης ἀπολειπόμενος.² . . . οὐθὲν εἰπεῖν
οὔτε ποιῆσαι πρὸς αὐτὴν ἰταμὸν ἐτόλμησαν,³ ἀλλ'
οὕτως ἐνεκαρτέρησαν ἀμφότεροι τῷ πρέποντι,
ὥσπερ ἀποδείξασθαι θέλοντες ὅτι πλεῖστον αἰδοῦς
ἔρωτι δικαίῳ μέτεστιν. ὅθεν ἔμοιγε πλεῖστον αὐτῇ
φαίνεται χρόνον ἀνὴρ συμβεβιωκέναι· πάντα γὰρ
διόλου τὸν δεκαετῆ χρόνον ὁμαλῶς συνεβίωσεν. αἱ
δ' ἄλλαι⁴ συνοικοῦσιν οὐ συμβιοῦσιν, ὅταν λυπῶσι
τοὺς⁵ ἄνδρας ἢ ζηλοτυπῶσιν ἢ διαφέρωνται περὶ
χρημάτων ἢ κακῶς λέγωσιν ἢ φεύγωσι θρυπτό-
μεναι τὰς φιλοφροσύνας καὶ συνδιαιτήσεις· ὥστ'
ἂν τοῦτον ἐξαιρῇς⁶ τὸν χρόνον ἐν ᾧ ταῦτα πράττουσιν, ἀπολείπεται βραχὺς ἐκεῖνος⁷ ὁ τῆς συμβιώσεως.

*205

Stobaeus, iv. 50. 29 (v, p. 1032 Hense).

'Εκ τοῦ Θεμιστίου περὶ ψυχῆς·

Καίτοι περί γε τῶν γερόντων ὁ Σοφοκλῆς εἴρηκε
χαριέντως,

σμικρὰ παλαιὰ σώματ' εὐνάζει ῥοπή·

καταγωγῇ γὰρ ἔοικεν ὁ γεροντικὸς θάνατος, ἐκβολὴ

---

¹ Meineke : ἄλλου M : ἀλλ' οὐ A.
² Meineke : ἀπολιπόμενος. Lacuna marked by Hense.
³ ἐτόλμησεν Meineke.   ⁴ Meineke : ἄλλαις.
⁵ μὲν after τοὺς omitted following Gesner.
⁶ Bernardakis : ἐξαίρης.   ⁷ ἐκείνοις Meineke.

*204 [a]

Themistius, from his *On the Soul* :

But in reality the chief cause of his death was longing for the wife he had lost : he loved her as she loved him. . . . They did not dare to treat her with any roughness of word or deed,[b] but both maintained such a decorum that it would seem they wished to demonstrate that an honourable love is associated with the deepest feelings of respect. So he seems to me to have shared his life with her as her husband for a very great length of time, for he shared it equably through the whole of those ten years. Other women share a house with their husbands, but not their lives,[c] at times when they give them pain or are jealous of them or quarrel over money-matters or abuse them or put on airs and avoid all affection and companionship. So that if you subtract the time in which they behave in this manner, that in which they share their life is but a brief remainder.

*205

Themistius, from his *On the Soul* :

Yet Sophocles has written a charming line about old men :

A small weight in life's scales brings old folk sleep.[d]

Death in old age is like reaching a harbour, but the

[a] Bernardakis suggested that this fragment comes from the *Amatorius*, having been lost in the lacuna at 766 D. This is improbable. If the fragment is Plutarchean at all, it is likely to come from the same book as frags. 172-178, 203, 205-206.
[b] The text is uncertain. Perhaps " he did not dare, etc."
[c] Cf. *Praecepta Coniugalia*, 142 F.   [d] *O.T.* 961.

δὲ καὶ ναυάγιόν ἐστιν ὁ τῶν νέων· ἐκπίπτει γὰρ ἡ
ψυχὴ βίᾳ συντριβομένου τοῦ σώματος.

*206

Stobaeus iv. 52. 45 (v, p. 1086 Hense).

Θεμιστίου ἐκ τοῦ περὶ ψυχῆς·

"Οπου τὸν ἀπὸ τῆς Στοᾶς φιλόσοφον Ἀντίπατρον
ἀποθνήσκοντα λέγουσιν ἐν εὐτυχήματος μέρει διανοεῖσθαι[1] καὶ τὴν ἐκ Κιλικίας αὐτῷ γενομένην εἰς
Ἀθήνας εὔπλοιαν.

*207

Stobaeus, iii. 33. 16 (iii, p. 681 Hense).

Πλουτάρχου·

Περὶ τῆς καθ' "Ομηρον ἐχεμυθίας διὰ τούτων
σαφῶς δείκνυται· λέγει γάρ,

Θερσῖτ' ἀκριτόμυθε, λιγύς περ ἐὼν ἀγορητὴς
ἴσχεο, μηδ' ἔθελ' οἷος ἐριζέμεναι βασιλῆι.[2]

καὶ τοῦ Τηλεμάχου εἰπόντος,

ἦ μάλα τις θεῶν[3] ἔνδον, οἳ οὐρανὸν εὐρὺν ἔχουσιν,

---

[1] Post: διακεῖσθαι. μερίδι θέσθαι Patzig after Meineke (μερίδι
κεῖσθαι).
[2] βασιλεῦσιν Homer.
[3] θεός Homer.

---

[a] Cf. Life of Marius, chap. 46, De Tranquillitate Animi,
469 D; Stoic. Vet. Frag. iii, p. 246.
[b] Wyttenbach guessed this fragment to come from
Homeric Studies (see p. 238). Diels, Doxographi Graeci,
380

death of young men is shipwreck and jettison : the soul is swept overboard, as the body is violently shattered.

*206

Themistius, from his *On the Soul* :

In this connexion the story is told that the Stoic philosopher Antipater on his death-bed counted among his pieces of good fortune even his prosperous voyage from Cilicia to Athens.[a]

*207 [b]

Plutarch :

Homer's approval of " holding the tongue " [c] is clearly shown by the following lines : he writes,

> Thersites, unconsidered are your words ;
> Keep quiet, ready speaker though you be,
> Nor wish alone to wrangle with the king.[d]

And when Telemachus said,

> Some god's within, a dweller in wide heaven,[e]

pp. 97-99, argues that it is a fragment of a pseudo-Plutarchean work, perhaps of the second cent. A.D., used in *De Vita et Poesi Homeri*, chap. 149. F. della Corte, *Riv. Fil.*, N.S. xvi (1938), p. 40, thinks that it is taken from a recension of a work by Plutarch, of which other versions are to be found in Pap. Lond. 734 and *De Vita et Poesi Homeri*.

[c] Often spoken of as a Pythagorean practice. On Pythagorean interpretation of Homer see M. Détienne, *Homère, Hésiode et Pythagore* (Coll. Latomus lvii).

[d] *Iliad*, ii. 246-247.

[e] *Odyssey*, xix. 40 ; the first half of the line is correctly cited at *Moralia*, 762 E.

ἐπιλαμβανόμενος ὁ πατὴρ ἔφη,

σίγα καὶ κατὰ σὸν νόον ἴσχανε μηδ' ἐρέεινε·
αὕτη τοι δίκη ἐστὶ θεῶν οἳ Ὄλυμπον ἔχουσι.

τοῦτο ἐκσίγησιν[1] οἱ Πυθαγορικοὶ καλοῦντες οὐδὲν
ἀπεκρίνοντο τοῖς περὶ θεῶν ὅ τι[2] τύχοιεν ἰταμῶς
καὶ εὐχερῶς ἐρωτῶσι.

*208

Stobaeus, iv. 36. 23 (v, p. 873 Hense).

Πορφυρίου ἐκ τοῦ περὶ Στυγός·

Ἥ τε ἰτέα αὕτη τὸν καρπὸν ἀποβάλλει πρὶν ἐκ-
θρέψαι· διὸ " ὠλεσίκαρπον "[3] αὐτὴν ὁ ποιητὴς ὀνομάζει. καὶ μέντοι ἱστόρηται ὡς μετὰ οἴνου δοθεὶς
ὁ ταύτης καρπὸς ἀγόνους ποιεῖ τοὺς πιόντας καὶ
κατασβέννυσι τὸ σπέρμα καὶ μαραίνει τὴν γόνιμον
ὁρμήν.

209

Stobaeus, iv. 41. 57 (v, p. 944 Hense).

Ἐκ τῶν Πορφυρίου περὶ Στυγός

Ἥ τε γὰρ αἴγειρος, ὥς φασιν ἄλλοι τε καὶ
Πλούταρχος, φιλοπενθὴς καὶ ἀτελὴς[4] πρὸς καρπο-

---

[1] ἐξήγησιν mss., corrected by Gomperz from Eustathius, *in
Odyss.* xxiv. 485, ἐκσίγησις Πυθαγορικῶς ἡ ἄκρα σιγή.
[2] Wyttenbach : ὅτε.

his father restrained him with the words,

> Silence ! Repress your thought and ask no questions :
> The dwellers in Olympus have this right.[a]

The Pythagoreans called this " firm silence," and
gave no answer to those who, recklessly and without
qualms, put indiscriminate questions about the gods.

*208 [b]

Porphyry, from the work *On the Styx* :

This willow also drops its seed before ripening it, so
that the poet calls it " seed-losing." [c] It is indeed also
recorded that, if given in wine, the seed of this tree
makes those who drink it infertile, drying up the
semen and withering their impulse to procreation.[d]

209

From Porphyry's *On the Styx* :

The black poplar, as Plutarch and others say, is a
sorrowful tree and unsuccessful in setting seed.[e]

[a] *Odyssey*, xix. 42-43.
[b] Claimed as Plutarchean by Bernardakis ; if in Porphyry
it originally followed frag. 209 (note τε . . . τε), there is a
good chance that he was right.
[c] *Odyssey*, x. 510 ; cited also by Theophrastus, *Hist.
Plant.* iii. 1. 3.
[d] *Cf. Geoponica*, xi. 13.
[e] Its resinous discharge was supposed to be tears ; for its
infertility *cf.* Theophrastus, *Hist. Plant.* iii. 4. 2, Arist.
Gen. Animalium 726 a 7 : the fact is that the great majority
of these trees are male.

---

[3] Gesner : ὀλεσίκαρπον.   [4] ἀτελὴς M : εὐτελὴς A.

γονίαν. διὸ καὶ Σοφοκλῆς ἔν τισι[1] φησιν,

οὐ χρή ποτ᾿ ἀνθρώπων[2] μέγαν ὄλβον ἀπο-
βλέψαι· τανυφλοίου γὰρ ἰσαμέριος
φύλλοις τις[3] αἰγείρου βιοτὰν ἀποβάλλει.

210

Stobaeus, iv. 50. 19 (v, p. 1024 Hense).

Πλουτάρχου·

Νέοις δὲ ζηλωτέον τοὺς γέροντας, κατὰ Σιμωνί-
δην,[4]

ἄθηλος ἵππῳ πῶλος ὣς ἅμα τρέχειν·

καθάπερ φησὶν ὁ Πλάτων ἐπὶ τοῦ μιγνυμένου πρὸς
ὕδωρ ἀκράτου μαινόμενον θεὸν ἑτέρῳ θεῷ νήφοντι
σωφρονίζεσθαι.

211

Syncellus, *Chronographia*, i. 625 Dindorf.

Οὗτος καὶ τὸν Ἰούλιον Κᾶνον,[5] ἕνα τῶν Στωικῶν
φιλοσόφων, ἀνεῖλε· περὶ οὗ παράδοξον Ἕλλησιν, ὡς
δοκῶ, πέπλασται. ἀπαγόμενος γὰρ πρὸς τὸ θα-
νεῖν ἀταράχως λέγεταί τινι τῶν ἑταίρων Ἀντιόχῳ
τοὔνομα, Σελευκεῖ, συνεπομένῳ προειπεῖν,[6] ὡς ἐν-
τεύξεται αὐτῷ κατὰ τὴν αὐτὴν νύκτα μετὰ τὴν

---

[1] ἐν Τηρεῖ Nauck, but see *Cl. Quart.* ii, p. 216.
[2] ἄνθρωπον Gleditsch.
[3] φύλλοις τις Pearson, adapting Gleditsch and Bergk : ὅστις.
[4] Σημωνίδην Wilamowitz.
[5] Bernardakis : κανὸν (and κανὸς below).
[6] Wyttenbach : προσειπεῖν.

OTHER FRAGMENTS

Hence Sophocles in certain verses says :

> Never admire men's great prosperity ;
> A man's days are like the slender poplar's leaves,
> As quickly his life is gone.[a]

210

From Plutarch :

Young men should be ardent followers of the old—
in Simonides' [b] words,

> Run like the just-weaned foal beside its dam.

Similarly Plato, speaking of the mixture of wine with
water, says that one god is chastened by another, a
mad god by a sober.[c]

211

He [d] also executed one of the Stoic philosophers,
Julius Canus, about whom the Greeks have invented
(or so I think) an extraordinary story. It is said that
as he was being led away to his death he calmly
prophesied to a friend who was accompanying him,
Antiochus by name,[e] from Seleucia, that on the very
night after his passing he would meet him and discuss

---

[a] Frag. 535 Nauck (593 Pearson), probably from Τηρεύς.
The meaning of τανύφλοιος is obscure, cf. Gow on Theocr.
xxv. 250.

[b] Really Semonides, frag. 5 Diehl, cited also at *Moralia*,
84 D, 136 A, 446 E, 790 F, 997 D.

[c] *Laws*, 773 D, cited also at *Moralia*, 15 E, 791 B. The frag-
ment is either carelessly written or has suffered abbreviation.
If the latter is the case, the source may be *An Seni Sit
Gerenda Res Publica*, 790 F—791 B. Stobaeus has other
extracts from that work, some abbreviated (iii. 29. 85, p. 653
Hense, iv. 4. 20, p. 189 Hense, iv. 13. 43, p. 363 Hense).

[d] The emperor Gaius.   [e] Not otherwise known.

ἔξοδον καὶ διαπορήσει τι τῶν σπουδῆς ἀξίων, καὶ
ὅτι μετὰ τρεῖς ἡμέρας Ῥεκτός, εἷς τῶν ἑταίρων,
ὑπὸ Γαΐου φονευθήσεται. ἃ καὶ γέγονεν, τοῦ μὲν
ἀναιρεθέντος τριταίου, τοῦ δ᾽ Ἀντιόχου τὴν ἐπ-
οψίαν εἰπόντος τῆς νυκτός, ὅτι φανεὶς Ἰούλιος
Κᾶνος τὰ περὶ διαμονῆς τῆς ψυχῆς καὶ καθαρω-
τέρου[1] φωτὸς μετὰ τὴν ἔξοδον διηγήσατο. ταῦτα
Πλούταρχος ὁ Χαιρωνεὺς ἱστορεῖ.

212

Theodoretus, *Cur. Graec. Affect.* i. 468 a.

Ὅτι δὲ καὶ τῶν Διονυσίων καὶ τῶν Παναθη-
ναίων καὶ μέντοι τῶν Θεσμοφορίων καὶ τῶν Ἐλευσινίων τὰς τελετὰς Ὀρφεύς, ἀνὴρ Ὀδρύσης, εἰς τὰς
Ἀθήνας ἐκόμισε, καὶ εἰς Αἴγυπτον ἀφικόμενος τὰ
τῆς Ἴσιδος καὶ τοῦ Ὀσίριδος εἰς τὰ τῆς Δηοῦς καὶ
τοῦ Διονύσου μετατέθεικεν ὄργια, διδάσκει μὲν
Πλούταρχος ὁ ἐκ Χαιρωνείας τῆς Βοιωτίας. . . .

213

Theodoretus, *Cur. Graec. Affect.* i. 510 b.

Πρώτους θεοὺς ἐνόμισαν καὶ Αἰγύπτιοι καὶ Φοί-
νικες καὶ μέντοι καὶ Ἕλληνες ἥλιον καὶ σελήνην
καὶ οὐρανὸν καὶ γῆν καὶ τἄλλα στοιχεῖα· τοῦτο γὰρ
δὴ καὶ ὁ Πλάτων καὶ ὁ Σικελιώτης Διόδωρος καὶ
ὁ Χαιρωνεὺς ἐδίδαξε Πλούταρχος.

[1] Goar : καθαρωτέρας.

an important subject,[a] and that Rectus,[b] one of his
friends, would be murdered by Gaius in three days'
time. These things did in fact happen. Rectus was
executed three days later, and Antiochus told of a
nocturnal vision, in which Julius Canus appeared and
informed him of the survival of the soul and the purer
light that succeeds its passing. This story is recorded
by Plutarch of Chaeronea.[c]

212

Plutarch of Chaeronea in Boeotia informs us that
the rites of the Dionysia and of the Panathenaic
festival, and indeed those of the Thesmophoria and
of the Eleusinian mysteries, were imported into
Attica by Orpheus, an Odrysian, and that after
visiting Egypt he transplanted the ritual of Isis and
Osiris into the ceremonies of Deo and Dionysus.[d]

213

Both the Egyptians and the Phoenicians, and indeed the Greeks too, thought that the first gods
were the sun and moon and heavens and the earth
and the rest of the elements. Plato,[e] Diodorus
Siculus,[f] and Plutarch of Chaeronea have informed
us of this.

---

[a] Seneca, *De Tranquillitate Animi*, 14. 4-9, recounts the
death of Julius Canus and how he promised to return to tell
his friends " quis esset animarum status."

[b] Not otherwise known.

[c] Patzig suggests with some plausibility that the source is
the work *On the Soul* ; compare fragments 173, 176.

[d] *Cf.* Herodotus, ii. 81, Diodorus Siculus, i. 11, 13, *Orphica*, frag. 237 Kern.

[e] ? *Laws*, 887 E.   [f] i. 96.

Tzetzes, *Chiliades*, i. 812-820.

Περὶ τοῦ ἱματίου ᾿Αντισθένους Συβαρίτου·

Τοιοῦτον τὸ ἱμάτιον ὑπῆρχεν ᾿Αντισθένους·
ἦν σοῦσον[1] ἁλουργὲς πεντεκαιδεκαπηχυαῖον,
ἔχον μὲν ζῷδα καὶ θεοὺς καὶ Περσικὰ καὶ Σοῦσα,[2]
μαργάροις ἠσκημένα τε καὶ λίθοις τιμαλφέσι,
χειρίδι δὲ θατέρᾳ μὲν εἶχε τὸν ᾿Αντισθένην
ἐν δὲ θατέρᾳ Σύβαριν, τὴν πόλιν ᾿Αντισθένους.
τοῦτο δὲ Διονύσιος ὁ πρότερος κραι ήσας
εἰς ἑκατὸν καὶ εἴκοσι τάλαντα νομισμάτων
Καρχηδονίοις ἐμπολεῖ. Πλούταρχος οἶμαι γράφει.

ΕΧ ΤΩΝ ΤΟΥ ΧΑΙΡΩΝΕΩΣ

*These notes are found in a number of mss., all descending
from Marc. gr. 196 of ix/x cent., which contains matter from
two sources, one providing a number of commentaries on
Platonic dialogues by Olympiodorus, the other a collection of
notes, of mixed origin, on the* Phaedo. *Among this collection
are three sets of matter which claim to be derived from
Plutarch ; unfortunately the ms., although indicating the
beginning, does not indicate the end of the second set. Wyttenbach, who first discovered it (in a later ms.), certainly included too much, and later editors of Plutarch have followed
him. I agree with Finckh and Norvin, the editors of
Olympiodorus, that only the first five notes [b] in this set are of
Plutarchean origin : what follows has a different, less individual, scholastic character. The third set of matter has the
same ultimate origin as the other two, with which it has*

[1] ἦν δ' αὐτὸ μὲν Ps.-Arist. (see note *a*). Tzetzes' motives
and meaning in writing σοῦσον are obscure.
[2] *Cf.* Ps.-Arist., ἄνωθεν μὲν Σούσοις (perhaps read Σκύθαις)
κάτωθεν δὲ Πέρσαις.

OTHER FRAGMENTS

*214

On the cloak of Antisthenes of Sybaris :

The manner of Antisthenes' cloak was like this. It was lovely as a lily (?), dyed purple, and fifteen cubits long, with animals upon it and gods and Persian scenes and Susa, all these tricked out with pearls and precious stones. On one sleeve was represented Antisthenes himself, on the other Sybaris, his native city. This cloak was sold by Dionysius the First, after he had got possession of it, to the Carthaginians for one hundred and twenty talents in cash. Plutarch, I think,[a] tells the story.

EXTRACTS FROM THE CHAERONEAN

many coincidences, but has been further abbreviated and modified in form. It is impossible to say what was the title or titles of the work or works thus laid under contribution. Possible candidates from the Lamprias Catalogue are nos. 48, 177, 209, and 226.

Ziegler, R.E. xxi. 753, is doubtful whether the fragments have anything to do with Plutarch, thinking that they are at best notes found among his papers. The coincidence between frag. 215 (k) and Moralia, 537 A, however, supports the ascription. Zeller, Phil. d. Griechen, iii. 2. 808³, supposed the extracts to be taken from the neo-Platonist Plutarch ; this view is rejected by W. Norvin, Olympiodorus fra Alexandria, p. 124, and R. Beutler, R.E. xxi. 970, s.v. " Plutarchos von Athen."

[a] No trust should be put in what Tzetzes thought or pretended to think. He derived the story from Ps.-Aristotle, *Mirab. Auscult.* c. 96, *cf.* Athenaeus, xii. 541 a, where the owner of the cloak is called Alcisthenes (Alcimenes in some MSS.).

[b] Doubt is possible about the sixth and seventh, which I have therefore included, but marked as uncertain.

(a) Ὅτι οὐ τὸ ἐπιστητὸν αἴτιον τῆς ἐπιστήμης, ὡς Ἀρκεσίλαος· οὕτω γὰρ καὶ ἀνεπιστημοσύνη τῆς ἐπιστήμης αἰτία φανεῖται.

(b) Ὅτι οὐχ ἡ ψυχὴ τρέπει ἑαυτὴν εἰς τὴν τῶν πραγμάτων κατάληψιν καὶ ἀπάτην κατὰ τοὺς ἀπὸ τῆς Στοᾶς. πῶς γὰρ αἰτία ἑαυτῇ γνώσεως ἡ ψυχὴ καὶ ἀγνοίας, μήπω αὐτὰς ἔχουσα ἀρχήν;

(c) Ὅτι μόνῳ τῷ Πλάτωνι ῥᾷστον ἀποδοῦναι τὸν λόγον, εἰς λήθην καὶ ἀνάμνησιν ἀναφέροντι τὴν γνῶσιν καὶ τὴν ἄγνοιαν.

(d) Ὅτι ἔνεισιν μὲν αἱ ἐπιστῆμαι, κρύπτονται δ' ὑπὸ τῶν ἄλλων ἐπεισοδίων ὁμοίως τῇ ὑπὸ Δημαράτου πεμφθείσῃ δέλτῳ.

(e) Ὅτι καὶ τὸ ζητεῖν καὶ τὸ εὑρίσκειν δηλοῖ τὴν ἀνάμνησιν· οὔτε γὰρ ζητήσειεν ἄν τις οὗ ἐστιν ἀνεννόητος οὔτ' ἂν εὕροι διά γε ζητήσεως· λέγεται γὰρ εὑρίσκειν καὶ ὁ κατὰ περίπτωσιν.

(f) Ὅτι ἄπορον ὄντως εἰ οἷόν τε ζητεῖν καὶ εὑρίσκειν, ὡς ἐν Μένωνι προβέβληται· οὔτε γὰρ ἃ ἴσμεν, μάταιον γάρ· οὔτε ἃ μὴ ἴσμεν, κἂν γὰρ περιπέσωμεν αὐτοῖς, ἀγνοοῦμεν, ὡς τοῖς τυχοῦσιν. οἱ μὲν γὰρ Περιπατητικοὶ τὸν δυνάμει νοῦν ἐπενόησαν· ἡμεῖς δ' ἠπορούμεν ἀπὸ τοῦ ἐνεργείᾳ εἰδέναι καὶ μὴ εἰδέναι. ἔστω γὰρ εἶναι τὸν δυνάμει νοῦν, ἀλλ' ἔτι ἀπορία ἡ αὐτή· πῶς γὰρ οὗτος νοεῖ; ἢ γὰρ ἃ

ᵃ Herodotus, vii. 239.   ᵇ 81 D.
ᶜ Aristotle, de Anima, 429 a 15.

(*a*) That it is untrue that that which can be known is the cause of knowledge, as Arcesilaüs maintained, since if this is so lack of knowledge will turn out to be a cause of knowledge.

(*b*) That it is untrue that the soul turns itself to the apprehension of facts and to error, as the Stoics maintain. For how can the soul be the cause of its own knowing or its own ignorance, if it does not already possess these things to begin with ?

(*c*) That a very easy explanation is open to Plato and to him alone, when he traces knowing and ignorance to forgetting and recollection.

(*d*) That various items of knowledge exist in us but are hidden under other supervening things, as with the tablet dispatched by Demaratus.[a]

(*e*) That both search and discovery prove the existence of recollection, since no-one could search for a thing of which he had no conception nor could he discover it—at least not by searching. We do also say, of course, that a man who comes across a thing makes a discovery.

(*f*) That the problem advanced in the *Meno*,[b] namely whether search and discovery are possible, leads to a real impasse. For we do not, on the one hand, try to find out things we know—a futile proceeding—nor, on the other, things we do not know, since even if we come across them we do not recognize them : they might be anything. The Peripatetics introduced the conception of " potential intuition " [c] ; but the origin of our difficulty was actual knowing and not knowing. Even if we grant the existence of potential intuition, the difficulty remains unchanged. How does this intuition operate ? It

οἶδεν ἢ ἃ οὐκ οἶδεν. οἱ δ᾽ ἀπὸ τῆς Στοᾶς τὰς
φυσικὰς ἐννοίας αἰτιῶνται· εἰ μὲν δὴ δυνάμει, ταὐτὸ
ἐροῦμεν. εἰ δ᾽ ἐνεργείᾳ, διὰ τί ζητοῦμεν ἃ ἴσμεν;
εἰ δ᾽ ἀπὸ τούτων ἄλλα ἀγνοούμενα, πῶς ἅπερ οὐκ
ἴσμεν; οἱ Ἐπικούρειοι τὰς προλήψεις· ἃς εἰ μὲν
διηρθρωμένας φασί, περιττὴ ἡ ζήτησις· εἰ δ᾽ ἀδιαρ-
θρώτους, πῶς ἄλλο τι παρὰ τὰς προλήψεις ἐπιζη-
τοῦμεν, ὅ γε οὐδὲ προειλήφαμεν;

(g) Ὅτι καὶ ἡ ἀλήθεια τὸ ὄνομα δηλοῖ λήθης
ἐκβολὴν εἶναι τὴν ἐπιστήμην, ὅ ἐστιν ἀνάμνησις.

(h) Ὅτι καὶ οἱ μητέρα τῶν Μουσῶν τὴν Μνημο-
σύνην εἰπόντες αὐτὸ τοῦτ᾽ ἐνδείκνυνται· αἱ μὲν γὰρ
Μοῦσαι τὸ ζητεῖν παρέχονται, ἡ δὲ Μνημοσύνη τὸ
εὑρίσκειν.

(i) Ὅτι καὶ οἱ πολλοὶ τὸ ἀγνοεῖν ἐπιλελῆσθαι
λέγοντες τῷ αὐτῷ μαρτυροῦσι· λανθάνειν γὰρ ἡμᾶς
φαμεν ἅπερ ἀγνοοῦμεν, καὶ λαθραῖα πράγματα καλοῦμεν τὰ ἀγνοούμενα.

(j) Ὅτι καὶ προβιοτῆς ἀναμνήσεις ἱστοροῦνται,
οἷα καὶ ἡ τοῦ Μύρωνος.

(k) Ὅτι καὶ ὅσοι γαλῆν φοβοῦνται ἢ σαῦρον ἢ
χελώνην, οὓς εἰδέναι αὐτός· καὶ ὁ Τιβερίου ἀδελ-
φιδοῦς ἄρκτους θηρῶν καὶ λέοντας, ὅμως ἀλεκτρυ-

---

[a] *Stoicorum Veterum Fragmenta*, ii. 104.

[b] Usener, *Epicurea*, p. 188. 25.

[c] Plato, *Theaetetus*, 191 D ; [Plutarch], *De Liberis Educandis*, 9 D ; Plutarch, *Mor.* 744 B ; Cornutus, chap. 14,
καλοῦνται δὲ Μοῦσαι ἀπὸ τῆς μώσεως, τούτεστι ζητήσεως.

[d] In Greek the three words all contain the root *lath-*,
" escape notice."

[e] The experience was that of Myron's boy-minion, who
remembered that in a previous existence he had driven a
lover, whom he had refused, to drown himself ; Aeneas of
Gaza, *Theophrastus*, p. 19 Boissonade, Migne, lxxxv. 904.

must be either on what it knows or on what it does not know. The Stoics make the " natural conceptions " responsible.[a] If these are potential, we shall use the same argument as against the Peripatetics ; and if they are actual, why do we search for what we know ? And if we use them as a starting-point for a search for other things that we do not know, how do we search for what we do not know ? The Epicureans introduce " preconceptions " ; if they mean these to be " articulated," search is unnecessary ; if " unarticulated," how do we extend our search beyond our preconceptions, to look for something of which we do not possess even a preconception ? [b]

(g) That the word alêtheia (truth) also proves knowledge to be a casting-out of lêthê (forgetting), and this is recollection.

(h) That they also indicate the same thing by calling the Mother of the Muses Mnemosynê (Memory),[c] since the Muses are the cause of search and memory the cause of discovery.

(i) That ordinary men too give evidence of the same thing when they call not knowing something being " oblivious of it." We say that what we do not know " escapes us," and we call things that are unknown " secrets." [d]

(j) That there are also recorded stories of the recollection of a previous existence, like for example the experience of Myron.[e]

(k) That ⟨similar evidence is⟩ also ⟨given by⟩ all those who are frightened of weasels, or lizards, or tortoises : he says that he personally knew such individuals. And Tiberius's nephew [f] used to hunt bears and lions, but could not abide even the sight of a

[f] Germanicus, cf. De Invidia et Odio, 537 A.

όνα οὐδ' ἰδεῖν ἠδύνατο· φαρμακοπώλην δέ τινα
εἰδέναι ὑπὸ μὲν δρακόντων καὶ ἀσπίδων μηδὲν πάσχειν, μύωπα δὲ φεύγειν μέχρι βοῆς καὶ ἐκστάσεως.
Θεμίσων δ' ὁ ἰατρὸς τὰ μὲν ἄλλα πάθη πάντα
μετεχειρίζετο, τὸν δ' ὑδροφόβαν εἴ τις καὶ ὠνόμασε
μόνον, ἐταράττετο καὶ ὅμοια ἔπασχε τοῖς ὑπ' αὐτοῦ
κατεχομένοις· ὧν αἰτίαν εἶναι τὴν ἀνάμνησιν τῆς
προπαθείας.

(l) Ὅτι αἱ τῶν προπαθειῶν σφοδρότεραι τυ-
ποῦσι τὰς μνήμας εἰς δύο γενέσεις· οἷον τὸ Πολε-
μάρχου καὶ τῶν ἐν Κορίνθῳ ὑπὸ τῷ μεγάλῳ σεισμῷ
καὶ τὸ ἐν Ἀμοργῷ τοῦ Δημητρίου ἐγγεγραμμένον
τῷ τάφῳ.

(m) Ὅτι ὅμοια πάσχουσι καὶ οἱ ποταμοὺς μᾶλλον ἢ θάλατταν δεδοικότες καὶ οἱ πρὸς τὰ ὕψη
ταραττόμενοι.

216

Παρὰ τοῦ αὐτοῦ συστάσεις ἕτεραι·

(a) Ὅτι τὰ νεογενῆ παιδία ἀμειδῆ ἐστι καὶ
ἄγριον βλέπει μέχρι τριῶν σχεδὸν ἑβδομάδων, ὑπνώττοντα τὸν πλείω χρόνον· ἀλλ' ὅμως ποτὲ καθ'
ὕπνους καὶ πολλάκις γελᾷ καὶ διαχεῖται. τίνα οὖν
τρόπον ἄλλον τοῦτο συμβαίνει, ἢ τῆς ψυχῆς τότε
ἀπὸ τῆς δίνης τοῦ ζῴου ἀναφερούσης καὶ κατὰ τὰς
ἑαυτῆς προπαθείας κινουμένης;

---

[a] On the meaning of δράκων, when not a generic term
for " snake," see Gow's note on Nicander, *Theriaca*, 438.

OTHER FRAGMENTS

cock. He says, too, that he knew an apothecary who
was unaffected by pythons[a] and cobras, but would run
away from a gadfly, actually shrieking and becoming
quite distracted. The physician Themison[b] would
handle any disease except hydrophobia : if that were
even mentioned, he would be disturbed and suffer
symptoms like those of patients in the grip of that
disease. These phenomena, he says, are all caused
by recollecting an experience in a previous life.

(*l*) That the more violent previous experiences
make an imprint on the memory for two reincarna-
tions, for example the case of Polemarchus and the
events in Corinth due to the great earthquake,[c] and
the inscription on the tomb of Demetrius at Amorgos.[d]

(*m*) That those who are more frightened of rivers
than the sea and those who are upset by heights are
similarly affected by a previous experience.

216

Further proofs from the same source :

(*a*) That new-born babies do not smile but have a
fierce look for about three weeks, sleeping most of
the time. But all the same at times in their sleep they
often laugh and relax. Now how else can this come
about, unless the soul then withdraws from the vortex
of animal life and its motions depend upon its own
previous experiences ?

[b] Founder of the " methodic " school of medicine, practised in Italy in the early first cent. A.D.
[c] Or possibly " and of those who were in Corinth at the
time of the earthquake."
[d] No other reference to these stories has been found.

(b) Ὅτι καὶ αἱ πρὸς τάδε ἢ τάδε εὐφυΐαι τοῦτον ἀποβαίνουσι τὸν τρόπον.

(c) Ὅτι τὸ μὲν λέγειν οὕτω πεφυκέναι παχύ τε καὶ ἰδιωτικὸν καὶ ἀρκοῦν πρὸς πᾶσαν ἀπόκρισιν. ἀλλ' οἷον τὸ πεφυκέναι ζητητέον ὅμως· ἄλλο γὰρ ἄλλου, ὡς τῆς λογικῆς ψυχῆς τὸ ἀπὸ τῶν προεγνωσμένων τὰ παρόντα ἀναγνωρίζειν.

(d) Ὅτι ἔσωθεν ἐκφέρομεν τὰς τῶν ζητημάτων ἐπιστήμας, δηλοῖ τὸ πρὸς τὴν εὕρεσιν συντεινομένους εἴσω βλέπειν.

(e) Ὅτι καὶ ἡ εὐφροσύνη ἡ ἐπὶ τοῖς εὑρήμασι δηλοῖ τὸν ἀναγνωρισμὸν τῆς ὅτι μάλιστα οἰκείας ἡμῖν ἀληθείας ἐν τῷ μέσῳ χρόνῳ οἷον ἀπολομένης.

*(f) Ὅτι Βίων ἠπόρει περὶ τοῦ ψεύδους, εἰ καὶ αὐτὸ κατ' ἀνάμνησιν ὡς τοὐναντίον γε, ἢ οὔ· καὶ τί ἡ ἀλογία. ἢ ῥητέον ὡς καὶ τοῦτο γίγνεται κατὰ τὸ εἴδωλον τοῦ ἀληθοῦς; τὸ δ' εἴδωλον εἶναι τοῦτο, ὅπερ ἀληθὲς οὐκ ἄν τις νομίσειεν, εἰ μή πῃ εἰδείη τὸ ἀληθές;

*(g) Ὅτι Στράτων ἠπόρει, εἰ ἔστιν ἀνάμνησις, πῶς ἄνευ ἀποδείξεων οὐ γιγνόμεθα ἐπιστήμονες· πῶς δ' οὐδεὶς αὐλητὴς ἢ κιθαριστὴς γέγονεν ἄνευ μελέτης. ἢ μάλιστα μὲν γεγόνασί τινες αὐτοδίδακτοι· Ἡράκλειτος, ὁ Αἰγύπτιος γεωργός, Φήμιος ὁ Ὁμήρου, Ἀγάθαρχος ὁ γραφεύς. εἶτα καὶ αἱ ψυχαὶ πολλῷ τῷ κάρῳ κατεχόμεναι τῆς γενέσεως πολλῆς πρὸς ἀνάμνησιν δέονται τῆς μοχλείας· διὸ καὶ τῶν αἰσθητῶν χρῄζουσιν.

---

[a] The inventor of agriculture.
[b] Odyssey, xxii. 347.

(b) That natural abilities, too, for this or for that, come about in the same way.

(c) That to say " that's its nature " is a clumsy amateurish phrase, that will serve as a reply to anything. It does not avoid the necessity of inquiring what sort of a thing this " nature " is. The nature of one thing differs from that of another ; thus the nature of the rational soul is to recognize what is before it from what was previously known.

(d) That we educe our understanding of problems from inside ourselves is shown by the fact that when we are concentrating on a discovery we look inwards.

(e) That our delight in our discoveries shows us to be recognizing truth that was absolutely our own but had been lost, as it were, in the meantime.

*(f) That Bion raised a difficulty about false belief, whether like its opposite it, too, arises by way of recollection, or not. He also asked what irrationality is. Should we say that false belief arises by way of an image of the truth ? And that this image is a thing one would not suppose to be true, unless one had some sort of knowledge of the truth ?

*(g) That Strato raised this difficulty : if " remembering " is a fact, how is it that we do not become possessed of knowledge without demonstrative proof ? And how is it that no-one has become a flute-player or a harp-player without practice ? Or have there in fact been some self-taught men—Heraclitus, the Egyptian farmer,[a] Homer's Phemius,[b] the painter Agatharchus ? [c] Then souls are overcome by much drowsiness at birth and need much therapeutic exercise if they are to recollect. And this is why they require sense-objects.

[c] An Athenian painter of the first half of the fifth cent. B.C.

Ἐπιχειρημάτων διαφόρων συναγωγὴ δεικνύντων
ἀναμνήσεις εἶναι τὰς μαθήσεις ἐκ τῶν τοῦ Χαιρωνέως Πλουτάρχου·

(a) Εἰ ἀφ' ἑτέρου ἕτερον ἐννοοῦμεν. οὐκ ἂν εἰ
μὴ προέγνωστο. τὸ ἐπιχείρημα Πλατωνικόν.

(b) Εἰ προστίθεμεν τὸ ἐλλεῖπον τοῖς αἰσθητοῖς·
καὶ αὐτὸ Πλατωνικόν.

(c) Εἰ παῖδες εὐμαθέστεροι, ὡς ἐγγίους τῆς προβιοτῆς, ἐν ᾗ¹ ἡ μνήμη ἐσῴζετο. ἐπιπόλαιος ὁ λόγος.

(d) Εἰ ἄλλοι πρὸς ἄλλο μάθημα ἐπιτηδειότεροι.

(e) Εἰ πολλοὶ αὐτοδίδακτοι ὅλων τεχνῶν.

(f) Εἰ πολλὰ παιδία ὑπνώττοντα γελᾷ, ὕπαρ δ'
οὔπω· πολλὰ δὲ καὶ ὄναρ² ἐφθέγξατο, ἄλλως οὔπω
φθεγγόμενα.

(g) Εἰ ἔνιοι καὶ ἀνδρεῖοι ὄντες ὅμως φοβοῦνται
φαῦλ' ἄττα, οἷον γαλῆν ἢ ἀλεκτρυόνα, ἀπ' οὐδεμιᾶς
φανερᾶς αἰτίας.

(h) Εἰ μὴ ἔστιν ἄλλως εὑρίσκειν. οὔτε γὰρ ἃ
ἴσμεν ζητήσειεν ἄν τις, οὔτε ἃ μηδαμῶς ἴσμεν πρότερον, ἀλλ' οὐδ' ἂν εὕροιμεν ἃ μὴ ἴσμεν.

(i) Εἰ ἡ ἀλήθεια κατ' ἀφαίρεσιν τῆς λήθης ἔν-
τευξις τοῦ ὄντος ἐστί. λογικὴ ἡ ἐπιχείρησις.

(j) Εἰ ἡ μήτηρ τῶν Μουσῶν Μνημοσύνη, ὡς ἡ
ἀδιάρθρωτος μνήμη τῶν ζητήσεων αἰτία.

---

¹ ἐν ᾗ] ἧς Duebner.   ² ὄναρ F. H. S. : ὕπαρ.

ᵃ Phaedo, 73 D.
ᵇ Phaedo, 74 D.
ᶜ See O. Luschnat, "Autodidaktos," Theologia Viatorum,
viii (1962), p. 167.

OTHER FRAGMENTS

217

A collection of various arguments to show that acts of learning are acts of remembering, from Plutarch of Chaeronea :

(*a*) Whether we think of one thing from another. We should not unless it had been known previously. The argument is Platonic.[a]

(*b*) Whether we mentally add to percepts that by which they are deficient. This too is Platonic.[b]

(*c*) Whether children are quicker to learn, as being nearer to the previous existence, in which memory was retained. The argument is an obvious one.

(*d*) Whether men differ in their capacity for different kinds of learning.

(*e*) Whether many men have taught themselves complete skills.[c]

(*f*) Whether many babies laugh in their sleep, though they do not yet do so when awake ; and many have spoken in their sleep, at a time when they still did not do so otherwise.

(*g*) Whether some men, although brave, are yet afraid of some ordinary things, such as a weasel or a cock, for no obvious reason.

(*h*) Whether discovery is otherwise impossible ; for none of us would search for what we know, nor for what we do not know at all previously, but we could not even find what we do not know.

(*i*) Whether truth (*alêtheia*) is to have converse with reality, by way of removal of oblivion (*lêthê*). The argument is a verbal one.

(*j*) Whether the mother of the Muses is Mnemosynê (Memory), since inarticulate memory is the cause of our inquiries.

(k) Εἰ, ἅπερ ἀδύνατον γιγνώσκειν, οὐδὲ ζητοῦμεν. ἀλλὰ τὸ ἐπιχείρημα πάλιν ἀπὸ τῆς εὑρέσεως.
(l) Εἰ τοῦ ὄντος ἡ εὕρεσις πάντως, ὅτι καὶ
θεωρημάτων· καὶ ποῦ οὖν ὄντων; ἢ δῆλον ὅτι ἐν
ψυχῇ;

(*k*) Whether we do not even look for what it is impossible to know. But this argument once again starts from the fact of discovery.

(*l*) Whether discovery is necessarily of what exists, since it is of objects of mental vision. And where then do these exist? Is it not clear that it is in the soul?

APPENDIX A

OTHER PSEUDEPIGRAPHA

Tradition as much as logic dictates the choice of spurious works to be printed in an edition of Plutarch. I give here a brief account of such as have found no place in the Loeb Classical Library.

1. John of Salisbury's *Policraticus* (xii cent.) contains extracts in Latin from an alleged letter of Plutarch to the emperor Trajan (Bernardakis vii, pp. 182-193). S. Desideri, *La " Institutio Traiani,"* Genova, 1958, concludes that there never was a Greek version, and that the forgery originated in the fourth or fifth century A.D.

2. *De Vita et Poesi Homeri* (Bernardakis vii, pp. 329-462) was included by Planudes in his Corpus Plutarcheum but, unlike such other spuria as he accepted, has been banished by more recent editors to an appendix. In its present form [a] it cannot be by Plutarch, but some scholars have held that it incorporates material from some lost Plutarchean work.[b] Coincidences between it and genuine works are,

---

[a] Or forms : there are two differing versions, and extracts from a third in Stobaeus, who does not ascribe them to any author.

[b] B. Baedorf, *De Plutarchi quae fertur Vita Homeri*, Münster, 1891 ; A. Ludwich, *Rh. Mus.* lxxii (1917–1918), pp. 537 ff., an important article ; Bernardakis, vii, pp. xi ff.

however, plausibly to be explained as due to common sources in the wealth of ancient Homeric exegesis.[a]

3. *De Metris* (Bernardakis vii, pp. 465-472) is an elementary manual, ascribed to various authors in different manuscripts.

4. *De Fluviis* (Bernardakis vii, pp. 282-328), preserved in Pal. gr. 398 only, contains mythological material and stories about plants and stones, laced with references to authors who are largely fictitious. It seems to be a fairly early forgery (see p. 2), perhaps by the same man who concocted the *Parallela Minora* (see L.C.L., Plutarch's *Moralia*, vol. iv, p. 254).

5. The third book of Zenobius' collection of proverbs has the subscription Πλουτάρχου παροιμίαι αἷς Ἀλεξανδρεῖς ἐχρῶντο. This was shown by O. Crusius, *Plutarchi de proverbiis Alexandrinorum*, Leipzig, 1887, to be a misplaced heading for a succeeding set of proverbs, which he there first published, claiming that it is a genuine work by Plutarch, entered in the Lamprias Catalogue as no. 142. Wilamowitz, in a Göttingen programme of 1888, replied that it was a mere compilation from Seleucus (an author who lived in the first half of the first century A.D.), and had been fathered on Plutarch to make it sell.[b] This seems to me to be highly probable : it is noteworthy that none of the material used in explanation of the proverbs is alluded to in any of the genuine works, whereas one or two of the proverbs are differently explained. Crusius, however, continued to maintain that the collection, although based on Seleucus, either contains [c] or may contain [d] additional material supplied

[a] So Ziegler, *R.E.* xxi. 878.
[b] Cf. his *Commentariolus Grammaticus*, iii (1880), p. xxiv.
[c] *Ad Plutarchi de proverbiis Alexandrinorum commentarius* (1895).   [d] *Sitz. Bericht. München,* 1910, p. 109.

by Plutarch ; and K. Rupprecht, *R.E.* xviii. 1763-
1764, *s.v.* " Paroemiographi," accepts the view that
we have a Plutarchean version of Seleucus. Since
the style is basically not one we associate with Plutarch, and since it is impossible to identify any specific
elements as Plutarchean, it seems reasonable to ex-
clude the work from this collection of fragments.[a]

6. Leutsch-Schneidewin, *Paroemiographi graeci*, i
343, print from Vat. gr. 16 a small collection of proverbs headed Πλουτάρχου ἐκλογὴ περὶ τῶν ἀδυνάτων.
Although this is reprinted by Bernardakis, vii, pp
463-464, the ascription to Plutarch is worthless.[b]

7. *De Nobilitate* (Bernardakis vii, pp. 194-281) is a
forgery made by someone with an imperfect knowledge of Greek, who passed off his work as Plutarch's
In it he embedded fragments from various authors
that he found in Stobaeus, including frags. 139-141
of this edition. The whereabouts of the original, if
it still exists, are unknown, but an abbreviated version
is found in a ms. of the Hamburg Stadtsbibliothek,
Philol. gr. ii. 4 C, which also contains transcripts of
the same text made by J. Grammius and J. L.
Mosheim ; these are the origins of the texts published by Fabricius in his *Bibliotheca Graeca*, xii (1724)
and J. C. Wolf in his *Anecdota Graeca*, iv (1724), pp.
173 ff. A longer text is known from a Latin version
published by Arnoldus Ferronus (Arnoul le Ferron,
1515–1563) at Lyon in 1556. All this was established
by M. Treu, *Zur Geschichte der Überlieferung von Plutarchs Moralia*, iii, Breslau, 1884. His guess, however,

---

[a] *Cf.* Bernardakis' rejection of it, vii, pp. xliv-xlvi. Crusius' text has been reprinted in *Corpus Paroem. graec.*, *Sup-
plementum* (1961).

[b] No. 29 should be corrected to read Ἁλιεῖ ἄροτρον (for
ἄντρον) παρέχεις.

that the original Greek was to be found in the Phillips ms. 4326 was wrong ; that ms., acquired in 1892 by the Deutsche Staatsbibliothek, Berlin, and now Lat. oct. 160, *Plutarchus de nobilitate*, is in Latin ; in 1962 it was at Marburg in the care of the Westdeutsche Bibliothek, having been sent away for safety during the war of 1939–1945 and never recovered.[a]

Ferronus' version was reprinted, with minor changes, by J. C. Wolf, *loc. cit.*, and later editors, including Bernardakis.   In his dedicatory epistle he says nothing of a Greek original, merely " offerimus Plutarchi Chaeronensis libellum magna cura conscriptum."   His Latin, however, contains errors only explicable as translations of a corrupt Greek text.

[a] An unexplained fact is that a manuscript note in the catalogue at Berlin, written by Valentin Rose, ascribes the text of Lat. oct. 160 to Johannes Bonacursius de Montemagno (G. Buonaccorsi, d. 1429) with the title " de nobilitate ad Carolum de Malatestis."   Another ms. of the Berlin collection, said also to be currently at Marburg, Lat. quart. 451, contains " Bonacursius de nobilitate."   I owe this information to the kindness of Dr Ursula Altmann of the Deutsche Staatsbibliothek ;   I have been unable to learn more from Marburg.

APPENDIX B

FRAGMENTA incerta 8-130 of Bernardakis' edition are taken from various gnomologia and anthologies : none of them deserves a place in an edition of Plutarch's fragments, although the majority may be derived from a collection of sentences fathered on him in antiquity. The extremely involved story of these " fragments " was unravelled by A. Elter in his *Gnomica Homoeomata*, Bonn, 1900–1904. Most of them come from the *Eclogae* ascribed to Maximus the Confessor (7th cent. A.D.), but probably of a later date, and from other anthologies which derived from this. Wyttenbach began their assembly, using the *Melissa* of Antonius and a gnomologium appended to John of Damascus in Laur. 8. 22, as well as Maximus himself.[a] For Maximus he had recourse to Gesner's popular edition of 1581, which omits many lemmata and alters others. He was not content, however, merely to collect sentences ascribed in Gesner's text to Plutarch ; he included some others in which he thought he detected Plutarchean colour. At one place, nevertheless, he expresses scepticism about the Plutarchean origin of all this material, which constitutes his fragmenta incerta ζ' to πα'. These were reprinted almost without change by Hutten (whence

[a] For the sake of simplicity I write Maximus, not " Maximus."

some 35 found their way to Orelli's *Opuscula Graecorum veterum sententiosa et moralia* and so to Mullach's *Fragmenta Philosophorum Graecorum*) and by Duebner. Bernardakis reproduced Wyttenbach's ζ'-οζ', οη'-πα' as 8-78, 80-83,[a] and then added as 79, 84-100 material which he found for the most part in manuscripts of Maximus or in the editio princeps of that author or in the derivative *Melissa* of Antonius. He again was not guided solely by the lemmata : for example his 79 has in Maximus the lemma Σωκράτους. Neither his motives nor his exact sources are always obvious : a few passages are taken from Stobaeus ; this he records, but does not add that Stobaeus does not ascribe them to Plutarch. Among the effects of his procedure is the inclusion of three passages from Isocrates or pseudo-Isocrates, one from Clement of Alexandria, and one from Dio Chrysostom.[b]

The larger part of the material drawn from Maximus consists of similes or of quasi-similes in the form of antitheses, Elter's " homoeomata." Many of these are found in other places, ascribed to Socrates, Pythagoras, Demophilus, Demonax, etc., while Stobaeus attributes some to the *Tomaria* of Aristonymus. Elter showed that these ascriptions are names for a number of overlapping selections from a great primary collection of such similitudes. In some gnomologia groups of these homoeomata bear the name of Plutarch, and allow the reconstruction of a selection that was fathered on him : 232 items can be assigned to it, perhaps fewer than the original total. Elter

[a] For Wyttenbach's κδ', which is to be found in *Moralia*, 523 E, he followed Duebner in substituting 25, itself also an unrecognized extract, discovered in the *Violetum* of Arsenius, from a surviving work, *Moralia*, 780 B.

[b] L. Früchtel, *Philologische Wochenschrift*, 1936, col. 1439.

APPENDIX B

guesses that this " Plutarch " may have been formed in the second century, a time when other works were falsely ascribed to him. The true Plutarch was very fond of similes, but the collection does not seem to have drawn on him ; only one or two of those it contains can be found, and then not verbatim, in his surviving works. Another selection of these homoeomata contributed to a gnomologium reconstructed by C. Wachsmuth, *Griechische Gnomologien*, pp. 162 ff., which was apparently entitled ἐκ τῶν Δημοκρίτου Ἰσοκράτους Ἐπικτήτου.[a] This had an infusion of ethical γνῶμαι, not in the form of similitudes.

To return to Maximus, he used a version of " Plutarch " preserved for us in Paris. gr. 1168, redistributing the material to suit his own chapter-headings. This ms. reproduces a corpus of gnomologia, Elter's Corpus Parisinum, which contained homoeomata drawn from other selections besides " Plutarch," including that just mentioned ; some of these, too, were incorporated by Maximus, along with associated γνῶμαι ; thus he provided a happy hunting-ground for Bernardakis and others who were prepared not only to accept his attributions to Plutarch, but also to include adjacent γνῶμαι, and to " emend " other ascriptions.

At first sight there is some hope of finding new fragments of Plutarch in Maximus, since he in fact gives a number of extracts drawn from surviving works. These are confined, however, to the *Lives* and the popular collection of Ἠθικά which Planudes later put in the forefront of his edition (Plan. 1-21) ; there is no reason to suppose that Maximus was able

[a] This explains why there is some overlap between the fragmenta incerta of Plutarch (Bernardakis), Isocrates (Benseler-Blass), and Epictetus (Schweighäuser).

409

to draw from any works now lost, except through Stobaeus as an intermediary. Neither Maximus nor any of the gnomologia, with their shifting ascriptions, provide a source for genuine new fragments. I have therefore omitted Bernardakis' fragments 8-130. He gives no reason for including 132, nor has Patzig any ground for claiming 139 as Plutarchean. 143 and 144 refer to the neo-platonist. 151 was, as Bernardakis himself notes, correctly rejected by Wyttenbach. The origin of 152 is the gnomologium of Georgidas (Boissonade, *Anecdota graeca*, i. 94).

The MS. in which Bernardakis found 149 is an anthology, and the ascription to Plutarch of these twenty-two notes, mostly concerned with physiology, must be suspect. If it were correct, one would expect to find some of their matter repeated elsewhere in his writings. As this seems not to be the case, I have excluded the fragment along with those mentioned above.

INDEX OF NAMES

[The letter L. before a number refers to that number in
the Lamprias Catalogue, pp. 8-29.]

411

INDEX OF NAMES

INDEX OF NAMES

413

INDEX OF NAMES

414

INDEX OF NAMES

INDEX OF SUBJECTS [1]

[the more important references and subjects]

" actual " and " potential," 63 ff.
affections, 35-39
almond, 229
anger, see rage
angle, 365
animals, man's treatment of, 353 ff.
arts, the, 273
Atticism, a feature of style, 347

bay-tree, connected with Hephaestus, 363
BEAUTY, 269-273 ; cf. " the beautiful (people)," 261
bronze, 113-115

CALUMNY, 281-283
cuttle-fish, 169

dawn, 175-177 ; cf. mist
death, 239, 313 ff., 369 ff., 379-381 ; cf. Miletus
demons, effect of bay tree on, 363
DESIRE, 39 ff.
destiny, see fate
Divine Cause, 365
drink, watering of, 179-181, 385

education, 299, 369
elephant, 237
envy, see calumny
etymology : P. explains the following (i) proper names :
  Adrasteia, 99
  Aeaea, 371
  Apollo, 291, 363
  Ares, 291
  Circê, 371

Elysium, 375
Hikesios, 133
Homognios, 133
Jordan, 347
Leto, 289
Mychia, 289
Nychia, 289
Peprômenê, 99
Pithos, 157
Xenios, 133
  and (ii) words :
  ainein, 183
  aletheia, 393
  aps, 345
  bios, 317
  demas, 317
  genesis, 315
  genethlion, 315
  koros, 325
  olôlenai, 317
  teleisthai, 325
  teleután, 325
  thanatos, 315

fate, 99-101, 371
fear, as an indication of our previous life, 393-395
filbert, 347
fire, 93 ; beauty's likeness to it, 261 ; wickedness compared to it, 263, 281 ; Hephaestus as god of, 363 ; Apollo identified with, 363
foreknowledge, 97-103, 129
forgetfulness, 245, 391
fortune, 131
FRIENDLINESS, 299 ff.
friends, 139, 189-191, 309

[1] An entry entirely in capitals denotes a title or part of a title.

417

INDEX OF SUBJECTS

Printed in Great Britain by R. & R. CLARK, LIMITED, *Edinburgh*

THE LOEB CLASSICAL LIBRARY

VOLUMES ALREADY PUBLISHED

THE LOEB CLASSICAL LIBRARY

Cicero : De Senectute, De Amicitia, De Divinatione. W. A. Falconer.

Cicero : In Catilinam, Pro Murena, Pro Sulla, Pro Flacco. Louis E. Lord.

Cicero : Letters to Atticus. E. O. Winstedt. 3 Vols.

Cicero : Letters to his Friends. W. Glynn Williams. 3 Vols

Cicero : Philippics. W. C. A. Ker.

Cicero : Pro Archia, Post Reditum, De Domo, De Haruspicum Responsis, Pro Plancio. N. H. Watts.

Cicero : Pro Caecina, Pro Lege Manilia, Pro Cluentio, Pro Rabirio. H. Grose Hodge.

Cicero : Pro Caelio, De Provinciis Consularibus, Pro Balbo. R. Gardner.

Cicero : Pro Milone, In Pisonem, Pro Scauro, Pro Fonteio, Pro Rabirio Postumo, Pro Marcello, Pro Ligario, Pro Rege Deiotaro. N. H. Watts.

Cicero : Pro Quinctio, Pro Roscio Amerino, Pro Roscio Comoedo, Contra Rullum. J. H. Freese.

Cicero : Pro Sestio, In Vatinium. R. Gardner.

[Cicero] : Rhetorica ad Herennium. H. Caplan

Cicero : Tusculan Disputations. J. E. King.

Cicero : Verrine Orations. L. H. G. Greenwood. 2 Vols.

Claudian. M. Platnauer. 2 Vols.

Columella : De Re Rustica, De Arboribus. H. B. Ash. E. S. Forster, E. Heffner. 3 Vols.

Curtius, Q.: History of Alexander. J. C. Rolfe. 2 Vols.

Florus. E. S. Forster ; and Cornelius Nepos. J. C. Rolfe.

Frontinus : Stratagems and Aqueducts. C. E. Bennett and M. B. McElwain.

Fronto : Correspondence. C. R. Haines. 2 Vols.

Gellius. J. C. Rolfe. 3 Vols.

Horace : Odes and Epodes. C. E. Bennett.

Horace : Satires, Epistles, Ars Poetica. H. R. Fairclough.

Jerome : Select Letters. F. A. Wright.

Juvenal and Persius. G. G. Ramsay.

Livy. B. O. Foster, F. G. Moore, Evan T. Sage, A. C. Schlesinger and R. M. Geer (General Index). 14 Vols.

Lucan. J. D. Duff.

Lucretius. W. H. D. Rouse.

Martial. W. C. A. Ker. 2 Vols.

Minor Latin Poets : from Publilius Syrus to Rutilius Namatianus, including Grattius, Calpurnius Siculus, Nemesianus, Avianus, with " Aetna," " Phoenix " and other poems. J. Wight Duff and Arnold M. Duff.

THE LOEB CLASSICAL LIBRARY

OVID: THE ART OF LOVE AND OTHER POEMS. J. H. Mozley.

OVID: FASTI. Sir James G. Frazer.

OVID: HEROIDES AND AMORES. Grant Showerman.

OVID: METAMORPHOSES. F. J. Miller. 2 Vols.

OVID: TRISTIA AND EX PONTO. A. L. Wheeler.

PETRONIUS. M. Heseltine; SENECA: APOCOLOCYNTOSIS
W. H. D. Rouse.

PHAEDRUS AND BABRIUS (Greek). B. E. Perry.

PLAUTUS. Paul Nixon. 5 Vols.

PLINY: LETTERS, PANEGYRICUS. B. Radice. 2 Vols.

PLINY: NATURAL HISTORY. 10 Vols. Vols. I-V and IX.
H. Rackham. Vols. VI-VIII. W. H. S. Jones. Vol. X
D. E. Eichholz.

PROPERTIUS. H. E. Butler.

PRUDENTIUS. H. J. Thomson. 2 Vols.

QUINTILIAN. H. E. Butler. 4 Vols.

REMAINS OF OLD LATIN. E. H. Warmington. 4 Vols.
Vol. I (Ennius and Caecilius). Vol. II (Livius, Naevius,
Pacuvius, Accius). Vol. III (Lucilius, Laws of the XII
Tables). Vol. IV (Archaic Inscriptions).

SALLUST. J. C. Rolfe.

SCRIPTORES HISTORIAE AUGUSTAE. D. Magie. 3 Vols.

SENECA: APOCOLOCYNTOSIS. Cf. PETRONIUS.

SENECA: EPISTULAE MORALES. R. M. Gummere. 3 Vols.

SENECA: MORAL ESSAYS. J. W. Basore. 3 Vols.

SENECA: TRAGEDIES. F. J. Miller. 2 Vols.

SIDONIUS: POEMS AND LETTERS. W. B. Anderson. 2 Vols.

SILIUS ITALICUS. J. D. Duff. 2 Vols.

STATIUS. J. H. Mozley. 2 Vols.

SUETONIUS. J. C. Rolfe. 2 Vols.

TACITUS: AGRICOLA AND GERMANIA. Maurice Hutton; DIALOGUS. Sir Wm. Peterson.

TACITUS: HISTORIES AND ANNALS. C. H. Moore and J.
Jackson. 4 Vols.

TERENCE. John Sargeaunt. 2 Vols.

TERTULLIAN: APOLOGIA AND DE SPECTACULIS. T. R. Glover;
MINUCIUS FELIX. G. H. Rendall.

VALERIUS FLACCUS. J. H. Mozley.

VARRO: DE LINGUA LATINA. R. G. Kent. 2 Vols.

VELLEIUS PATERCULUS AND RES GESTAE DIVI AUGUSTI.
F. W. Shipley.

VIRGIL. H. R. Fairclough. 2 Vols.

VITRUVIUS: DE ARCHITECTURA. F. Granger. 2 Vols.

THE LOEB CLASSICAL LIBRARY

ACHILLES TATIUS. S. Gaselee.

AELIAN: ON THE NATURE OF ANIMALS. A. F. Scholfield. 3 Vols.

AENEAS TACTICUS, ASCLEPIODOTUS AND ONASANDER. The Illinois Greek Club.

AESCHINES. C. D. Adams.

AESCHYLUS. H. Weir Smyth. 2 Vols.

ALCIPHRON, AELIAN AND PHILOSTRATUS: LETTERS. A. R. Benner and F. H. Fobes.

APOLLODORUS. Sir James G. Frazer. 2 Vols.

APOLLONIUS RHODIUS. R. C. Seaton.

THE APOSTOLIC FATHERS. Kirsopp Lake. 2 Vols.

APPIAN'S ROMAN HISTORY. Horace White. 4 Vols.

ARATUS. *Cf.* CALLIMACHUS.

ARISTOPHANES. Benjamin Bickley Rogers. 3 Vols. Verse trans.

ARISTOTLE: ART OF RHETORIC. J. H. Freese.

ARISTOTLE: ATHENIAN CONSTITUTION, EUDEMIAN ETHICS. VIRTUES AND VICES. H. Rackham.

ARISTOTLE: THE CATEGORIES. ON INTERPRETATION. H. P. Cooke; PRIOR ANALYTICS. H. Tredennick.

ARISTOTLE: GENERATION OF ANIMALS. A. L. Peck.

ARISTOTLE: HISTORIA ANIMALIUM. A. L. Peck. 3 Vols. Vols. I and II.

ARISTOTLE: METAPHYSICS. H. Tredennick. 2 Vols.

ARISTOTLE: METEOROLOGICA. H. D. P. Lee.

ARISTOTLE: MINOR WORKS. W. S. Hett. "On Colours," "On Things Heard," "Physiognomics," "On Plants," "On Marvellous Things Heard," "Mechanical Problems," "On Indivisible Lines," "Situations and Names of Winds," "On Melissus, Xenophanes, and Gorgias."

ARISTOTLE: NICOMACHEAN ETHICS. H. Rackham.

ARISTOTLE: OECONOMICA AND MAGNA MORALIA. G. C. Armstrong. (With METAPHYSICS, Vol. II.)

ARISTOTLE: ON THE HEAVENS. W. K. C. Guthrie.

ARISTOTLE: ON THE SOUL, PARVA NATURALIA. ON BREATH. W. S. Hett.

ARISTOTLE: PARTS OF ANIMALS. A. L. Peck; MOTION AND PROGRESSION OF ANIMALS. E. S. Forster.

ARISTOTLE: PHYSICS. Rev. P. Wicksteed and F. M. Cornford. 2 Vols.

THE LOEB CLASSICAL LIBRARY

ARISTOTLE: POETICS; LONGINUS ON THE SUBLIME. W. Hamilton Fyfe; DEMETRIUS ON STYLE. W. Rhys Roberts.
ARISTOTLE: POLITICS. H. Rackham.
ARISTOTLE: POSTERIOR ANALYTICS. H. Tredennick; TOPICS. E. S. Forster.
ARISTOTLE: PROBLEMS. W. S. Hett. 2 Vols.
ARISTOTLE: RHETORICA AD ALEXANDRUM. H. Rackham. (With PROBLEMS, Vol. II.)
ARISTOTLE: SOPHISTICAL REFUTATIONS. COMING-TO-BE AND PASSING-AWAY. E. S. Forster; ON THE COSMOS. D. J. Furley.
ARRIAN: HISTORY OF ALEXANDER AND INDICA. Rev. E. Iliffe Robson. 2 Vols.
ATHENAEUS: DEIPNOSOPHISTAE. C. B. Gulick. 7 Vols.
BABRIUS AND PHAEDRUS (Latin). B. E. Perry.
ST. BASIL: LETTERS. R. J. Deferrari. 4 Vols.
CALLIMACHUS: FRAGMENTS. C. A. Trypanis.
CALLIMACHUS: HYMNS AND EPIGRAMS, AND LYCOPHRON A. W. Mair; ARATUS. G. R. Mair.
CLEMENT OF ALEXANDRIA. Rev. G. W. Butterworth.
COLLUTHUS. Cf. OPPIAN.
DAPHNIS AND CHLOE. Cf. LONGUS.
DEMOSTHENES I: OLYNTHIACS, PHILIPPICS AND MINOR ORATIONS: I-XVII AND XX. J. H. Vince.
DEMOSTHENES II: DE CORONA AND DE FALSA LEGATIONE. C. A. Vince and J. H. Vince.
DEMOSTHENES III: MEIDIAS, ANDROTION, ARISTOCRATES TIMOCRATES, ARISTOGEITON. J. H. Vince.
DEMOSTHENES IV-VI: PRIVATE ORATIONS AND IN NEAERAM. A. T. Murray.
DEMOSTHENES VII: FUNERAL SPEECH, EROTIC ESSAY EXORDIA AND LETTERS. N. W. and N. J. DeWitt.
DIO CASSIUS: ROMAN HISTORY. E. Cary. 9 Vols.
DIO CHRYSOSTOM. 5 Vols. Vols. I and II. J. W. Cohoon. Vol. III. J. W. Cohoon and H. Lamar Crosby. Vols. IV and V. H. Lamar Crosby.
DIODORUS SICULUS. 12 Vols. Vols. I-VI. C. H. Oldfather. Vol. VII. C. L. Sherman. Vol. VIII. C. B. Welles. Vols. IX and X. Russel M. Geer. Vols. XI and XII. F. R. Walton. General Index. Russel M. Geer.
DIOGENES LAERTIUS. R. D. Hicks. 2 Vols.
DIONYSIUS OF HALICARNASSUS: ROMAN ANTIQUITIES. Spelman's translation revised by E. Cary. 7 Vols.
EPICTETUS. W. A. Oldfather. 2 Vols.

5

EURIPIDES. A. S. Way. 4 Vols. Verse trans.

EUSEBIUS : ECCLESIASTICAL HISTORY. Kirsopp Lake and J. E. L. Oulton. 2 Vols.

GALEN : ON THE NATURAL FACULTIES. A. J. Brock.

THE GREEK ANTHOLOGY. W. R. Paton. 5 Vols.

THE GREEK BUCOLIC POETS (THEOCRITUS, BION, MOSCHUS). J. M. Edmonds.

GREEK ELEGY AND IAMBUS WITH THE ANACREONTEA. J. M. Edmonds. 2 Vols.

GREEK MATHEMATICAL WORKS. Ivor Thomas. 2 Vols.

HERODES. *Cf.* THEOPHRASTUS : CHARACTERS.

HERODIAN : C. R. Whittaker. 2 Vols. Vol. I.

HERODOTUS. A. D. Godley. 4 Vols.

HESIOD AND THE HOMERIC HYMNS. H. G. Evelyn White.

HIPPOCRATES AND THE FRAGMENTS OF HERACLEITUS. W. H. S. Jones and E. T. Withington. 4 Vols.

HOMER : ILIAD. A. T. Murray. 2 Vols.

HOMER : ODYSSEY. A. T. Murray. 2 Vols.

ISAEUS. E. S. Forster.

ISOCRATES. George Norlin and LaRue Van Hook. 3 Vols.

[ST. JOHN DAMASCENE]: BARLAAM AND IOASAPH. Rev. G. R. Woodward, Harold Mattingly and D. M. Lang.

JOSEPHUS. 9 Vols. Vols. I-IV. H. St. J. Thackeray. Vol. V. H. St. J. Thackeray and Ralph Marcus. Vols. VI and VII. Ralph Marcus. Vol. VIII. Ralph Marcus and Allen Wikgren. Vol. IX. L. H. Feldman.

JULIAN. Wilmer Cave Wright. 3 Vols.

LIBANIUS : SELECTED WORKS. A. F. Norman. 3 Vols. Vol. I.

LONGUS : DAPHNIS AND CHLOE. Thornley's translation revised by J. M. Edmonds ; and PARTHENIUS. S. Gaselee.

LUCIAN. 8 Vols. Vols. I-V. A. M. Harmon. Vol. VI. K Kilburn. Vols. VII and VIII. M. D. Macleod.

LYCOPHRON. *Cf.* CALLIMACHUS.

LYRA GRAECA. J. M. Edmonds. 3 Vols.

LYSIAS. W. R. M. Lamb.

MANETHO. W. G. Waddell ; PTOLEMY : TETRABIBLOS. F. E. Robbins.

MARCUS AURELIUS. C. R. Haines.

MENANDER. F. G. Allinson.

MINOR ATTIC ORATORS. 2 Vols. K. J. Maidment and J. O. Burtt.

NONNOS : DIONYSIACA. W. H. D. Rouse. 3 Vols.

OPPIAN, COLLUTHUS, TRYPHIODORUS. A. W. Mair.

PAPYRI. NON-LITERARY SELECTIONS. A. S. Hunt and C. C.

Edgar. 2 Vols. LITERARY SELECTIONS (Poetry). D. L. Page.

PARTHENIUS. *Cf.* LONGUS.

PAUSANIAS : DESCRIPTION OF GREECE. W. H. S. Jones. 5 Vols. and Companion Vol. arranged by R. E. Wycherley.

PHILO. 10 Vols. Vols. I-V. F. H. Colson and Rev. G. H. Whitaker. Vols. VI-X. F. H. Colson. General Index. Rev. J. W. Earp.

Two Supplementary Vols. Translation only from an Armenian Text. Ralph Marcus.

PHILOSTRATUS : THE LIFE OF APOLLONIUS OF TYANA. F. C. Conybeare. 2 Vols.

PHILOSTRATUS : IMAGINES : CALLISTRATUS : DESCRIPTIONS. A. Fairbanks.

PHILOSTRATUS AND EUNAPIUS : LIVES OF THE SOPHISTS Wilmer Cave Wright.

PINDAR. Sir J. E. Sandys.

PLATO : CHARMIDES, ALCIBIADES, HIPPARCHUS, THE LOVERS. THEAGES, MINOS AND EPINOMIS. W. R. M. Lamb.

PLATO : CRATYLUS, PARMENIDES, GREATER HIPPIAS, LESSER HIPPIAS. H. N. Fowler.

PLATO : EUTHYPHRO, APOLOGY, CRITO, PHAEDO, PHAEDRUS. H. N. Fowler.

PLATO : LACHES, PROTAGORAS, MENO, EUTHYDEMUS. W. R. M. Lamb.

PLATO : LAWS. Rev. R. G. Bury. 2 Vols.

PLATO : LYSIS, SYMPOSIUM, GORGIAS. W. R. M. Lamb.

PLATO : REPUBLIC. Paul Shorey. 2 Vols.

PLATO : STATESMAN, PHILEBUS. H. N. Fowler : ION. W. R. M. Lamb.

PLATO : THEAETETUS AND SOPHIST. H. N. Fowler.

PLATO : TIMAEUS, CRITIAS, CLITOPHO, MENEXENUS, EPISTULAE. Rev. R. G. Bury.

PLOTINUS. A. H. Armstrong. 6 Vols. Vols. I-III.

PLUTARCH : MORALIA. 16 Vols. Vols. I-V. F. C. Babbitt. Vol. VI. W. C. Helmbold. Vol. VII. P. H. De Lacy and B. Einarson. Vol. VIII. P. A. Clement, H. B. Hoffleit. Vol. IX. E. L. Minar, Jr., F. H. Sandbach, W. C. Helmbold. Vol. X. H. N. Fowler. Vol. XI. L. Pearson, F. H. Sandbach. Vol. XII. H. Cherniss, W. C. Helmbold. Vol. XIV. P. H. De Lacy and B. Einarson. Vol. XV. F. H. Sandbach.

PLUTARCH : THE PARALLEL LIVES. B. Perrin. 11 Vols.

POLYBIUS. W. R. Paton. 6 Vols.

THE LOEB CLASSICAL LIBRARY

Procopius: History of the Wars. H. B. Dewing. 7 Vols.
Ptolemy: Tetrabiblos. *Cf.* Manetho.
Quintus Smyrnaeus. A. S. Way. Verse trans.
Sextus Empiricus. Rev. R. G. Bury. 4 Vols.
Sophocles. F. Storr. 2 Vols. Verse trans.
Strabo: Geography. Horace L. Jones. 8 Vols.
Theophrastus: Characters. J. M. Edmonds; Herodes, etc. A. D. Knox.
Theophrastus: Enquiry into Plants. Sir Arthur Hort. 2 Vols.
Thucydides. C. F. Smith. 4 Vols.
Tryphiodorus. *Cf.* Oppian.
Xenophon: Anabasis. C. L. Brownson.
Xenophon: Cyropaedia. Walter Miller. 2 Vols.
Xenophon: Hellenica. C. L. Brownson.
Xenophon: Memorabilia and Oeconomicus. E. C. Marchant. Symposium and Apology. O. J. Todd.
Xenophon: Scripta Minora. E. C. Marchant and G. W. Bowersock.

VOLUMES IN PREPARATION

GREEK AUTHORS

Aristides: Orations. C. A. Behr.
Musaeus: Hero and Leander. T. Gelzer and C. H. Whitman.
Theophrastus: De Causis Plantarum. G. K. K. Link and B. Einarson.

LATIN AUTHORS

Asconius: Commentaries on Cicero's Orations. G. W. Bowersock.
Benedict: The Rule. P. Meyvaert.
Justin–Trogus. R. Moss.
Manilius. G. P. Goold.

DESCRIPTIVE PROSPECTUS ON APPLICATION

CAMBRIDGE, MASS.   LONDON
HARVARD UNIV. PRESS   WILLIAM HEINEMANN LTD